Rough Waters

ROUGH WATERS

NATURE AND DEVELOPMENT IN AN EAST AFRICAN MARINE PARK

Christine J. Walley

PRINCETON UNIVERSITY PRESS

PRINCETON AND OXFORD

Library of Congress Cataloging-in-Publication Data

Walley, Christine J., 1965–
Rough waters : nature and development in an East African
marine park / Christine J. Walley
p. cm.
Includes bibliographical references and index.
ISBN 0-691-11559-1 — ISBN 0-691-11560-5 (pbk.)
1. Mafia Island Marine Park (Tanzania)   2. Marine parks
and reserves—Tanzania—Mafia
Island—Social aspects.   3. Economic development
projects—Tanzania—Mafia Island—
Social aspects.   I. Title.
QH91.75.T5W35 2004
338.4'79167823—dc21   2003053606

British Library Cataloging-in-Publication Data is available

Portions of Chapters 6 and 7 were previously published in
Ethnography 3, no. 3, 265–298 and *Anthropological
Quarterly* 76, no. 1, 33–54.

This book has been composed in Times Roman

Printed on acid-free paper. ∞

pup.princeton.edu

Printed in the United States of America

10   9   8   7   6   5   4   3   2   1

This book is dedicated to the memory of Bi Zubeda Mohammed, Bi Hadija Bacha, Bi Saida Mohammed Kimbau, Mzee Rajabu Fadhili, Mzee Imani Farijala, Abdallah Gomba, and especially Mzee Issa Ally, better known in these pages as "Mzee Bakari," as well as the other Chole residents who contributed to this endeavor but who passed away before it was completed.

Contents

Illustrations

Acknowledgments

It is difficult to express the debt of gratitude that I owe to the residents of Chole Island who emerge as the central protagonists in this book. Like many visitors to Chole, I initially fell in love with the beauty of the island; yet, it is the friendships that emerged over the course of months and years that I will continue to cherish. Although those friends and acquaintances who helped me must remain anonymous, I trust that my gratitude and appreciation are apparent in the pages that follow. As I imagine they are aware, during the course of my research I came to think of Chole not simply as a "field site," but as a second home.

I would also like to express my appreciation to numerous others in Tanzania who assisted this research in various ways. The use of pseudonyms to protect the privacy of those depicted in these pages once again excludes formal acknowledgments. Nevertheless, I would like to thank the government officials who agreed to speak with me; the partners of what is herein referred to as the Chole Kisiwani Conservation and Development Company who offered a place to live and various kinds of support; the numerous hotel operators, tourists, development workers and visiting professionals whose insights provided grist for this anthropologist's mill; and those WWF employees in Washington, D.C., Dar es Salaam, and Mafia who graciously consented to be interviewed and offered their viewpoints. In particular, I owe special thanks to the WWF staff on Mafia who were a constant source of aid, providing lifts in their boat and jeep when there was no other source of transportation and offering help when my own equipment ceased to function. I would especially like to thank the person referred to in these pages as "David Holston" for his unflinchingly principled belief in institutional transparency. Without his rare openness and willingness to address difficult questions, this "social drama" could not have been written. It is my hope that this book will vindicate this trust by encouraging constructive debate among environmental activists as well as academics.

I also owe my thanks to a number of institutions and individuals that *can* be named. COSTEC and the Zanzibar Ministry of Information, Culture, Tourism and Youth provided permission to conduct research in mainland Tanzania and Zanzibar respectively. A variety of institutions funded the various stages of this research. The Social Science Research Council supported a preliminary research trip to Zanzibar. The Research Institute for the Study of Man (RISM) and an Elaine Brody Fellowship in the Humanities from New York University funded the main body of research on Mafia. New York

University provided much-needed write-up funds through a Dean's Dissertation Fellowship. And, finally, the Massachusetts Institute of Technology provided the financial means necessary to conduct follow-up research, to create the maps, and to index this volume.

My dissertation committee at New York University deserves special acknowledgment. Faye Ginsburg inspired me to shift my research to the environment, and she and Connie Sutton provided continual intellectual stimulation and support over the years. Timothy Mitchell fundamentally transformed the ideas and conclusions of my dissertation by offering me the opportunity to be a teaching assistant in his ground-breaking class, "What is Capitalism?" Fred Cooper graciously agreed to be my "outside" reader and asked incisive and provocative questions that challenged the limits of my thinking in ways for which I am deeply grateful. And, finally, Lila Abu-Lughod was a superb adviser. She offered not only perceptive analytical insights and astute editorial skill, but also the kind of support and encouragement for which every graduate student hopes. Her own work has been a source of constant inspiration, combining theoretical rigor, an artist's attention to the craft of writing, and a profoundly humanist vision. I suspect I would not have become an anthropologist without her care and attention.

A great many others offered various kinds of assistance with this book. I would like to thank Bill Bissell, Laura Fair, Jonathon Glassman, Garth Myers, Rachel Eide, and Martin Benjamin, not only for their insights and experience as fellow researchers in East Africa, but for their good company as well. Thanks to Marty Baker and Lisa Cliggett whose visits helped me to see these islands through fresh eyes. Avelin Malyango provided help with the translations in Chapter 1 and generously opened his home to me in Dar es Salaam. Rob Barbour, Jackie Barbour, Deb Ash, and Dudley Iles shared a heartfelt appreciation for Chole Island. Two writing groups, one in New York and one in Cambridge, offered perceptive comments and made the writing process a far less lonely one; thanks to Alice Apley, Ayala Fader, Teja Ganti, Jerry Lombardi, Barbara Miller, Lotti Silber, Sara Friedman, Ann Marie Leshkowich, Sandra Hyde, and Tuulikki Pietila. My colleagues in the anthropology program at MIT, Susan Slyomovics, Jim Howe, Jean Jackson, Hugh Gusterson, Susan Silbey, Arthur Steinberg, and Mike Fischer, have been wonderfully supportive throughout the writing of this book. I am grateful to them, as well as to Pat Caplan, Celia Lowe, Dorothy Hodgson, Rick Schroeder, and two anonymous reviewers for their insights and perceptive criticisms. My sincere thanks to Mary Murrell at Princeton University Press for her enthusiastic interest in this project as well as her patience. In addition to the friends already mentioned, I would also like to thank Beth Epstein, Kris Sowa, Mike Putnam, Nina Browne, and Heather Kirkpatrick, as well as my family, for their companionship and moral support.

Finally, my thanks to my husband and partner in all things, Chris Boebel, who has lived with this project in all its incarnations. Early on, he suffered long absences and, later, endured equally long periods of distraction as I stared at a computer in our tiny New York apartment strewn with files and papers. In the ensuing years, he visited Chole with me, befriended those I cared about, and obligingly supported my passions. He has read every chapter in this book many times over, pushed me when others were satisfied, and suggested ideas when I was tired or unable. As an artist, film maker and writer, he constantly forced my attention to both the power of narrative and the rigor of argument. This book as a final product owes more to him than anyone else. For all this, simple thanks are not enough.

Glossary of Kiswahili Terms

Boma	government building; fortress
bui-bui	black and loose-fitting veil worn draped over the head and body (but not the face), generally fastened with a piece of elastic under the chin.
dini	religion, i.e. Islam
jahazi	the largest category of wooden hand-made sail boats along the coast
kanga	a set of two colorful pieces of cloth imprinted with KiSwahili proverbs that are the most common form of dress for women along the coast
kofia	muslim skull cap for men
maendeleo	"development"
mashua	a category of wooden sailboat smaller than *jahazi*, and the most common on Mafia
mganga	(plural-*waganga*) healers
mzungu	(plural-*wazungu*) Europeans
mila	"tradition" or "custom"
mtaalamu	an expert
mwenyeji	(plural-*wenyeji*) an inhabitant or someone belonging to and having proprietorship of a place
shamba	(plural-*mashamba*) agricultural fields or gardens
sheria	Islamic law
wageni	(singular-*mgeni*) visitors, guests, strangers, outsiders
waungwana	the freeborn, elites
wazungu	(singular-*mzungu*) Europeans
wenyeji	(singular-*mwenyeji*) the inhabitants, owners or proprietors of a place

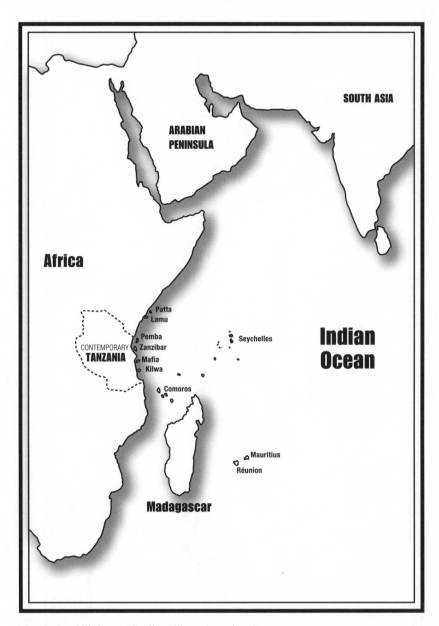

Map 1. Swahili Coast (Credit: Allison Associates)

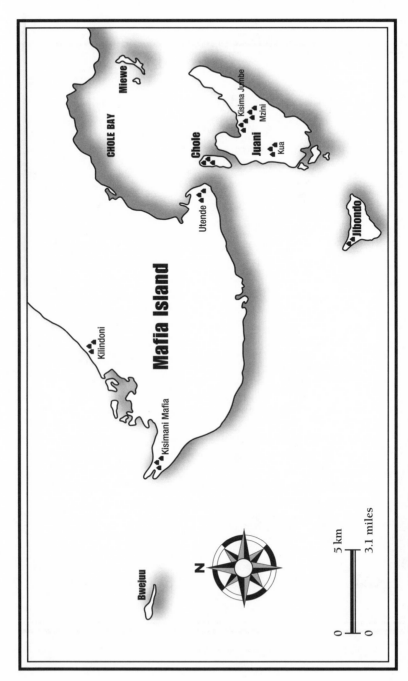

Map 2. Southern Mafia (Credit: Allison Associates)

Preface

THIS BOOK ANALYZES the political struggles surrounding Tanzania's first national marine park, located in the Mafia archipelago off the coast of East Africa. According to park planners, the Mafia Island Marine Park was to be a premier example of an integrated conservation and development project, which would encourage the participation of Mafia residents in decision-making processes. Despite the initial support of Mafia residents, however, the park quickly became mired in controversy and conflict. In this book, I analyze the struggles over the marine park as it was being implemented during the mid- to - late 1990s—what I refer to as its "social drama"—as such struggles played out among international organizations, national government officials and island residents. These conflicts, I argue, offer a fascinating, if often troubling, window onto power relationships in a post–Cold War world. Although the current period has been widely touted as an era of growing "global" integration, in sub-Saharan Africa the rapidly expanding influence of donor organizations has, ironically, occurred within a broader context of increasing economic and political marginalization. My book uses the "social drama" of Mafia's marine park to offer a grounded exploration of the dynamics of this contemporary period from the point of view of what many characterize as an increasingly peripheral region.

In this work, I have considered the possibilities and problems associated with a new generation of conservation and development projects, the range of meanings that Mafia residents, government officials and representatives of international organizations attach to "nature" and "development," the social positioning of these actors in relation to each other, and the range of ways in which international projects can be used to contest or buttress existing power relationships in local, national, and international contexts. Ultimately, this book provides a portrait of power relationships in the contemporary era that challenges commonplace understandings of globalization and asks what impacts—both intended and unintended—this and similar projects might have for both poorer individuals and the environments upon which they depend.

Yet, as I write this preface early in 2003, the concept of the "global" is itself currently in flux. My research and much of the writing of this book was completed prior to the events of September 11 and the economic downturn that has affected so many parts of the world. Even now, it remains unclear how such transformations will affect the concept of the global. The most effusive rhetoric surrounding globalization that appeared in the business press before 2000 has since dissipated, although the concept itself appears to have survived. The current "war on terror" may be seen, on the one hand, in terms of a deterritorialized threat that needs to be understood in global terms, and, on the other, in relation to a resurgence of nationalism and increasingly centralized state authority in the United States and elsewhere. Although such events are laying to rest glib statements about the irrelevance of nation-states, the current period also represents an historic crossroads. The expanding role of international bodies like the United Nations is being redefined vis à vis the authority of the strongest state actor in the contemporary period, the United States, and it is unclear in which direction the future lies. Thus, the dynamics referred to as globalization are being revealed, not as an inevitable force, but as a product of human agency and historical contingency and thus, itself, subject to transformation. In this book, I have taken pains to insist that the "social drama" of the Mafia Island Marine Park represents merely one act in an ongoing struggle, as the vivid changes revealed in the epilogue clearly demonstrate. Similarly, we must also recognize that the debates surrounding globalization—their trend, direction, and multiple meanings—also form part of an ongoing story.

New York City, February 2003

Conservation and Development in the Age of the "Global"

OFF THE EASTERN coast of Africa, a series of islands form a chain, beginning just below the continent's protruding horn and ending in the region now known as Mozambique. These islands, from Pate and Lamu in the north to Kilwa in the south, together with adjacent coastal settlements, have historically formed the "Swahili" coast.[1] At a time when Europe was experiencing what is sometimes known as the Dark Ages, this region formed part of a dynamic Indian Ocean trading world, serving as a gateway between the peoples of Africa and the regions to the east.[2] Following the seasonal monsoon winds, dhow traders plied their wares between East Africa, the Arabian peninsula, Persia, India, Indonesia and beyond, creating far-flung social and economic networks (Chaudauri 1985; J. Abu Lughod 1989; Frank 1998; Ghosh 1992). As part of this cosmopolitan milieu, African coastal residents regularly interacted with visiting traders and immigrants from Arabia, India, and other regions, as well as with African peoples living farther inland, who supplied such goods as ivory, animal hides, amber, and human slaves. The fluid interactions of this ocean-centered world defined the East African coast for centuries before it was interrupted by the land-based logic of European colonization and, eventually, the formation of independent nation-states.

Of all these islands and coastal settlements, Mafia Island is perhaps the least well known today. Long dominated by neighboring Kilwa Island that had controlled the medieval Sofala gold trade, Mafia came under the suzerainty of Zanzibar Island to the north in the eighteenth and nineteenth centuries. During this period, Zanzibar emerged as coastal entrepot for Indian Ocean trade as well as terminus of the mainland caravan routes, and later served as a site of clove plantations that fed a growing international economy hungry for spices. Eventually, however, the economic and political heart of the region shifted to the city of Dar es Salaam, located on the mainland to the south of Zanzibar. Founded in 1862 by Zanzibar's Sultan Majid, Dar es Salaam later became the colonial administrative center for mainland Tanganyika under the Germans and, after World War I, the British. In 1890, Mafia Island, which had been a dominion of Zanzibar, was "traded" to the Germans and became a mainland territory, economically and politically oriented toward Dar es Salaam.[3] As part of the "mainland," Mafia gained its independence along with the rest of Tanganyika in 1961. However, it was only after the 1964 political merger between Tanganyika and the newly independent revolutionary government of Zanzibar that the contemporary nation-state of Tanzania was formed.

Located a mere 20 km from the mainland, the Mafia group of islands appears at the point where the massive delta formed by the Rufiji River meets the Indian Ocean. Some have argued that the name "Mafia" derives from the KiSwahili "Ma-afya" referring to a healthy place, an intimation of the alleged healing properties of waters on the islands (Saadi 1941). Others link the name to the medieval town of Kisimani Mafia and note that it was historically popularized as "Monfia" by visiting Arabs (Baumann 1957 [1896]). In the nineteenth century, however, residents themselves referred collectively to these islands as "Chole," after the smallest inhabited islet that at the time served as the urban center for the entire chain.

Although Mafia's residents participated in global trading networks centuries before the arrival of Europeans, Mafia, ironically, became increasingly "remote" over the course of the twentieth century. Indeed, Mafia residents today agree with those in other parts of the country that their island is lamentably isolated from the rest of Tanzania as well as regions beyond. During the mid-1990s, Kilindoni, Mafia's government seat, constituted an unremarkable settlement of concrete block offices and houses that were tenuously linked to each other by a few telephone and electricity lines. Although there had been a prodigious traffic of wooden sailing vessels in the past, the number of dhows in the region had since been reduced to an anemic trickle, and larger "modern" ships docked infrequently at Mafia in part due to the dangers of Kilindoni's shallow port. On the main island, a mere handful of motorized vehicles traveled the sandy roads that became impassable with the onset of the rainy season, and tiny single-engine airplanes made only rare, erratically scheduled landings on an airstrip barely distinguishable from the surrounding sand.

Ironically, however, Mafia's current "remoteness" has attracted a new kind of attention, one that serves as the impetus for the dynamics to be explored in this book. According to a certain symbolic logic, isolation signals not hardship but the "pristine" nature of the islands and their environment—a situation attractive to both conservationists and the international tourism trade. Such dynamics are not entirely new on Mafia. During the British colonial period, a European-owned fishing lodge operated in Utende, a village on the southeastern coast of Mafia's main island. During the post-independence period, this lodge was supplanted by a government-owned and managed hotel on a nearby site. During the late 1980s and 1990s, however, tourism increased dramatically along the Tanzanian coast due in large part to the encouragement of international donors as well as policy reforms that were designed to pull poorer regions more tightly into an international economy.

By the mid-1990s, signs of expanding tourism activity were widely apparent in the otherwise quiet village of Utende. Gangs of workers laid cement foundations, pounded coral rock and set mangrove beams, while hotel staff traveled the unpaved roads in four-wheel drive vehicles in order to meet supply-laden planes at Kilindoni's landing strip. During this period, four new tourist establishments came under construction in Utende. The first completed lodge exhibited striking differences from the existing government hotel, despite a common wish to attract a prosperous international clientele. The older establishment, built in the "high modernist" architectural style that was favored by so many newly independent African states in the 1960s and 1970s, emphasized such (often nonfunctioning) luxury items as flush toilets and air-conditioning. In contrast, the new private lodge sought to attract a clientele interested in understated, although also luxurious, ecotourism. Comprised of a series of thatched bungalows surrounding a central terrace and overlooking Chole Bay, the new lodge exuded an air of peacefulness and discrete isolation. Soothing and artful shades of ocher and blue dominated the decor. Impressionistic paintings of underwater marine life graced the wall behind the circular bar; hand-blown glassware rested delicately on the heavy wooden tables and bamboo chairs festooned with floral-patterned pillows invited sun-weary tourists to rest on the shaded terrace. Although guests stubbornly continued to arrive on Mafia only in trickles, Utende's new tour operators, largely Euro-American expatriates and white Africans, had hope. Their gamble in building on Mafia was a calculated one, premised on the rise of a new tourist attraction—the Mafia Island Marine Park.

THE ECOTOURISM SEMINAR

Gazetted in 1995 and covering approximately one-quarter of Mafia's main island and most of the surrounding smaller islands and ocean, the Mafia Island Marine Park is the first national park within Tanzania to focus on the marine environment. In a country where nearly 25 percent of the land mass has been dedicated to some form of nature protection, it is also the first park to legally incorporate the people who live there,[4] a pointed departure from the European colonial belief in the inherent incompatibility of people and wildlife. Mafia's internationally funded park was designed to be a premier example of a new kind of natural area—one that would encourage conservation *and* development through "sustainable development" based on ecotourism. Planned by international donors and environmental organizations in cooperation with national government officials, the park called for the participatory involvement of area residents, a position that echoed the calls for greater democracy being made throughout Africa at the time.

During the first week of October in 1995, the new tourist lodge was unusually full. The source of the bustle was not tourists, however, but dozens of Tanzanians and Europeans, arranged purposefully around the tables of the terraced dining room. The meeting, called by park staff, included representatives of environmental organizations, Tanzanian government officials, tour operators, a handful of European development workers and academics, and, finally, representatives of Mafia's villages. The latter, a quiet group of men, some dressed in frayed, white Islamic robes and skull caps, others in worn but neat Western shirts and trousers, had been popularly elected by their home villages. If they felt uncomfortable in these surroundings—the hotel grounds being a place well known for prohibiting island residents from "trespassing"—their composure offered no trace of it.

The gathering was a seminar on "ecotourism," which was hosted by the World Wide Fund for Nature (WWF), an international environmental organization. The meeting was intended to call together the "stakeholders" in the newly formed marine park, but it soon became clear that these stakeholders possessed widely differing agendas. Scientists had described the region as "pristine," a site of ecological biodiversity of importance not only for Mafia but also for regions beyond. Like the coast's own complex history, marine life in the Indian Ocean clearly ignored the penciled-in national boundaries of contemporary maps and, as environmentalists pointed out, Mafia appeared to serve as a crucial seed bank for other parts of the world. Spurred by a spate of research on Mafia's marine environment that was conducted during the late 1980s, representatives of national and international bodies had lobbied hard for a marine park. Responding to criticisms of preservationism as practiced within Tanzania's older wildlife parks, conservationists involved in park planning for Mafia, like many of their counterparts in the world of development, stressed the need for community participation rather than the exclusion of area residents as had been standard in the past. Participation, it was argued, was not only crucial for ethical reasons, it was also more efficient, and ultimately cheaper than the elaborate enforcement required to police the use of island resources.

For their part, Tanzania's national officials had long recognized the ability of protected areas to attract international tourism. In this debt-ridden country, which is also one of the poorest in the world,[5] national parks have served as a crucial source of foreign exchange. In addition, during the 1980s and 1990s the World Bank and IMF were presiding over attempts to transform Tanzania's socialist economy to a market-oriented form of capitalism through "structural adjustment" policies. These financial institutions, along with other multilateral and bilateral development agencies, were anxious to encourage tourism—one of the largest items in global GNP[6]—as a development strategy for Tanzania and other poorer countries. Thus, the marine park fit comfortably into the agendas of both government officials and development organizations. Consequently, in a joint effort between international organizations and Tanzanian national ministries, an organizational and legal framework was ultimately approved in the mid-1990s that would serve as the basis not only for the Mafia Island Marine Park, but as a prototype for future marine parks throughout Tanzania.

Unlike the situation in many wildlife parks on the mainland, Mafia's residents were largely supportive of the concept of a marine park.[7] Many depended heavily on fishing for their livelihoods and were angered by the practice of "dynamite fishing," an illegal technique used primarily by non-resident fishers from Dar es Salaam operating in the waters around Mafia. The dynamite blasts created underwater shock waves, which killed or stunned the fish that then floated to the surface and were scooped into boats, providing fishers with large harvests that required minimal (although risky) effort. Dynamiting, however, also ravaged the coral reefs that shelter fish and on which fish feed—reefs that are known on Mafia as the *nyumba ya samaki* or "home of the fish." According to residents, the underwater landscape was increasingly turning into a "desert" (*jangwa*) and the numbers of fish were decreasing. Although many residents on Mafia had reservations about the creation of a marine park, and worried in particular about potential restrictions on their own fishing practices, most were more concerned with the need to stop dynamiting. In a planning workshop held on Mafia in 1991, representatives of Mafia's villages, once assured of residents' rights to participation, of help in halting dynamiting, and of the creation of jobs and economic opportunities within the park, enthusiastically agreed to support the incipient marine park (MTNRE 1992; T. R. Young 1993).

However, the 1995 Ecotourism Seminar was the first meeting—as representatives of the ten villages located within the marine park would ruefully point out—to which they had been invited since the initial planning workshop in 1991. While the seminar had been called by WWF to discuss ways to ameliorate any detrimental social and environmental effects associated with tourism within the park, village representatives politely but persistently steered the discussion to more fundamental issues about the set-up and running of the park. Although the park had been described in the project's draft general management plan as "for the people and by the people" (GMP 1993:iv), residents made it clear that even the most basic information about the park had not been shared with them. The growing tensions surrounding the park emerged in striking form that afternoon. When television journalists from Dar es Salaam and their camera crew began conducting interviews on the hotel's luxurious patio, village representatives, after conferring in hushed tones, put forward a spokesperson to address the television camera in KiSwahili. In a move that would startle national and international representatives at the seminar, the village delegate boldly told the camera that members of the government agency that was entrusted with overseeing the creation of the marine park had in fact been "cooperating" with dynamite fishers, and that Mafia residents wanted the government agency removed from involvement in the park. Although the content of the message surprised few present, the openness of the accusation created a stir at the workshop (although many non-KiSwahili–speaking participants would only belatedly hear of the accusation, if at all). Perhaps even more startling than the words of the village representative was the subsequent broadcasting of this interview on national television and radio in the heady days preceding Tanzania's 1995 multiparty election, the first since the beginnings of one-party rule in 1965.

CONSERVATION AND DEVELOPMENT IN THE AGE OF THE "GLOBAL"

The contestation at the 1995 Ecotourism Seminar offers a brief glimpse of the social struggles which occurred during the implementation process of the Mafia Island Marine Park between 1994 and 1997. The goal of this book is to capture the nature of those struggles—what I refer to as the "social drama" of the marine park—in terms of the day-to-day tensions and alliances found among Mafia residents, government officials, and representatives of international organizations as each group attempted to control and define the incipient park. Although Mafia residents were initially both hopeful and wary of the marine park, their position had turned to one of strong support by the time I finished my fieldwork in 1997. Yet as documented in the epilogue to this book, the "social drama" of the marine park has been an ongoing one filled with occasionally dramatic reversals. When I returned to Mafia in 2000, many residents now claimed they hated the park, stating that it was waging a "war" against them and their livelihoods. In this book, I have attempted to make sense of these evolving struggles, considering the broader socioeconomic, political, and historical contexts in which such contestation has occurred. The goal of attempting to understand how this once promising project came to be widely hated by Mafia residents is, I believe, an important one. The answers suggest issues that should be addressed, not only by scholars of East Africa, environmentalists, or aid workers, but also by those interested in thinking critically about interactions between various parts of the world in the first years of a new millennium.

Increasingly, we hear the world in which we live characterized as a "global" one. In both the popular media and among academics from many regions, ideas of globalization have emerged as a dominant framework for thinking about the contemporary era.[8] Although the concept itself has taken on different meanings among various observers, this range of perspectives has been linked by a common assumption that interactions among regions across the globe are intensifying at an unprecedented rate. In the business press, globalization is linked with growing integration powered by an invigorated form of free market capitalism; in anthropological and cultural studies, it is associated with an intensification of cultural "flows" and population

movements between various parts of the world; and in post–Cold War political theory, it has led to debates over the ability of global processes to bypass,
and thus undermine the integrity of, nation-states. Yet, how does a place like
Mafia and its social drama fit into such conceptual frameworks?

Within accounts of globalization, sub-Saharan Africa holds a peculiar
place. An apparently exceptional region, in recent years it has experienced
greater isolation on many fronts, leading James Ferguson (1999) to theorize
that globalization in Africa may mean a state of "disconnect" rather than
intensifying interconnections. In recent decades, many regions of the continent have suffered not only growing impoverishment and, in all too many
cases, violence, but also a contraction, rather than expansion, of international
trade and an increasing sense of neglect on a world scene. In Africa, a
heightened interdependency with other regions has appeared; however, as
the 1995 Ecotourism Seminar suggests, this has occurred more in relation to
international organizations than to the free market mechanisms championed
by neoliberal reformers. And, ironically, the will to give among richer countries has decreased at the same time that the realities of crippling international debt and growing poverty have generated an intensified reliance upon
international development institutions and organizations. Yet, development
institutions have also been transformed during this period. Recent years have
witnessed an exponential growth in non-governmental organizations, or NGOs,
which are increasingly charged with carrying out development interventions,
while development paradigms now counterpoise market models with ideas
of environmental sustainability and local participation or "empowerment." It
might be argued that an analysis of globalization in Africa should focus on
precisely these themes. Indeed, some scholars have identified the harbingers
of a global era in such trends, stressing either their potentially progressive
political possibilities or pointing to the disturbing specter of new forms of
governmentality.[9] Although this book centers upon these transformations, it
nevertheless makes a different argument. Rather than providing evidence for
the impact of globalization, I argue that the social drama of Mafia's marine
park instead serves to challenge the concept of the global itself.

When I began my research on Mafia in the mid-1990s, I had not intended
to make such an argument. Initially, I conceived of my project as providing a
portrait of globalization from the perspective of sub-Saharan Africa by way
of anthropology's trademark emphasis on the "local." A global analytical
framework seemed useful in challenging assumptions that states, cultures,
and societies are bounded and relatively autonomous entities—a popular
viewpoint in previous decades even if many observers recognized far mess-
ier realities. Eric Wolf once colorfully described this perspective as a world
conceived as so many billiard balls careening off each other on a global pool
table (1982:6). In my research on Mafia, the "billiard ball" view of the world
made little sense given the long history of cosmopolitanism along the

Swahili coast, the failure of fish in Mafia's waters to observe national borders, and the fact that struggles over the Mafia Island Marine Park regularly crossed—and cross-cut—not only national boundaries but those presumed to exist between so-called First and Third Worlds. Indeed, globalization seemed an apt way to understand the social drama of the Mafia Island Marine Park, which focused on the power-laden interactions among individuals and institutions with origins on a range of continents. In writing this book, however, it became increasingly clear that the concept of globalization, even in its many manifestations, failed to fully account for what had been occurring on Mafia. In order to understand why, it is necessary to take a brief detour and consider the assumptions commonly bound up with this concept.

"Globalization": The New Narrative of Modernity

As Gibson-Graham (1996/1997) and others have argued, globalization is associated with a certain set of ideas.[10] Commonly imagined as an abstracted, even supralocal, force, globalization is often thought to happen "above" day-to-day life in ways that determine what occurs at the local "level" below and to be integrating various parts of the planet in an almost evolutionary fashion. Although many early discussions of "global" dynamics had been formulated by scholars on the political left, who were interested in the far-ranging impacts of European colonialism as well as capitalism,[11] this terminology came to be widely superceded during the 1990s by usages common on Wall Street and among the business press. This shared vocabulary suggests not only a common assumption among many on both ends of the political spectrum that capitalism is systemic and proceeds in a teleological fashion, but also a mutual desire to understand how capitalism has been changing in the contemporary era. Eventually, the concept of the global developed into a belief vigorously propounded in business circles that, in a post–Cold War era, globalization was an inevitable and unstoppable process of expanding free markets, and that those governments and individuals who failed to adapt to the juggernaut would be left behind. As such, globalization has come to be either celebrated or castigated by a range of commentators.[12]

Many anthropologists have also drawn upon the framework of the global, both challenging and supporting some of its central tenets.[13] For example, scholars of anthropology and cultural studies have contested the belief that local people are simply victims of broader processes, noting that people throughout the world give new meaning to borrowed goods and concepts, thereby "localizing" global phenomena. They have also pointed out that global cultural flows do not simply represent a one-way traffic between such power centers as the United States and their peripheries, as models of cultural imperialism presuppose, but also regularly occur across regions of the "Third World" (Appadurai 1996).[14] Nevertheless, some anthropological accounts have perhaps not gone far enough in their critical engagement with conceptions of the global. The language of "flows" can give such dynamics an abstract and homogenizing quality that contradicts anthropologists' own ethnographic focus on the specific. More seriously, there has sometimes been a tendency to accept, rather than challenge, the belief that the contemporary period represents a radical break with the past that has created a new and fundamentally different era. In the introduction to a recent anthropological volume on globalization, for example, history itself has been relegated to a single footnote.[15] As anthropologists and other scholars move to adopt the framework of the global, it might be helpful to ponder more closely why this concept has proven to be so successful as a theoretical construct in recent years. Is the exponential expansion of global discourse to be attributed solely to serious observation and analysis, or is there something more at work?

Some might argue that globalization narratives are appealing simply be-cause such accounts describe real changes happening in the contemporary world. Indeed, the shifting nature of capitalism, the social implications of new technologies, and the post–Cold War realignments of people and places *are* having significant impacts in many regions. However, the important question, I would suggest, is not whether change is occurring, but whether common narratives of globalization serve to elucidate—or to obscure—the nature of those changes. From the vantage point of Mafia, I would argue that many of the assumptions commonly equated with globalization have proven problematic. Although it might be possible to view Mafia's internationally sponsored marine park and its growing (if still tiny) tourism trade in terms of heightened global connections, a historical perspective suggests a more com-plicated reality. Mafia as part of the ancient and dynamic Indian Ocean trad-ing world was, if anything, more thoroughly associated with cultural borrow-ing, interregional trade, and mixed populations than Mafia in the present, an observation that challenges the idea that the contemporary period represents a new and radically different condition.[16] Although acknowledging that global dynamics occurred in the past does not address the crucial question of how those dynamics potentially differed from those of the present, it does usefully challenge the assumption that the contemporary period represents a radical break in human history and makes clear that the present can only be understood *in relation to*, rather than apart from, the past.

Mafia's social drama further contradicts commonplace accounts of global-ization by challenging ideas of how power works in the current era. Many contemporary debates center upon the ability of global dynamics to side-step and thus undercut the authority of nation-states, whether through new tech-nologies, the movements of capital, or a growing body of international organizations (for example, Strange 1996). And, indeed, expanding NGO networks and other international institutions are playing an increasingly powerful role in determining national agendas in heavily indebted countries like Tanzania. I argue in this book, however, that the expanding influence of international organizations, like those involved in the Mafia Island Marine Park, is having a more complicated effect, and ironically may serve to buttress governmental elites while potentially undermining the state itself. Other accounts of globalization have implied that power moves in a single direction, with global forces impacting upon local residents whether for good or ill. On Mafia, however, we see island residents who are actively creating alliances or attempting to bypass more powerful actors, representatives of international institutions who are failing to control the course of events, and presumably marginalized national elites who are moving to centerstage—all dynamics unexplored in commonplace accounts of the global.

Globalization d progress

If the dynamics on Mafia are not unique—and I strongly suspect they are not—why then have the assumptions associated with globalization narratives proven so persuasive? Some scholars have pointed to the parallels between ideas of globalization and those of "modernity" and "modernizaton" (Cooper 2001; Tsing 2001; Rouse 1999). In this analysis, I seek to push such insights further by contending that these concepts are not merely similar, but that the idea of globalization itself represents the latest incarnation of modernist narratives. Although the concept of the modern may take on different meanings and be put to a range of uses in various parts of the world (Pigg 1997; Rofel 1998; Donham 1999; Piot 1999), modernist narratives in their dominant form generally suggest that history moves progressively "forward," that it is characterized by ever increasing rationality and prosperity, that capitalism (or its modernist alter ego, socialism) serves as the primary motor for social transformation, and that a profound rupture exists between the supposedly antithetical conditions of the modern and the traditional. Like globalization, modernization has been similarly portrayed as an evolutionary force, which serves to determine what happens "below" and which penetrates, connects or infiltrates various parts of the world and transforms preexisting social processes in its own image. Indeed, the excitement and the worry that is generated by the scepter of globalization shows striking parallels with that linked to ideas of the "creative destruction" of modernity in previous eras.[17]

This is not to say that ideas of globalization do not in any way differ from prior modernist narratives. Most crucially, the meanings of nation-states, culture, and ethnic difference have shifted noticeably. During the twentieth century, the nation-state was generally held up as the proper embodiment of cultural and ethnic difference as well as identity (despite nineteenth century linkages between cosmopolitanism and capitalism [Polyani 1944]). In the contemporary period, the value of cosmopolitanism has once again been resurrected, ostensibly in a more egalitarian postcolonial fashion, while the role of nation-states has been downplayed and the idea of fixed cultural and national identities has been challenged. Even here, however, older understandings of modernity can quickly reassert themselves. For example, some observers have viewed the apparent post–Cold War surge in fundamentalism, civil wars, and identity movements as a particularist response to the homogenizing tendencies of globalization (Giddens 2000; Friedman 2000), much as the traditional once served as a counterpoint to a universalizing modernity.

Just as the categories "modern" and "traditional" have been used to label types of people, there is also an emerging tendency to map the ostensibly spatial metaphors of global and local onto particular groups. For example, Mafia residents, along with many other rural-dwellers of what used to be called the Third World, are now commonly classified by visiting international tourists as "locals." This terminology encourages the tendency to think of residents as strictly bound to a particular place, despite the cosmopolitan histories of places like the East African coast. Paralleling the use of the term "native" under European colonialism, the label "local" implies a similar kind of incarceration in space. Not surprisingly, there has also been a vicarious association of Euro-Americans with global dynamics which are thought to emanate from places like the United States, and, on Mafia, Euro-Americans were widely assumed to be cosmopolitan and influential actors in a way that island residents were not. Such usages ignore the reality that all people are necessarily both local and global actors (if we choose to use those terms). All people are global actors because everywhere individuals exist in relation to—affecting as well as being affected by—dynamics that extend beyond the borders of the nation-states in which they live. At the same time, all individuals are local actors who operate in both time and space, whether within corporate boardrooms in Tokyo or the United States, factory shop floors in Mexico, or tiny islands in the Indian Ocean.

This is not to deny that some actors wield considerably more power in transnational arenas than others. Buying a Coca-Cola in rural Tanzania is not equivalent to deciding to close three clothing factories on different continents, although both are acts with global implications. The concept of the global, however, encourages us to attribute such disparities in influence to the apparent reality that certain actors operate at global rather than local *levels*, thereby offering a false spatialization of social processes that ignores the particular mechanisms by which some individuals come to be more powerful than others. Given contemporary anthropologists' skill at critiquing the loaded symbolism of the terms *modern* and *traditional*, a dualism with numerous links to the concept of the global and local, anthropologists are well positioned to help disentangle the implications of these more current ideas for how we think about the contemporary world.

Analyzing a Social Drama

It has become a familiar trope in cultural analyses to muse about the presumed historical ruptures of the current globalizing period by opening with a series of "snapshots" of culture-out-of-place, perhaps African cloth sellers operating in France, rural-dwellers in Asia driving water buffalo past gleaming multinational factories, American tourists photographing former headhunters in the Amazon, or even poor fishermen on an Indian Ocean isle attending an international ecotourism conference. The excitement generated by such images relies upon the symbolic transgression of the locations where stereotypically modern and traditional peoples should be and what they should be doing. Thus, such tropes ironically reproduce rather than transcend these categories, while they ignore the possibility that social and cultural "hybridity" may be more the historical norm than the exception. As historian Frederick Cooper (2001) asks (in a sentiment that many anthropologists might echo), should we not instead be concerned with following the specific pathways and connections, as well as disconnections and breaks, that make up the contemporary social terrain—pathways that patently fail to be captured in the image of a snapshot or even the concept of the global? These pathways, networks, and institutional linkages are not uniform across space, as the idea of flows suggest, but rather uneven, discontinuous, and contested, or "lumpy" in Cooper's terminology. In this book, I have joined other anthropologists in seeking to capture this lumpiness, combining the insights of ethnographies of global dynamics with a critique of the concept itself.[18]

This book also seeks to convey a humanist portrayal of those individuals and groups who participate in, or are excluded from, various interconnections across geographic regions. Like Abu-Lughod (1993) and others, I worry about the potential of abstracted discourses, including those of conservation and development as well as globalization, to erase particularities of people, places, and history in ways that serve to dehumanize those being discussed. Following her lead, I have similarly sought to create an "anthropology of the particular" that relies upon tactical humanism as a representational strategy (Abu-Lughod 1991, 1993). At the same time, I have tried to create an ethnography that is sensitive to transregional dynamics without resorting to potentially misleading assumptions of supralocal global forces. George Marcus (1998) has made the excellent suggestion that anthropologists should create multisited ethnographies, or works based on research conducted in several geographic locations, as a tool for capturing complex regional interdependencies. *Rough Waters* attempts to achieve this same objective by utilizing yet another methodology, one drawn from a prior period in anthropology's history—the social drama.

According to Victor Turner's 1950s formulation, "social dramas," or analyses of conflict over extended periods of time, help to elucidate the broader structures at work within societies, as well as how such tensions come to be resolved (1957). My own use of a social drama draws even more heavily upon the work of Max Gluckman, who was Turner's teacher and the intellectual force behind the Manchester school of anthropology (Kuper 1973:137–

47). In a groundbreaking analysis that departed from then existing norms of presenting societies as static and bounded, Gluckman analyzed a power-laden event which occurred in 1938—a "social situation" in his parlance—the ceremonial opening of a bridge in Zululand attended by British colonial officials, European expatriates, and African aristocrats and commoners (1958). Although Gluckman's and Turner's accounts were directed toward more functionalist questions of how conflict and tension are overcome in order to maintain societal cohesiveness, my own analysis offers a more open-ended exploration of the ways in which conflicts and alliances among different categories of actors can serve as a map of broader power relationships. Following the various strands of the social drama of the Mafia Island Marine Park outward in order to explore their historical, institutional, socio-cultural, and economic linkages (as well as their disconnections) offers a window onto a contemporary social terrain that crosscuts presumed boundaries of First World and Third World as well as global and local "levels," while remaining focused on the day-to-day lives of actual people. Utilizing such a perspective allows those social spaces that are excluded from snapshots of the global to come into view, and permits us to explore the myriad (although still lumpy) linkages between various regions of the world.

The Lessons of a Social Drama

But where exactly does the social drama of the Mafia Island Marine Park take us and what can we learn from it? As a self-reflexively "new" kind of international project, the Mafia Island Marine Park has sought to combine the institutions and ideas of conservation and development into a form of sustainable development that centers around ecotourism and that ostensibly counters more authoritarian institutional models by encouraging community participation among residents. The hopes, worries, and conflicts surrounding the many facets of the marine park draw attention to a broad range of issues. These issues include islanders' perspectives on the region's history, the meaning of "community," and the role of fishing in economic life. It also includes the history of conservation and development policies, the role of knowledge, bureaucracy, and tourism in structuring social relationships, and the different meanings given to nature, development, and participation among various park actors. Finally, this analysis considers the fit—or lack of fit—between such dynamics and overarching frameworks of globalization.

In trying to make sense of the numerous strands of this social drama, this book has had to rely upon a broad range of literatures, two of which I will single out for attention here. Rather than utilizing the ecological models historically common in anthropological theorizing of the environment, this book has drawn inspiration from the work of political ecologists, primarily geographers, who have brought political and historical questions to bear on environmental analyses (although I have sought to add a more "cultural" perspective to such accounts, as fellow anthropologist Donald Moore [1993] has suggested).[19] To an even greater degree, this book has been influenced by an emerging critical literature on development. Rather than simply contributing to technical discussions of why particular projects succeed or (more often) fail, this literature takes "development" itself as its object of analysis and explores the ideas, knowledge practices, and organizational dynamics of international and national projects and policies (Ferguson 1994; Gupta 1998; Pigg 1996, 1997; Escobar 1995; Hodgson 2001; Benjamin 2000; Cooper and Packard 1997; T. Mitchell 1995; Crush 1995). In particular, James Ferguson's now classic account of a development project in Lesotho (1994) offers an important model for rethinking international projects. In addition to addressing how ideas of development have been premised on particular power-laden assumptions about First and Third World countries, Ferguson examined the social consequences of the institutional apparatus of a development project itself. He argued that the technocentric orientation of development ideas and institutions disguised the political effects of development projects, including such unintended consequences as the way governmental elites might use such projects to further their own authority and control. This book draws upon Ferguson's work, but also focuses on a different kind of project and utilizes a somewhat different analytical and methodological orientation. Consequently, it explores a range of issues left unexamined in Ferguson's account.

As a new type of international project, the Mafia Island Marine Park was consciously created to counter critiques leveled against an older generation of projects, including the one analyzed by Ferguson. The marine park was intended to address charges that national parks, which generally have been based upon exclusionary preservationist models, disregard the economic welfare of poor citizens and are authoritarian in their orientation. Paralleling common trends among development institutions, the design of the marine park sought to encourage "sustainable development" through ecotourism and to incorporate the participation of affected communities. This book suggests that Ferguson's insights into the social implications of technocentrism continue to hold relevance for the ways in which participation and communities are conceptualized within this new generation of projects. However, as the analytical focus of this book shifts from the institutional apparatus privileged by Ferguson to the human interrelationships occurring in and around the marine park itself, still other dynamics come into view.[20] Such dynamics include the ways in which such institutions are contested (successfully or not) by "target" populations, how individuals and groups create alliances as well as suffer exclusions, and the ways in which ideas of development, nature, and participation are variously understood, appropriated, disputed, and used.

Such points of contestation and reinterpretation, in turn, raise questions about the theoretical paradigms that have increasingly been used to understand development. Many critical development scholars, as well as social theorists concerned with "modern" institutions more broadly, have drawn heavily upon the work of French philosopher Michel Foucault. And, indeed, the insights afforded by Foucault have been powerful. His work has drawn attention to power dynamics in arenas outside of formal state authority through its focus on the "disciplinary" techniques of modern institutions and forms of knowledge (for example, Foucault 1972, 1977, 1978, 1994). In contrast to liberal assumptions that emphasize the role of modern institutions in creating free individuals, Foucault's account suggests that modern disciplinary techniques as well as the forms of subjectivity that such disciplines generate and through which individuals learn to "discipline" themselves, are inherently implicated within broader power relationships. As utilized by critical development theorists, such perspectives have offered important insights into how development institutions and paradigms, as forms of modern social organization and knowledge, underwrite broader international hierarchies and serve to shape how individuals conceptualize themselves and a larger social world. Foucauldian insights, as will become clear, are evident throughout this volume.

Yet, there are also aspects of this legacy that are potentially limiting. Despite Foucault's critique of teleological ideas of history, there is an implicit sense in his accounts in which "modernity," or the transition to it, continues to exist as something that requires explanation. Such accounts thereby implicitly draw attention to what is presumed to be qualitatively unique about Western societies or "modernity" more generally. At the same time, the Foucauldian emphasis upon institutions and discourses, rather than human actors (even while acknowledging the ability of disciplinary regimes to generate new subjectivities as well as resistance), draws attention away from the multiple interpretations and uses to which development and conservation—along with other modern ideas and institutions—may be put.

There is a growing interest in examining the multiple interpretations and uses of development (for example, Hodgson 2001; Pigg 1996, 1992; Walley 2003). Although the concept of development has disturbing historical origins in colonial-era European evolutionary thought, like all concepts, it is open to ambiguities, conflicting meanings, and reinterpretation. For example, as Cooper and Packard note, independence-era nationalists appropriated the colonialist conception of development and sought to transform it into a language of entitlement (Cooper and Packard 1997). On Mafia, rather than politically appropriating the concept of *maendeleo* or development, residents have instead mapped it onto broader historical understandings of wealth and economic relations. Similarly, what are often referred to as modern institutions have also been put to multiple uses within the marine park. For example, contestation over the apparatus of park bureaucracy itself formed a significant strand in the social drama of Mafia's marine park (see chapter 7). In addition, the fact that bureaucracies *can* institutionalize rights and counter abuses of power (while also imposing their will upon the less powerful) is a point that may be too easily neglected in some Foucauldian accounts. On Mafia, the vigorous attempts of certain government officials to oppose the institutionalized participation of islanders in an effort to consolidate their own authority underscores such a reality. In sum, this analysis of daily interactions within an international project draws attention to the conflicting ways in which "modern" institutions and ideas are understood and used by particular individuals and groups. This is not to suggest, however, that social phenomena are infinitely malleable or that contestation and reinterpretation should be invariably romanticized as the "resistance" of marginalized groups (particularly since the powerful engage in similar tactics). In the end, the ability of individuals to contest, appropriate, and reinterpret may be most useful in analytical terms because it draws into relief the broader power relationships in which all actors are embedded.[21]

Ultimately, the social drama of the Mafia Island Marine Park suggests a reality in which history is both structured by existing power relationships and open-ended, and in which everyday social relationships consist of practices and ideas with multiple historical and social genealogies. Although such practices and ideas often come to be labeled either modern or traditional, particularly in non-western contexts, there is nothing inherently oppositional about such phenomena. For example, Mafia residents countered their exclusion from park bureaucracy (despite the official language of participation) by drawing upon historically salient models of patron–client relationships in an effort to find individuals who could influence the bureaucracy on their behalf. Similarly, Mafia residents depended upon noncommodified networks of reciprocity, at the same time that they were thoroughly enmeshed in markets, and they failed to view scientific paradigms in opposition to popular knowledge.

Such "mixed" phenomena can be, and have been, interpreted in various ways. The most common interpretation in both First World and Third World countries is to assume that such realities represent an incomplete transition from traditional to modern ideas and practices. For postcolonial theorists, some of whom seek to make Foucault's ideas applicable to nonwestern parts of the world, such phenomena may instead suggest a condition of "hybridity," a terminology that implies that the modern and the traditional are simultaneously distinct and intertwined, much as a biological hybrid mixes two separate species.[22] For some Marxists, the persistence of "traditional" practices stems from their functionality within the contemporary world. For example, the tendency of capitalists to pay lower wages to laborers who also utilize subsistence strategies has been seen in this light.[23] In their own way, each of these viewpoints privileges the perspective of the modern, assuming the "modern" to be the dominant factor or the logic to which other logics must defer. Even theories of "hybridity" problematically assume the unique ability of modernity to create such "mixed" social dynamics.

In yet another theoretical vein, some anthropologists have emphasized that "traditions" are constantly reworked and assume new meanings in different contexts (without necessarily presuming a functionalist purpose),[24] while others have emphasized the very different symbolic understandings that "modernity" may take on for various groups (for example, Donham 1999, Pigg 1996, Rofel 1998). Pushing such assertions further might suggest an alternative way of thinking about the world that does not unduly privilege the modern. I would argue that such apparently "mixed" phenomena might instead force us to recognize that the social worlds in which we all live are comprised of a patchwork of dynamics with varying social and historical origins, not all of which follow or are being subsumed by an overarching logic of capitalism or modernity. In this patchwork world, techniques of power and the subjectivities they create may reflect different histories, may overlap, coexist, and be in a constant state of transformation (with non-modernist dynamics being as potentially problematic as modern ones). It is toward this view of the world that some scholars, who are pushing the boundaries of poststructuralist paradigms, appear to point (Mitchell 1998; Gibson-Graham 1996). At the same time, however, depicting social life in terms of a diversity of ideas and practices does not necessitate throwing one's hands up in despair at the world's complexity. Historical trends do indeed "move" in certain directions. However, this is a product of the social logics at work within particular social and economic relationships, networks, and institutions. It is not because there is a teleological totalizing force at work that is transforming the world as narratives of modernity and, their latest offspring, globalization, both suggest. In short, rather than arguing that abstracted global processes bind people in different parts of the world to-gether, might we not instead emphasize a common humanity that is uni-formly worked from patchwork cloth?

Finally, it should be clearly stated that although this analysis is often criti-cal of the processes at work within the Mafia Island Marine Park, it is not intended as an attack on development—if what is meant by "development" is an increased standard of living and greater equality for more than a small percentage of a population. Nor is this work a critique of environmentalism. On the contrary, it demonstrates how crucial environmental issues are to poorer people such as those on Mafia, who are heavily dependent upon natu-ral resources, even if such issues are discussed in terms not easily recognized by many Western environmentalists. Although I do not believe, as some imply, that poorer or "indigenous" people are inherently better ecologists, I do believe that a "better" environmentalism is necessarily one that addresses the inequities of poverty and access to natural resources both across and within so-called First World and Third World. Perhaps most importantly, this book does not imply that all efforts at reform are useless. Rather it argues that current efforts to reform the ideas and practices of development and conservation institutions have been, at best, superficial and that there is a pressing need for more radical forms of change. Finally, if the dynamics presented in this book are messy and complex, this should not be a cause for despair. Such messiness might represent the appropriate starting point from which both our thinking and our political action should begin.

On Mafia, residents speak of *maji makali* or the "fierce" or "rough" waters that endanger the lives of fishers as well as travelers. Yet, this sense of the ocean as dangerous is paralleled by the recognition that the possibility of sustaining life rests on their ability to harvest from the sea, a need that has dramatically increased in recent years. Residents have held a similar ambivalence toward the Mafia Island Marine Park. On the one hand, they have expressed high hopes that the park can assist them in maintaining the marine resources upon which they depend; on the other, the park holds the potential to forbid access to natural resources necessary for survival. It is through these rough waters that this book follows the social drama of the Mafia Island Marine Park.

NEGOTIATING THE ROLE OF RESEARCHER

In an ethnographic project that focuses on the interrelationships among a range of actors, it is crucial to acknowledge how the researcher is positioned in this mix. Anthropologists have increasingly come to recognize that, while accustomed to thinking of ourselves as observers, we are also actors, and our own particular social location is an inescapable part of our work. The point in analyzing our own positioning is neither narcissism nor the belief that this is somehow more "objective." Rather, it points to the recognition that cultural anthropology is in essence dialogic, the product of interrelationships and interactions among people, and that this interaction is intrinsic to the work we produce (for example, Haraway 1983; Rabinow 1977; Crapanzano 1980; Clifford and Marcus 1986; Marcus and Fischer 1986; and Clifford 1988).

Before describing my relationship with other individuals and groups on Mafia, I should mention how I myself arrived there. I did not originally intend to conduct research on the Mafia Island Marine Park. In fact, I had not intended to work on Mafia at all, but rather to study tourism on neighboring Zanzibar Island. A growing interest in environmental issues and a desire to do something "useful," however, made me dissatisfied with this choice. Consequently, I was intrigued when I was invited by an expatriate from the United States who owned a hotel in Zanzibar to come to Chole Island in the Mafia archipelago where he and a partner were setting up a community-based tourism initiative. At the time, I knew little about Mafia, which lay well to the south of Zanzibar, other than what I had gathered from reading Pat Caplan's 1975 ethnography, at that time almost the only published social scientific work done on Mafia since a German geographer visited the islands in the 1890s.[25] Mafia seemed to be best known among tourists, academics, and many Tanzanians themselves for being "unknown." Intrigued by the idea of working with island residents as they negotiated the economic and social shoals of tourism development via this community-based project, I decided to split my research time between Zanzibar and Mafia. In exchange for a place to live, I agreed to help the budding tourism initiative by teaching English to adults on Chole and by offering various kinds of assistance to the elected committees of island residents that were to help run the project. I quickly became drawn into life on Chole and eventually moved my research entirely to Mafia. I shortly realized, however, that Chole's residents were more concerned with fish than with tourists. This realization led me to redirect my attention to the growing controversy surrounding what was ultimately the catalyst for Mafia's expanding tourism industry as well as the potential protector of its fish—the Mafia Island Marine Park.

In 1994, when I first arrived on Chole, an island with less than 800 residents, my own social positioning would prove instrumental to the types of relationships that I would develop. Because I was initially known to the island's residents as someone who had volunteered to teach English, a subject many people were eager to learn, and because I was associated with a project that many viewed with high hopes, I was in the enviable position of being viewed as someone useful to have around Chole. During my first weeks, I was surprised by the small gifts I received when I walked around the island, and invariably returned home with my hands and pockets full of oranges, mangoes, unripe coconuts, and boiled eggs. Because Chole was so small, and because most of its residents were bound by ties of kinship and marriage, it was relatively easy to forge links to the various social networks on the island, and I quickly developed a sense of belonging that contrasted sharply with my prior experiences in East Africa, first as a high school teacher in rural western Kenya and later as a student and researcher in Zanzibar Town. As my attachment to certain individuals and families on Chole grew, so did my desire to repay their hospitality and generosity.

My growing desire to be useful, was, I believe, paralleled by the desire of many people on Chole that I *be* useful. Although many residents were never entirely clear about the nature of anthropology as a discipline—most preferred to think of me in terms of the known and respected category of "teacher"—they, nonetheless, were interested in my assuming roles that might be of use to them. When I first arrived, there was only one person on Chole who spoke English. Many islanders were therefore eager for assistance in communicating with the growing number of Euro-Americans who were coming to Mafia as a result either of the tourism industry or the marine park. Some of these visitors held positions of considerable influence and represented a potential source of jobs or other benefits to islanders; others were merely vacationing, but residents hoped that the visitors would stimulate a market for local wares and services. Even though many tourists and expatriate workers seemed untroubled by their failure to speak KiSwahili, people on Chole, in accordance with the cosmopolitan spirit that has long characterized the coast, were troubled by their inability to communicate or even greet these newcomers, an unthinkable affront to coastal standards of politeness. An older man on Chole expressed a common frustration when he informed me that, "People are coming to our island, yet we stand around like *bubu* (deaf-mutes), unable to speak to them." Thus, in addition to teaching informal English classes, I was often called upon to serve as translator.

The roles that people on Chole most desired for me to play, however, were those of information source and potential liaison. As a researcher and a "European," I had access to people and to information that they did not. In an atmosphere where secrecy and the withholding of knowledge was a primary technique for consolidating and maintaining power, a willingness to share information was highly valued. I was also at times called upon to serve as an intermediary with individuals involved in Chole's tourist camp or with the marine park. Some people clearly hoped that what I might say, or later write in my book or *ripoti*, could serve as a means to communicate with more powerful others who could not, or would not, otherwise hear their viewpoints.

Although my relationships with people on Chole were marked by a closeness built, in some cases, on affection and friendship, and in others on mutual self-interest, my relationships with other actors on Mafia were at times more fraught. As is already clear, government officials played a central role in the unfolding marine park drama, both by virtue of their being members of a national and educated elite and in their role as an interface between international organizations and Mafia's residents. Government officials assigned to Mafia District, the Maritime Division,[26] and the marine park were overwhelmingly male, hailed from the mainland, and lived in the government administrative center of Kilindoni on Mafia's main island.

Although government officials were central actors in the marine park drama, I had considerably less interaction with them than I did with people on Chole. Difficulties were posed both by geography and my own social positioning. The journey to and from the government center, while not far in terms of kilometers was a difficult one, often requiring an entire day's travel.

Those living on Chole regularly complained of the erratic service of the "ferry," a sailboat dependent on the vagaries of wind and weather that was the only public transportation on or off of Chole Island (the ferry captain himself was kept to this thankless job only by the social pressure of island elders). Once the ferry deposited Chole residents in Utende village on the main island, passengers faced even greater difficulties trying to travel the 15 km into Kilindoni. One often-broken and dangerously overcrowded pick-up truck traveled from Utende into Kilindoni and back each day (following a schedule even more erratic than the winds that powered the ferry). Like other Chole residents, I considered myself lucky if I was able to squeeze into or on top of the truck—especially since the less fortunate were left to walk through the sand and heat. Even when I managed to make my way into Kilindoni, I found that my ability to interact socially with government bureaucrats was limited. Formal interviews, not surprisingly, elicited vague pronouncements meant for public consumption. Informal interactions, the stuff of which anthropological understandings are built, were limited for other reasons. As a young, unmarried woman, any attempts on my part to spend time informally with male government officials would have been misinterpreted by both Mafia's residents and by the officials themselves—a situation of which I was keenly aware.

This situation posed a striking contrast to the one on Chole where I had informal access to many homes, and would spend hours visiting and gossiping with friends, hearing what people said in relaxed moments both to myself and others. Although I worried about this unevenness of access, I also recognized that overly close relationships with government officials would have threatened the trust I had developed with people on Chole who viewed such officials with suspicion. People on Mafia often complained about government bureaucrats, arguing that the officials preferred to spend their time in Kilindoni rather than addressing the needs of district residents. Many felt that government officials were not to be trusted and best ignored, or viewed them, as in the case of dynamite fishing, as outright adversaries. As time progressed, I also noticed that as I became closer to island residents, some government officials appeared increasingly wary of me, a dynamic that, ironically, further cemented my relationships with Chole residents. Increased trust in one arena clearly meant increased suspicion in another, and in the end I was forced to recognize that there was no "objective" space outside of already existing social relationships in which I could conduct research.

My research possibilities on Mafia were also strongly shaped by my being an *mzungu* (the KiSwahili term which encapsulates all "Europeans" including those from the United States), as well as by where I lived and the access to other categories of people that this position afforded. When I first arrived on Chole, I stayed in one of two tents pitched in a deserted portion of the island that would eventually become the tourist camp, a location that turned out to be an excellent observation point for the social interactions with which my research was concerned. Initially I was the only *mzungu* in residence, and during my stays in 1994 and 1995, those who frequented the camp were largely Chole residents—the committee members overseeing community aspects of the project, day laborers working construction, and long-term employees of the camp. The camp quickly became an informal social gathering place for those who worked there and for many who did not. Consequently, there were always opportunities to participate in casual conversations, to ask questions, and to watch the processes by which residents were negotiating this tourist initiative.

During the 19 months (over the course of three years) in which I lived on Chole, the camp grew to the point where it was difficult to recall the plot of bush on which it was originally sited. When I left Chole in 1997, the camp consisted of seven large canvas safari tents under plaited palm frond roofs built with mangrove poles. There was also a coral and cement office and store room, several latrines (I had originally used the bush), landscaped showering stalls, and a canopied dining area with a large table around which various European and American workers as well as the odd tourist, would gather for meals. (By the time of my visit in 2000, the camp had become even more elegant and luxurious, with magnificent wooden tree houses perched in the baobob trees along the water's edge and with guests enjoying lantern-lit meals within the island's stone ruins with *zumari* or horn music playing in the background.)

Although during my latter periods of fieldwork in 1996 and 1997, I often missed the "old days" spent socializing and chatting with Chole residents in the camp, these changes brought new research possibilities as well. Conversations held at the central dining table, over meals of beans and rice when there were only "workers," or crab claws, fancy hors d'oeuvres, pastas, and grilled fish when there were guests, became an important source of information for my work. When the tour operators who had created Chole's camp were in residence, they brought news of the expatriate-dominated tourism industry, as well as development and conservation circles in Dar es Salaam and Zanzibar. In addition to friends and guests, they also brought various volunteers or others who agreed to work on Chole for several month stints, often with minimal pay. At various points, development workers, tourism industry personnel, naturalists, construction workers, journalists, teachers, filmmakers and an eclectic assortment of others, including an archaeologist, a geologist, a landscape architect, and a performance studies professor all spent time in Chole's camp. Although a few Africans stayed at various points, including several Zanzibari employees and a handful of professionals from mainland Tanzania and Kenya, the vast majority of those who worked and stayed in the camp were *wazungu* (pl. of *mzungu*) hailing from all parts of the "West," including Britain, the United States, Holland, Germany, and Italy.

Over those evening meals, I learned far more about the social workings of East Africa's development world, as well as its tourism industry, than I could have anticipated. Particularly on those occasions when dinner guests included central figures in the expatriate worlds of Zanzibar and Dar es Salaam, or those involved in Mafia's tourist industry and marine park, dining table conversation centered on the inner workings and political machinations of government ministries, international organizations, and expatriate-owned businesses involved in conservation and development within Tanzania as well as on Mafia. Just as information, both accurate and inaccurate, rapidly circulated through gossip networks among Mafia residents, so too gossip was equally central to the expatriate world—with one major difference. Because development workers, employees of international organizations, and even moderate-level investors play a substantial role in determining national policies in a country like Tanzania, one of the peculiarities of expatriate circles was that individual "Europeans" (to use the KiSwahili translation) could travel in far higher social and political circles in such countries than they could have in their home countries—a phenomenon as consistent today as it was under colonialism. Even Europeans visiting for short periods could with relative ease gain access to these numerically small networks by virtue of national and cultural ties. Thus, "Europeans" could routinely gain informal access to information far beyond the reach of most nonelite Tanzanians.

Although there were various shoals to negotiate in dealing with government officials, there were also more shoals than I had anticipated in interactions with fellow *wazungu*. Although I was deeply dependent upon, and grateful for, the support and assistance provided by numerous fellow Euro-Americans, living in a tourist site within an expatriate-dominated industry at times presented unanticipated moments of awkwardness. We all possess "cultural scripts" for imagining what "others" are like, and many Tanzanians held particular visions of *wazungu* just as most Europeans held particular assumptions about Africans. However, it is undeniable that these scripts are also implicated in power relationships between groups, and living in a tourist site meant that I was often in the uncomfortable position of having to negotiate between these power-laden scripts, not only for myself but for others. On numerous occasions, I was asked by European tourists to act as a translator or in other ways to mediate their relationships with people on Chole. If visitors behaved in ways that were impolite by coastal standards (as sometimes happened), it was difficult not to worry that such behavior would reflect badly on me as a fellow *mzungu*.

Although in general Chole residents were remarkably welcoming of visitors, they were annoyed by the failure of some *wazungu* to dress appropriately, to take photos without asking permission, or to fail to respond to greetings that they did not understand. "They don't know this is not the proper way to act here," many people would tolerantly acknowledge. However, at times, such cultural "miscommunications" seemed to shade into something more disturbing, namely, the particular constellation of power relationships in which we are all enmeshed as residents of so-called First and Third Worlds. Perhaps influenced by stereotypical images of Africans common in the news media or having grown accustomed to Tanzanians as service personnel in high-end hotels and restaurants, some visitors treated Chole's residents as cultural backdrop rather than individuals. Whereas most European visitors came to East Africa precisely because they were open-minded, others shared the dismissive stereotypes about Africans common to much of European history. Such attitudes were disturbing to me, not because they were different from those with which I had grown up, but precisely because they were embarrassingly similar. Although island residents acknowledged the problematic behavior of some *wazungu,* I think I sometimes found these incidents more awkward than Chole residents, who were busy worrying about their own cultural literacy in relation to visitors.

At the same time, other Europeans may also have felt ambivalence about having an anthropologist in their midst. Although some short-term visitors to Mafia seemed to romanticize the role of the anthropologist, as well as the act of establishing "rapport" with islanders, a few Europeans, particularly those who were well established within expatriate circles in places like Utende tended toward the opposite extreme. Some *wazungu* who had been born in East Africa or had lived there for long periods were justifiably tired of the stream of researchers who came for short stays and then left to publish grand pronouncements about the region. Others simply assumed that research such as mine was unimportant: After all where were the educated research assistants, expatriate-style housing, four-wheel drive vehicle, and large-scale budget associated with "serious" academics (particularly those linked with the ubiquitous aid projects)? In general, such tensions suggest the need to examine the social positioning of different groups of Euro-Americans in relation to each other (for instance, as researchers, businesspeople, aid workers, missionaries, environmentalists, tourists, and African citizens), just as it would be necessary to identify the social divisions found among diverse groups of Tanzanians.

Finally, I had to admit that my own social positioning, including a particular class background, worked to shape my perceptions of, and interactions with, various park actors. However unlikely it seemed, Chole, with its diverse population bound by a dense web of social and familial ties rooted in the area over several generations, held strong parallels with the ethnic, working-class urban neighborhood in the United States where I was raised. On Chole, both women and men made sure that I maintained the social networks to which they had introduced me, by encouraging me to attend weddings, funerals, and other *mashuguli* (social events) when appropriate, by hinting that it was time to visit particular individuals who might be feeling slighted socially, or by using guilt to chastise me when I let other concerns like my research take precedence over social obligations. Their concerns spoke of a place where the maintenance of thick networks of social ties was highly valued and reminded me of my own family and neighborhood. In addition, the cynical indifference that men and women displayed in casual conversation toward those in power spoke volumes about how they felt themselves to be positioned outside such structures. Despite the obvious differences in culture and standard of living between Chole and the Southeast Side of Chicago, there were structural similarities that at times made life on Chole feel strangely familiar. In particular, I was disturbed by the condescension many educated "experts" and government officials showed Chole's residents, in part because it reminded me of more muted social slights that my own family members, some with similarly limited educational backgrounds, had also experienced.

Although anthropologists regularly find themselves mediating between cultural worlds and even class positions, I was often aware of the similarities between the role that I played on Mafia and at home in Chicago. On Chole, I was often asked to help deal in small ways with a bureaucratic and elite world outside Mafia. For example, one afternoon, I found myself sitting in the home of a family to which I had become close, helping an elderly man who had gone blind from diabetes and his unschooled wife make logical piles out of heaps of medical bills, prescriptions, and instructions, many of which were written in English, the language of expertise, rather than KiSwahili, the language of communication. Earlier that day, I had read aloud to them from the KiSwahili version of the self-help medical guide "Where There Is No Doctor," which I had found in Dar es Salaam after much difficulty, and we shared information about his illness. Sitting on that floor, I was struck by the parallels with my situation only a few months earlier when I had been called home from Tanzania to visit my ailing father in Chicago. At that time, I had similarly sat on the floor sorting through medical bills and insurance forms, explaining bureaucratic procedures and pill schedules, and offering condensed readings from books about heart disease. The contexts were very different, and yet similar structural positions were at work. This incident, along with countless others, underscored for me that First and Third Worlds were far less distant than I had been raised to believe.

WRITING THE PARTICULAR: THE ORGANIZATION OF THIS BOOK

Although the process of building relationships with various actors during fieldwork is a complex one, so too is the process of committing the ambiguities of research into a written form. Writing an ethnography of the "particular" can also create specific problems when the topic is as politically charged as the one addressed in this book. Descriptions of real people and events risk invading the privacy of the people presented therein, a risk only partially offset by the use of pseudonyms. Focusing on particular events and struggles not only at the village level but in the context of public forums also means potentially alienating public figures and organizations whose identities are not easily concealed (and, clearly, the primary players in the struggles over the Mafia Island Marine Park will be recognizable to those involved in the park regardless of my efforts at disguise). As anthropology increasingly invades the territory of journalism and takes as its subjects public figures more accustomed to its conventions, it is appropriate to consider how this affects the ethics of doing anthropology. While an insight offered in an unguarded moment of personal confession is often considered the most telling kind of information for anthropologists, when our subjects are public figures whose identities are less easily concealed, should this alter the nature of what we commit to paper? I have tried to address this issue in two ways. First, I have followed anthropological conventions and used pseudonyms when referring to individuals, as well as to tourism establishments and a government ministry, in an admittedly imperfect effort to protect the privacy of those involved. I have also, at times, given less-detailed descriptions than I would have liked. In particular, writing about corruption, a topic not easily documented or cited, poses difficulties for researchers. Corruption, however, is central to how Mafia residents understand the dynamics of the marine park and other international projects, and there is no way to make sense of their actions without addressing this issue. Although many Mafia residents *believe* such claims to be true, causing them to act in particular ways that are important to this research, this book, clearly, can itself make no claims to the accuracy or inaccuracy of such views.

In writing this book, I have begun with the conceptual heart of the analysis, the "social drama" itself. Part 1 consists of a single chapter, "Battling for the Marine Park," and examines the struggles over the Mafia Island Marine Park among Mafia residents, government officials and representatives of international organizations during the period of the park's implementation between 1994 and 1997. The second part of this book includes three chapters focusing on those actors in the preceding drama with which I am most concerned—residents of Chole Island within the Mafia archipelago. Although Chole residents may be seen by some as exemplars of the "local," I contest such a view, considering how life for Chole residents is shaped in complex ways by national, regional, and transregional dynamics both in the present and in the past. Chapter 2, "'When People Were as Worthless as Insects': History, Popular Memory, and Tourism on Chole," explores the historical narratives told by Chole residents and asks what such narratives reveal about residents' understandings of power and their relationships with groups and institutions beyond Mafia. Chapter 3, "The Making and Unmaking of 'Community,'" considers the various meanings of "community," a central concept to planners of participatory conservation and development projects and one that, along with the "local," is often used as a counterpoint to ideas of the "global." Chapter 4, "Where There Is No Nature," challenges the tendency of Euro-American environmentalists to view rural residents of the Third World as embedded in "nature" without exploring what nature means—and does not mean—to people like those on Mafia. It explores fishing practices on Chole as well as the relationship between market and nonmarket practices and considers how such processes are related to broader national and transnational hierarchies.

The third and final section of this book includes three chapters focusing on the marine park itself, its historical predecessors and how the implementation of the park has played out in day-to-day life on Mafia. Chapter 5, "Establishing Experts: Conservation and Development Policies from Colonialism to Independence," considers the historical rise of national parks, conservation policies, and development paradigms within Tanzania and how such histories shape the social drama of the Mafia Island Marine Park. Chapter 6, "Pushing Paper and Power: Bureaucracy and Knowledge within a National Marine Park," acknowledges that although "globalization" is widely associated with the spread of multinational capitalism, it has also been linked to the expanding influence of international organizations and the bureaucracies that they create. This chapter considers bureaucracy itself to be a site of struggle within the marine park and explores how the valorization and exclusion of particular kinds of knowledge within park institutions works to marginalize Mafia residents despite the official emphasis on participation. The final chapter, "Tourist Encounters: Alternate Readings of Nature and 'Development,'" considers the different meanings assigned to development by various park actors as well as the social implications of the particular form of "development" being championed within the marine park—tourism.

Finally, the epilogue, "Participating in the Twenty-First Century," resumes the social drama of the marine park which began this book. Based on information gathered during a return visit to Mafia during the summer of 2000, it follows the contestation over the marine park since 1997, exploring some occasionally dramatic reversals. In offering this final installment of Mafia's "social drama," I argue for the necessity of gaining critical distance on commonplace narratives of globalization as well as technocentric understandings of conservation and development in order to explore the complex power relationships at work in the contemporary era. I argue that the drama of the marine park offers a vision of the world in which modern and nonmodern elements comingle in a way that contests totalizing narratives of both modernity and globalization. By taking into account such complex dynamics, we might be better able to understand the interrelationships between humans and the natural environments of which we are a part, allowing us to explore possibilities for countering the degradation of nature in ways that address, rather than exacerbate, broader social inequalities.

PART ONE

Figure 1. Mafia Island Marine Park sign in Kilindoni. (Credit: Pat Caplan)

CHAPTER ONE

Battling for the Marine Park

THE "SOCIAL DRAMA" of Tanzania's Mafia Island Marine Park forms the core of this analysis. Between 1994 and 1997, island residents, national government officials, and representatives of international organizations struggled to define and control the fledgling marine park, a drama that points to the central issues that will be explored in subsequent chapters. In order to understand these events, it is necessary to locate this drama within the broader international transformations which were occurring during the 1990s. Such transformations included: a post–Cold War reworking of geopolitical alignments, a resurgence of belief in the free market, demands by multilateral institutions that poorer countries adopt the market-oriented economic reforms known as Structural Adjustment programs, a rapid expansion in the influence and number of international organizations, and the ascendency of the language of "sustainable development." In addition, yet another transformation occurred that holds particular relevance for this social drama. In response to expanding post–Cold War discourses of democratization, "participatory" frameworks began to appear at the center of many international projects.

Although this growing interest in "participation" was still relatively new at the time of my fieldwork on Mafia, activists and social theorists have recently begun to direct attention toward understanding the social and political implications of such frameworks (for example, Craig and Mayo 1995; Ribot 1996, 1999, 2000; Cooke and Kothari 2001; Paley 2001; Peters 2000). While supporters have hoped that the emphasis on participation would encourage the "empowerment" of poorer people in the so-called Third World, critics suggest that the language of participation merely disguises the ways in which powerful international bodies continue to impose their own agendas and disenfranchise the poor. My own interest lies in shifting discussions of participation away from the dualistic poles of either utopian hope or cynical skepticism. Instead, this analysis seeks to consider the broader social and political dynamics at work in a "participatory" project, as well as the range of ways in which "participation" comes to be understood, appropriated, and used by various park actors ranging from Mafia residents to government officials and international organizations (see also Paley 2001). While the concept of participation is useful in drawing into relief decision-making authority within projects and in offering a space in which the allocation of those rights might be contested, it is also clear that the effects of participation on Mafia have been radically different from those envisioned in planning documents.

At the same time, the "social drama" of the marine park underscores the inability of commonplace narratives of globalization to account for the contradictory impact of international organizations on Tanzania's national scene. Assumptions that social dynamics occur at global or international, national and local "levels"—with international organizations involved in a zero-sum game of power with national officials—disguises the symbiotic relationship between national and international institutions. Many narratives of globalization also fail to identify the channels—often ones with long histories—through which power is wielded within this contemporary park. In presenting this social drama, I begin by depicting a crucial moment in Chole residents' relationship with the incipient marine park, then consider its "cast of characters," and, finally, offer an expanded discussion of three critical moments in the struggles over the Mafia Island Marine Park.

A MEETING

When I began my fieldwork in 1994, the Mafia Island Marine Park was still a vague and distant prospect to residents, and the only activity occurring in relation to the park seemed to be happening in faraway offices. It *was* clear, however, that dynamite fishing formed an overwhelming concern on Chole. I first heard an explosion while conducting an English class held at Chole's tourist camp, then in its earliest stages of construction. Unable to recognize the far-off sound, I ignored the blast and continued teaching. However, the dozen or so men, who were seated upon wooden poles, cement blocks, and other building paraphernalia, cocked their heads and listened anxiously;[1] all were fishers or had been in the past. Shaking their heads in disapproval, they informed me how dynamiters from Dar es Salaam were destroying the fishing around Mafia, and throughout the rest of the day a palpable sense of worry hung over the island.

Over the next several months, I would learn more as men on the island repeatedly turned conversations to the issue of dynamiting. Women on Chole hunted octopus and shell fish at low tide, but fishing from boats or with the use of hand lines or traps was considered to be men's work. Consequently, although dynamiting was a worry for all residents, it fell particularly within men's sphere of concerns. Some men ruefully explained how they were powerless to stop the dynamiting: if they went after the culprits, dynamite would be thrown into their own boats. Others complained about the futility of seeking help. They claimed that people had often tried to report dynamiting to the government's Maritime Division in Kilindoni, either making the long trip into town themselves or attempting to report the blasts more quickly by begging the use of the telephone at the government-owned Mafia Island Lodge in Utende. But, they contended, help never arrived; all they received were protests that there was either no boat or no engine fuel available at the maritime office. When these men mentioned the marine park, it was invariably to express hope that the park would set up regular *doria* (patrols) capable of halting the dynamiting.

In an impromptu meeting on Chole in July of 1995, nearly a year later, the tensions that linked dynamiting with the politics of the newly formed marine park would become strikingly clear. Through expatriate networks linked to Chole's tourist camp, I had met David Holston, an employee of WWF who had appeared on Mafia as the park's technical adviser. This position was conceived as a counterpart to the government post of acting warden, an official with whom Holston would share joint responsibility for setting up the marine park. As we talked, Holston revealed that some national officials opposed implementing the park as it had been planned, particularly its community participation aspects. As a non-KiSwahili speaker who was thereby limited in his interactions with residents, he further speculated that Mafia's villagers themselves did not fully support the marine park. Worried that the viewpoints of island residents had failed to reach such an influential figure, I offered my services as translator and suggested that Holston visit Chole to speak informally with residents.

On the appointed day, however, the idea that this would be a casual visit was quickly dispelled. After Holston arrived, I accompanied him to the home of the island's village chairman for an introductory visit—an obligatory act of politesse in Mafia's villages. The popularly elected chairman of Chole village, Mzee Maarufu, with his tattered *kofia* (Muslim skull cap) and his slow, philosophical speech was a widely respected man with a reputation for integrity that extended throughout Mafia's villages. When he discovered that the *mzungu* (European) from the marine park was visiting Chole and willing to talk to residents, Mzee Maarufu seized the opportunity. Shortly afterwards, I was informed that a meeting had been convened at the school house on Chole's waterfront and that people had already assembled and were waiting expectantly for Holston. I was startled that this informal occasion had so quickly been turned into a "meeting." On an island where only a handful of people possess watches and where tides, winds, prayers, and mealtimes structure the pace of daily life far more than the hands of nonexistent clocks, gathering people for meetings was generally an extremely slow process. However, by the time we arrived, approximately thirty people had already congregated in the school—a striking turnout for an unplanned event.

Serving as translator, I conveyed Holston's few words of self-introduction and his open call for questions to the mostly middle-aged men who had gathered. Despite the emphasis along the East African coast on social proto-col and the delicate, even circuitous, wording of sensitive issues, the ques-tions at this meeting came with unusual insistence: If the point of the marine park was to "protect," why was there as yet no patrol boat capable of doing so? Why was the governmental Maritime Division patrolling the area around Kilindoni rather than the other side of the island where the fish were concen-trated? Why, when villagers traveled personally to Kilindoni or sent mes-sages to alert the Maritime Division that dynamiting was in progress, were their requests for assistance ignored by the very government body that was supposed to be stopping the illegal dynamiting? The forthrightness of such questions spurred forthrightness in turn. In a tacit acknowledgment of the political forces at work, Holston prefaced his comments by stating that he had been prohibited from speaking with villagers without the accompani-ment of Maritime officers. Thus, he asked that this meeting be kept confiden-tial. The brazenness of restricting communication with residents in a project widely advertised as "community-based" clearly disturbed those present and generated snickers and looks of disgust. Finally, in response to the ongoing deluge of questions, Holston resorted to a sweeping response: while he sym-pathized with residents' complaints, his hands were tied, he could not act alone. Despite the vagueness of this answer, it was greeted with knowing looks from those gathered in the schoolhouse.

Holston then revealed an important piece of information—the Maritime Division was seeking to relocate the temporary marine park headquarters from Utende to Kilindoni, which lay outside the marine park boundaries. This revelation provoked not only more snickers but outright anger, and what had previously been mere innuendo now became explicit. Several peo-ple stood up to interject that they were well aware that *wageni wanakula tu* (the "visitors" just eat), *wageni* being a reference to centrally appointed gov-ernment officials in Kilindoni who come overwhelmingly from the mainland and "eating" being a well-known metaphor for taking bribes.[2] In the ensuing discussion, it became evident that Kilindoni symbolically represented a site of disenfranchisement to residents and that the location of the temporary headquarters was perceived as a key strategic point in determining who would control the fledgling marine park. A dynamic, young man, Hemedi Hussein, stood up and turning to his fellow villagers began an impassioned and angry speech. With sweat beading on his forehead, he ended with a rueful smile and an apology for losing his temper. The thrust of his soliloquy paralleled that of other residents—"the 'visitors' have not yet understood that the park is ours!"

Arguing that they had long fought for this park, some of those present began organizing representatives to alert villagers on the neighboring islands of Juani and Jibondo about the possibility of the temporary headquarters being moved to Kilindoni. They thanked Holston for this information and the meeting closed with mutual acts of entreaty. Mzee Mohammedi, a large man with a deep and sonorous speaking-voice who was often called upon to speak on behalf of his fellow villagers, stood up and holding his hands open in a gesture of supplication—a customary act in an area that has long known patron–client relationships—asked that Holston continue his fight on behalf of the people on Mafia. Holston, clearly drawing on an alternate political ideology centering around participatory activism, entreated those gathered to let their views be known in Kilindoni. He argued that their voices must be heard—he could accomplish nothing alone. As it was, he revealed, the Maritime Division was looking for a reason to dismiss him, as well as the recently hired community development staff member who was from Chole. The village chairman, Mzee Maarufu, responded to this revelation with disarming simplicity, "We will protect you."

Still naive about the politics of fish and the fledgling park, I felt as if I had eavesdropped on a conversation in which the stakes were clear to everyone except myself. Only later would I realize just how subversive this seemingly innocent "meeting" had been, because it offered village residents an opportunity to speak with a crucial NGO representative without the presence of government officials from the Maritime Division. While I had heard hints of corruption before, and would increasingly hear such comments the longer I stayed on the island, this was the first time I encountered explicit charges that government officials were accepting bribes to ignore dynamiting or were even cooperating (*wanashirikiana*) with dynamiters. The tendency of residents to use veiled language in talking about power—a legacy of slavery and colonialism as well as interactions with the post-independence state—had been temporarily cast aside at this meeting as the high stakes involved encouraged less ambiguous forms of expression.

In retrospect, I am also struck by the way in which the power dynamics of this meeting contradicted easy assumptions about the nature of "global" processes or about relationships between so-called First and Third Worlds. In contrast to familiar depictions of First World donor organizations as the most powerful actors in international projects (depictions common to both supporters and critics of such organizations), at this meeting the WWF technical adviser was clearly struggling with, rather than directing, the course of events, while the power of national officials to shape the outcome of this international project was central in the minds of all present. In addition, Chole's residents did not portray themselves as objects of an externally generated project, whether as its victims or beneficiaries. Instead they saw themselves as central actors in a park they perceived as their own, and they depicted themselves as able to offer help and even protection. Whether or not residents were as central in the struggles surrounding the marine park as they themselves implied is a debatable issue, as later events will demonstrate. Nevertheless, I argue that residents' self-depiction did not stem from naivete. Rather it emerged from their desire, and indeed what they perceived as their right, to be regarded as primary actors, a perception encouraged by the language of "community participation." Finally, when Mzee Mohammedi requested assistance from the WWF technical adviser on behalf of island residents, he was not seeking the technical expertise that international organizations depict themselves as offering, but rather an alliance that would bypass existing power relationships in ways villagers desired. In short, at this meeting, islanders located themselves, not on the periphery of a technical exercise in conservation management, but at the center of a highly politicized power struggle.

DRAMATIS PERSONAE

In order to understand this social drama, it is first necessary to consider its cast of characters. The various actors involved in the Mafia Island Marine Park are socially positioned in particular ways both in relation to each other and to national and international institutions—social locations which have had a profound impact upon this social drama. These actors are easily grouped into three categories: Mafia residents, Tanzanian government officials, and the predominantly Euro-American representatives of international organizations. At first glance, such categories appear commonsensical and to correspond to international, national, and local arenas. In reality, however, such groupings are porous, with cross-cutting alliances and oppositions. For example, Euro-Americans, as representatives of international organizations, tourists, tour operators, researchers, and individuals share common understandings, yet also engage in vigorous debates amongst themselves over the meaning of nature and development (see chapter 7). Even though many influential international organizations are of "European" origin, development and conservation NGOs regularly employ educated elites in places like Tanzania. These elites often share the language and concepts of international conservation and development with their Euro-American colleagues, thereby creating a space that is both "national" and "international" and to which rural residents, such as those living on Mafia, rarely have access. And, finally, Mafia residents often seek alliances with "outsiders" such as representatives of international organizations, rather than with state elites with whom they have strained relationships—a situation that challenges assumptions of homogenous interests within nation-states. In short, while the social relations among this cast of characters are structured in important ways, such relationships are also porous, rather than rigid, and may be based upon common (if continually shifting) interests rather than identity.

Wazungu *(Europeans) and International Organizations*

The involvement of international aid agencies within Tanzania has a long history. Since its independence in 1961, Tanganyika (later Tanzania) has been a primary recipient of foreign aid from both socialist and capitalist countries and, while such aid has been viewed as necessary, the country has also suffered the drawbacks of this position. Increasingly, however, non-governmental organizations or NGOs are coming to replace governmental bodies and national aid agencies in implementing development and conservation projects within Tanzania (Fisher 1997; Keck and Sikkink 1998). The growing importance of NGOs stems in large part from increasing skepticism towards state bodies in the post–Cold War era, as well as the reality that massive international debt makes the governments of poorer countries increasingly dependent upon donors and unable to refuse "international" agendas. While some see international organizations as offering progressive political possibilities for the future (Keck and Sikkink 1998), others perceive a new world order in which international organizations constitute a new and disturbing form of governmentality.[3] Such disparate viewpoints are further complicated by the reality that international organizations are highly varied, ranging from extremely powerful, quasi-governmental bodies to oppositional grassroots organizations. Thus, the roles played by such organizations may differ markedly within particular contexts.

The primary non-governmental organization involved in the Mafia Island Marine Park, the World Wide Fund for Nature or WWF, is a prominent example of the growing number of non-governmental organizations that focus on environmental issues (Keck and Sikkink 1998). Like all international organizations, WWF possesses a unique institutional history and its activities fall at a particular point along a spectrum ranging from heavy government involvement to more oppositional "non-governmental" positions. Although WWF is considered to be an independent non-governmental organization, it historically grew out of quasi-governmental international bodies and continues to work in strong partnership with national governments. WWF was conceived in 1961 as the offspring of the International Union for the Conservation of Nature or IUCN (formerly the International Union for the Preservation of Nature or IUPN and now known as the World Conservation Union). The IUPN was brought into existence in 1948 amidst debate over whether it would become part of the United Nations system, and hence be an official intergovernmental body, or whether it would exist as a non-governmental organization (McCormick 1989:31–36). The resulting compromise was a hybrid institution initially funded by UNESCO, which included both government and private representatives working to promote cooperation between national governments, as well as between national and international organizations concerned with nature preservation and conservation (McCormick 1989:34–35).

WWF later emerged as an offshoot of the IUCN charged with fund-raising for international conservation efforts. Its expanding size and success as an independent organization, however, meant that it eventually came to overshadow the IUCN itself (McCormick 1989:41–41). True to its origins within the IUCN, WWF continues to work closely with government leaders of various nations, international organizations, donor agencies, and individual contributors, and its board of trustees includes corporate leaders as well as aristocrats. WWF currently operates in more than a hundred countries and claims nearly 5 million supporters internationally. Over the years, its agenda, like that of numerous other "sustainable development" proponents, has shifted away from preservation and now reflects the belief that conservation can be achieved in conjunction with the development process itself (a reformist philosophy that differs sharply from more radical environmentalist positions which assume a fundamental tension between environmentalism and capitalist development). Although WWF works in strong partnership with national governments, it has also increasingly come to emphasize the "participation" of those groups affected by its projects. Although WWF employs Tanzanians in its program office in Dar es Salaam as well as a handful of East Africans in its international offices, its headquarters are located in Gland, Switzerland, and most of its high-level staff members are Euro-Americans. In general, Mafia residents, along with most other park actors, conceived of WWF as a "European" organization.

Although a large literature now exists on international organizations at an institutional level, very little has been written about how Euro-Americans working within development and conservation organizations are perceived "on the ground" (although this situation may be changing with the growing number of ethnographies on development [for example, Benjamin 2000; Pigg 1996; Hodgson 2001]). On Chole, during the mid-1990s, it was stated as a general principle that "Europeans" or *wazungu* were necessary to development projects and that, after *wazungu* left, such projects would invariably fall apart. According to the park's community development staff, such assumptions were commonplace throughout all the villages of the marine park. Initially, I found such comments highly disturbing. I assumed that such theories implied that residents believed that *wazungu* possessed greater competence than Africans, and I privately attributed such ideas to *kasumba* or the legacy of colonial-era thinking. Over time, however, it became clear that this was far too simplistic an understanding. Despite a long history of cosmopolitan tolerance along the coast, many Mafia residents were deeply ambivalent about *wazungu*. On the one hand, Euro-Americans *were* accorded high status within Tanzania on the assumption that they possessed wealth and technical knowledge as residents of countries presumed to have greater *maendeleo* (development). On the other hand, this did not mean that people necessarily viewed *wazungu* in positive ways. Indeed, the historical narratives of Chole residents described in chapter 2 emphasize the harsh (*ukali*) nature of European colonialism and the pride and joy Mafia residents felt at independence in 1961. The rise of expatriate-led tourism on Mafia was also opposed by some residents who speculated that *wazungu* once again desired to "rule" (*tawala*) the region. Indeed, despite the tendency to lump Euro-Americans into a single amorphous category, distinctions were made, for example, between aid workers and those *wazungu* business operators who, particularly in places like Zanzibar to the north, were rumored to engage in land grabbing, corruption, or worse.[4]

When I asked people on Chole why they, nonetheless, saw *wazungu* as important to the proper functioning of development projects, they invariably pointed to examples of development projects that had failed after *wazungu* had left. Many mentioned the boat-building "factory" (*kiwanda*) begun on Chole in the 1970s with aid from a Scandinavian development organization. This project had sought to "modernize" the historical art of boat building by adding a generator and power tools. After the Scandinavian development worker and his family left, however, the tools were stolen and the boatyard reverted to its prior state. The failure of this project could easily be explained in terms of its naive focus on the importance of inappropriate technology (for example, on the use of power tools in a location with no electricity, spare parts, or ready access to generator fuel), and how the project unknowingly inserted itself into social relationships in a way ensured to cause conflict.[5] However, people on Chole, once again, chose to depict themselves as central actors, even in this negative instance, attributing the demise of the project to jealousy (*wivu*) and greed (*tamaa*) among residents. In a relatively egalitarian but impoverished social world where jealousy *was* a crucial source of contention, development projects seemed to invariably heighten conflict by allocating coveted resources in a manner oblivious to existing social relationships, and which allowed such projects to be readily subverted by the opportunistic. In such contexts, Chole residents not only worried about the "greed" of their neighbors but also the propensity of government officials who presided over development projects to "eat" at their expense.

Eventually, I realized that when Chole residents stated a desire to have *wazungu* involved in such efforts, many were in fact offering an analysis of the political economy of international projects. Given the social conflicts and lack of accountability associated with such projects (as well as the lack of independent legal organs to which residents could appeal), it was not surprising that Mafia residents would resort to a longstanding historical practice of seeking outside mediators. Because Euro-American aid workers possessed nonlocal sources of prestige and resources, and because they generally existed on the fringes of local social relationships (due in part to the pervasiveness of short-term contracts), they could be potentially viewed as likely candidates. It was equally clear, however, that in such instances Mafia residents desired "outsiders" to mediate—not control—international projects. Residents did not accept European-defined priorities for the marine park and other projects and clearly wished to shape the agendas of such projects according to their own interests. In sum, many Mafia residents were engaged in a calculated effort to use third parties to bypass those already considered to be implicated in an economy of corruption.

Government Elites

At the same time that Euro-American representatives of international organizations were positioned in particular ways in relation to Mafia residents, so too were government officials from Kilindoni. While the overwhelming majority of island residents were Muslims who spoke KiSwahili as their first language, government officials were almost invariably educated Christians who hailed from the mainland and who stayed on Mafia for only a short time. It is striking to note, for example, that the only Mafia resident in a position to directly influence the marine park (aside from the district member of Parliament) was the relatively low-placed assistant community development officer, whose appointment by WWF was vigorously opposed by Kilindoni officials. It is equally striking to note that a preponderance of crucial players within the marine park hailed from such upcountry ethnic groups as the WaChagaa and included the acting warden of the marine park, the director of the Maritime Division in Dar es Salaam, numerous maritime officers, the former Tanzanian WWF country office representative in Dar es Salaam, the WWF community development officer, the former director of the Institute for Marine Sciences, the chief of security for Mafia District, and several of Mafia's high-level district officials. The irony that so many influential players in a coastal marine park hailed from the land-locked Kilimanjaro region was frequently commented upon by both Mafia residents and European expatriates.

It is a common assumption in the international media, as well as among many Tanzanians themselves, that social divisions within African countries unambiguously mirror tribal, ethnic, religious or other sorts of "primordial" boundaries. I would argue, however, that the power relationships evident between national elites and Mafia's residents were, on the contrary, built upon something far more mundane—the educational policies of European colonizers. As Issa Shivji (1976) noted, business professionals and white collar union leaders were largely disenfranchised in Tanzania's post-independence era, resulting in a national elite that consisted almost entirely of those government civil servants whom Shivji acerbically referred to as the "bureaucratic bourgeoisie." Consequently, prior colonial policies determining which regions would gain access to the formal schooling necessary for civil service professions would, ironically, have a profound influence in shaping the distribution of power within socialist Tanzania.

Although some schools were built by the Germans prior to World War I (including one on Chole), the British colonial administration largely neglected public education.[6] Before World War II, less than 10 percent of children in Tanganyika were being educated in "modern" schools. The situation was even more severe for girls and, as late as 1947, not a singe female African student in Tanganyika had been educated beyond the primary school level (Coulson 1982:90). Because formal education during the colonial period was provided primarily by Christian missions, Muslim coastal residents, who were resistant to proselytization, were largely marginalized. The colonial government's failure to incorporate Quranic schools into modern school systems resulted in a post-independence situation in which coastal Muslims were widely excluded from government positions (Illife 1979:345).

The impact of this situation is clearly apparent on Mafia today. While many older women on Chole have had no access to schooling at all, even those elderly men trained in Quranic schools (*madarasa*) have been rendered "illiterate" by their inability to read and write KiSwahili in the now standard Roman alphabet rather than Arabic script. Despite the post-independence expansion of primary schools, educational opportunities have been severely limited on Mafia. Until the mid-1990s, Chole's primary school served only young children, forcing higher-level primary students to cross on foot to neighboring Juani Island when low tides permitted. Mafia is also rumored to be the last district in the entire country to have a high school—Kitomondo Secondary School being built during the course of my fieldwork—a telling indication of Mafia's status as a marginal "backwater" within contemporary Tanzania.

Despite the striking lack of educational institutions on Mafia and the subsequent absence of coastal Muslims in the ranks of government appointees in the district capital of Kilindoni, historically, education took starkly different paths in other regions. The Mount Kilimanjaro area, for example, was an early site of intensive missionary activity as well as colonial-era school building,[7] resulting in a level of education that differed radically from that available in other parts of Tanganyika Territory. By the 1950s, Africans around Kilimanjaro had achieved universal primary education and, by independence in the 1960s, students of WaChagga origins would, unsurprisingly, dominate the enrollment of the University of Dar es Salaam (Coulson 1982: 89). Despite efforts in the post-independence era to smooth over the ethnic divisions that had been exacerbated by British colonial policies, this geography of education and privilege would often continue to be read in ethnic terms.

Within contemporary Tanzania, educated elites tend to view themselves as progressive in relation to other groups and to self-identify as the "nation." Chole residents, however, instead often portray governmental elites as "big people" (*watu wakubwa*) with a tendency to "eat" at the expense of the poor and uneducated. Although it is common in Western popular accounts to assume that corruption is endemic in the so-called Third World, clearly corruption is a result of particular structural situations within both richer and poorer countries rather than something intrinsic to particular types of people or "levels" of development. Within Tanganyika, British colonial policies of indirect rule created a situation in which "traditional" leaders were accountable upward to colonial authorities rather than to the populace, creating an association between government posts and financial opportunism. Given the highly centralized nature of the colonial government—a structure that was transferred largely intact to the post-independence state—this lack of public accountability would later feed clientalist tendencies within independent Tanzania (although perhaps less so than in many other regions of Africa given President Nyerere's own highly ethical stance). Within Tanzania, however, it was not the socialist period, but the era of structural reform and a movement away from socialism during the late 1980s and 1990s in which corruption was popularly perceived to explode.

During this latter period, a new generation of donor projects and loans were bringing free-flowing resources into the country, at the same time that inflation and the currency devaluations associated with Structural Adjustment Programs made the official salaries of public employees a mere pittance. Given the inadequacy of salaries to provide for individuals much less families, even those rare individuals who possessed jobs in the formal sector were forced to turn to the informal economy. In Dar es Salaam and elsewhere, such informal activities might range from the street-vending projects of the poor to the elaborate siphoning of goods and resources by the better placed (for example, Tripp 1997). It is important to note, however, that this process was a class-based one. While the poor were limited to producing informal goods and services, government bureaucrats and elites through whom international funds were channeled possessed the ability to extract resources at the expense of both donors and poorer residents and, thus, to potentially reproduce and even expand their own elite status. Such dynamics have not been limited to Tanzania or Africa but are common in many parts of the world, including formerly socialist Eastern Europe, which has undergone similar structural transformations (Verdery 1996). It was this broader context that created a situation on Mafia in which government bureaucrats were widely perceived to simply "eat."

Mafia Residents

Mafia residents, in turn, have their own particular social location in relation to other park actors, as well as a unique history that affects their perception of the participatory frameworks being promulgated by international projects. Swahili coastal culture, with which most of Mafia District's approximately 40,000 residents identify, is the historical product of the cosmopolitan Indian Ocean trading economy. Although those who were historically involved in this economy were highly diverse, Arabs, who came to the region as immigrants, traders, and colonizers, had a particularly profound impact upon coastal Africans. A relatively small but powerful group of Arab male immigrants intermarried with Mafia's families and engaged in relations of concubinage with women from the most numerically populous group, slaves, who in the nineteenth and early twentieth centuries consisted largely of Yao and Nyasa from Central Africa as well as WaNgindo from the Rufiji. Mafia inhabitants also intermarried with individuals from other regions, including immigrants and traders from islands ranging from Lamu in the north to the Comoros in the southeast. It is therefore not surprising that the ethnic backgrounds of Chole's 800 residents are highly diverse. Yet, with the exception of a group of relatively recent Makonde Christian arrivals from southern Tanzania, Mafia residents are overwhelmingly Muslims who have assimilated into coastal society regardless of their backgrounds.

Just as Tanzania is one of the poorest countries in the world (Tordoff 1997), Mafia district is one of the most marginalized districts within Tanzania. Educated elites and government officials in Dar es Salaam and Kilindoni tend to depict it as a remote and "backward" region, both because of its lack of "modern" conveniences and because the Islamic faith is often perceived by Christian mainlanders as being mired in "tradition." In addition, many mainlanders continue to resent coastal Muslims whom they perceive as the historical perpetrators of the highly destructive nineteenth-century slave trade (although the ancestors of Mafia residents were themselves as likely to have been slaves as slave traders, see chapter 2). While Mafia residents may serve as symbols of "backwardness" to national elites, it is precisely this marginalized status that makes them an appropriate "target" for intervention by international non-governmental organizations.

The particular positioning of Mafia residents in relation to other park actors is also expressed through their conceptions of participation. International organizations have tended to describe participation in terms that range from the desire to encourage greater efficiency to the need to protect human rights, while Tanzanian government officials have largely viewed participation through the prism of the top-down "self-help" discourses of the socialist era. Mafia residents, however, instead draw upon longstanding coastal concepts in making sense of participation. Long-term inhabitants view themselves as the island's *wenyeji,* or the true "owners" of the region's natural resources and a group ideally bound together by consensus, an understanding that has been mapped onto the community participation framework espoused by international organizations (see chapter 3). At the same time, however, Mafia residents recognize the need to cultivate patron/client relationships in order to influence the powerful, a recognition drawn from the hierarchical relationships of slavery, colonialism, and a highly centralized post-independence government. In short, Mafia's residents combine a belief in the moral validity of their own "participation" as *wenyeji* with a pragmatic recognition of the need to find patrons who are willing to represent their interests within the marine park.

In their interactions with both representatives of international organizations and national government officials, Mafia residents reveal themselves to be actors with particular agendas as well as individuals who have been strongly influenced by the broader power relationships in which they find themselves. Residents' attempts to further their interests in relation to the marine park may best be visualized, not as a frontal assault, but as a series of sorties. During the course of my fieldwork, Chole residents strongly expressed their views in certain contexts, yet retreated in situations in which such viewpoints appeared too risky. For example, the outcome of the impromptu meeting in 1994, which began this chapter, was not the march on Kilindoni by representatives of Chole, Juani, and Jibondo envisioned at that meeting, but rather the more passive and covert act of disseminating potentially subversive information to other islanders. As the marine park drama unfolded, village representatives did take increasingly vocal stands in support of residents' interests. However, they also drew upon strategies for insulating themselves against risk by resorting to the covert forms of resistance found among the less powerful in many parts of the world, such as foot dragging and the use of gossip and informal information networks to create blocks of passive opposition (Scott 1985).[8] However, despite the park's promises of participation, residents were ultimately forced to contend with the reality that crucial decisions continued to be made in distant offices, while their most strongly expressed wishes were ignored by government officials as well as international organizations. It is to this story which we now turn.

THE SOCIAL DRAMA OF THE MAFIA ISLAND MARINE PARK 1994–1997

Prelude to a Drama: At the Birth of the Park

The genesis of the Mafia Island Marine Park demonstrates the symbiotic relationship between international and national institutions. The Institute of Marine Sciences (a division of the University of Dar es Salaam) and the Frontier-Tanzania Project (a joint initiative between the University of Dar es Salaam and the Britain-based Society for Environmental Exploration) sponsored a number of studies of Mafia's marine environment during the late 1980s, which spurred interest in the formation of the marine park. However, the idea for a marine park was considerably older, having first been proposed for Mafia in 1968. During the early 1970s—a period in which widespread damage from dynamite fishing began to appear along other parts of the Tanzanian coast—two marine protective reserves were established on Mafia at Tutia Reef and Chole Bay (Horrill and Mayers 1992; Bryceson

1981; Salm 1983). It was widely acknowledged, however, that these reserves were "paper parks" with little real impact.

The impetus for the new Mafia Island Marine Park and its participatory framework stemmed from the combined efforts of the Tanzanian director of the Institute of Marine Sciences or IMS (who would later work for the IUCN in Gland, Switzerland) and a British expatriate who had first worked on Mafia for Frontier and himself later became the IMS's deputy director. The interrelationship between international and national institutions is apparent in the various marine park planning initiatives, reports and meetings which included such sponsors as the Tanzanian Ministry of Tourism, Natural Resources and Environment (MTNRE), The Frankfurt Zoological Society, the Food and Agricultural Organization of the United Nations (FAO), the European Union, the Norwegian Agency for Development Cooperation (NORAD), and the World Wide Fund for Nature (WWF). WWF would become a primary sponsor of the Mafia Island Marine Park in 1991, acting as a central conduit for technical expertise in constructing the park for both the government and other donor organizations.[9]

Mafia Island residents, however, who worried about potential restrictions on their fishing practices, initially opposed the idea of a marine park. Although there had been some discussion between IMS representatives and residents, Mafia islanders would only become formally involved in deliberations over the park in 1991. At that time, a workshop was held at the Mafia Island Lodge to determine the feasibility of a marine park and which brought together future "stakeholders" within the park, including national government officials, representatives of international environmental NGOs, academics in the natural sciences, district government officials, and the chairmen and secretaries of several villages within the proposed marine park. Although village leaders originally attended the workshop in order to *oppose* the idea of a marine park, they changed their minds after receiving assurances that community participation would be legally mandated within the marine park and that the park would offer protection against dynamiting as well as jobs through the tourism industry (T. R. Young 1993:172, 175). Although there was widespread support for the marine park when I began conducting research on Mafia in 1994, if one scratched below the surface, a number of concerns quickly emerged that resembled those initially expressed at the 1991 workshop (MTNRE 1992). Residents continued to worry about potential restrictions on their fishing practices, fears that were related to the widespread recognition that Tanzania's mainland national parks and reserves had long served to dispossess area residents from access to land and other natural resources (see chapter 4).

In the end, the concept of the Mafia Island Marine Park gained the support of a wide range of actors by claiming to offer something for everyone. International environmental organizations were promised conservation measures and the sustainable management of natural resources; government officials were promised assistance with development and a national park that offered possibilities for tourism and much-needed foreign exchange; and Mafia residents were promised participation, jobs, and help against dynamiting. In addition, the concept of "participation" was vague enough that all park actors could ostensibly agree to it. As Craig and Mayo (1995) argue, some participatory models assume that power is infinitely expandable and, thereby, presume that the "empowerment" of local residents can occur without a decrease in authority among other actors. An alternate possibility, namely that expanding area residents' rights to participation would require significant political changes (although presumably acknowledged informally), was significantly missing from park planning documents, an omission that created an aura of a technical rather than a political transformation.

In the years following the 1991 workshop, Mafia residents would remark upon the frustrating lack of activity surrounding the marine park. Rumors, however, circulating through elite and expatriate networks in Dar es Salaam and Zanzibar suggested that battles were, in fact, being fought on other terrains. According to such gossip, efforts to legislate community participation in a national marine parks bill had met considerable opposition in Dar es Salaam. At the same time, staffing decisions for this prestigious and heavily funded project were the subject of speculation and debate in the offices of NGOs and research organizations in Gland, Switzerland, Washington, D.C., Dar es Salaam, and Zanzibar. Yet, Mafia residents would hear little about these controversies. Despite the proclamations of support offered by Mafia's villagers (and a picture of residents prominently gracing the cover of the 1991 planning workshop report), islanders would receive almost no information about the park over the next several years. The park, however, *was* preceded by a burst of another kind of activity—the construction of a handful of new tourist hotels and lodges in Utende and Chole. Although the concept of development has a long and complex history (Cowen and Shenton 1996), such activity suggests the particular fissures occurring in international uses of the concept during the 1990s. While the term *development* in English is often taken to imply the rationally planned, controlled and altruistic economic activities ideally associated with donor agencies, it can also refer to the relatively unplanned, profit-oriented construction and real estate development that accompanies tourism in a free market. Over the course of the 1990s, the kind of development promised by international projects would be increasingly located in free market models such as that of tourism.

The Park Stalled

Around the time of the gazetting of the Mafia Island Marine Park, boxes of gear and luggage intended for future offices began to appear on Mafia, the first concrete signs that the long awaited park was coming into being. Yet, after the Mafia Island Marine Park was finally legally incorporated or "ga-zetted" in April of 1995, the implementation of the park immediately stalled as conflict emerged between the two ostensible "heads" of the marine park—the government-appointed acting warden and WWF's technical ad-viser. Despite the symbiosis between international organizations and national state structures previously described, this emerging conflict instead reveals the tensions between the two. During this period, several points of conflict hardened the relationship between these two sides, which stemmed in large part from tensions over the role that Mafia residents would play—or not play—within the incipient marine park.

According to park documents, the management structure of the marine park was to take the following form. The park would exist under the juris-diction of the Ministry of Tourism, Natural Resources, and the Environment and, through its Maritime Division, would appoint an acting warden and, eventually, a permanent warden for the park. WWF would hire a technical adviser, a temporary position already mentioned as the counterpart to the acting warden, and the two would jointly implement the park during a pro-jected four-year initial phase. In addition, WWF would also hire members of the permanent core staff, including a community development team to inter-face with island communities. The acting warden and technical adviser would continue working together until a board of trustees and a permanent warden had been selected and the park came into full operation.

As the park began to stir to life, the acting warden in the person of Pius Mseka, a maritime official who had worked on the marine park during its planning stages, began to make occasional appearances on Mafia. In April, David Holston, the Australian selected by WWF to be the park's technical adviser moved onto the island. Although hired the previous year, Holston had been forced to wait in Dar es Salaam during the long period preceding the park's gazetting. Once on Mafia, however, he quickly set up a temporary office in a rented house in Utende and appointed the park's community de-velopment staff led by a mainlander, Charles Mtui, and assisted by a Chole resident, Rashidi Hemedi (one of only a handful of Mafia residents who had been selected to attend high school on the mainland).

Although the official marine park documents circulating in national and international offices appeared to spell out the management structure of the park in unambiguous terms, in reality, the nature of this dual power structure was distressingly vague. Some WWF documents implied, for example, that the WWF technical adviser and acting warden would be on equal footing during these initial stages. According to the 1994 WWF document *Support for Establishment of Mafia Island Marine Park*, "The project will be imple-mented by a core WWF-funded staff, in strong collaboration with the 'Act-ing Warden' and the village committees. A Technical Advisor will be re-sponsible for ensuring implementation of WWF-funded activities. The TA and 'Acting Warden' will function as counterparts" (1994:5). Other documents, however, suggested that the acting warden as the representative of the presiding Tanzanian ministry would be in a position of higher authority. On Mafia, however, such ambiguities were a moot point since these documents were written in English, the lingua franca of international development, and thereby unavailable to Mafia's residents. Consequently, island residents were forced to rely on rumor and observation to piece together an ad hoc understanding of the power relations at work—a reality that differed significantly from that envisioned by planners.

The reality that quickly emerged on Mafia was not the ideal of cooperation between the two halves of the marine park structure, but a situation of conflict and increasing polarization. Tensions centered around three main issues: corruption charges brought by the technical adviser, David Holston, against the acting warden, Pius Mseka; access that community development staff would have to villagers within the marine park; and the location of the park's temporary headquarters. In all three areas, the ideals of the park as written in planning documents would differ radically from dynamics "on the ground," and the opinions of Mafia residents would remain largely ignored by actors within national and international institutions.

In May of 1995, the Maritime-appointed acting warden was accused by the WWF technical adviser of having embezzled WWF funds earmarked to pay village residents for work conducted during a demographic survey two years earlier.[10] After having been approached by a Mafia resident who complained that he had not been paid, the technical adviser, David Holston, submitted a report to the director of the Maritime Office in Dar es Salaam including signed statements from island residents and xeroxed copies of apparently forged payment receipts submitted by Pius Mseka. Although the charge was dismissed by an investigative team made up of Mseka's colleagues (who alleged that, among other factors, discrepancies in signatures were due to the inability of illiterate villagers to write their names consistently), this incident contributed considerably to the hardening rift between the two sides.

Underlying this conflict, as well as numerous others, there existed a fundamental disagreement over whether WWF was a "partner" to the government as an autonomous organization or whether it was operating under the government umbrella of the marine park and hence subject to its authority and jurisdiction. While in interviews Holston stated his resentment of the alleged embezzlement of funds and the potential tarnishing of WWF's reputation on Mafia, Mseka and the Maritime Division in turn repeatedly complained that the technical adviser was acting "autonomously" or outside the control of government officials. At stake were decision making over budgets and resources more generally, the extent to which information would be made publicly available, and the degree of "participation" that island residents would have in the park. While the conflict was embodied in the persons of the technical adviser and the acting warden, Mseka and Holston were linked to broader social networks and groups of supporters. Although the various "sides" that emerged during the social drama of the marine park would shift over time (particularly at the higher political levels), the stance of area residents would remain constant during the implementation stage. Deeply suspicious of the Maritime Division and its motives for ignoring dynamiting prior to the formation of the marine park, villagers offered their cautious support for WWF field staff even at a point when relatively little was known about the incipient park. In short, the emerging conflict within the park revealed tensions stemming from the shifting and ambiguous boundary between "non-governmental" and "governmental" institutions, and both sides drew upon a range of supporters who had their own stakes in marking such divisions.

The second point of contention involved island residents in a more direct manner, centering around the access that WWF Community Development staff would have to villagers. During much of 1995, the Community Development officers, Charles Mtui and Rashidi Hemedi, were forced to sit idle. According to the park's general management plan, the community development staff was to interface with residents living within marine park boundaries. They were to provide and gather information as well as help organize a marine park committee in each village, which would provide representation in marine park deliberations. However, the acting warden along with a high-ranking district official refused to provide the written permission necessary for the community development staff to hold meetings with villagers (Scherl 1995:9). Thus, Mafia residents were cut off from the only official channel by which they might influence the implementation of the park or even obtain basic information concerning the park's boundaries, its management structure, its content, and, indeed, the villagers' own role. This situation was exacerbated by the acting warden's refusal to allow the marine park legislation, which offered some legal recognition of village residents' rights to participation, to be translated into KiSwahili and made public. Even the accusations of corruption made against the acting warden, although discussed in national and international offices, would not be publicly shared with Mafia's residents. Thus, the only information available to those living on Mafia during this stage of the park's implementation would arrive via rumor and speculation.

This impasse was finally resolved in September of 1995 when a visiting consultant sent by the WWF-US office succeeded in securing Mseka's permission for the community development staff to have access to the villages and to begin their work (Scherl 1995). In the ensuing months, Charles Mtui and Rashidi Hemedi made repeated visits to each of the ten (later twelve) villages within the marine park. After confronting the villagers' frustrations over the long delays as well as their own apparent idleness, the Community Development staff began a flurry of activity that included assisting each of the ten villages to elect marine park committees and recording information about each village and its residents' concerns in a voluminous KiSwahili-language report, the "Village Holistic Study" (WWF 1996). In general, this period marked the beginning of increasingly close ties between WWF staff and residents of Mafia's villages, who hoped that the international organization would act to further their own interests.

The third point of conflict—the location of the temporary marine park headquarters—was a subject of considerable concern to island residents as the opening pages of this chapter demonstrate. On Chole, anger that the temporary marine park headquarters might be located in Kilindoni reemerged on the day slated for the election of Chole's village marine park committee. In response to the disturbingly low attendance at this crucial village meeting, Rashidi Hemedi turned to his fellow villagers and began an impassioned speech. Interpreting the poor attendance of his neighbors as a form of passive resistance and expression of anger regarding the siting of the temporary headquarters, Rashidi Hemedi eloquently pleaded with those few present that "times were changing in Tanzania," that they were now living in an era of "multipartyism" (*vyama vingi*) and should openly speak their minds rather than show their anger by more passive means. Although village representatives had not gone to Kilindoni to protest the move as had been suggested at the impromptu meeting with David Holston, some residents now expressed the desire to directly question the highest-ranking government official on Mafia, the District Commissioner, concerning the location of the temporary park headquarters. Consequently, it was decided that the village marine park committee elections should be postponed until the district commissioner could be invited to Chole, particularly since he had neglected a customary visit to the island after his recent appointment. On a September morning a few weeks later, I sat patiently with friends on the coral wall beneath the stone ruins that bordered Chole's waterfront, waiting for the scheduled arrival of the district commissioner's boat. As the minutes turned to hours—a common but nonetheless frustrating aspect of official gatherings in Tanzania—some expressed their disgust at the "oppressiveness" (*unyonge*) of the situation. One elderly man, the island's Quranic teacher, told me emphatically as he left that he was thoroughly angry and had no intention of returning even if the district commissioner should arrive.

When in midafternoon, the district commissioner finally set foot on Chole accompanied by an entourage of officials from Kilindoni as well as the WWF Community Development officers, the long-anticipated meeting began in the village schoolhouse along the waterfront. Although all the officials, including Charles Mtui, the mainland Community Development officer, were formally introduced and applauded, Rashidi Hemedi, the Community Development assistant, was pointedly ignored on his home island. After several long and formal speeches, the district commissioner agreed, with some reluctance, to accept questions from the floor. Mzee Mohammedi, the elder who had opened his arms in entreaty to David Holston, the WWF technical adviser, in the meeting described in the opening of this chapter, once again took the floor. After begging pardon for speaking as one of the "uneducated" (*sisi tusiosoma*) to the educated, he asked the district commissioner to publicly state whether the marine park headquarters would in fact be moved to Kilindoni. The district commissioner responded with vigorous protest that this was a false rumor. "Where did you hear this?" he asked. "Who is trying to stir up trouble?" After continuing in this vein for some time and stating emphatically that the marine park headquarters would be built in Utende, he finally added in a quick and dismissive undertone, "[I]t is only the *temporary* headquarters that will be located in Kilindoni!" By playing on potential confusion about the status of the temporary versus the permanent park headquarters and by ignoring the possibility that "temporary" in a slow moving project could extend over several years, the DC had finessed this explosive question with consummate skill. He quickly called an end to further questions and went to drink sodas in the tourist camp with his entourage.[11]

Although Mzee Mohammedi seemed satisfied with this answer and sought my assurances after the meeting that he had spoken boldly on behalf of Chole, the next day rumors and discussion around the island indicated that others were less satisfied with the meeting. Many had criticized the district commissioner's avoidance of questions and his patronizing attitude toward people on Chole. This was the first meeting that I had attended between district government officers and Chole residents and it prompted me to ask how government officials perceived those living on the island. Most of the people I asked simply shrugged their shoulders and responded "they scorn us" (*wanatudharau*). When I pressed for further elaboration, I was told, "It is because we are not educated" (*kwa sababu sisi hatujasoma*). When I expressed surprise at the way in which Rashidi Hemedi as Community Development assistant had been humiliatingly ignored at this meeting, one middle-aged man simply explained that Rashidi Hemedi "defends" (*anatetea*) Mafia residents.

The desire that the temporary park headquarters be located in Utende also found expression in other forums that included residents of the ten villages located throughout the marine park. At the WWF-sponsored Ecotourism Seminar held in Utende in October of 1995, the newly elected chairs of the village marine park committees were offered the first opportunity residents would have to officially speak with government officials, donors, tour operators, and other park "stakeholders" since the 1991 Planning Workshop. As the various stakeholders broke into groups to write down their goals and concerns for tourism within the park, village representatives continued their ongoing efforts to shift discussion to the park itself and away from tourism, stating clearly that "It is necessary that the temporary and the permanent marine park headquarters be in Utende" (*lazima makao makuu ya muda na makao makuu kudumu ya Hifadhi yawe Utende*) (WWF 1995). The written minutes of the first meetings of the various village marine park committees submitted to WWF also demanded that the temporary park headquarters remain in Utende.

Despite the rhetoric that the Mafia Island Marine Park would be a park "for the people and by the people," as stated in the draft General Management Plan, and despite repeated assurances to the same effect during the Ecotourism Seminar, the viewpoints of Mafia's residents were ignored when the final decision was made to locate the temporary marine park headquarters. The issue was instead decided in a flurry of correspondence among the WWF offices in Dar es Salaam and Utende, the acting warden's office in Kilindoni, and the Maritime Director's office in Dar es Salaam. When David Holston, the WWF technical adviser protested the location of the temporary headquarters in Kilindoni, he highlighted cost effectiveness and convenience as the most persuasive arguments, mentioning community opposition to the move as only the sixth on a long list of points. Holston's arguments were then relayed to the maritime authorities by the WWF Tanzanian country representative, an elite Tanzanian who offered a far more conciliatory stance and failed to even mention the presumably irrelevant point that area residents opposed the move. During this period of contest, letters were issued by both the acting warden of the marine park and the director of the Maritime Division in Dar es Salaam stating unilaterally and without elaboration that the temporary park headquarters would be located in Kilindoni and that WWF field staff would be relocated accordingly. Despite the recognition that this was a battle lost for the WWF field staff, the conflict was not yet over. Holston's tactics now shifted to the passive resistance techniques wellknown to Mafia residents. During the rest of my stay on Mafia, the WWF field staff simply stalled by ignoring the order to move. In an internal letter within WWF, Holston presented the case that "WWF maintains it [sic] right to act as an independent NGO and as such believes it is not in the best interest of WWF or the community of Mafia to relocate its office to Kilindoni."[12] In short, while Mafia residents' perspectives were ignored in official channels, support for their viewpoints would hinge upon the advocacy of influential figures within the park structure itself. While the tensions among various camps within the marine park would harden considerably during this period, the most heated struggles centered around dynamiting, an issue of crucial concern to all park actors.

At the Drama's Climax: Dynamiting and the Politics of Identity

The conflict over dynamite fishing within the Mafia Island Marine Park presented the most striking example of the discrepancy between the language of participation found in national and international planning documents and actual events happening "on the ground." In these struggles, confusion over the identity of dynamiters underscored the failure of park officials to acknowledge the social and economic complexities that underlay destructive fishing practices and also pointed to the centrality of political conflict within the marine park.

It became clear to me just how widely discordant views of dynamiting were on Mafia on a November day in 1995. That afternoon, I arrived in Kilindoni to interview the marine park's acting warden, Pius Mseka, at the tiny storefront that served as his makeshift office. Mseka began the interview by informing me that he had just returned from participating in a dynamiting patrol (*doria*) near Jibondo Island. I already knew something of the situation. On a trip through Utende a few days earlier, Bakari Hassan, the newly elected chair of Jibondo's village marine park committee, had asked me to assist him as a translator. Distraught over recent dynamiting near Jibondo, he wanted to discuss the need for a patrol with the English-speaking WWF technical adviser, David Holston. I later learned that this conversation had prompted the patrol on which Mseka had participated and that Bakari had volunteered the use of his own boat for the operation. Although cynics implied that the acting warden had decided to take a more aggressive stance toward dynamiting because Holston's participation on several *doria* was making the acting warden "look bad," the move, nevertheless, seemed positive from residents' point of view.

I was startled when the acting warden informed me at the beginning of our interview that on this patrol several Jibondo residents had been apprehended for dynamiting, disproving, he claimed, the "myth" that local residents do not participate in this form of illegal fishing. Surprised by this turn of events, I asked why he thought Mafia residents would participate in dynamiting. Mseka argued that local residents participate simply because they are unaware of the impact that dynamiting has on the marine environment. How could it be otherwise, Mseka asked, given the lack of education on this issue and the absence of informational meetings and awareness programs on television and radio? Not wishing to begin our interview on an awkward note, I listened in silence. Nevertheless, such comments were wildly incongruent with the vivid descriptions that Chole's fishers repeatedly gave me of the destruction that dynamiting caused the reefs or "the home of the fish" (*nyumba ya samaki*). I also pondered the detachment implicit in advocating informational television programs on an island where electricity, much less television sets, were virtually nonexistent.[13] The acting warden continued his analysis by arguing that this lack of information could be remedied by additional funding from international donors for conferences and educational programs to raise awareness about dynamiting. After the formal interview ended, he pressed me for information on organizations or institutions in *Ul-*

aya (Europe) which could help in these matters and with whom he hoped I could intercede.

As I later considered this conversation, I was struck by how Mseka's use of the language of participation sat uneasily with a viewpoint that was clearly guided by modernization ideology and which conceived of education as the solution to "underdevelopment." From this perspective, it is villagers' presumed lack of education that hinders economic development and suggests the need for "experts" to instruct villagers, underscoring the importance of conferences and educational programs funded by international donors and presided over by national elites. The alternative perspective put forward by Mafia's residents, which emphasized charges of corruption within the Maritime Division as well as the political, economic, and social dimensions of fishing, as described in chapter 4, conveniently fell away in this scenario. In this view, the popular knowledge of residents about the marine environment could be safely ignored. Instead, islanders were to be molded by experts and expert knowledge, a position that exposed the tensions with "participatory" ideals.

After returning to Chole, I began asking people what they had heard about the recent arrests near Jibondo, an incident that had already become widely discussed throughout southern Mafia. The conversation I had with a group of five young fishermen a few days later was typical. These young men claimed that, as far as they knew, the Jibondo men had not been "cooperating" with the dynamiters. On the contrary, they suggested that the men who had been arrested had themselves gone to Kilindoni to report dynamiting in the days prior to the patrol and their calls for assistance had been ignored by the Maritime Division. When the men subsequently went out fishing, they approached an area that had been recently dynamited; feeling "bitter" (*uchungu*) and pressured by the "need to feed their children," they scooped the dead fish out of the water which had been left behind by the dynamiters. It was at this point that the patrol with the acting warden arrived and apprehended them. Although it is impossible to know the actual context for the arrests and whether they had in fact been participating in the dynamiting, these men, nonetheless, had widespread sympathy on Chole and this version of events was repeated by other Chole fishers and corroborated by a Jibondo man who had participated on the patrol.

The Jibondo incident as well as the comments of the acting warden raised numerous questions about dynamiting as a practice as well as the political implications of dynamiters' identities. In explaining the perspectives of Chole residents on the arrest of the Jibondo men, I found myself arguing to those European expatriates who were chronically skeptical of residents' viewpoints that in general "Mafians" did not dynamite. Although this was largely true at the time I conducted my research, it was discomforting to shunt the argument off along this problematic track. Obviously, if the Mafia residents I knew did not dynamite, it was not simply because they were from Mafia. On Zanzibar, KiSwahili-speaking individuals from the coast—people who shared sociocultural, religious, and ethnic bonds with those on Mafia—themselves engaged in dynamiting. And despite the romantic strain in some environmentalist thinking, because people on Mafia were engaged in a more "traditional" fishing economy, it could not be assumed that they were somehow living in harmony with the environment. Economic difficulties on Mafia were leading some to overfish and some men, despite the disapproval of many of their peers, engaged in a highly destructive fishing practice involving the use of a plant poison called *mtupa*. Clearly, either opposition to, or participation in, dynamiting stemmed not from identity, but from the broader social and economic contexts in which people found themselves.

In order to understand why some people dynamited and others did not, I sought to learn more about those who engaged in dynamite fishing. On Chole, most people simply stated that dynamiters came from Dar es Salaam. Others gave more detailed information, including one Mafia resident who claimed to have done some "investigating" while in Dar. The general consensus was that dynamiters were poor men who operated out of Kigamboni, or the dock region of Dar es Salaam. They were hired as wage laborers by elites (*watu wakubwa*) who provided them with the dynamite. Expatriates and national elites also gossiped that people at "high levels" were involved and that the dynamite, which was illegal to purchase in Tanzania, came from road and quarry projects sponsored by international donors. Unfortunately, given the difficulties of gathering information about an illegal economy, particularly one that operated out of Dar es Salaam rather than Mafia, I was unable to learn more about these intriguing speculations.

I also asked close friends on Chole whether Mafia residents themselves ever engaged in dynamiting. The answers I received were complex. In general, my friends argued that it was impossible (*haiwezekani*) for "them" to dynamite (by which they meant the inhabitants of the socially knit villages of southern Mafia that formed the core of the marine park). They argued that the exceptions to the rule were Makonde Christians who had recently immigrated to Mafia from southern Tanzania and socially marginal individuals, particularly "drunkards" (*walevi*), who often lived in Kilindoni. Tiny Bwejuu island, on the opposite side of Mafia from Chole and located halfway between Mafia and the mainland, was also mentioned as a notorious hideout for dynamiters. It was said that dynamiters from Dar es Salaam set up temporary residence on Bwejuu and then persuaded local young men to show them the best fishing spots or to rent them boats.[14]

Although it might be argued that my friends were simply scapegoating marginal individuals, the anomalous Makonde Christians, or the distant Bwejuu islanders, I contend the key to their response was actually located in how they conceptualized their own group identity. Whereas coastal society has been known historically for its ability to assimilate people from a variety of backgrounds, there is also a common distinction made in Swahili coastal culture between *wenyeji*, that is, the original inhabitants or "owners" or a place, and *wageni*, strangers or guests who have fewer rights. Through marriage, *wageni* can assimilate relatively quickly into the thick web of social ties that link together the families, villages, and islands of southern Mafia. It is through such social networks that men and women, and their children after them, gain rights to land and other natural resources as well as to sources of economic support when times are difficult (see chapters 3 and 4). Thus, it is this thick web of social interconnections that exercises informal control over individual behavior. Although some individuals, such as alcoholics in a Muslim society, might be shifted to the margins of such social networks, *wageni* like the Makonde who, as Christians are less likely to intermarry, are more likely to remain perpetually on the fringes.

Whereas the social networks of Mafia's *wenyeji* discourage them from taking part in dynamiting and hence incurring the potential anger of friends and family on whom they depend or from damaging the resources on which their children will rely, those who are marginal to such networks are more likely to engage in activities that are personally profitable but are an anathema to other Mafia residents. Clearly, those who have less access to resources to begin with, and who possess few alternatives, will be those most likely to take such risks. On Mafia, this includes not only "strangers" (*wageni*), or alcoholics (*walevi*), but those in resource-poor regions like Bwejuu, and, potentially in the future, those young men throughout the islands who lack access to natural resources because of growing population and because they have not yet inherited, making it difficult for them to marry and continue their life on Mafia. The case of dynamiters in Dar es Salaam is the extreme end of this process in which individuals are thoroughly alienated from the natural resources they use except through the short-term interests of wage labor, a very different relationship to Mafia's marine environment than that of Chole's *wenyeji,* as will be described in chapter 4.

Although the park's acting warden attributed dynamiting to a lack of knowledge, WWF officials and the organization's literature about environmental degradation attributed such activities to poverty. This viewpoint usefully points to the social and economic dynamics at work; however, it fails to specify what those dynamics might be or how they would shape actual uses of the environment. Ultimately, it is not simply poverty that leads to environmentally destructive practices. Dynamite fishers, for example, could easily be considered prosperous in comparison to Mafia residents, while well-endowed companies and businesspeople located in wealthy countries regularly engage in practices such as factory trawling that are even more destructive of the marine environment (McGoodwin 1990; McEvoy 1986). In order to understand environmental practices, it is therefore necessary to consider the broader social and economic contexts in which people make choices about their lives. As will be explained in chapter 4, these contexts on Chole are far more complex than a presumed dualistic split between a "modern" cash economy and "traditional" fishing practices might suggest. Indeed, social pressures and interpersonal obligations on Chole are central to how fish are caught and sold.

Despite residents' support for the elimination of dynamiting, the existence of the marine park initially did little to halt the dynamiting around Mafia. In December of 1996, however, this situation was radically transformed by the long-anticipated arrival of a sleek, double-engined Boston Whaler speedboat purchased by WWF to patrol the region's waters. Within the structure of the marine park, the enforcement of antidynamiting legislation came under the jurisdiction of the government Maritime office with the assistance of district police. Despite the recent apprehension of the men on Jibondo, no convictions had ever resulted from the activities of the Maritime Division either on Mafia or anywhere else along the coast since the legislation had been passed in the early 1970s. After the arrival of the speedboat, however, responsibility for *doria* (patrols) shifted radically. Although only Maritime staff and district police officers who participated on such patrols held the power to arrest, the patrols were now led by the WWF technical adviser, David Holston, the only person at that time who knew how to operate the new boat and had been trained in antidynamiting enforcement procedures.

The arrival of the Boston Whaler was viewed as a radical breakthrough in Mafia's villages although many people were unaware of the prolonged struggle that had preceded its arrival. The boat, which had been custom-designed with powerful engines and a water cannon, had been shipped by sea from the United States, but when it arrived in Dar es Salaam in June of 1996, crucial parts were missing and had to be specially ordered. A much more fundamental problem, however, quickly emerged. The Maritime director in Dar es Salaam and the district executive director on Mafia both refused to authorize the boat's operation, an ironic state of affairs given that, once again, the Maritime Division was itself charged with stopping dynamiting in Tanzania's waters. It was only after the principal secretary of the Ministry of Tourism, Natural Resources, and the Environment had herself personally authorized the boat to operate temporarily without the required signatures that the boat was actually put to use Thus, after the arrival of the Boston Whaler in Dar es Salaam, it took 6 months before regular patrols would begin on Mafia.

In a meeting called on Mafia by WWF field staff shortly after the boat's launching, the leaders of the village marine park committees voted to name the boat the *Ukombozi*, meaning "liberation" or "deliverance"—an indication of the seriousness with which they viewed the patrols. Much to the delight of island residents living within the marine park, the patrols had their intended effect. Within one month, eight dynamiters had been arrested near

Bwejuu Island in two separate incidents, and dynamiting appeared to make an abrupt halt in Mafia's waters. Videotapes of the arrests on Bwejuu show pleased crowds surrounding the patrol boat and the arrested dynamiters. The success of the *Ukombozi* also generated a flurry of publicity, newspaper accounts and expressions of support for the Mafia Island Marine Park, praising the only successful effort to halt dynamiting within Tanzania and one of only a few internationally. An Italian film crew even sought to incorporate the *Ukombozi* into a documentary, and the WWF field staff, Maritime officers, and district police spent a week simulating fake dynamiting attacks for the cameras. Not everyone was happy with the success of the *Ukombozi*, however. It was around this time that the chief security officer for Mafia District sent a memo to the WWF field staff warning them to hire additional security guards because there were rumors of plans being made in Dar es Salaam to sabotage the boat. According to the police chief "I . . . suspect that a lot of prominent persons in Mafia and Dar-es-Salaam have suffered a big monetary loss since the arrival of this 230 HP boat."[15]

When I returned to Mafia after a visit of several months to the United States and shortly after the *Ukombozi*'s debut, I was struck by the upbeat feeling on Mafia about the marine park. Villagers seemed less hesitant to make their perspectives known in public. As one fisher from Chole explained to me, the Maritime Division had never caught a single dynamiter; however, the WWF technical adviser had now demonstrated "through actions rather than words" that he was serious in his opposition to dynamiting and had thus consolidated the support of Mafia residents. Residents living within the marine park now began to make pointed distinctions between branches of the marine park—the Utende office was increasingly referred to as simply "WWF" while the "marine park" (Hifadhi ya Bahari) was used exclusively to refer to the acting warden and the Maritime Division in Kilindoni. Discussions of marine park politics had also become strikingly more open. Previously, when people I knew from Chole visited Kilindoni, they would invariably look over their shoulders before speaking about the marine park (a habit that I had acquired as well); now, talk about park politics had become far more casual even within the hearing range of those individuals widely rumored to be "spies."

In the months following the *Ukombozi* arrests, I spoke with people on Chole about their relief at the recent turn of events. One young fisher on Chole, who like many other men sold his fish at sea to an "ice boat" that came periodically to Mafia from Dar es Salaam, noted that many former dynamiters were now working as laborers on the ice boat. One individual had told this young man that dynamiters now feared being arrested by the *Ukombozi* and had nicknamed Chole Bay "the jail" (*jela*). The fact that former dynamiters would be working the ice boat, which bought fresh fish at sea and paid area fishers relatively high prices, did not surprise me. While one activity was illegal and the other was not, both of these wage labor occupations operating out of Dar es Salaam were oriented toward national and international markets in which fish existed only as commodities, and both positions indicated a lack of long-term stakes in Mafia's waters.

No one on Chole, however, mentioned the identities of those dynamiters who had been arrested. When I asked both the WWF technical adviser and the mainland Community Development officer who the dynamiters were, they both admitted that they were unsure but they believed that individuals with origins on Mafia were included among the apprehended. A perusal of the district police report filed with the WWF office, however, which listed not only the names of the arrested but their ethnicities and places of residence, painted a more complex picture. While half of the dynamiters were from Dar es Salaam, as people on Chole generally claimed, others were listed as Mafia residents. Although all of the latter possessed common Muslim "Swahili" names, their ethnicity in each case was listed as "Makonde." I could only surmise that these Makonde had taken Swahili names to facilitate their assimilation into coastal society and that the ensuing confusion made it difficult for nonresidents of Mafia, including many prominent persons within the marine park, to distinguish between *wageni* and *wenyeji,* or recent versus long-term residents, as well as their potentially very different motivations.

After reading the police report, I shared its contents with Rashidi Hemedi, the Community Development assistant from Chole, who breathed a sigh of relief. As we both knew, and as had become pointedly clear during my interview with Pius Mseka, the question of the dynamiters' identities was a politically charged one. The potential involvement of Mafia's *wenyeji* in dynamiting might be understood in national and international offices, not as a complex statement about social and economic life on Mafia, but in terms of a presumed lack of knowledge about the marine environment. This presumed lack of knowledge could in turn easily buttress the belief in a need for increased control of, and oppressive surveillance over, area residents, a topic that will be further addressed in chapter 6. The easiest defense against this potentiality was to simply assert that those Mafia residents who participated in dynamiting were not "real" Mafians, demonstrating the disturbing way in which identity politics could easily replace more substantial social insight into the dynamics of how and why people use the environment as they do.

*The Final Scene: Participation and the Contradictory Role
    of International Organizations*

Shortly before I left Mafia in 1997, a new series of events once again dramatically altered the course of the marine park drama. During this period, the tensions apparent in WWF's contradictory position of being a "non-governmental" advocate of "community participation" and simultaneously supporting and working through governmental elites would finally come to a head. Ironically, as residents were making their strongest efforts yet to appropriate the discourse of participation in a way that would allow them to shape the course of the marine park on their own terms, the lack of democratic accountability within the park would result in a very different outcome.

The first few months of 1997 were a period of growing optimism within Mafia's coastal villages. There was excitement and relief at the success of the *Ukombozi* against dynamiting and also a sense that power relations within the marine park were shifting. Due perhaps to a new level of accountability brought by "multipartyism" within Tanzania as well as the positive publicity the park was receiving for its antidynamiting efforts, more government officials in Dar es Salaam and Kilindoni seemed to be taking positions supportive of the WWF field staff and hence, indirectly, in support of villagers. The acting warden appeared increasingly marginalized on Mafia, the new district commissioner was publicly critical of the Maritime Division's role in the marine park, and villagers themselves were increasingly assertive in their demands concerning the park. However, rumors were circulating that alarmed some members of the village marine park committees. When the acting warden and the Mafia District Council requested to review David Holston's contract, speculation grew that there was an *njama* (plot) against him. Some residents as well as expatriates believed that the goal of such actions was to find a loophole that would allow for the termination of the technical adviser's contract, given the central role that he was playing in antidynamiting patrols.[16]

It was during this period that village leaders seized an opportunity to alter the dynamics of the park when, in February of 1997, the prime minister of Tanzania made an official visit to Mafia Island. During the customary open meeting held between political leaders and the district's elders (*wazee*), one aged man stood up and delivered a speech in angry and impassioned tones to the prime minister. According to others present, this elder had been chosen by his peers as someone who could "speak freely" because he lived in a village safely outside of marine park boundaries. His words, as transcribed from a videotape of the event, were as follows:

> [Concerning] that dynamiting, we here [on Mafia] have been complaining long and hard about it. So we made a plan [to deal with it, i.e., community agreement to, and participation in, the marine park] and we were brought an expert [i.e., Holston], praise be to God, we are grateful. But there are great battles being waged against us. He [reference to the acting warden] wants to have that expert who has knowledge of this kind of work removed, and another one brought in. If we are brought this other person, we the citizens of Mafia will be dying. This is because the produce that we get—some people don't have food to go with their rice! They

don't have anything at all because of that illegal fishing. Therefore, Mr. Prime Minister, we ask you that the European expert not be taken away from us here on Mafia so that he can protect us and our ocean.[17]

The new district commissioner (the third since I had arrived on Mafia in 1994) then elaborated on the situation for the prime minister: "WWF has a patrol boat that goes out with the police patrol. They are catching those people who have been causing the destruction. Now in my reading of the situation, the people of the marine park [i.e., Maritime Division] have an *interest* in those dynamite fishers. Should that boat leave Mafia, the dynamiting will continue. This is as I read the situation."[18] After listening to what had been said, the prime minister publicly charged the district commissioner to investigate these matters and report back to him.

This turn of events—the pointed speech by one of Mafia's elders, the apparent support of the latest district commissioner, and the promise of investigation by the prime minister—heartened many Mafia residents who heard of what had occurred. This was particularly true for those most involved in the marine park drama, including village leaders, members of marine park committees, and the park's community development staff. Yet, not all Mafia residents shared such optimism. When I returned to Chole later that day with news from Kilindoni of the prime minister's visit, a friend working in the tourist camp quickly put the optimism that the meeting had generated into perspective. Words, he countered, mean nothing; government officials always promised to "investigate" matters and usually did nothing. Personally, he would wait to see the outcome. His fear that authorities beyond Mafia might not be responsive to the interests of residents proved well founded, although trouble would next emerge from a different quarter.

A few days after the meeting with the prime minister, I accompanied a Chole woman to a town on Mafia's main island where her husband, who had been injured in a fall from a coconut tree, was convalescing at his parents' home. On arriving, I was surprised to recognize the husband's father as the chair of his village's marine park committee. I had previously met this man at the Ecotourism Seminar in October of 1995 and remembered him as being widely respected by other village leaders. I later discovered that he had also been one of the original participants in the 1991 Planning Workshop that had resulted in the formation of the marine park. Inevitably, conversation veered toward the park, and this elder asked if I was acquainted with the *mzungu* (European) with the technical skill (*ujuzi*) [i.e, the WWF technical adviser who led the *Ukombozi* patrols]. He described this man as "highly capable" or "praiseworthy" (*hodari sana*) because he refused to allow matters to be settled "in the corners" (*pembeni*), that is, in a corrupt manner, and that, for this reason, he was disliked by the acting warden. This elder then confided in a conspiratorial but optimistic tone that he and other village leaders were making plans to have the acting warden removed from Mafia and the technical adviser retained. When I ventured to suggest that decisions might be made beyond the borders of Mafia, where villagers held no control, the elderly man's face clouded but his optimism held. He asserted vigorously, "We will not allow this *mzungu* (European) to be taken away from us. We will not agree to it."

As it turned out, however, during the same week that the prime minister was visiting Mafia, a report was being faxed to the WWF regional office in Dar es Salaam. This report contained the recommendations of a review team sent briefly to Mafia in January of 1997 by NORAD, the Norwegian development agency that had donated funds to the marine park that were placed under the unilateral authority of the acting warden. The WWF field staff had long worried that the NORAD funds were being used inappropriately. Most recently, according to the community development staff, "projects" funded with NORAD monies and with little connection to the overall goals of the marine park, were appearing in the hands of village leaders who had once opposed the acting warden. For example, the elected chairs of two village marine park committees who had been vigorous opponents of the acting warden at the 1995 Ecotourism Seminar had suddenly undergone a change of heart. According to the community development staff, other village representatives were complaining that their committees had ceased to function properly and there was an assumption by those involved that these leaders had been "bought."

After receiving repeated complaints from the WWF field staff that NORAD funds were being "inappropriately" used, a commission consisting of five members—three Europeans chosen by NORAD and two Tanzanians from the Ministry of Tourism, Natural Resources, and the Environment in Dar es Salaam—arrived on Mafia to investigate the situation. The commission members, much like other consultants sent to Mafia, spoke primarily to the main participants in the battle within the marine park structure, Acting Warden Pius Mseka, Technical Adviser David Holston, the community development staff and Maritime officials. Although the commission made some attempt to speak with village residents, this generally occurred in the context of formal meetings with Maritime Division officials present.

The report that the commission issued several months later (NORAD 1997) offered the following analysis and recommendations. It stated, "Discussions with the [acting warden] revealed a serious lack of necessary technical competence in matters of marine conservation and poor capability in relation to community development approaches." In addition, "disturbing allegations have been made against the [acting warden] concerning forging of signatures and embezzlement of WWF funds," and "The accounts availed to the review team did not reveal the actual expenditures in the project for the various project activities." In relation to David Holston, the report commented that "The WWF Technical Adviser (TA) appears to be technically competent in matters of marine conservation and management . . . ," however, "The WWF TA acts autonomously and with his own budget. He behaves in an arrogant and contemptuous way towards the [acting warden] and others that disagree with him." The review team's recommendation was that "For the smooth running of the project in the future the MTNRE [Ministry of Tourism, Natural Resources, and the Environment, p. 91] is advised to ensure the replacement of both the [acting warden] and TA with immediate effect. It must be clearly stated that the MIMP administration should have authority over the WWF TA in all park matters."

The NORAD report would result in the resignation of the technical adviser and the removal of the acting warden over the ensuing six months, concluding the primary period of research on which this book is based and ending the earliest phase in the marine park's implementation. Although I have little information about how this report was received by the Maritime Division, it is clear that within WWF there were conflicting responses to its contents. When David Holston left, some international funding, including that of WWF-UK and the WWF-International office located in Gland, Switzerland, was withdrawn because of "a lack of confidence" in the project. However, the WWF-U.S. office based in Washington, D.C., maintained its support of the marine park and agreed with the WWF-Tanzania office that it was necessary to find a technical adviser who was more amenable to working with the Maritime Division. Although when interviewed WWF representatives in the United States tacitly acknowledged potential problems with the Maritime Division, they also expressed an overriding belief that it was necessary to find a technical adviser who was more amenable to working with the Maritime Division. In general, there was a pronounced tendency in many international and national offices to reduce the conflict over the marine park to a "personality clash" between two individuals. By implying that the root cause of the problem was managerial, this perspective readily accorded with technocentric assumptions common in conservation and development paradigms and conveniently ignored the political basis for this conflict.

More broadly, the position taken by the NORAD report ignored the contradiction implicit in having a marine park that was ostensibly dedicated to fostering community participation and the eradication of dynamiting being placed under the directorship of a government division whose officials were accused of supporting the very practices they were charged with eliminating. In the end, the refusal to acknowledge the power struggles within the park meant supporting—and potentially exacerbating—the social hierarchies at work. When faulting Holston for acting independently of, and displaying "arrogance" towards the acting warden, the report failed to consider that the technical adviser's willingness to challenge elite perspectives might be interpreted on Mafia itself as a willingness to defend the interests of island residents. In short, NORAD's report validated the perspective of elites who self-identified as the "nation" in contrast to those of Mafia residents, perpetuating a fiction central to the park, namely, that national interests and those of people on Mafia were the same.

The report's insistence that "the MIMP administration should have authority over the WWF technical advisor in all park matters" acknowledges that, despite globalization narratives that emphasize the growing power of international organizations at the expense of states, international organizations like WWF are often careful to emphasize that they work through and are supportive of national states. Although nation-states in Africa *are* being undermined by economic impoverishment caused by devalued prices for agricultural goods, by massive and unforgiving international debt that makes them dependent upon the agendas of external actors, and by increasing economic and political marginalization in a post–Cold War era, it is equally important to recognize that international organizations may simultaneously buttress governmental elites through whom such organizations channel resources and influence. Indeed, governmental and many non-governmental organizations exist in a symbiotic relationship. Thus, power relations between states and NGOs are not a zero-sum game. Rather, state actors (potentially acting as individuals rather than on behalf of a "nation") may utilize non-governmental organizations as sources of resources and influence within a broader context of increasing impoverishment and marginalization. In sum, the situation which has unfolded on Mafia is not simply international organizations seeking to bypass national governments to pursue their own agenda, as some have contended, but rather state and international actors mutually supporting complementary agendas potentially at the expense of those they are claiming to "empower."

In recent years, many critics of globalization have expressed the hope that the expansion of non-governmental organizations can aid the disenfranchised and help to protect the environment. But, given such an analysis, can the expansion of international organizations and their new "participatory" frameworks serve as a democratizing force in the contemporary world? Clearly, within the Mafia Island Marine Park, the concept of "participation" has been vague and subject to conflicting interpretations. Among some representatives of international organizations, participation has merely meant greater efficiency in getting residents "on board" in terms of conservation agendas, while, for others, it has signaled a new way of doing development and conservation that encourages greater accountability toward rural residents and perhaps even their empowerment. Indeed, among WWF staff, wildly different understandings of participation became apparent, resulting in palpable confusion. Some like Holston argued vociferously that participation entitled island residents to decision-making powers, while others implied that participation merely conferred the right to consultation with higher authorities retaining the ultimate responsibility for decision making.

For government officials, ideas of participation have a different genealogy. Rather than being an innovation introduced by international organizations, ideas of "participation" or "self-help" (*kujitegemea*) emerged as a central political discourse under Tanzania's socialist government. For government officials on Mafia, participation appears to have retained much of this earlier meaning, suggesting a process by which rural residents are recruited to work toward goals that have been predetermined by centralized authorities.[19] From this viewpoint, participation does not signal a shift in decision-making power, but rather the need for island residents to take responsibility for acting out nationally determined agendas. And, finally, Mafia residents have appropriated and understood the concept of participation on their own terms, interpreting it as a right to decision making, which they view to be justly theirs as the *wenyeji* or "proprietors"of the region (see chapter 3). While all ideas are subject to multiple readings, the extraordinary vagueness of the concept of "participation" has achieved a striking political effect within the Mafia Island Marine Park by obscuring the issue of whether Mafia residents have— or do not have—enforceable rights within the park.

In the end, it is distressingly easy to conclude from this social drama that "participation" has been a hollow and even cruel promise. Given that participation within the marine park grossly failed to provide accountability to residents or to transform underlying power relationships in relation to national and international institutions, it is all too clear that participation does not necessarily entail democratization (see also Ribot 1996, 1999, 2000; Paley 2001). This does not mean, however, that the participatory rhetoric of the marine park has had no effect. The concept of "participation" *has* suggested a more inclusive language that Mafia residents have sought to appropriate, thereby shifting the terms in which existing power relationships are negotiated. At the same time, the possibility of alliances with outside organizations have been welcomed by residents as a means to counter existing power relationships. While such trends hold out the possibility of shifting political discourse in ways potentially desired by Mafia residents, there are less encouraging scenarios as well. Just as the failed promises of the socialist era encouraged cynicism about state authorities on Mafia, so too a new generation of "participatory" projects might simply exacerbate a sense of ongoing political disillusionment or lead to the further disenfranchisement of residents by encouraging a rhetoric of "participation" that serves only external agendas (see also Paley 2001).

In sum, this social drama has pointed to the ongoing exclusion of residents within the Mafia Island Marine Park and to the deep lines of conflict existing among park actors. The efforts of planners to paper over these differences have not obscured the power hierarchies that have emerged in this drama. Although narratives of globalization commonly purport to describe such power relationships in the contemporary period, these accounts often fail to elucidate the complex nature of these relationships. As the latest narrative of modernity, the concept of globalization implies a distinct historical break with the past. Yet, as will be elaborated in ensuing chapters, the social drama of the marine park suggests that power in the contemporary era continues to operate through well-worn channels, building upon historical dynamics associated with colonial and post-colonial states (which also relied upon the operation of power at a distance), patron–client relationships, and particular workings of institutional bureaucracies. Even as power relationships in the contemporary period shift, such shifts occur in relation to—rather than apart from—those of the past.

Thus, in order to fully understand this drama, it is necessary to examine a range of dynamics usually excluded both from narratives of globalization and from technocentric frameworks of conservation and development. Part Two of this book begins to do so by considering the historical experiences of Mafia residents and the contemporary implications of such experiences, how Chole residents conceptualize and live "community" in ways distinct from assumptions found in international participatory projects, and how fish and fishing on Mafia reflect complex ideas and practices that fail to accord with assumptions of the "indigenous" or "traditional" as suggested in much of the recent NGO literature on conservation. After revisiting the Mafia Island Marine Park in greater depth in part 3, the epilogue will once again resume the social drama of the marine park. It will consider the dramatic reversals that had taken place within the marine park by the year 2000 and what such transformations reveal about the nature of international conservation and development in a contemporary world increasingly described in "global" terms.

PART TWO

Figure 2. Sailing in Chole Bay. (Credit: Chris Boebel)

"When People Were as Worthless as Insects": History, Popular Memory, and Tourism on Chole

THE MOST NOTICEABLE feature of Chole's landscape, as viewed from the shore in Utende across Chole Bay, is a prominent two-story stone structure on the tiny island's waterfront that juts out from a green leafy background of palm and mango trees. Chole's residents refer to this ruin as "the Boma" stating that it was built, along with the other abandoned stone buildings on the island, by Arabs during the reign of "Abu Saidi," a reference to the nineteenth-century Omani dynasty which, from its base in Zanzibar, had once dominated the East African coast.[1] By the century's end, German colonialists had added a second floor to this building and converted it into that forerunner of European imperial institutions—the Customs House—the title by which it is still known to contemporary tourists. The ferry, a wooden sailboat that serves as the only transportation on or off the island for most of its 800 residents, deposits it passengers on the beach at the base of this ruin. On this sandy strip stands a lone casuarina tree where, according to Chole's elderly residents, the Germans hung those who violated their ideas of justice. Beginning at this tree, a broad and neatly angled coral "boulevard" rises out of the sand, passing in front of the Boma. Oscar Baumann, a German geographer who visited Mafia in 1895, derided the Arab official responsible for this boulevard and other early efforts at "town planning" on Chole as a "ludicrous reformer" who in "his blind enthusiasm" had "spoil[ed] this attractive place with embellishments" (1957[1896]:14). Castigated by Baumann for its "modernist" pretensions, this crumbling boulevard—once the main thoroughfare of bustling Chole Town—is now largely deserted, and signals for contemporary Euro-American visitors, not "modernity," but the charm and romance of a bygone era. By the mid-1990s, stillness had come to pervade the waterfront. On most days it was interrupted only by the occasional sounds of fishermen stretching and drying their nets or the quiet conversation of would-be ferry passengers as they waited along the coral wall of the former thoroughfare in the shade of flowering frangipani trees.

Past the gaping ruins of the Boma, this now decrepit boulevard leads to other relics of Chole's past. A short distance from the waterfront, an array of stone structures rise above the undergrowth. The remains of a building that had served as the German jail appears across from a now imaginary street and the stone pillars of a long-abandoned market. A little further along, the ruins of several multistoried stone dwellings, once the homes of Chole's elite merchants, jut upward from the vines and brush. Nearby, a partially intact Indian mosque emerges from within a cluster of gargantuan baobab trees. The plant life enveloping these stone structures acts not only as a covering but as an integral part of the ruins. Birds have deposited the seeds of "strangler fig" trees along the tops of the roofless ruins and, with the passage of time, trees have sprung from these seeds. In seemingly miraculous fashion, the trunks of the fig trees are now perched upon the top of the stone walls 15 to 25 ft in the air with their roots fanning out across the walls in a downward push towards the soil. As the roots pry into the crevices between the coral blocks, they both destroy and bind together what remains of the buildings. Underfoot, the sand hides the coral pavement of the former boulevard, and the grassy underbrush serves as a home for a range of small animal life, including green and yellow speckled monitor lizards several feet in length and a group of reclusive, ring-tailed civet cats who appear during twilight hours. Overhead, shimmering green, blue, and purple sunbirds flit in the humid ocean air, alongside the ubiquitous yellow and black weavers and an occasional paradise flycatcher graced by long, trailing red tail feathers. Although this northern end of the island has long been abandoned to the remains of the past, the ruins of stone houses, mosques, walls, and cemeteries crop up in other parts of Chole as well. Recently built mud and thatch homes abut walls that are centuries old, patches of brush hide a crumbling mosque embedded with decorative porcelain bowls, mango trees shelter pyramid-shaped grave stones, and broken bits of painted glass bowls litter the beaches and sandy paths that are trod upon by contemporary feet.

While far removed from the bureaucratic battles that constitute much of the social drama of the Mafia Island Marine Park, Chole's overgrown ruins are, nonetheless, crucial to the story. The marine park has been conceived by national and international institutions as centering around tourism. When park planners argued for the integration of conservation with development on Mafia, it was international tourism that they meant by "development." This choice was not a surprising one given that tourism has been increasingly touted as an economic strategy by development organizations and lenders like the World Bank and IMF (Crick 1989; Bishop and Robinson 1998). As previously mentioned, tourism also corresponds well with the perspectives of national officials in Tanzania who have long valued the foreign exchange generated by safari tourism in the country's wildlife parks (Neumann 1992, 1998). Unlike government-sponsored tourism development in Tanzania in the 1960s and 1970s, however, when the government itself actively built hotels and entered the tourism trade (Curry 1990), new models of "free market" development serve to encourage private investment, which, given the large amounts of capital required by tourism, almost invariably means foreign investors. Thus, tourism development has been left to the vagaries of the market while also being incorporated into park planning in highly specific ways. For example, the original management plan for the marine park projected that after the start-up funds of the major donors had been depleted, the marine park would run on revenues generated by entrance fees from tourists (GMP 1993). In addition, wages from jobs generated by the tourist industry are to serve as a source of income for local residents, allowing them an alternative to fishing and presumably aiding the conservation of marine life. Overall, the logic of the park rests not only on the assumption of tourism expansion, but on the belief that tourism will transform caretaking of the environment into an economic necessity, thus encouraging a mutual dependency between conservation and development (see chapter 7).

As planners hoped, the newly formed marine park has served as a catalyst to tourism development on Mafia, encouraging the formation of the Chole Kisiwani Conservation and Development Company as well as the new hotel construction in Utende. Tour developers "sell" the idea of conservation within the park to attract divers and snorkelers who wish to experience the colorful marine life below the water's surface, as well as to game fishers eager to test Mafia's reputation as one of the best, if least-known, fishing grounds in the world. However, the historical ruins on Chole and other islands have also been conceived by tourism developers as an important secondary attraction. Indeed, the developers of the community-based tourism project on Chole have focused their attention on the stretch of ruins along Chole's waterfront, commissioning architectural plans that seek to incorporate the overgrown ruins into their designs for a future hotel and tourist area. This commingling of nature and the ruins is not the result of chance. Planned by expatriates and geared towards the sensibilities of Euro-American tourists, both the ruins and "nature" hold similar symbolic positions within the European romantic tradition—both are thought capable of evoking a soothing sense of solitude and "other-worldliness" which can transcend both time and the perceived banalities of the "modern" world.

When I first arrived on Chole in 1994, the Chole Kisiwani enterprise, like the park, still existed only on paper and, like other Euro-American visitors to the island, I was struck by the "magical" quality of Chole's overgrown ruins. I sought odd moments to explore them, gingerly climbing over the fallen masonry and pushing my way through the brush, charmed by the combination of flitting birds, crumbling walls covered with tangled overgrowth, and the images my own imagination conjured of Mafia's past. In letters home, I described Chole as more like a "fairy tale" than a research site. Although I was slightly embarrassed to be so easily seduced by this island, I nevertheless congratulated myself on my lucky choice of fieldsite. I had read numerous historical accounts of the coast, but Mafia was mentioned only in passing if at all and I initially knew little about the history of these ruins. In retrospect, I wonder whether it might have been this lack of concrete knowledge that allowed my imagination free rein to create whatever ghosts it chose. Ultimately, I also wonder, was it history that these ruins evoked for me or was it, ironically, an attempt to escape history?

I would soon discover that the "reading" Chole residents offered of the ruins differed radically from own initial impressions. This was brought home to me one hot afternoon, shortly after my arrival, when I stopped to chat with Saidi, a young man hired by Chole's nascent tourism development enterprise to clear brush in the ruins near the waterfront. As Saidi cut grass with a machete, I admired the stone columns inside the building. Saidi, polite to a fault like most people on Chole, nevertheless, curled his lip and let escape a slightly disgusted look as he asked whether I knew about the "Arabs" who had built these ruins. "Do you know what Arabs did to slaves in the past?" he added. "They forced slaves to husk rice with their fingertips! One Arab slit open the belly of a pregnant woman!" Throughout my stay on Chole, I would hear a similar litany of stories about the ruins. For most people on Chole, the ruins symbolized not the romance of the past but a physical reminder of its oppression. As I learned more about Mafia's history from those who lived there, over time I too came to associate particular ruins with particular groups from Chole's past; I learned the functions of many of the buildings and even the names of some individuals who had inhabited them; and I became painfully aware of the moral associations these ruins held for people like Saidi. Rather than embodying a romanticized past conveniently free from both history and moral content, the ruins symbolized the tensions and conflicts of an earlier historical epoch. The past, I found, was not refreshingly devoid of content, but rather full of meaning that was also part of the present.

READING THE RUINS

In this chapter, I argue that an examination of how Chole residents talk about Mafia's history helps illuminate the struggles that surround the marine park. It does so by offering insight into how residents conceive of themselves as historical subjects as well as how they think about power, oppression, and the nature of social relationships as evidenced by the particular histories they choose to tell. These perspectives in turn offer insight into the range of actions residents view as available to the less powerful in their efforts to influence the more powerful. Thus, these histories offer crucial context for the ways residents choose to act—and not act—in relation to influential outsiders, including national and international institutions. In addition, these historical accounts underscore that Mafia's residents, far from being incarcerated in the realm of the "local," have for centuries, if not a millennium, operated in a context of "global" processes. While most of this chapter will address perspectives on the past held by people on Chole, I begin by considering alternate readings of Mafia's history evident in the tourism industry and the planning documents for the Mafia Island Marine Park. I argue that despite the tourism industry's fascination with the ruins, the view of history operative for many tourists is an abstracted one that ultimately works to distance contemporary residents from their own past. In contrast, the scientific and managerial traditions evident in park bureaucracy encourage an emphatic focus on the present that renders Mafia's history irrelevant. Both these ahistorical perspectives form a sharp contrast to residents' views of themselves as historical subjects—a subjectivity that strongly shapes their involvement with Mafia's marine park.

Alternate Readings of Mafia's Past

During my stay on Mafia the number of international tourists reaching Utende were still very few, but those who did come were often ferried by hotel speedboat to spend a morning on Chole wandering through its ruins. Many would also walk through Chole's not-yet-operational tourism camp, passing the tent where I stayed. In the conversations that often ensued, I occasionally ventured bits of information learned from the oral histories of island elders that I was collecting with the assistance of Ally Ahmadi, a young man from Chole. In relating such information, I generally commented upon the cosmopolitan nature of Mafia's history and the outlook of its residents. These comments often elicited looks of surprise from European visitors. Although tourists came to the island to see its historical ruins, somehow the ruins and their history seemed distant from Chole's living residents, much as the ruins had for me when I first arrived on the island. Instead, many tourists (and expatriates) preferred to turn the conversation to worries that tourism development could easily "ruin" Chole and its residents. While tourism development does raise serious concerns (see chapter 7), many visitors expressed their fears in a particular way, namely, that potential "ruin" stemmed from the possibility of the "outside" world intruding upon and changing remote Mafia. This scenario entailed an assumption that Chole's residents were, and had been in the past, cut off (in a social as well as geographical sense) from other parts of Tanzania as well as the world in general. When I mentioned that many people I knew on Chole often traveled within Tanzania (despite the hardships posed by difficult transportation) and that some of the older men in their youth had worked on ships, traveling along the East African coast and even to the Middle East and beyond, such comments met with looks of even greater surprise, creating a dissonance that more easily ended conversations than began them.

This situation on Chole in many ways parallels that described for Greece by Michael Herzfeld, who argued that the Western European tourist imagina-

tion draws a rigid conceptual line between those who built the ruins of ancient Greece and the country's contemporary inhabitants (1987), or in the
distancing ways that former Arab homes are romantically described as ahistorical ruins by some contemporary Israelis (Slyomovics 1998). Although on
Chole the time lag between the building of the ruins and the present is
reckoned in centuries rather than millennia (as is the case in Greece), the
same perception holds true. Despite the physical presence of the ruins, history, for many visitors, appears to have little to do with contemporary residents. Clearly, this perspective relates to a long-standing European tradition
of portraying non-Westerners as outside of history, as "natives" rooted and
immobile in space (Appadurai 1988; Fabian 1983; Wolf 1982). Another dynamic, however, is also at work. On Chole, the contradictory tendency for
tourists to be fascinated with the historical remains of the past but to see this
past as segregated from the present, may have to do with the kind of history
that the ruins are thought to embody. As previously mentioned, in the Euro-
American romantic tradition, ruins hold a similar symbolic position to nature, suggesting not so much history as its transcendence. Like "pristine"
nature, "natives" are thought to be untouched and unchanging, a contested
but still powerful strain of thought among Euro-Americans. In a similar
manner, both nature and "natives" are conceived as fragile and threatened by
the forces of modernity and the changes it is thought to wrought. According
to such thinking, change in places like Mafia is not so much a product of
history as the transition between the binary states of being "traditional" and
being "modern."

The tenacity of these strains of Euro-American thought are evident among
those visiting Chole. For example, one visitor who was writing a brochure
about Chole during the time that I was there, interpreted the current explosion of small stores or selling stalls (*maduka*) on Chole as representing the
introduction of money into a subsistence economy. Despite my protest that
currency had been in use on Mafia for nearly a millennium, as evidenced by
the abundance of old coins found on Mafia dating to at least the fourteenth
century, she good-naturedly persisted in this interpretation, presumably because it more closely corresponded with her preconception that Chole residents were traditional whereas money was modern. Residents were often
also taken as archetypal exemplars of a traditional past common to all hu-
mankind. One young American man with artistic leanings who worked for a
time in the Chole tourist camp waxed eloquent about the ancient wisdom
apparent in the craggy visages of Chole's elders. On one occasion, he spoke
at length about his fascination with the face of one man visiting the camp
and how he could see the "sea" in his eyes—a transcendental image that
downplayed this man's individuality (and ignored the reality that this particular individual rarely fished). Similar archetypal images appear throughout
European literature about the East African coast. One of the few travelogues
that mention Mafia, *Heaven Has Claws*, which was written by the game-

fishing son of Sir Arthur Conan Doyle, the creator of Sherlock Holmes, describes Chole as "a smallish island lusciously green and girdled with water of crystal clarity," and "an infringement on Heaven's patent" (Conan Doyle 1953:185). Remarking upon the deserted ruins, the author notes that "the natives themselves, occupying a straggling village tucked away in the vivid heart of the forest, were a dying race consisting almost entirely of ancient men and women who still preserved the natural courtesy which belongs to the Africa of the past" (1953:186). While for the author, Chole represented an archetypal image of decay with its inhabitants signaling "the remnants of expiring tribes" (1953:188), his observations reflected a highly particular historical moment after Chole had been depopulated by the demise of the slave trade and the transfer of the urban capital.

The peculiar tendency of the tourism trade to both fetishize historical remains and to reflexively deny historical processes is evident in a more pronounced way on Zanzibar Island to the north of Mafia. Zanzibar experienced an explosion of tourism in the 1990s, much of it focusing on history and the old "Stonetown" area of the island's capital. Historical accounts prepared for international tourists often combine images of swashbuckling Arabs and their harems, sensationalistic accounts of the slave trade, and nostalgia for British colonialism, while conveniently ignoring the impact of the less than romantic power relations of the past on Zanzibar's contemporary residents.[2] Once again the discourse of potential "ruin" is prominent, with numerous visitors expressing worries that tourism development will "spoil" the island.[3] Such transcendental perspectives on coastal history do not go uncontested, however. For example, the eminent Zanzibari historian Abdul Sheriff (1987) has been involved in numerous attempts to create more balanced accounts of Zanzibar's past for tourists, serving as adviser and curator for the Zanzibar Museums. The developers on Chole Island have also demonstrated a more substantial interest in the island's history, encouraging the collection of oral narratives of island residents. However, the power of such transcendental images is difficult to escape in an economy dominated by tourism. For example, a photographic historical essay on Zanzibar geared toward tourists and prefaced and captioned by Sheriff comes to be titled "Historical Zanzibar—Romance of the Ages" (1995). Similarly, Chole's tour developers rely heavily on the "romance" of the ruins to generate tourist interest about the island.

While the tourism industry has drawn its reading of history from the transcendentalism of the European romantic tradition, the conservation and development bureaucracies involved in the Mafia Island Marine Park offer a very different perspective on Mafia's history—its erasure. Conservation and developmental planning, as embodied in the marine park, are historical heirs to yet another eighteenth- and nineteenth-century European perspective, a technocentric vision of science that rejects "tradition" and centers around a reductionist philosophy concerned with uncovering universal laws, thereby making attention to history unnecessary. In planning documents for the Mafia Island Marine Park (including Horrill and Ngoile 1991; Horrill and Mayers 1992; and GMP 1993), Mafia's history is neither mentioned nor assumed to hold relevance for the future marine park. The only mention of history that I was able to find in any marine park document was contained in the Village Holistic Study (WWF 1996), which devoted a few sentences to the history of each village within the marine park.[4] In general, although Mafia residents are portrayed as being "marine resource users" or "stakeholders" in the park, they are never portrayed as historical actors. The ahistorical perspective found in both the tourism industry and the marine park, however, poses a sharp contrast to the importance of history in terms of how residents perceive themselves and the world in which they live. For it is through understandings of the past that Mafia residents come to make sense of the workings of power and the possibilities for their own actions in relation to both the marine park and the tourism industry.

THE HISTORICAL NARRATIVES: A LEGACY OF GLOBAL PROCESSES

Talking History

In general, history on Mafia is a spoken affair. Except for a handful of references in English and German, by far the most extensive by Oscar Baumann, the German geographer who visited Mafia in the late nineteenth century (1957[1896]), written histories of Mafia's islands in any language are virtually nonexistent. In English, the historical record of Mafia must be pieced together largely from a handful of notes in the colonial-era volumes of the Tanganyika Notes and Records (TNR) or from articles about the history and archeology of neighboring Kilwa Island rather than Mafia itself (for example, Chittick 1959; Dorman 1938; Freeman-Grenville 1958, 1962; Gray 1951, 1952; Piggott 1941; Revington 1936; Saadi 1941; Wheeler 1955). Despite an occasional academic article elsewhere (N. King 1917; Sunseri 1993) or a fleeting sentence or two in the histories of other parts of the coast (for example, Trimingham 1964; Illife 1979; Nicholls 1971), most of Mafia's history remains undocumented. In any case, however, written historical accounts are largely irrelevant to daily life on Mafia, given that books and written matter of any kind, regardless of language, are extremely difficult to come by. Consequently, *historia* for Mafia residents refers almost exclusively to a lengthy tradition of shared oral accounts passed across generations. Although both male and female elders (and certain individuals in particular) are assumed to be particularly knowledgeable, all residents theoretically have access to these narratives.

When I began my research, I did not intend to systematically collect historical material. However, after serving as a translator for another researcher who worked briefly on an oral history project on the island, I was struck by the enthusiasm of Chole's participants and fascinated by what I heard.[5] Consequently, I jumped at the chance to continue the project when the researcher offered to leave his video camera behind. With Ally Ahmadi now acting as cameraman, we videotaped oral histories that included fifteen of Chole's elderly women and men. On two separate occasions, Ally and I screened these historical narratives for Chole residents. We borrowed a television, VCR, and generator from the WWF office in Utende, carefully wrapping the precious items in plastic. With the help of willing hands, we lugged the equipment through the shallow water onto the ferry and then across to Chole. The two showings took place on the soccer field near Chole's primary school in the shadows of the Boma. Hundreds of residents came to watch the island's elders as they appeared on the television screen, recognizable despite the jerky motion and raspy sound, and much to the amusement of their giggling grandchildren and great-grandchildren.

In these videotapes, as in daily life, the telling of history takes on a variety of styles. Some accounts, generally those offered by men, were presented as uninterrupted oral performances in accordance with the social conventions of public speaking; others, particularly those of the women and others less accustomed to speaking in public, were offered as part of the give-and-take of a dialogue or a question-and-answer session. However, the most common form of historical commentary, found among residents of all genders and generations, was one in which historical narratives came to be collapsed into a distilled form of moral commentary, such as that offered by Saidi as he cut grass in the ruins. In such instances, only a brief reference need be made to "slaves husking rice with their fingertips," for example, to conjure up for listeners the often repeated, almost mythic, stories of the horrors of the slave trade and the injustices of the past. Quietly contested by a few, such commentaries nonetheless served to draw Chole residents together into a world of shared moral viewpoints.[6] Although some children, eager to imagine places beyond Mafia's shores, wistfully asked whether I could arrange to show kung fu movies on future occasions, the historical commentaries captured on these videotapes, and the reflections on power they encapsulate, remain pregnant with meaning for the present as well as the past.

Following the lead of Chole's elders, I have divided Mafia's history into three general time periods: (1) the period up until the early nineteenth century, which focuses on the medieval towns of Kua and Kisimani Mafia; (2) the Omani Arab colonial regime of the mid-to-late nineteenth century in which plantation slavery was pervasive and Chole was the urban capital of Mafia; and (3) the history of German and British colonialism from the very end of the nineteenth century to the mid-twentieth century.

Kua and Kisimani Mafia

The interview that offered the most historical detail was that of Mzee Bakari Ally. During my time on Chole, Mzee Bakari and his wife Bi Sharifa Mohammed had become close friends—almost surrogate parents. He was a highly intelligent and kindly man, known for his skill as a speaker as well as his mischievous sense of humor. On the day that Mzee Bakari had been videotaped at the waterfront near the schoolhouse, he knew exactly what he wanted to say and spoke uninterrupted for nearly an hour. His hand movements and facial expressions resembled those of a professional stage actor's and, with a backdrop of sand glittering in the reflected light of Chole Bay, he acted out the raising of flags, the shooting of rifles, and the capture of slaves. A year after this videotape was made, Mzee Bakari would go partially blind and would be forced to spend long days in his house protecting his eyes from sunlight and the smoke from cooking fires. Frustrated by his confinement, he chided me when I neglected my daily visit, and he relished the chance to speak into my tape recorder and continue to teach me about Mafia's history. Assuming a mild air of self-importance, he would hush his youngest children and grandchildren and politely make excuses to visiting neighbors so that we could continue our work. This account of Mafia's history relies heavily upon his words.

Mzee Bakari began his account with an introduction intended for posterity and for those who might hear his words from beyond Mafia's shores. He then described the way in which history is learned on Chole.

My name is Mzee Bakari, and I am the son of Ally, who was the son of Maarufu, who was the son of Bahari. My lineage is Luatwami. I am a resident here of Chole and I was born here on Chole. My father, my mother, my elders—all were from here. At the period when the Arabs came, they encountered our family ancestors, and when the Europeans came they also met our ancestors.

We learned history in encounters with our elders who would sit on their porches talking and we would listen to them. They would speak of things that were both praiseworthy and things that were disturbing. . . . I had a grandfather, Mohammed Bahari, whose nickname was "Octopus". . . . At the time when I encountered him and heard his stories, I was perhaps a child of ten.

He would sit and explain about the history of Kisimani Mafia and Kua. Indeed, Kisimani Mafia was the first city on all of Mafia beginning about five hundred or so years ago.

The people at Kua and Kisimani Mafia had kings and our elders would tell accounts of how this one would do something to that one, and how that one would do something to the other. I had the opportunity to hear them talking—Mzee Mohammed bin Bahari [his grandfather] and Mzee Mwalimu Nyundo. During their game of bau [a boardgame], they would talk about those things which happened in the past. As they would play bau, they would say to one another, "You! You are doing to me what the people of Kua and Kisimani Mafia did to each other. Don't do such things to me—it is foolish and ignorant!" We would listen as they argued back and forth. We would ask, "Grandfather, why did the people of Kua trick the people of Kisimani Mafia?" or, "Why did those kings compete with each other?" And they would begin telling stories.

Mzee Bakari then recounted the story of the rivalry between Mafia's two oldest cities, Kua and Kisimani Mafia, the starting point of virtually all historical narratives on Chole. Perhaps the most important aspect of such accounts is that they demonstrate how, for Mafia's residents, there is no historical golden age of unproblematic power relationships. Instead, history begins in a vortex of conflict, rivalry, colonial relationships, and slavery.

[Mzee Mohammed and Mzee Nyundo] related how the people at Kua were invited to Kisimani Mafia where they were building a *jahazi* [a large wooden sailboat]. Now, there was to be a celebration as the *jahazi* was launched from on high ground where it was built towards the water. It was customary to inform people of such events. Even today if a *jahazi* is built, everyone is called in from the surrounding areas to come and push. We lay down logs and then the jahazi passes along them on its way to the ocean.

So the people of Kua were informed of this event, and the children of the elite of Kua arrived there. After their arrival, the people of Kisimani Mafia forced the children of the elite of Kua to lie down. In other words, the *jahazi* would pass over their backs on its way to the sea. Do you understand? There was nothing the people of Kua could do. They were bound and laid on the ground, and the *jahazi* passed on top of their backs. Out of all those who died, they left behind one person who was given a letter and when he reached his home at Kua the letter was read. When they had read it, the king said, "Lo! Indeed, is this the sort of thing they have done to my people?" The king was troubled but, when asked what they should do, the king replied, "Wait."

Then the people of Kua began to dig deep down—they built a chamber beneath the ground. Our elders told us that five or ten years had passed by this point. They dug down deep, deeper and deeper and deeper until finally it was done. They made a small door and put many beautiful decorations inside. Then the people of Kisimani Mafia were informed of a wedding—the child of the ruler of Kua would be married to her cousin. The people at Kisimani Mafia were sent a letter informing them of the wedding saying "please come." The people of Kisimani Mafia had completely forgotten about what had happened earlier—ten years or more had passed. "Fine," they responded; they would make the journey. The people at Kua had decorated the underground chamber beautifully and everyone was to go down there for the celebration. The party and feasting for the wedding were to take place there, so they would all be sitting down below. When the guests arrived, they were welcomed and sent down into the chamber. At one o'clock, it was time. The hosts brought the food and welcomed the guests to eat.

There was one person from Kua who was serving the guests and who had volunteered to sacrifice himself. . . . There was another person who was standing up above bringing the food, and the man who had volunteered to sacrifice himself was serving it. When they had finished the food, the person who was up top left, shutting the door. Boom! It was closed off completely. The people of Kisimani Mafia sat inside there until the air was gone and then, one by one, they died. One person was left behind to bring back the news to Kisimani Mafia. He told his king, "Over there at Kua, Bwana, our companions were buried in the ground! Revenge was the reason—five or ten years back, you had taken their children and killed them and now they are exacting revenge. If you are able, make war!" The king agreed, "Then go, all of you!"

Although the people at Kisimani Mafia were very angry, they were afraid—they didn't have any weapons of war. As a result it was just a war of words; it didn't amount to anything.

The world in which the rivalry between Kua and Kisimani Mafia occurred, as described by Mzee Bakari, was a complex one full of "global" processes. As already mentioned, the East African coast had long been part of the trading world of the Indian Ocean. The region was mentioned in ancient Greek and Roman texts as the land of "Azania" and the monsoon winds ensured widespread links between the coast, the Arabian peninsula, North Africa, India, Persia, Madagascar, the Comoros, Indonesia, and beyond. This heritage is evident in the complex hodgepodge of cultural practices and material items still found along the coast, including a Persian New Year's festival, Indian decorative styles, Islamic architecture, and an Indonesian design of outrigger canoes, not to mention the ubiquitous foreign loan words which have been incorporated into KiSwahili, constituting perhaps 20 percent to 30 percent of KiSwahili terms (Freeman-Grenville 1962 as cited in Romero 1997:7).

It was into this complex coastal world that a small group of migrants from Shiraz, Persia entered in the tenth century as they searched for a new home in East Africa. One group settled in Kilwa Kisiwani, a tiny but powerful islet to the south of Mafia near the present-day border of Mozambique (Chittick 1959; Dorman 1938; Freeman-Grenville 1958; Gray 1951, 1952). In the ensuing centuries, the city-state of Kilwa, led by an elite of Shirazi who had intermarried with Kilwa residents and Arab immigrants, came to dominate the East African coast through its control of the Sofala gold trade while also serving as the primary slave entrepot in the south. According to the Kilwa Chronicle (*Sunna al-Kilawia*) the city-state's first sultan, Hassan bin Ali, shortly after founding the colony in the tenth century, sent one of his sons,

Bashat, to subjugate Mafia.[7] For the next eight hundred years or so, Mafia would remain to varying degrees a dependency of Kilwa (Gray 1951:7). According to archaeologists, the strength of the bond between Kilwa and Mafia is demonstrated by the fact that more coins minted in Kilwa have been found on little-known Mafia than on famous Kilwa itself (Gray 1951:7). Indeed, some of Kilwa's sultans appeared not only to have ruled at Mafia but to have "retired" or spent considerable time there suggesting a degree of prominence for Mafia itself (Chittick 1965:276, 289).

The oldest ruins on Mafia are located at the former site of Kisimani Mafia on the main island near contemporary Kilindoni. Although many of the ruins have now washed into the sea, the earliest strata of mosques at this site date from perhaps the tenth and eleventh centuries (Chittick 1966). There is considerable speculation, however, over the date of the ruins at Kua on the neighboring island of Juani. A British archaeological expedition uncovered coins at Kua dating from the thirteenth to fifteenth centuries (Freeman-Grenville 1957). Although some surmise that Kua itself was built in the following centuries, still other contemporary archaeologists suggest it may have been built far earlier. According to Chole residents like Mzee Bakari, the *waungwana* (elites, freeborn) of Kua were descendants of the Shirazi who had intermarried with other coastal people. An oral account given in 1955 by an elder of Juani, Shaikh Mwinchande bin Juma, to archaeologist G.S.P. Freeman-Grenville (1962) tells a similar story of the rivalry between Kua and Kisimani Mafia (indeed this story appears in every oral account of Mafia's history of which I am familiar. See also Saadi 1941). Shaikh Mwinchande, however, prefaces his account of the *jahazi* launching and wedding trickery by arguing that this state of affairs emanated from tensions between the long-settled Shirazi at Kua who had intermarried with local residents, and a newer group of Arab immigrants. Presumably, this group of Arabs were MaShatiri, a group of Sharifu, or descendants of the Prophet, who originated in the Hadhramaut of contemporary Yemen and were known to have intermarried with the Shirazi elite at Kua.[8] Indeed, there was a continuous history of Arab immigration along the East African coast, much of it from Oman and Hadhramaut. Significantly, most of these immigrants were men traveling without wives who quickly intermarried with coastal women, leading to their relatively rapid assimilation into coastal life (Trimingham 1964:9). The rivalry between the Shirazi and the Arabs in Mwinchande's account, in which the Arabs used deceit to take over the town from its rightful owners, the Shirazi, with whom they had intermarried, contains many similarities with other coastal accounts of the origin of city-states like Kilwa and Lamu (El-Zein 1974; Gray 1951). In all these stories, a new group of immigrants replaces the original inhabitants of a place through trickery, apparently a common narrative trope along the coast to explain power shifts among various groups.

The rivalry between Kua and Kisimani Mafia is a common theme in historical narratives on Chole. Even more common, however, are the references made by both young and old about the treatment of slaves at Kua. At times consisting of only a sentence or two, these "stories" are less attempts to explain events than to provide a condensed form of moral commentary that captures in an almost ritualized way the horrors of slavery. Mzee Bakari continues:

> [at Kua] Rice had to be husked by hand. . . . Here on Chole, we pound rice with either a machine or a pestle and then the husks are sifted out. Now the ruler at Kua, would force you to husk rice with your fingertips, and it had to be entirely whole . . . so it could be cooked with each kernel intact. You weren't to break it! If you broke the kernels, there was a very tiny chamber [under the palace stairs], which is still there today . . . and you would be put in there as your punishment.

The act of slaves being forced to husk rice with their fingertips rather than using the customary pestle, seemed to be a form of abuse that captured the imagination of most people on Chole, and constituted the bulk of the references made to Kua (similar references are found in the oral traditions collected on Mafia by Kadhi Amur Omar Saadi and translated by D.W.I. Piggott [1941]). While the ruins at Kua invariably elicited this story, at times the young, along with those less well-versed in Mafia's oral traditions, would indiscriminately transfer this story to any ruins on Mafia from any period. Thus, stories about slavery from very different eras would at times merge together in a narrative of common oppression. Still other stories elaborated the abuse suffered in the past by slaves at Kua. Some people described how one or more artisans, presumably slaves, had their hands cut off or their eyes put out by Kua's elite to prevent them from creating buildings of equal splendor for any of their rivals. Many, like Mzee Bakari, mentioned the tiny chamber that is still evident under the staircase at Kua's "palace," contending that it was used to punish recalcitrant slaves.

Bi Rehema Hassani was another chronicler of Chole's past. She was an articulate elderly woman whose teeth were stained with tobacco and who often wore her short white hair covered with the customary colorful *kanga* cloth. Like many women and men on Chole, she had been married several times in her life. At the time of my first visit to Chole, she was temporarily living with one of her sons while she waited to move into her own new mud-and-coral house. Bi Rehema informally presided over the courtyard life of her daughters-in-law whose homes formed a near-by cluster. Like most other women, she offered her history as a dialogue rather than an oral performance but, like the other elders who agreed to be videotaped, she also wanted to look her best for the camera. On the day that Ally Ahmadi and I videotaped her, she brought out of her house her faded black *buibui* (veil), an article of clothing rarely seen on Chole these days, and laughing both proudly and sheepishly, donned a pair of broken spectacles. The video camera captured her sitting in her courtyard, her hands like those of many women on Chole preoccupied with mat weaving, and her grandchild Mariamu's tiny face peering out toward the camera from behind her grandmother's back.

Bi Rehema described Kua in the following terms:

> *BR:* The Shirazi, indeed those were the people of Kua. If you hear of a person who was from Kua, then they were from that group. They were Arabs, and they built those large buildings. The [skilled laborers] who built those buildings had their hands cut off so they wouldn't be able to build again. They had their hands cuts off. Others had their eyes put out so they wouldn't be able to build buildings like those again. . . . And there was a ruler there who was a woman! Truly they had a ruler that was a woman.
>
> *CW: Really? What was her name?*
>
> *BR:* Her name was Mwanaharua of Kua.

In Bi Rehema's account, the Shirazi are "Arabs" although Shiraz itself is in Persia. This interpretation is a common one on Chole, because the Shirazi were perceived to be, as Mzee Bakari put it, "'Arab-like' if not actual Arabs," presumably because they intermarried with MaShatiri Arabs and held similar structural positions of dominance. Like other elders, Bi Rehema reveals that at the time of Kua's demise, (approximately 1817 or 1818 according to Alpers [1977]), the city was ruled by a woman named Mwanaharua (presumably an error since she is referred to as Mwanzuwani in older accounts;[9] see Saadi 1941, Mwinchande in Freeman-Grenville 1962). According to Bi Rehema: "Her husband had been king and, when he died, she was given the position of regent and took on the status and responsibility of her husband. . . . This ruler stayed on the top floor of the palace saying, "It is better to be burnt in a fire than to be burnt by the sun." In other words, because going out of the palace meant being in the sun, Mwanazuwani refused to leave the palace. According to Mzee Bakari she had "never set foot on the ground one day in her life." This refusal signaled the seclusion that marked the high status of elite Arab/Shirazi women along the coast.[10] In the popular imagination today, however, the regent's behavior suggested an overbearing pride, a sense of superiority that was an affront to others. Like veiling, the seclusion of women along the coast was not only a statement about gender, but also very prominently about social status (Strobel 1979; Fair 1994).

Kua met its downfall in 1817 or 1818 when it was sacked by a group of raiders from Madagascar who attacked the East African coast in a flotilla of *laka* or outrigger canoes (Alpers 1977).[11] Accounts on Chole link the attack of the Sakalafa to local resistance against Kua's oppressive rulers. In Mwinchande's account, as in many of the accounts I collected, the sacking was attributed to the machinations of the head artisan who had his hand chopped off by Kua's Arab elites to prevent further building (Freeman-Grenville 1962). According to Mzee Bakari, abuses such as forcing people to husk rice with their fingertips caused the people at Kua to ask,

"Why are we ruled by a person [Mwanazuwani] who oppresses us in this way?" . . . But there was nothing they could do. So they hurriedly built canoes. They carved canoes in the bush [on Juani] where there were big trees; they carved until they had perhaps four. Then they began to escape and went towards land. But the country they went to existed only in the past; it was inhabited by a different people from those who live there today. In this place [Madagascar], there were people called Sakalafa. These people were very fierce and fought each other with axes. If you tried to hide yourself from them, you would be discovered. There was no place you could go to hide. Now, some of those people who had escaped from Kua went there and told the Sakalafa, "We have come to your land asking for help. Go and fight the ruler of Kua. After you have beaten the regent, you can rule us. We will allow you to rule us, because we are not able to overcome the problems we face ourselves—their punishment is too great."

In this telling, rather than being a single slave artisan as in Mwinchande's account, it was a small group of people who escaped to Madagascar. The oppressed, even if unable to directly challenge existing power relationships at Kua, retained their ability to act. They sought more powerful outside actors to intervene on their behalf and to take revenge on Kua's elite. Mzee Bakari continues:

The Sakalafa agreed and then the Sakalafa built their canoes. . . . After some time, the Sakalafa entered Kua to fight. Now some people already understood what was happening and told the ruler. "People are coming. Don't you know there will be war? Let's run away. There is war—people will come to kill you!" But she wouldn't leave. She spoke some words that Bwana Mzee often used to tell us, but unfortunately, they were not written down and we have lost those words of long ago. Anyway, the Sakalafa entered. They fought until they reached the top floor of the palace and they attacked the ruler.[12] Some people from Kua had run away into the forest while others were hiding themselves at Kua. When the ones who were hidden were discovered, they would be attacked. It is said that the people of Kua chased each other out of their hiding places. They would say, "You, who are hiding, come out! Better that I should hide here beneath this chair." Oh, here's another person! That person would be caught, and if that person was caught then another person says, "You who are hiding, come out! It's better that I should be here behind this door frame." Oh, here's another person! It continued like this until they were all caught. Now others had escaped into the forest, into the area with big trees over on Juani. The Sakalafa had maps which permitted them to find their way in that forest. They went and found those people who had gone to hide in the caves. Then God sent a plague and, in the end, the corpses of all of those Sakalafa who had died far from home were removed. I believe that history relates that even today the chains of the Sakalafa can still be found there on Juani. Thus, the Sakalafa were finished off; they died without getting the chance to rule—they didn't get anything at all.

Although Norman King (1917) also mentions an outbreak of smallpox around the time of Kua's downfall, other oral accounts collected by Saadi (as well as written accounts like Brown 1976 and Piggot 1941) add that some Sakalafa who attacked Kua carried off large numbers of slaves and booty taking them to the small island of Msimbati. Here they were pursued and defeated by a retaliatory expedition sent by the sultan of Zanzibar (who had begun taking tribute from Mafia in 1812 [Kirkman 1964]).[13] In Bi Rehema's account, the focus is not on the violence of the Sakalafa, a point which contrasts with Mzee Bakari's telling, but on the plight of the captured slaves who were said to have been transported as booty to Madagascar. In her words, "God has cried over the graves of those people who were brought to Kua as slaves: not only were they given punishment like this [husking rice with their fingertips], they came to Kua only to be captured again by the Sakalafa. They were captured once again and knew nothing of their homeland."

The period of Kua's demise would turn out to be a transitional period between types of colonialism on Mafia. Although in earlier centuries, Mafia had been associated with or subordinated to Kilwa, that island in turn had come under the control of the Portuguese at the very end of the fifteenth century (Gray 1951, 1952; Dorman 1938). The Portuguese, including the famous explorers Vasco da Gama and Amerigo Vespucci, attacked and sub-jagated Kilwa in their efforts to gain control of that city-state's lucrative gold trade and also subordinated Mombasa further to the north. The Portuguese were more interested in booty and control over Indian Ocean trade routes, however, than in establishing systematic political control (Young 1994:49–54). Consequently, while the Portuguese had a blockhouse and agent on Mafia, their presence was relatively superficial (Baumann 1957[1896]). They are perhaps best known in popular accounts for bringing new animals to Mafia such as cattle, pigs, and monkeys (see also Saadi 1941). In his histori-cal account, Mzee Bakari describes how the Portuguese were eventually forced down the coast toward Mozambique by Omani Arabs located at Zan-zibar, an event estimated to have occurred around 1669 (Piggot 1941:38). According to Mzee Bakari, it was the power of a *hirizi* (charm) made by the Omanis that insured that the Portuguese remained south of the Ruvuma river.

Ultimately, however, the dominance of Kilwa, based on intermarriage as well as overlordship, and that of the Portuguese, based on control of trade routes rather than substantive contact, would prove very different from the colonialisms to follow. Both the colonialism of the Zanzibar-based Omani state and, later, that of the Europeans would develop in response to the "global" phenomenon of expanding capitalist relationships. In the historical narratives of Chole residents, the emphasis now shifts to the visceral images of later colonialisms, images which continue to resonate powerfully in the minds of those living on Chole.

Plantation Slavery and the Rise of Chole

As is clear from the accounts of Kua told by Chole residents, slavery had long existed on Mafia. Nevertheless, it was during the expansion of Omani Arab economic and political influence along the coast in the nineteenth century that the slave trade on Mafia exploded, a trade that would not officially end until 1922 and which would continue informally even later. Indeed, it is the slavery of the Omani period that serves as the focal point of almost all historical narratives told on Chole, serving as the center of a moral discourse which remains pervasive even in the present. Prior to the nineteenth century, many forms of slavery had existed in East Africa. Among some mainland groups, both war captives and persons "pawned" for debts or crimes often ended up as slaves, although the practice of pawning also held out the possibility that kin groups could ransom family members. In other instances, pawned persons and war captives might be incorporated into the kin groups of their "owners" including those from chiefly lineages (Robertson and Klein 1983; Miers and Kopytoff 1977). In East African coastal society, slaves served as household servants, soldiers, personal dependents, and laborers. Slaves held varying degrees of autonomy, in some cases having the right to own and lease property (including houses and other slaves), to sell their labor, and to work as artisans or in other professional capacities (Cooper 1977; Glassman 1991, 1995). Slaves might also use their position as the *watu* (people) of the *mamwinyi* (masters) to appeal for help or protection. Thus, the idiom of slavery along the coast was less one of outright ownership than of an extreme form of patron–client relationships in which slaves were in positions of strong personal dependency upon a powerful "owner" (Glassman 1991, 1995; Cooper 1977).[14]

The relative harshness of slavery along the coast has been the subject of debate (Morton 1990). However, it is clear that the rise of a plantation economy along the East African coast—the result of attempts to grow spices, copra, and other products tailored for expanding capitalist markets centered in Europe—meant the rise of a much harsher and more dehumanizing form of slavery, which acted to make slaves resemble commodities more closely than clients (Cooper 1977; Glassman 1995). Indeed, it was this type of plantation slavery that would become pervasive on Mafia (Sunseri 1993). Although cloves dominated the extensive plantations of Zanzibar and Pemba, Mafia's plantations grew coconuts for the production of copra which was used in making oils and soaps. These plantations emerged relatively late in the 1860s under Sultan Bhargash, a period in which the Omanis were firmly entrenched in producing raw materials for a world market and in which Zanzibari plantation owners were reeling from depressed prices due to an overproduction of cloves (Cooper 1977; Sheriff 1987). Thus, rather than slavery being simply a holdover from a more "traditional" era, the expansion of slavery along the East African coast was a response to transformations in a "global" capitalist economy (Sheriff 1987), just as the centrality of slavery in the American South was a response to the need for cotton to supply Britain's expanding textile mills (Wolf 1982).

The shift in types of slavery on Mafia corresponded loosely with the transfer of influence from the sacked city of Kua to the budding capital of Chole. It was during this period that Sultan Seyid Said consolidated his control over the East African coast, moving his capital from Oman on the Arabian peninsula to Zanzibar in 1840. According to most accounts, the survivors of the Sakalafa raids moved to Chole and the leader of the retaliatory Zanzibari expedition against the raiders, Abdulla bin Jumaa, built the original Boma there during the reign of Seyid Said (Saadi 1941:25). When the German geographer Oscar Baumann (1957[1896]) visited Mafia in 1895, he described the plantation owners of this period as being a combination of Omani Arabs and another "local" group that he referred to as the "Shatri" (already familiar in this book as the MaShatiri, originally Hadrami Arabs who had extensively intermarried). Aside from administrative officials, Omanis resident on Mafia also included immigrants from Zanzibar who had feuded with Sultan Seyid Said and who later established large plantations on the main island (Nicholls 1971:36–37 as cited in Caplan 1982).

Historical accounts identify the MaShatiri as Chole's new elite, noting that they had intermarried with and supplanted the Shirazi from Kua. Chole's stone structures were largely built by MaShatiri—buildings that Bi Rehema describes as "shining with sugar" from a plaster made with sugar rather than the coral limestone used today. Although the coconut plantations of elites were located on Mafia's main island, many slaveowners preferred to reside in Chole Town. Although Baumann claimed that the "Shatri" were easy masters, it is rare on Chole today to hear the term MaShatiri without someone adding the adjective *wakali* (harsh) and launching into a story about abuses committed against slaves in the past. Most of the slaves who were brought to Mafia to work the plantations were from mainland groups, including the Nyasa and Yao, who originated near present-day Malawi and arrived via Kilwa, and the Ngindo, who lived in the Rufiji Delta region on the mainland directly opposite Mafia. The growth of slavery was also encouraged by a series of natural disasters occurring in the late nineteenth century, some of which resulted from changes brought by incipient European colonialism, including smallpox and rinderpest epidemics as well as tse tse fly infestations (Kjekhus 1977). The result was widespread famine on the mainland and a growing willingness to sell humans into slavery.

On Chole, residents overwhelmingly emphasize the dehumanization of slavery, and underscore the tragedy of the commodification of human beings and their treatment as objects or animals. Bi Rehema began her historical account with a discussion of slavery:

> The period of slavery was difficult—those were hard times. People took their children and sold them to get food. Because slavery existed and because people were in difficult straits, they sold their children. The Arabs [from Kilwa Kisiwa] would go in their ships over to the mainland; you would go to them with your children and then send them away as slaves. It was a business. . . . The Arabs bought the children on the mainland and brought them here to Chole to be sold in the market. . . . There were slave markets in that Boma [the Customs House] which you see on the beach. The market for selling children was once in those ruins. . . . The "big people"—the rich people of that era—were here on Chole. . . . They would buy the children and make them farm slaves. There was hardship in the land where those children and their people had come from, but when they reached here, once again they faced hardship.

Numerous residents offered moral commentaries about the slave trade, stating that "people were considered to be as worthless as insects" or were considered only as objects to be sold "like coconuts in the market." As Bi Rehema stated, "In truth, slaves were sold like fish in that market—they were auctioned off like fish! You buy this one; that person would buy that one. . . . They bought and sold slaves in the same way that people today would sell coconuts from Mafia in Dar es Salaam."

The dehumanizing aspects of plantation slavery were also related to the obstacles slaves faced in marrying, reproducing or carrying on a family life (Glassman 1991)—essential aspects of personhood along the coast. As Bi Rehema added:

> A slave didn't marry. . . . Men didn't marry and women didn't marry. All they had was their work. . . . You would farm all day long until you finished in the evening. Wasn't that the only thing you were wanted for—work? . . . If you were a woman and had children on the sly, you would just put them aside—throw them away— and continue with your work. . . . The women would put the children aside all day long while they were working. When you returned in the evening to try to rescue your child, you didn't know whether it would be dead or alive.

The conflicts of the slave era emerged at the center of Ibrahim Abdallah's history of Mafia. In the mid-1990s, Ibrahim Abdallah was a middle-aged man and a respected fisherman and farmer on Chole. While not young, he was not old enough to consider himself an *mzee* or elder. Thus, he felt it important to justify his right to speak about Mafia's history by emphasizing the care with which he had listened to the stories of his own elders, a care which became apparent in the detailed and eloquent account of slavery that he offered. Ibrahim also alerted me to the ongoing politics of talk about slavery on Chole. In describing himself as unafraid and willing to speak openly, he contrasted himself to some older people on Mafia whom he argued would be nervous to do so—particularly to a "European" or *mzungu*. His comment rang true and helped explained a telling encounter that I had with an older woman, a relative of his. Although Ally Ahmadi, my enthusiastic coworker in collecting oral histories, was known by, or related to, everyone on Chole, many residents were, with good reason, less clear of my own motivations. Among the people we interviewed, those whom I either knew well or with whom I maintained ties with other family members were usually frank. A few, however, seemed to agree to be interviewed either out of politeness or because they were intrigued by the novel possibility of being videotaped, and were carefully noncommittal in their responses. One of the latter, an elderly woman, Halima binti Hassani, who lived on the far side of Chole and whom I knew only in passing, expressed an interest in being interviewed but, on the appointed day, parried questions about Mafia's history with one sentence responses. Months later, when she realized that I was friends with her younger sister, Bi Rehema Hassani, she came to me insisting that we do another interview. "But," she muttered in embarrassment, "I didn't know. . . ." and, as if she needed to make a conciliatory gesture, she promptly began to smooth my unruly hair, an affectionate gesture between female friends. Even her younger sister, open and forthright from the start, nevertheless characterized her discussion of slavery in a hushed tone as "the hidden memories of slavery" (*siri ya makumbusho ya utumwa*).

In the videotape of Ibrahim, he is sitting cross-legged in front of his mud and thatch house, bare-chested and wearing a purple *serenge* cloth wrapped around his waist. Proudly nonchalant about the boldness with which he expresses himself, he offers the following uninterrupted account of Chole's past:

I have learned about many things which happened in the past . . . especially concerning slavery. Indeed, slavery was begun by Arabs during the reign of Abu Saidi [i.e., Sultan Bhargash, the son of Seyid Said]. . . . Slavery had progressed until the point when it became a big business, and, here on Chole, a slave market was built and an auctioneer installed. The market existed, although I [was not born in time] to see it personally. But at Mikindini, I saw with my own eyes a market which had been used for auctioning slaves—nothing else had been sold there except slaves. It exists until today although it is now being used for other kinds of business.

So, things continued, and slaves were brought here. Slavery was based on the use of force and on struggles and competition between people. To give an example, I might leave here and go to a place like Juani. When I reach Juani, perhaps I meet some children and steal them. After stealing those children, I take them to the market and auction them off and people would buy them—yet the government was there! It knew that people stole children, but the government didn't concern itself with such matters because the government itself was made up of Arabs, and, indeed, they were the ones who had instituted slavery.

Time passes, and passes, and passes. Finally, the point comes when the Abu Saidi dynasty leaves [Mafia] and the Germans take over. The Germans followed in the footsteps of the Arabs by not opposing slavery. Thus slavery continued and even people of my generation could meet people who had been bought as slaves. I knew an old man who has since died who was bought in the market. I asked him, "In your home area [on the mainland], did you know about slavery?" He said, "No, at home, I did not understand." I asked, "Why?" He replied,

> I stayed in a place with about ten other children. When the slave raiders came, my older companions ran away; I alone remained and was carried off. I was immediately put on board a vessel in the Rufiji where these things happened, and when I reached [Mafia] I was sold. I was still a small child and incapable of doing any work. After being sold, and to tell the truth up until now, I still don't know the region where I'm from or who my father and mother were. As a consequence, this had a very profound impact on me. It was easier for those people who were older and understood where they came from.

After being sold, a slave went to a master who could punish you to any degree he pleased. The "big people" who were the owners and who had the financial means to buy slaves were a group called the MaShatiri. Those who had the money to buy slaves would arrive at Chole's market near the Customs House on the beach—the place where they are now building the hotel. A slave owner might have fifteen, twenty, or thirty slaves. The master would sit in his house, like this, with his arms crossed, and he would divide up the slaves whom he had bought. Some would be sent to Bweni, some to Juani, others to the Rufiji, but all to work on the master's farms. These people didn't have permission to eat any of the produce that they had farmed. Instead, they were required to bring it to their master and put it inside [his store rooms]. Everything they worked for was brought to the master. They no longer had any authority over themselves; they were reduced to the work of being "sent."[15]

Things continued and continued like this. The arrogance increased until the point when, if a slave did anything wrong at all, it was possible to butcher that slave and throw him or her away. Yes, It is true! And the government was there! Such things were done, but the government didn't care at all. In the past, a person was treated as if he or she were some kind of insect—they thought slaves didn't have any more value than that! If some kind of [government institution] had existed that was interested in defending people it would have concerned itself with such cases, otherwise, it would have been impossible for people to have suffered this kind of oppression.

It even reached the point when people like the slavemaster known as Masunda forced a person to climb a coconut tree and shot him with bullets to see if he would fall out of the tree the way a monkey would—a person was forced to climb a tree and killed just to be experimented upon! The government knew and saw this, but this was done by a master and so nothing was done to him. Nunu [the wife of Masunda] told her husband, "Bwana, I don't know how a child lies within a woman's stomach; how does it lie?" Therefore a female slave who was pregnant was sought and brought to them. She was made to lie down and was cut open in order to show Nunu the anatomy of a fetus. This was done to a young woman! The government knew, but didn't do anything. I say a prayer that God lessen the punishment of those who did such things because, of course, God is punishing them for what they have done. These things were not right!

In all truth, these things ended immediately after the British arrived. The British didn't agree with slavery. They issued an order that starting from that moment even the word "slavery" would no longer exist. But there were some slaves who hated the end of slavery. They thought, "Why remove it?" [Speaking sarcastically] Perhaps they felt it held benefits for them; perhaps they didn't care that they could be punished for nothing—it didn't bother them. Of course, for many others, the end of slavery made them very happy because now they were free.

The major participants in the slave trade had been the MaShatiri, but it began with the [foreign] Arabs. During the time of Abu Saidi's reign, any master at all was like a king. It shows the abjectness of that period that any slave master could think of himself as a king: after all, wasn't he able to do anything he wanted and not be judged?

Thus, the situation as I understand it was that people were very oppressed and that this was unlawful. Toward the end of the time of slavery, it was no longer even necessary to go steal people to be slaves over on the mainland. Let me use the example of my young relative here [gesturing toward Ally Ahmadi]. At that time, if I were cunning, I would take Ally Ahmadi and tell him, "Grandchild, let's go. We're going for a visit." So we would go to the home of a slavemaster. We would be sitting on his porch, eating and drinking and I would go inside. I would tell the master, "I'll sell this child to you" and the master would buy him. I would myself sell my own grandchild and this master would buy him. Then I would tell my grandchild, "Wait here, I'm coming." But instead I would leave and go on my way. When this child decides to go, the master would inform him, "You can't go out again. You've already been sold. Go into the courtyard and sweep." The deed would already have been done. For some people, if they were reduced to selling their own children, it was because they needed food. Yet, a person's own child! This person might think I have ten children or fifteen and so would take three children and sell them. Thus slavery occurred by many means. Slavery was not approved of by God—it was about oppression and force. Indeed, a point even came when our ancestors did it to get money. Perhaps the problems we are experiencing today are retribution for this. In other words, our elders did things which were inconceivable and outside of religion, for in no religion is there anything about having slaves. Therefore, it is possible that this is their payment. Perhaps the punishments we are experiencing today are payment for what our ancestors did. May God relieve the punishment they are surely experiencing. Indeed this is as I understand it.

Ibrahim's account was both a passionate and intriguing one. There is an interesting accusatory refrain about the government. Ibrahim asserted that the government "knew" of injustice, but turned a blind eye to it, an interpretation that potentially reflects on the *watu wakubwa* (big people) of the present as well as the past. Ibrahim also argued against the injustice of individual slave owners being allowed to act as "kings" without being subjected to a higher political authority, an analysis that might also suggest a desire to temper the power of local potentates who would choose to oppress Mafia's majority in the present.

Moral retribution emerged as a primary principle of historical causality in this account. Indeed, it was extremely common in all historical narratives told on Chole, which were used not simply to convey "objective" facts but to offer an interpretation of the past that also held lessons for the present. For example, the sacking of Kua as well as the reality that the ruins at Kisimani Mafia eventually washed into the sea were considered by Chole residents to be moral retribution for the atrocities committed during the period of their rivalry. Kua's downfall was also attributed to the cruelty of Kua's elite toward slaves, while the smallpox plague that later decimated the invading Sakalafa was, in turn, seen as punishment for their own attack on the town. Like other Chole residents, Ibrahim suggested that their current problems might be divine punishment for the inhumanities of the slave trade. Because of the complexity of the backgrounds of Chole residents, this could, ironically, be interpreted as punishment for either mainland African ancestors selling their children into slavery, or, alternately, for Arab ancestors participating in the slave trade or owning slaves.

In general, slavery was the overwhelming focus of Ibrahim's account. In contrast to the accounts of slavery at Kua, which had focused on the image of slaves being forced to husk rice with their fingertips, even more visceral images were used to imply the negation of slaves' humanity during the period of Omani colonial hegemony. Chole residents in particular focused on the image of a male slave being shot out of a coconut tree to see if he would fall to the ground like a monkey and of the belly of a pregnant slave woman being cut open to observe how the fetus lay inside the womb, both acts attributed by several of Mafia's elders to a man they named as Masunda of

Kaziwa. These stories construct a portrayal of slavery in which slaves are so dehumanized that they could be killed to serve as objects of inhuman experimentation. Whether or not these accounts were literally true, these images functioned symbolically for both speakers and listeners to encapsulate what one woman on Chole referred to as the "oppression of the past" (*uonevu wa zamani*). The man being shot out of a coconut tree to see if he would fall like a monkey argues for a lack of boundaries between humans and animals under slavery, as does the comment which serves as the title for this chapter, namely, that slaves were considered to be "as worthless as insects." The vivisection of the woman and fetus graphically illustrates the lack of control slaves had, not only over their bodies, but over reproduction—the ability to bear children and be a part of a kin group being an essential part of personhood throughout East Africa. Interestingly, identical stories circulated in other parts of the East African coast and were at one time used to consolidate support for the bloody 1964 revolution in Zanzibar (Mwanjisi 1967).[16] Although the factual accuracy of these stories is unclear, it is evident that such accounts offer a historical analysis of power dynamics couched in symbolic terms that carry great resonance for Chole residents.

The legacy of slavery on Mafia, and along the coast in general, is complicated by the mixed backgrounds of many residents and by the fact that distinctions between "Arabs" and "Africans" are often unclear. Because Arab immigrants to the East African coast were usually men without wives who drew upon traditions of both polygyny and concubinage, assimilation with coastal residents was rapid (Trimingham 1964). Whether Arab men married women from elite coastal families or took African slave women as concubines (*masuria*), the children of these unions were considered legitimate and were entitled to inheritance under Islamic law (although differences in status existed in practice). The ethnicity of a person or their *kabila* (a term commonly translated into English as "tribe") was not based on biology or racial phenotype, but upon family lineage (which in the case of patrilineal Arabs meant through the father's side). Thus, an individual with only a distant Arab ancestor could identify as an "Arab" although he or she might be predominantly African in appearance. In short, the intermixing of Shirazi, various Arab groups, coastal residents, and Africans of other backgrounds (particularly the numerically dominant group of former slaves) makes easy categorization impossible and complicates the issue of how residents might choose to self-identify. As Margaret Strobel suggests, despite the high status historically accorded to things "Arab" and the low status accorded to slaves, it is perhaps most accurate to think of both Arabs and slaves as having assimilated into coastal Swahili society (1979).

Although the historical legacy of slavery is central to Chole residents' understanding of the world, this issue does not smoulder in the context of contemporary relationships as it does in the more politicized regions of

Zanzibar and Pemba. Some individuals, whom I knew to be descendants of slaves, insisted that *ubaguzi* (discrimination) based on such backgrounds was a thing of the past: They did not know the *kabila* of others, nor did they care. A number of people spontaneously informed me that their parents were either Nyasa or Yao (implying slave backgrounds) without any apparent self-consciousness. And, when I asked Chole residents to identify the *kabila* of their neighbors, many people were genuinely stumped and insisted that only the *wazee* (elders) would know such things today. At the same time, however, Ally Ahmadi in the course of conducting our kinship survey, declined to ask fellow residents what their "tribe" or "lineage" was, fearing this question might give offense if it implied a slave background. Furthermore, only elderly Mzee Hodari stated openly and unequivocally that his parents were not simply "Yao" but slaves. After Ally Ahmadi and I videotaped Mzee Hodari's historical account, he went into his house and gingerly brought out an official document that crackled with age in his knotted hands. The document, dating from 1891 and stamped by the German colonial government, stated that his parents had ransomed themselves from slavery and were declared free. Perhaps Mzee Hodari's relatively prominent social position, described in the following chapter, gave him the strength to be more open than many of his peers.

In general, the historical accounts of most Chole residents strongly identified with the slaves of the past. In part, this may be because most of the people who would have been considered "Arabs" had long since died or left Mafia in search of more prosperous economic horizons, while those who remained had heavily intermarried with less elite residents. Unlike the situation in Zanzibar, where prosperous Pembans and Zanzibaris pack the weekly Gulf Air flights to visit relatives in the Middle East, no Mafia resident that I know has relatives in Oman or other Arab countries. Even some of Chole's residents who because of their own mixed backgrounds might have claimed "Arab" descent, nevertheless offered historical accounts in which they passionately identified with the plight of slaves (which would presumably have included their ancestors as well). For example Ibrahim Abdallah himself belonged to one of the few families on Chole that could still realistically speak of having an "Arab" past; a male relative of his had been one of three persons (all men) on Chole listed as an "Arab" in the British census of 1957. Despite this (or perhaps because of this?), Ibrahim's moral passion is obviously on the side of the slaves. Similarly, Bi Rehema's account sympathizes strongly with the plight of slaves although one of her grandfathers was a Baluchi (a group described as "Arab" on Chole that had served as mercenaries for the Zanzibari sultans), while another grandmother was an Mgunya or mixed "Arab" from the Lamu region.

A few other residents, however, equally mixed in their backgrounds, quietly offered an alternative historical reading, one which identified more closely with the conservative Arab past. Bi Safiya Abdallah, a large, regal older woman with heavily Bantu features that signaled the many Africans in her own background, nevertheless, referred to slaves as "them" and felt the need to quickly exonerate herself stating that she had not owned slaves even if her ancestors might have. Mzee Bakari himself was quietly ambivalent in a way that initially surprised me. One day, at his house, I flippantly mentioned the "*MaShatiri makali*" (harsh MaShatiri) as they were generally described by people on Chole, including his wife. Expecting a smile of recognition that I had picked up this term, he instead looked grave and hurt. He explained how he himself had been raised as a child in one of Chole's stone houses, the home of his relative Binti Saidi Ahmadi—one of the last of the MaShatiri. Overall, however, in contrast to the pervasive hierarchy of the past, the dual processes of intermarriage and assimilation along the Swahili coast have worked on Mafia to alleviate the historical conflict between groups, creating a situation in which almost everyone (at least publicly) identifies with the plight of former slaves.

The historical narratives about slavery offered by Chole residents suggest, not only the centrality of such bondage in the past, but also ways of thinking about human relationships, social hierarchy and morality that have strong implications for the present, including the social drama of the Mafia Island Marine Park. The impact of this history on contemporary residents extends beyond a wariness about challenging powerful figures or the perceived necessity of appealing to the influential through patron–client relationships. These accounts also point to the inevitability of divine justice and retribution, perhaps a particularly meaningful form of belief for those who possess relatively few mechanisms for achieving worldly justice. Indeed, the attitudes of those like Chole's village chairman, who maintained a quiet conviction that justice would of necessity prevail in contemporary struggles over the marine park, suggests another counterlegacy of this disturbing history— hope for the future.

Other Colonialisms: The Germans and the British

On Mafia, those referred to as "Arabs" were both the most hated and the most respected of the various oppressors in Mafia's history. Certainly, they were those with whom residents most closely identified and with whom they shared the Islamic religion and the ideal of *ustaarabu* (literally, "Arabness" perhaps best translated as the state of being civilized). However, the Omani period was not an era of "tradition," as contemporary tourist accounts suggest, but rather the harbinger of European colonialism. Omani political expansion itself came into existence in response to the demands of an increasingly integrated global capitalist economy, which provided opportunities for some to grow rich as suppliers of raw materials and such valued commodities as copra and spices (Sheriff 1987). Eventually, however, this same logic, as expressed by European desires for "captive" markets and secure sources of raw materials, as well as the desire to enhance national pride through the acquisition of colonies, would lead to the so-called Scramble for Africa. At the very end of the nineteenth century, almost the entire African continent would be divided among various European powers (Hobsbawm 1987; Illife 1995). Despite the reality that it was global capitalism which initially brought intensified forms of plantation slavery along the coast, ironically, the logic of wage labor and the liberal individualism on which Euro-American forms of capitalism were based, would in turn lead to the demise of slavery and Arab plantation life (Cooper 1977).

Just as the European colonial takeover would happen at a particular moment in the history of capitalism, it would also happen at a particular point in the history of state making. European colonies in Africa formed the last great wave of colonization and, thus represented a particularly advanced form of modern state (C. Young 1994). Although European colonization brought relatively few Europeans to Mafia (and those who did arrive segregated themselves socially unlike earlier waves of Arabs), it did lead to the creation of a new form of state relying upon "modern" instruments of control. The Omani state had a relatively loose relationship with its dependencies, functioning according to the logics of kinship, patronage, and tribute. For example, the Omani State in Zanzibar was considered to be the familial property of Sultan Said and was inherited by his thirty-six living children upon his death in 1857. As a result, his royal successor was required to spend large sums buying back the apparatus of state from his siblings (Fair 2001:301–2, ftn 23). While Arab colonialism had a large cultural, religious and legal impact along the coast, European colonialism would have a substantial institutional impact. Although modern states, like patrons and slave owners, must negotiate power with those they seek to control (Foucault 1977; Mitchell 1988), such states also rely upon a range of "modern" modes of organizing political life that include particular variants of bureaucracy, civil service, police, and military. It would be this form of state, created by European colonialism and inherited by the independent Tanganyikan government in 1961, that would constitute the political apparatus governing Mafia's marine park.

Mzee Bakari describes the beginnings of European colonialism in the following terms:

[O]riginally, the [Abu Said] Arabs ruled all the way from Kilwa and Zanzibar to Mombasa and Tabora. The Arabs lived here for perhaps twenty or twenty-two years, and then the Europeans started going about, investigating things, and saying "I want the country." The Europeans reached the interior, and the Germans took a piece of land here, and the Germans took a piece of land there. They continued until they reached Mafia. After reaching Mafia, they passed along this route with *merikebu*. Vessels in the past were called *merikebu*, not "man-of-wars" or something else. There were two kinds that passed here, *merikebu* and *manchani*, [author's transcription] and they had many sails. I don't know whether these kinds of vessels exist any longer, but when I traveled outside the country as a young man, I myself was shown these kinds of ships.

Now, the Germans came to raise the war flag. It was red. They raised the flag and they entered with their trumpets of war. The Arabs were there relaxing on the beach, and they saw that war was coming. They said, "We don't have weapons of any kind, nor do we have any expertise in war. We don't have a volunteer militia. We don't have anything to display at all." They decided to raise the flag of peace. They raised the white flag high [he acts out raising the flag]. The Germans disembarked, and when they came, they saw the flag of peace. Thus, when they arrived there was no war—there wasn't anything at all. The Arabs explained, "We accept your rule here." It was done. They wrote the treaty conditions and then the Germans received possession of this place. I think that in their negotiations it was decided that Zanzibar and Mombasa would remain in the arms of the Arabs of Abu Saidi and not in the arms of the Germans; Do you understand? Indeed it must have been so because in our own century we encountered the rule of the Abu Saidi Arabs in these places.

During the latter half of the 1800s, European powers were scrambling to gain control of various parts of the African continent. In the 1880s, a group of German adventurers attempted to gain territory on mainland Tanganyika by obtaining treaties through force and stealth (Glassman 1995). In 1885, the Germans formalized this situation by declaring a Protectorate over the Tanganyikan mainland. In 1890, Britain declared a protectorate over the territory of the sultan of Zanzibar, where it had been exercising a strong behind-the-scenes influence, and it continued to rule indirectly through the sultan until Zanzibari independence in the mid-1960s. In a last-minute addendum to an 1890 Anglo-German agreement, the British traded Mafia, part of the sultan's territory, to the Germans in exchange for Stephenson Road between Lake Nyasa and Lake Tanganyika (Baumann 1957[1896]). Following this fluke of fate, Mafia would, except for one brief interval after World War I, henceforth be governed as part of the mainland rather than as part of Zanzibar. According to Oscar Baumann (1957[1896]), the German flag was hoisted on Chole by Emil von Zelewsky, a member of the German East Africa company then dominated by a group of men who were known for their cruelty and arrogance (Glassman 1995). Their reputation was such that an embarrassed Otto von Bismarck had nicknamed them the "conquistadors" (Glassman 1995: 177–198). Although few Germans would actually stay on Chole, a Sudanese garrison was at one point stationed on the island.

In Ibrahim Abdallah's account of Mafia's history, it was the freedom of each master under the Omanis to conceive of himself or herself as a ruler that led to atrocities committed upon the bodies of slaves. Under European colonialism, however, control over and abuse of bodies came not from a lack of government, but from government itself. In the historical accounts of Chole's residents, many references to European colonialism focus on the hangings and beatings that took place at the Boma for infractions of European justice. As Bi Rehema relates:

> If someone did something wrong, that person would be hanged at the Boma there on the beach. . . . [T]hat person would be imprisoned and then hanged near the casuarina tree at the spot along the beach where people today like to sit. It was an open place and a box would be placed below and the person's neck would be placed in a rope. At that time, it was the Germans who had arranged to use that place in this manner, and indeed they were the ones who did the hanging. . . . The Germans were harsh. . . . Didn't they beat you for any kind of mistake you could make? Any error at all. You would go there to be accused, and then you were summoned, then you would be beaten, and then locked up. People were locked up right over there where the jail was.

Although elites along the coast may have initially preferred the German presence to the British (given Britain's more vigorous stance against slavery), nonelite residents of southern Tanganyika were not so quick to accept this overlordship. After the so-called "Arab" rebellion against the Germans centered in Bagamoyo (Glassman 1995), southern Tanganyika was galvanized by the Maji Maji War in 1905–1907.[17] In this conflict, people from across a broad range of tribal and ethnic backgrounds joined together in a precursor to later national movements, operating under the religious belief that their leaders possessed magic water that would render their followers invincible to the guns of the Europeans (Illife 1979).

According to historian John Illife's account (1979), the Maji Maji movement began inland among various stateless people. Although Mzee Bakari mentions mainland figures in his narrative, it is the coastal peoples of Kilwa who instigated the Maji Maji War after being angered by the presumptuous behavior of the Germans towards their ruler. He states:

> [The Maji Maji combatants] fought a war with those Germans. They fought each other very hard. They fought the Germans for close to two or three years. . . . [The combatants] went out with just arrows. There were many of them at that time. People came from all over to fight the Europeans. The Europeans had guns [he mimics shooting a gun] and [the combatants] are just shooting arrows. Even though they were only shooting arrows, many people [on the European side] still died.

Mzee Bakari argues that the Germans eventually won this war by importing new kinds of automatic rifles, a technology they obtained from the British.

In the case of the Maji Maji War, resistance against oppression resulted in an outright revolt against the imposition of European colonial rule. However, this act of resistance was brutally put down by greater military might, and, in the future, the Germans would punish southern Tanganyika through both oppression and neglect for its involvement in the Maji Maji War (Illife 1979). The repression was such that half a century later, many people in southern Tanzania were hesitant to support TANU, the party that led Tanganyika to independence in 1961, for fear of further European reprisals (Illife 1979).

What disturbs Chole residents most in their accounts of German colonialism is that the Germans did not end slavery. According to the historian Thaddeus Sunseri, the Germans feared that the demise of slavery would undermine the colonial economy and were critical of British abolitionist efforts in Zanzibar (1993). Consequently, they established a policy whereby slaves could purchase their freedom by working on the German coconut plantations that were replacing Arab plantations on Mafia's main island. Conditions, however, were often not much better than slavery (Sunseri 1993).

Although Mzee Bakari, some of whose ancestors were MaShatiri, is quick to exonerate the "Arab" way of life, he is critical of the Germans:

> The Arabic life and the way people were living here on Chole was very good. In other words, it was a religious life; it wasn't a life of decadence. It was a religious life based on fellowship. However, there was slavery. And the Germans did not remove slavery. . . . Do you see that building there? [pointing to the ruins of the Boma or Customs House]. Indeed, it was there that people were sold, sold as if they were coconuts. And if a person made a mistake, they were whipped there with a hippopotamus-hide whip by the Germans.

In 1915, during World War I, Mafia became the first area in German East Africa to be captured by the British.[18] Bi Rehema describes how some Mafia residents helped Germans trapped on the island to escape by hiding them from the British. She adds that some of these Germans later returned after the war bringing gifts for those who had aided them. While Bi Rehema implies that these Mafia residents merely felt sorry for the Germans, Sunseri's suggestion that plantation-owning elites favored the Germans as a result of Britain's greater commitment to the abolition of slavery suggests a less altruistic motivation (Sunseri 1993). Once captured by the British, Mafia was used as a base for airplane reconnaissance missions over the Rufiji Delta in the search for the German cruiser, the *Koenigsberg* (Revington 1936; Piggott 1941; Hatchell 1954). Mzee Bakari colorfully describes the British search for this vessel and the mythic qualities attributed to the elusive *Koenigsberg*. He describes how the cruiser was like a "chameleon" and capable of disguising itself as it entered a group of British ships by appearing to be

English, as well as how it continued to elude the British in the *Kikali* branch of the Rufiji Delta with a disguise of leaves and branches that made it indistinguishable from the surrounding river banks.

During the war, many slaves on Mafia ran away or severed ties with their masters (Sunseri 1993). Later, after Tanganyika had become a British territory under a League of Nations mandate in the postwar period, slavery was finally abolished in 1922. According to the oral accounts collected by Saadi (1941), while the slaves rejoiced, many masters were bitter because they had no one to work their plantations. Some masters died, others went mad, and still others were frustrated that they had not been compensated for the loss of slaves, as slave owners on Zanzibar had been (1941:26). According to Mzee Bakari, the loss of labor caused many slave owners to move to Mafia's main island to guard and work their plantations, and eventually many former masters left the islands altogether.

As Cooper points out, the British motivation for abolition was more closely related to the dissonance caused by the incompatibility of slavery with ideas of individual "free labor" rather than aversion to racism per se (Cooper 1977). Nevertheless, Chole residents view the ending of slavery in moral terms and frequently comment that it was the British who freed the slaves. Like Ibrahim Abdallah, Mzee Bakari states, "The Germans had pretended that they would quickly end slavery, but they actually only did it little by little until the country was finally taken by force by the British." Ibrahim Abdallah tells us, "In all truth, these things ended immediately after the British arrived. The British didn't agree with slavery. They issued an order that starting from that moment even the word 'slavery' would no longer exist." Despite the abolition of slavery, however, former slaves faced great economic insecurity, causing some to prefer to continue their relationships with former masters. Sunseri speculates that women in particular would have found it difficult to achieve economic independence for themselves and their children, and might have chosen this option (Sunseri 1993, see also Saadi 1941).

The British, however, hoped to replace slavery with their own labor regime designed to enhance the economic productivity of the territory. Consequently, they imposed policies designed to force Tanganyikan residents to participate in wage labor as well as cash cropping. One way to encourage wage labor was to impose onerous taxes on residents to force them to work for cash. One elderly man on Chole, Mzee Shomari, described on videotape how he had been unable to pay his taxes and was sentenced to 3 years of hard labor at Kua. In another interview, Bi Rehema and I discussed the British taxes:

> BR: The house tax—it was 20 shillings. That tax existed until the time of [President] Nyerere [after independence], then it was removed. It was the men who paid it, not the women. The head tax was 3 shillings. This head tax was calculated

every year. Every year they would pass by the houses and you would pay the tax and be given a receipt. But it was only adults—children like that one [pointing to a teenager] weren't yet charged the tax.

CW: And if you weren't able to pay?

BR: Then you would be imprisoned. You were imprisoned at the jail. You would be given difficult work.

CW: Were many men unable to pay?

BR: Many!!!

CW: Really? It was a big problem?

BR: A big problem! There was a lot of economic hardship at that time and getting even ten cents was difficult.

With the demise of slavery, many free residents and former slaves refused to work on plantations—work that was associated with slave status. As in Zanzibar (Fair 1994), it became increasingly common for the British to encourage contract laborers from the mainland to work on Mafia's coconut plantations, which were now largely owned by Europeans. Archival records include requests by European plantation owners to track down "runaway" workers who had left before the expiration of their contracts (TNA L 1/3). Verbal traditions on Mafia also suggest the harshness of European plantations. Indeed, under European colonialism, wage laborers were subjected to corporal punishment and were unable to end their contracts at will (Illife 1969). Thus, although labor for wages came to supercede slavery, the extent to which such labor was "free" is a debatable point. European colonialism also began a period in which the state would increasingly take on new forms of authority. On Chole, although people might still be beaten, it was no longer by individual slave owners. One elderly man on Chole, Mzee Kichigi, impoverished in old age as he was in his youth, recalled how he was whipped at the Boma because he had not planted a cassava plot required by the British. Thus, the demise of slavery meant only the transformation, not the end, of "the oppression of the past" (*uonevu wa zamani*).

The Demise of Chole Mjini

The era of Chole's dominance as the urban center of Mafia was soon to end, resulting in what residents perceive as the current "backwardness" of the island. In 1913, the Germans resolved to move the administrative capital of Mafia from Chole to Kilindoni because of Chole's poor harbor and the dangers posed to ships by the Kinasi Pass entrance into Chole Bay. Oral accounts indicate, however, that the move was not completed until later during the British period. The combination of the demise of slavery, the emigration of slaves and plantation owners, and the movement of the capital to Kilindoni resulted in what is commonly referred to by residents as the "death" of

Chole Town. As a result, Chole would undergo a radical depopulation in subsequent years. Although Chole residents still joke that villagers on Mafia's main island live on *Chole Shamba* or Chole's farm region (as it was called during the nineteenth century when the entire archipelago was known to its inhabitants as "Chole"), those living on the main island in turn tease Chole residents about living in "town" when Chole's contemporary reality is clearly one of rural poverty.

Mzee Bakari offers this account of the island's depopulation:

> After the slaves received their freedom and left, the wealthy free-born were also forced to disperse. Some went to their farms, others died, some went to supervise their property in the rural areas, only a few remained here on Chole. Those who remained were the elderly; do you see? And also the young "sprouts," the children who were growing up and would be the people whom my own generation encountered. There was no one left on Chole; all those people left. Those who were able, traveled back and forth between Chole and other places until, finally, they didn't come back again.

The current chairman of Chole Island, Mzee Maarufu states that when he was a child there were only 14 other children of his age on Chole. For people of this generation, the more recent repopulation of Chole is considered to be a blessing. Mzee Bakari states:

> Praise be to Allah, we are grateful to God, we have been fertile. . . . When the British began to rule here, there were no people on Chole. . . . Now our brothers have given birth, and we have given birth to the point where those blessings of our fertility, our children, are filling our primary school. . . . We have other children who have traveled here and there and who are living in other places. We have others who are here with us and praise be to Allah, they are now marrying.

Mzee Maarufu expands,

> At that time there was no "development" (*maendeleo*) in terms of parenthood. There were old people and then some younger people, perhaps 25 years of age, who were with them. . . . After this time, our brothers began looking for young women. They married them, and then, thanks be to God, they started to give birth. We have produced children and produced children until we had 20 [on the island] and then 30, then, 50 until now in terms of the history of young children, praise be to God, we don't know how many children have been born. . . . The number of people [on this island] is perhaps 1,200 including everyone [including those living elsewhere], instead of what it was during that period, in which as I remember there were only a hundred people here including the children as well as the elderly.

Many of Chole's residents, particularly the elderly who remember when the island was a proper "town," hope that the incipient tourist project on Chole will generate wealth for the community and revive Chole's earlier position of importance on Mafia. Many express a longing for the lost grandeur of Chole Town, ignoring the contradiction that such wealth was based on a slave economy that most contemporary residents of Chole abhor.

THE RUINS AND THE PAST IN THE PRESENT

It is common knowledge on Mafia that *wazungu* (Europeans) are fond of visiting ruins and interested in other material relics of the past. On numerous occasions, friends from Chole made the crossing to Juani with me, wading through the shallow water and mangrove trees at low tide to view the ruined town of Kua on Juani. Although Kua was described as "worthless" architecture by Baumann after his visit in 1895 (much of it being presumably covered by bush at the time), it was described in glowing terms by Sir Mortimer Wheeler as "potentially the Pompeii of East Africa" (Wheeler 1955). Kua was cleared in 1955 by the British archaeologist Freeman-Grenville and later by Neville Chittick in 1964. The site spreads across approximately 35 acres and includes, in addition to the two-storied palace, seven mosques, two cemeteries and the ruins of many stone houses which would presumably have been interspersed with the mud-and-thatch homes of poorer residents (Freeman-Grenville 1957).

Even after I had been to Kua numerous times, friends in customary displays of unflagging hospitality would always suggest an excursion whenever I had visitors. On one particular afternoon in 1997, several of my closest female friends on Chole escorted me and a visiting American friend to the ruins at Kua. On this day, I had packed a knapsack of packaged biscuits, pounded rice and bottled water and after arriving at Kua, we crouched in the shade of the ruins chewing biscuits and talking. As invariably happened, the remains of Kua's former "palace" elicited now familiar stories. Hadija and Rukia pointed out the tiny chamber underneath the crumbling staircase in which recalcitrant slaves were said to have been punished and told how a female ruler at Kua had refused to leave the second story of the palace. When the women's stories strayed from well-worn paths and contradicted each other, they argued good-naturedly, trying to recall the particular accounts they had heard from elders either on Chole Island where they had married, or else in their home areas on other parts of Mafia.

Bi Sharifa, the eldest of the group and perhaps the person who had drawn me most vigorously into her social world, asked what I would do with the historical narratives that I had gathered on Chole after I left. I had often explained about my dissertation, but the concept was vague and the world of American academia and its theoretical interests were distant here. I mentioned an idea with which I had been toying: perhaps I should transcribe the videotapes and make a booklet of the historical narratives? Such a booklet might be useful to the elementary school teachers on the island, I reasoned, and some of the teenagers on Chole claimed they had not even heard their grandparents' stories of the past. Bi Sharifa strongly supported the idea arguing that many people on the islands did not know enough about Mafia's history. She lamented, "They see the ruins but they don't know how severe the punishment (*adhabu*) of the past was." Looking thoughtful, she suggested that knowing about the oppression of the past (*uonevu wa zamani*) was an important lesson that could give people in the present the courage to face hardship in their own lives.

In general, Mafia residents, unlike Euro-Americans, were little interested in preserving the ruins—they were inauspicious spaces that would crumble and decay with time just as living things did. Indeed, during my stay, one elderly man, who was rumored to be involved in black magic, moved in among the ruins at Kua and set fire to the remains in order to plant a rice crop. The fire helped turn the ancient limestone mortar to powder, hastening the disintegration of the ruins as I would discover when I returned in 2000. While a few residents opposed his actions as damaging a potential asset in the budding tourism trade, for most Chole residents such actions were inconsequential. For them, history was not located in the ruins, but in the stories, the moral lessons that the past encapsulated and offered to the living. Such a position contrasted sharply with the lack of history found in the documents for the Mafia Island Marine Park and with the romantic and transcendental portrayal of history found in tourist narratives. It also contrasted with the view of some visiting Euro-Americans that "history" meant little to Mafia's residents. For example, when I described Mzee Hodari's aged document which had conferred freedom on his parents, several European visitors asked whether I had "taken" it from him. Presumably, this perspective was based on the belief that Euro-Americans had a deeper appreciation for such artifacts and, thus, had a "right" to protect such objects in the interests of history. After all, I imagined them arguing, were Mafia residents any more "educated" about conserving the past than they were about the environment?

Yet what emerged in the words of Bi Sharifa and from the pervasive moral commentary about the past on Chole was that history was indeed a powerful force for residents. History taught that oppression and abuse had existed long before European colonialism, yet it also suggested that the powerful would ultimately be punished for their oppression of the weak and that justice in the end would prevail. Both these ideas were apparent in residents' attitudes toward the struggles over the Mafia Island Marine Park—attitudes that were based on a longstanding skepticism about those in power combined with a belief in the possibility of justice and, therefore, the need to hope.

CHAPTER THREE

The Making and Unmaking of "Community"

THROUGHOUT MY STAY on Chole during the mid-1990s, I savored two plea-sures each morning. The first was being awakened, not rudely by an alarm clock as at home in New York City, but by the sun making its first tentative appearances through my tent windows and by birds riotously singing from surrounding orange trees. The second was "hiding" in my tent, even as the camp and nearby homes were already bustling with activity, and enjoying the early morning BBC world news reports in English on my short-wave radio. For myself, as well as for those people on Chole who could afford such luxuries, radio was the only reliable source of information about the rest of Tanzania, as well as the world beyond its borders. Although there had been an explosion of newspapers in Tanzania's new "multiparty" era, and despite the ubiquitousness of such papers in the daily life of Dar es Salaam and Zanzibar, printed matter of any sort was difficult to come by on Mafia. Consequently, it was through the radio and the BBC that I followed the conflict and peace negotiations in Bosnia, the attempts to reconstruct Rwanda in the aftermath of genocide, the controversy surrounding the exe-cution of writer and social activist Ken Saro-Wiwa in Nigeria, and the outcry over France's nuclear bomb tests in the Pacific.

In listening to these and many other reports, I was struck by the contin-uous evocation of something called the "international community." Whether national leaders were being chastised for flouting its views and warned of its sanctions, or whether they were busy reassuring the international community and seeking its help, the assumption that an international community existed was taken for granted. In a context of an imploding "Second World" and increasingly porous boundaries between First and Third Worlds, this evoca-tion of community worked to symbolically construct a "new world order" under reassuringly benign leadership and to help counter the apparently cha-otic transformations widely portrayed as globalization.

Talk of community on Mafia was not limited to BBC news reports, but also pervaded the language of the newly instituted Mafia Island Marine Park as well as the Chole Kisiwani tourism enterprise which the park had helped to foster. The vocal interest in community within the marine park, as well as among some Euro-American expatriates, in turn reflected broader transfor-mations that extended far beyond Tanzania. Although the policies of many international donor organizations were still based on the post–World War II faith in the power of centralized bureaucracies and technically trained experts to orchestrate economic and social transformation, the language of such institutions had shifted. During the 1980s and 1990s, these organizations increasingly came to rely upon the language of community (Craig and Mayo 1995; Western and Wright 1994; Nelson and Wright 1995; Pottier 1993; Alcorn 1997; Kempf 1993; Adams and McShane 1992).

The widespread appeal of this language stemmed in part from the ability of the concept of community—much like that of participation—to draw support from across the political spectrum. As Raymond Williams noted, community is one of those few "keywords" in English that can always be viewed in a positive light (Williams 1976:76). Community-oriented initiatives appealed to critics of mainstream development and conservation who hoped to empower poorer actors and change existing power relationships, as well as to conservative supporters of the free market who viewed the shift from state to community as coincident with decentralization, the valorization of market actors and family values, and the necessity of cost sharing (Craig and Mayo 1995, Peet and Watts 1996). As Peet and Watts suggest, the language of community also easily melds into a populist rhetoric that valorizes "the people" without taking the more contentious step of identifying who exactly "the people" are and what their relationships are to each other (1996). Thus, it is precisely the vagueness of the concept of community, much like that of "participation" and "sustainable development," that accounts for its ability to unify a range of divergent actors with disparate agendas. Perhaps just as importantly, the growing emphasis on communities as emblematic of the "local" serves as a symbolic foil to the universalizing assumptions of the "global," just as ideas of the traditional once served to anchor the "modern."

The previous chapter explored the centrality of history for Chole residents, despite the radically ahistorical perspective offered by the planners of the marine park and much of the development and conservation literature. In this chapter, I examine the concept of community and what it means for different actors involved in the Mafia Island Marine Park, particularly for residents of Chole Island. In order to understand the associations that representatives of international organizations and Tanzanian government officials bring to the concept, it is helpful to begin with a brief exploration of the term *community* in English as well as in ideas of *ujamaa* socialism within Tanzania. Such ideas both parallel and pose striking contrasts with concepts such as *wenyeji* or "the owners of a place" by which Chole residents themselves make sense of their relationships with others. It is also important to consider the relationship between such concepts and the realities of daily social life on Chole, which include dynamics that push residents apart as well as those which bind them together. In the final section of this chapter, I consider an incident that occurred in the Chole Kisiwani tourism camp that draws such dynamics into graphic relief. Incidents such as this one suggest the contradictory impact that community-based projects can have on social groups, serving both to draw people together to act as a "community" and simultaneously introducing resources and inequalities that exacerbate existing tensions. In conclusion, I argue that the possibilities and problems associated with "community-based" projects cannot be understood simply at a "community" level. Just as the BBC's focus on the "international community" draws attention away from power relationships among countries, so too the focus on "community" within international projects can work to obscure the national and international dimensions of power dynamics *within* communities.

CONCEIVING "COMMUNITY"

"Community" in English

Among development and conservation organizations, the language of community has become increasingly prominent (if rarely defined), and communities are assumed to be central partners in projects such as the Mafia Island Marine Park. Yet, what exactly does the term *community* suggest for representatives of international organizations with origins in the United States and Europe? In this brief overview, I consider the use of the word *community* in English, which has become the lingua franca of the development world. According to Williams, the use of the term *community* for English-speakers can be traced back to the thirteenth century. However, it was during the nineteenth century, when new forms of social organization based on capitalism were radically transforming first Britain, and then the rest of Europe, that the term took on the symbolism it would carry into the present (Williams 1976:75–76). It was during this period that community came to be understood in opposition to the emerging concept of *society*. Whereas *society* suggested atomistic groupings of individuals which were linked in relatively abstract ways within emerging modern nation-states, community connoted smaller social groupings that were presumed to share deeper social bonds and which were based on homogeneity and common interests. In short, society was seen as a distinctly modern phenomenon; community evoked a "premodern" quality of human relationship that was presumably being lost in the transition to the modern.

One of the most powerful influences on the concept of *community* in English came from Germany. In 1887, German scholar Ferdinand Tonnies theorized the difference between community and society as that between *gemeinschaft* and *gesellschaft*. *Gemeinschaft* suggested that community was a "natural" grouping based on kinship, geographic proximity, and shared culture in contrast to *gesellschaft*, which signified "society" based on contractual and legal relationships rather than shared identity or other similarities. Within this formulation, the concept of community was used, not only to represent "premodern" social groupings, but also as a form of symbolic critique of capitalism or modernity. A range of critics drew upon the concept of community, from reactionary conservatives (for whom community foreshadowed the exclusionist ideology of ultranationalism) to revolutionary radicals, including Karl Marx and Frederick Engels among others. Marx and Engels drew upon a social evolutionary framework that posited an early state of "primitive communism" (recall that the words community and communism share a common root) and believed that modern society, after passing through other historical stages, would ultimately return to a utopian communalism (Engels 1978[1884]). Thus, the concept of community has been centrally intertwined with the history of both of the major "modern" forms of social and economic organization—capitalism and socialism.[1]

Contemporary uses of the term, however, are increasingly distant from Tonnies version of *gemeinschaft*, which portrayed community in terms of blood relationships, face-to-face interactions, and geographic proximity. In an era in which new technologies make it easier to communicate as well as to develop and maintain social ties across vast distances—developments generally described as influencing the rise of "globalization"—the term "community" is increasingly used to delineate groups that do not share geographic spaces, for example, "communities" of users on the Internet. Indeed, we increasingly find the term invoked in the political terminology of a post–Cold War world that has been dominated by such communities as the European Economic Community (the predecessor to the European Union), the donor community and—as the BBC alerted us—the international community. Although the terrain for what constitutes a community is shifting, the concept continues to suggest strong and unproblematic social bonds and to direct attention away from issues of power, hierarchy, or conflict. The creation of "communities" that are not tied to geographic places, however, is not as "new," as commonplace narratives of globalization might suggest. In fact, such usages may be quite old. For example, the concept of *umma* or a community of believers in Islam has been used for centuries to unite Muslims from radically different backgrounds who live at great distances. A more pertinent issue to explore might be to consider why the concept of community has generated such widespread interest in recent decades and what kind of social work this concept is being asked to perform in the contemporary world.

"Community" and Ujamaa in Tanzania

Government officials within the Mafia Island Marine Park also draw upon ideas of community that are a product of political discourses within Tanzania. Given that "modernity" was forged, not simply in Europe, but in the relationship between Europe and other parts of the world (Piot 1999; Comaroff and Comaroff 1991, 1997), it is not surprising that Tanzania's own history suggests the influence of European conceptions of community. In the 1960s, the newly elected president of a newly independent country, Julius Nyerere, pronounced his intention to lead Tanzania toward a version of socialism based on the philosophy of *ujamaa*. Whereas Marx and Engel's understandings of social evolution were based on presumptions about "primitive" social organization in the non-Western world, Nyerere's philosophy drew in turn upon socialist ideologies formulated by European intellectuals. His goal, however, was to create a variant of socialism that was distinctively African. In Nyerere's formulation, *ujamaa* was a philosophy of community drawn from ideas of familyhood that he saw as characteristic of African "tradition" (his literal translation of *ujamaa* was "familyhood"). He wrote: "In our traditional African society we were individuals within a community. We took care of the community, and the community took care of us. We neither needed nor wished to exploit our fellow men." (1966:166). In short, Nyerere espoused the romanticized ideas of communalism found in Marx and Engels's ideas of "primitive communism," yet he appropriated it as characteristically "African" and found within it a source of superiority to European-based ideas of socialism that portray class struggle and conflict as intrinsic social processes.

In describing his policy of establishing *ujamaa* villages, Nyerere expressed his own utopian vision of what an African socialist nation would be like, a vision very much caught up in ideas of community. In such villages, he argued: "most of our farming would be done by groups of people who live as a community and work as a community. . . . Their community would be the traditional family group, or any other group of people living according to ujamaa principles (1968:351). . . . A nation of such village communities would be a socialist nation." (1968:353). Thus, Nyerere argued that the essence of true socialism was the extension of community based on *ujamaa* out from the family to the entire nation, the African continent, and, ultimately, "the whole society of mankind" (1967:171), demonstrating how community could be used metaphorically to forge other types of ties in a "modern" world.

Nyerere's vision of *ujamaa*, however, was clearly not a product of a homogeneous tradition within Tanzania. Referred to as Mwalimu (the "Teacher") and educated in Christian mission schools, Nyerere hailed from the Zanaki, a small group characterized by nonstratified social relationships (Stoger-Eising 2000). The historical egalitarianism of the Zanaki, however, bore little resemblance to "traditional" social relationships in other parts of Tanganyika, which ranged from the aristocratic kingdoms of the Shambaa (Feireman 1990) to the slave-based societies of the coast. Nyerere, however, drew upon his own background to create a generic and romanticized image of a "traditional" nonhierarchical African past—one which readily corresponded with the concept of community in English—upon which to build his variant of socialism. Yet, such understandings of community also served to deflect attention away from power relationships within the Tanzanian polity. Indeed, the idea of a generic African traditional community helped foster the illusion that all Tanzanians shared common interests that the state merely served to articulate. Thus, the interest expressed by international organizations in "community" in the 1990s did not prove to be a new phenomenon for Tanzanians, but a more recent manifestation of a concept with a long and hybrid history.

Conceptualizing Community on Mafia

Residents of Chole Island themselves used a range of terms to signify social bonds in ways that both parallel and differ from the uses of community in English as well as *ujamaa* in KiSwahili. Nyerere built his socialist philosophy on the abstract form of the word *jamaa* (the prefix "u" in KiSwahili denoting the quality or state of a thing). However, the form *ujamaa* is one that is almost never used by Mafia residents unless they are explicitly discussing politics. *Jamaa* itself is a generic term for relatives that is commonly used as a short hand way of signaling kinship ties without specifying how complex or distant those ties might be. In daily life, *jamaa* is often used on Mafia to refer to nonrelatives in a way that suggests inclusiveness and social bonds, even though no blood ties exist, thereby creating what anthropologists would call "fictive kinship." As a consequence, Pat Caplan defines *jamaa* for Mafia residents as "personal networks" that can refer to either relatives or nonrelatives (1975). In accordance with this logic, people signal respect for others by addressing unrelated younger women as *dada* (sister), older women as *mama* (mother) or *bibi* (grandmother), and elderly men as *mzee* (elder) or *babu* (grandfather). When individuals on Mafia enter or leave large groups of people, which potentially include kin as well as non-kin, their greetings and leave takings are collectively made to *jamaa*. Similarly, visitors from outside of Mafia who desire to create a sense of connection with area residents will often address them as *jamaa*. It is this tendency to use *jamaa* to suggest a social inclusiveness characteristic of kinship that presumably led Nyerere to translate the term as "familyhood" and to offer it as an equivalent to "community."

The concept, however, through which Mafia residents conceive of their collective rights within the marine park does not draw upon the ideas of community found in political discourses of *jamaa*, but from another cultural framework. As mentioned in previous chapters, *wenyeji* in KiSwahili literally refers to the "owners" of a place and is often translated as "inhabitants" (although John Middleton suggests that a more accurate translation would be the "proprietors" of a place [1961]). This term exists as part of a symbolic dualism and is conceived in opposition to *wageni*, a word that connotes guests, visitors, strangers or outsiders, depending on the context. Thus, this term is not only used to mark or create ties between people, as is the case with *jamaa*, but to underscore distinctions between people. It is as *wenyeji* that people are felt to have rights and obligations in a place in contrast to others. Significantly, one is not a *mwenyeji* by virtue of ethnic or racial identity (a reflection of, or perhaps a contributing factor to, the heterogeneity of coastal society), but rather by virtue of kinship ties and long-term residence. Being a *mwenyji* suggests assimilation, not only into Muslim coastal society (although this is crucial), but also into those social networks that are grounded in a particular place. Thus, being a *mwenyeji* is, in some sense, less about *who* one is than about *how* one acts. It is both an ascribed identity and a relational one, as a person is always to varying degrees a *mwenyeji* or *mgeni* in regards to a particular spatial location. Thus, people commonly argue about their degree of *mwenyeji*-ness in relation to others. For example, those residents who have a longer history on Chole are quick to point out that they are Chole's *wenyeji* in relation to more recent immigrants from Juani and other parts of Mafia or Kilwa. At the same time, however, virtually all Muslim KiSwahili-speakers on Mafia are considered *wenyeji* in relation to *wageni* or "strangers" from other places. It is as *wenyeji*, that is, as the rightful proprietors of an area's natural resources, that residents understand their rights within the marine park and the justice of participation, and it is through this logic that Chole residents, during their meeting with David Holston documented in chapter 1, described the park as "theirs."

Although the concept of being *mwenyeji* is part of Chole residents' assumptions about how the world should work, it is also a coastal conception (presumably linked to historical, and in some cases ongoing, ideas of communal ownership based on *ukoo* kin groups in rural areas and small towns along the coast). Communities, however, are also products of broader political structures, and Mafia residents are aware that such ideas carry little weight within the political landscape of contemporary Tanzania. Consequently, Chole residents also draw upon another concept that forms part of the political discourse of the nation-state, that of *wananchi* (the citizenry or people of a country). This term is an overtly political one, suggestive of the populist language of "the people" that was a central part of the discourse of Nyerere's post-independence socialist government. When Chole residents discuss their rights within the park, they often use the term *wananchi* to contrast themselves with government bureaucrats in Kilindoni and other park actors. This language suggests the rights of the "citizenry" and the need for government bureaucrats to serve "the people" rather than their own ends, and it often carries implicit critiques of presumed corruption or inactivity on the part of officials. (This usage also contrasts strongly with that of NGOs, which often treat sovereign states and national elites as synonymous). Most pertinently, the use of the word *wananchi* suggests that residents conceive of their relationship to the marine park in overtly politicized terms, unlike the apolitical assumptions of the discourse of community used by park planners. In general, it is through this largely unacknowledged range of concepts based on particular histories and social locations that various park actors understand the meaning of "community" on Mafia.

COMMUNITY ON CHOLE: THE TIES THAT BIND

Before considering points of social tension on Chole, it is first necessary to sketch out the kinds of social relationships that draw island residents together. In fact, during the mid-1990s, social relations on Chole were remarkably egalitarian, creating a sense of "community" that in some ways mirrored assumptions associated with the term in English. This situation, however, was not the result of Africans being innately predisposed to being egalitarian, as President Nyerere's *ujamaa* ideology might suggest. Rather, such relations stemmed from a variety of factors, including shared poverty and a range of social ties, such as those based on kinship. Before considering such factors in more depth, it is important to contextualize such relations in terms of the social and historical realities of the demise of a slave-based plantation economy in southern Mafia and the end of colonialism. The social hierarchies that were so central to the narratives of Chole residents in the previous chapter had dissipated by the 1990s for a range of reasons, the most important being the outlawing of slavery in 1922 and the end of the various colonialisms that had long ruled Mafia by 1961.

At the same time, additional social dynamics were also at work. After the demise of southern Mafia's slave-based plantation economy, Arabs and other wealthy elites either left the island or continued to assimilate into Mafia's "Swahili" population, as did large numbers of former slaves. In a context in which no new forms of wealth were appearing, both Islamic law and customary practices encouraged the fragmentation of wealth by mandating the division of property among all children (although under Islamic law female children would receive half the inheritance of males). After independence, Nyerere's socialist government also implemented measures that encouraged greater egalitarianism, including changes in land tenure policies, and it sought to discourage the class and ethnic divisions that had been fostered by European colonial regimes. Although the post-independence government did create a new elite of educated Africans, Mafia residents, as already described, were almost entirely excluded from this social group. In fact, the isolation and neglect of Mafia District, ironically, allowed more egalitarian social relationships to emerge on Mafia than if it had been more thoroughly incorporated into the socialist state.

Any discussion of "community" invariably raises the question of where one draws boundaries. If social relationships on Chole suggest a "community," is this community limited to Chole, or does it extend to the ten other villages within the marine park or, more broadly, to the entire group of islands?[2] As is almost always the case, drawing boundaries around groups of people is extremely difficult in practice. During the time that I was on Chole, residents did not make rigid distinctions between themselves and those from other villages in southern Mafia. Instead, social life was fluid and residents participated in a thick web of social relationships that linked the villages in the southern half of the island. This fluid sense of identity stemmed in large part from the reality that many, if not most, people on Chole had themselves originated in other parts of Mafia or, at the very least, had widespread family ties in other areas.

However, the web of social ties binding people together was tighter in some parts of Mafia and thinner in others. For example, people on Chole identified closely with the residents of two other small islands, Juani and Jibondo (which together with Chole comprised a government ward or *kata*), as well as with residents in other villages sprinkled throughout southern Mafia such as Utende, Kigeani, Marimbani, and, to some extent, the capital, Kilindoni. This network of social ties, however, was more tenuous with the northern half of the main island.[3] Some people on Chole suggested that Mafia residents from the north were "different" from those to the south, or at least had been so in the past. Although all are Muslims and share in a common Swahili coastal culture, the reality of almost nonexistent roads and the lack of motorized transportation meant that the southern half of the island (which could be traveled by sailboat or on foot), was far more accessible for Chole residents than the north. In addition, the southern part of the island had historically served as the heart of the colonial plantation economy. This meant that the customary practices of *mila* had continued in a more uninterrupted fashion in the north and that different populations predominated (although all groups would assimilate to become part of "Swahili" culture). In the north, for example, there were more descendants of the Wambwera, who may have been the original inhabitants of Mafia (Baumann 1957[1896]), as well as such mainland groups as the Pokomo. The south, in contrast, saw a higher influx of "Arab" and other elites as well as Nyasa and Yao from Central Africa who were brought to Mafia as slaves. This informal division between north and south has been perpetuated by the boundaries of the Mafia Island Marine Park, which encompasses southern Mafia and the four smaller adjacent islands, but excludes the north.

Despite difficulties in transportation, Chole residents also maintain connections with other coastal areas to which they have been historically linked, such as Kilwa, the Rufiji, Dar es Salaam, Zanzibar, and even Mombasa across the Kenyan border. In fact, many Chole residents had more ongoing social ties with these regions than with northern Mafia. Thus, "community" on Chole is not bounded in any simple way by geography, but exists within a broader social field that is determined by patterns of history and social networks rather than by the physical boundaries of sea and coral rock that constitute this group of islands.

A Community of Shared Poverty

During the 1990s, the reality of shared poverty was a primary cause behind the relative egalitarianism on Chole, one that contrasted sharply with the social and economic inequalities of Mafia's slave-owning past. In order to understand what such material realities meant on Chole during this period, I describe two men: one considered to be "rich" on Chole; the other, "poor."

Although in his seventies, Mzee Hodari often came to English classes during my first period of fieldwork on Chole. He was thin and bony with gray hair and a single, tobacco-stained tooth pointing out at an extreme angle from under his lips. Everyday, he wore the same torn *kofia* and a ragged cloth wrapped around his waist; his feet like most peoples' on Chole were bare. Like many elders on the island, he desired to learn some English if only to be able to greet the European visitors who were increasingly coming to Mafia, a role which most elders saw as an extension of their informal responsibility for representing the island to *wageni* (guests, outsiders). Whereas to my unpracticed eye, Mzee Hodari appeared to be among the poorer men on the island, I was surprised to hear from the British divers of the Frontier organization who stayed for a period on Chole that the land they were renting belonged to Mzee Hodari. Eventually, I learned from discussions with Chole residents that Mzee Hodari was in fact the wealthiest man on Chole, and owned hundreds of orange and coconut trees as well as one of only eight wooden sailboats on the island. Not only was Mzee Hodari wealthy in terms of trees, he was wealthy in an equally important way on Mafia—in terms of children. Although he had recently lost his wife of many years, he had thirteen living children, most of whom resided near him, as well as numerous grandchildren and great-grandchildren. Mzee Hodari's progeny now included a sizeable portion of the island's population and there was scarcely a family into which his children or grandchildren had not intermarried. Although his children farmed his *shamba* (garden or farm) and his sons assumed responsibility for using his wooden *mashua* to fish, he continued to be active, earning extra money by occasionally burning coral rock to make limestone plaster and, more importantly, serving as the respected teacher at the island's mud-and-thatch Quranic school.

I also learned, however, that other old men, equally bedraggled in appearance, did not share the relatively comfortable old age of a man like Mzee

Hodari. Mzee Suli, for example, who was also a widower, was as poor in trees as he was in people. In addition to a handful of trees, he had only one living child, a son who had in turn fathered only one son before divorcing. Although Mzee Hodari might have appeared to be no more prosperous than Mzee Suli, Mzee Hodari could afford to spend his time sitting on his porch conversing, while his grandchildren played around him. Mzee Suli, in contrast, was reduced to bumming cigarettes from younger men in the tourist camp and earning a few cents by banging chunks of dead coral into smaller pieces called "kokota," which were mixed with cement as building aggregate. On Chole, Mzee Hodari and Mzee Suli exemplified two social extremes, yet their differences, like the similarities of their dress, were potentially deceptive. The difference between "rich" and "poor" on Chole was in fact easy to miss. Although Mzee Hodari's house was finished in limestone rather than being simply made of mud and branches and, although he had greater security in knowing that he would have a meal at the end of the day, both men ate similar foodstuffs, both lacked ready access to cash, both dressed in similarly tattered clothes, and both eventually died on the island on beds made of coconut fiber rope and mangrove poles, far removed from access to medical care. In contrast to many other places in the world, the differences in wealth that existed between them were in amount not in kind. During the period when I conducted research, for example, no individual on Chole possessed sufficient wealth to regularly hire the labor of others, nor was any able-bodied person exempted from labor in order to survive.

The differences—as well as lack of differences—in wealth between individuals like Mzee Hodari and Mzee Suli on Chole were very much related to the dynamics surrounding Tanganyika's independence in the early 1960s. During my stay on the island, there were only a handful of people who were considered "affluent" on Chole and these were generally older people, usually, but not always, men. Although some of the relatively "affluent" residents, like Mzee Bakari, Mzee Maarufu and Bi Safiya, could claim descent from the old *waungwana* or elites of Chole, others, like Mzee Hodari, were the descendants of former slaves. What ultimately differentiated the more prosperous from the less prosperous was not their social backgrounds, but whether they had been residents on Chole during the time when land tenure practices radically changed after independence. During this period, Chole was relatively depopulated, and residents were able to claim as much land on this tiny island (including that of former absentee landlords) as they were able to clear and farm. Since the clearing of land is generally considered to be men's work, land went disproportionately to the dozen or so adult men then residing on the island. This situation poses a sharp contrast, not only to Nyerere's stated socialist ideal of greater equality for women, but with customary practices on Mafia in which women possessed equal rights to use land through their *ukoo* or kinship groups.[4] Thus, while Mzee Hodari benefited from his early residence on Chole and his industriousness, Mzee Suli, similarly a descendent of slaves, arrived on Chole after most of the land had already been claimed. When I asked one young man whether other residents of Chole resented the greater prosperity of elders like Mzee Hodari, he shook his head, no. Everyone, he asserted, was aware that this wealth would dissipate with the deaths of the older generation as their property came to be divided among their progeny. And indeed the wealth of Mzee Hodari, who died during the course of my fieldwork, was fragmented into modest tree holdings for the benefit of his thirteen children.

A wealth survey that I conducted on Chole during the mid-1990s confirmed this pattern of shared poverty, cross-cut by patterns of inequality across gender and generation.[5] When Chole residents discussed the relative prosperity of themselves and their neighbors, they focused on the ownership of coconut and orange trees, the fruits of which could be sold for cash, as the key element of wealth. Although Chole residents also counted houses, boats, and the few goats and handful of cows that lived on Chole as wealth or *mali*, the emphasis on trees was a powerful reminder of the legacy of the Arab plantation era. Land itself, however, was not conceived as something that could be "owned." Historically, usage rights to land had been conferred through *ukoo* or communal kin groups. Under colonial and socialist governments, ownership of land came to be vested in the state, which allowed residents usage rights at its discretion. Following the historical precedents of the plantation era, however, trees could be counted as private property (with ownership of trees conferring usage rights to the land beneath the trees). As documented in this survey, less than a dozen individuals, mostly men with long histories on the island like Mzee Hodari, owned between 90 and 150 trees while a few of these individuals also owned wooden sailboats. The vast majority of adult residents, however, owned only between fifteen and fifty trees while some young adults and divorced women had no assets at all. Because there was no more room on Chole for planting trees, tree wealth was generally transmitted by inheritance, meaning that older generations almost invariably possessed more than the young. Inheritance of trees and boats also followed Islamic law, meaning that women inherited half of what their brothers did. Consequently, although older women owned trees, they owned fewer than men, while some young women owned none. In sum, it was young adults of both sexes, divorced women, and newcomers to the island who were the poorest of the poor on Chole.

In contrast to my own cultural preconceptions, money or *pesa* was considered to be a distinct category from "wealth" or *mali* on Chole. In general, *mali* referred to those assets that were durable and had the ability to reproduce social life such as boats, trees, and houses, while money was considered to be far more ephemeral. Given a reality of currency devaluations and inflation, as well as a context in which cash attracted numerous requests for aid from friends and relatives, this was a highly realistic assessment. Although young men had great difficulties obtaining *mali*, they had some ability to earn cash by laboring for a share of the catch on the island's fishing boats or through new opportunities for wage labor in the budding tourism industry. (Women once again had extremely few opportunities to earn cash.) Wage labor was poorly paid and fish catches erratic, however, meaning that even the cash that young men were able to earn did not ensure their ability to support themselves or other family members as Islamic law dictated. Although older people often chided younger people for being seduced by the ephemeral pleasures of cash and the consumer goods it could buy, younger generations often countered that they themselves desired "wealth," but that such assets were increasingly impossible for younger people to obtain. In general, everyone who lived on Chole during the mid-1990s was poor, although this poverty was deeper for some residents than others.

Kinship

While the reality of shared poverty on Chole contributed to the dissipation of social inequalities inherited from the past, it was ties of kinship that were the strongest glue binding people together across Mafia's villages (even as social divisions within families offered the most persistent remaining form of hierarchy). A visit that I made with Bi Sharifa in 1994 illustrates the diffuse nature of kinship bonds that were common among Chole residents. During the time I was on Chole, Bi Sharifa often returned to what she called *nyumbani kwetu* ("our home"), the standard way people referred to their natal families, even though she, like many other women on the island, had lived on Chole for many years with her husband.[6] Her family home was located in Baleni near the center of Mafia's main island, at the outer reaches of those villages from which Chole residents tended to marry. Like other people on Chole, she frequently returned home for weddings and funerals, to help farm, to aid sick relatives, to rest during pregnancy as is customary for women, or simply to visit. In 1994, as she prepared to travel to Baleni to help with the rice harvest, Bi Sharifa made me promise to visit her there. A week later, I accompanied her then healthy husband, Mzee Bakari, and his three young grandsons on the *mashua* or wooden sailboat that he had borrowed from his old friend, Mzee Maarufu. In the mid-1990s, there was no regular transportation by boat anywhere on Mafia except for Chole's erratic ferry service to Utende. Consequently, to reach more distant destinations like Baleni, people generally waited until they heard someone was traveling by boat and then begged a lift. Consequently, when I reached the Boma with Mzee Bakari and the children shortly after sunrise, a small crowd of people had already gathered at the *mashua*. After sailing across the choppy waters in the widest part of the bay, we eventually reached a distant part of Mafia's main island and began searching for a break in the mangrove trees, which indicated a place where boats could be safely anchored. Once on land, and after taking leave of the other passengers, we scrambled up over the sandy hillside, walking single file over the narrow footpaths in the hot sun, and carrying bags of oranges and other foodstuffs wrapped in plastic bags tied with coconut fronds. After about an hour and a half, we finally approached the scattered homes, coconut trees, and grazing cattle of Baleni.

We arrived to find Bi Sharifa working in the fields alongside her adult daughter, Amina, while her three youngest daughters played nearby. Expecting us the following day, she was chagrined by our arrival—she hadn't had a chance to slaughter a chicken or cook the special foods she had intended to prepare for me as a guest. However, what was most important to her was that I should begin visiting her numerous relatives as soon as possible, and we soon set off on a whirlwind of visiting. Bi Sharifa's parents were divorced, a common occurrence along the coast; consequently, we walked a considerable distance from the plot she was farming to reach first her mother's house and then her father's, making sidetrips to visit various siblings and other unspecified relations. Some of Bi Sharifa's relatives were considerably better-off than others; for example, her father owned a comfortable, well-plastered home and many cattle, while her mother lived only in a ramshackle mud *kibanda* (hut). Nevertheless, all generously proffered whatever food or snacks they could afford, sometimes with pride, at other times with embarrassment, and, despite an increasingly painful and full stomach, I continued to eat in an attempt to uphold my end of coastal hospitality. When we finally left Bi Sharifa and her daughters that evening to race back to the boat before the sun set, I was overwhelmed by this stream of new faces, names, and homes and was weighted down with the gifts we had acquired at each stop—bags of pounded rice, giant papayas, eggs, and other foods, in addition to the live chicken that Bi Sharifa gave me in apology for having failed to cook it herself. What was striking to me about this visit, as well as subsequent trips to other parts of Mafia, was the remarkable degree to which she, like most other Chole residents, possessed a wealth of social ties in other areas of Mafia, ties which served to bind them together into a common social world.

In general, the flow of women, men, and children who traveled between the villages of Mafia was constant. Some of these visits were conducted en masse over short periods as people traveled for an endless stream of weddings, funerals, and other *mashaguli* (ritual events). Other visits were longer, lasting for several weeks or even months at a time. It was particularly common to see women, with bundles on their heads and small children in hand, waiting at the ferry to embark on these longer visits. This tendency was clearly related to the pattern of "patrilocality" on Mafia, that is, for a woman to move near her husband's family after marriage.[7] Thus, it was women who generally lived away from their families of birth and who had the closest relations living off of the island (although this situation was mitigated by the fact that numerous women married within their home areas and many divorced women returned to live near their parents, particularly their mothers). Therefore, as an anthropologist, participation in daily life on Chole meant meeting a constantly changing mosaic of visiting relatives and accompanying Chole residents as they themselves visited relatives in other parts of Mafia.

The kinship networks in which Mafia residents participate are unusually diffuse and malleable ones. In most areas of Africa, kinship is reckoned unilaterally, that is, either patrilineally (on the father's side) or, less commonly, matrilineally (on the mother's side). However, descent along the East African coast has historically been reckoned bilaterally or through both mother's and father's sides. Thus, people on Chole say they have four *ukoo* or kinship groups, one for each grandparent. Although kinship organization has sometimes been discussed among anthropologists as if it were a self-evident label that defined a static and rigid type of society, kinship arrangements are not determinative of social life. Nevertheless, kinship patterns do encourage particular social logics, even as their arrangements are fluid, changeable, and under constant negotiation. On Mafia, this logic centers around the diffuse and wideranging ties that *ukoo* bonds generate. In unilineal descent systems, it is relatively clear who is inside or outside a kin group; however, within bilateral kinship arrangements (particularly ones with high divorce rates like this one) those who count as "family" may differ for each individual, thereby encouraging each person to maintain his or her own unique ties.[8] Because relationships are traced through a variety of individuals, such ties generally extend to a range of villages.

Ties based on *ukoo* are also the primary means of soliciting social and economic support in southern Mafia. Anthropologist Pat Caplan has described how residents obtained rights to farm and use land as part of corporate kinship groups in the village of "Minazini" in northern Mafia in the 1960s (1975, 1982). Older persons on Chole suggest that a similar system once operated in the past on southern Mafia, although kin groups no longer act as corporate units on Chole. (One man surmised that the reason for this was land scarcity on Chole, which left no unoccupied "meadow" land available for kin groups to distribute.) This bilateral form of kinship organization has both gender and generational implications. Because women hold equally valued connections with their natal families as men and because such ties provide them and their children with inheritance, rights to land, and other resources, women are widely conceived as independent social actors in a way that is not always true, for example, within patrilineal kinship arrangements. In addition, individuals draw inheritance from several *ukoo* to which they can also appeal for aid. As a result, younger generations are less subject to the authority of particular elders than in many societies that are based upon unilineal descent. By allowing individuals to access resources at varying times from different groups (Caplan 1984), membership in different *ukoo* enables people to maximize social ties with a wide range of others, a strategy that can be particularly useful in contexts of poverty.[9] Overall, the bilateral kinship patterns found on Mafia encourage a constant movement around the region as people maintain ties and fulfill social obligations and duties in a range of locations, creating a "community" of shared social bonds among the villages encompassed by the Mafia Island Marine Park.

Although bilaterality is the "traditional" form of kinship organization along the Swahili coast, it is not the only way of reckoning kinship in the region. The historical influence of Shirazi Persians and Hadrami and Omani Arabs, as discussed in the last chapter, encouraged a shift toward more patrilineal forms of kinship organization associated with Middle Eastern countries. Even though *sheria* or Islamic law had historically encouraged the reform of patrilineal practices in the Arabian peninsula, for example, by allowing women to inherit, it also incorporated much of its patrilineal logic. Although coastal residents have been Muslims for centuries, the implementation of *sheria* and an attendant shift toward a more patrilineal kinship arrangement were given a powerful boost by the establishment of *kadhi* courts by Zanzibar's Sultan Barghash in the late nineteenth century (Caplan 1982). This position was later buttressed by the British who established indirect rule through the Omanis at Zanzibar and who supported *sheria* as "tradition." In addition, other forms of reckoning kinship have also been at work historically along the coast. Nyasa and Yao slaves originating in Central Africa themselves brought matrilineal influences to both Mafia and the coast more generally.[10] Although such practices lacked the high status of *sheria* associated with Arab countries, the sheer number of slaves, the practices of concubinage between Arab men and slave women, and the assimilation of many former slaves into coastal society suggest that such influences were considerable (Eastman 1988).

Although kinship dynamics are always under negotiation, the social complexity of the East African coast suggests that kinship practices may be more contested in this region than in some others. As Pat Caplan has pointed out in her work, the division between *sheria* (Islamic law) and *mila* (customary practice) has been a source of ongoing tension on Mafia.[11] In general, higher social status and upward mobility have been linked to "Arab" cultural forms along the coast. For example, the state of being "civilized" has been defined as *ustaarabu* (literally, the state of being "Arab"). Thus, *sheria* is symbolically linked, not only to monotheistic Islam, but to Arab social and cultural practices such as patrilineality, and the more hierarchical social relationships fostered by Arab colonialism. Such viewpoints, however, find a counterpoint in *mila* or "custom" that encompasses "traditional" bilateral kinship forms as well as matrilineal practices brought by slaves.[12] It also encompasses other coastal beliefs and practices, as well as those brought by mainland Africans, including belief in spirit possession and witchcraft, and a comparatively less-stratified vision of social relationships. In short, *sheria* and *mila* have been associated with two broadly opposing worldviews on Mafia (Caplan 1982:40). Nevertheless, as Caplan notes, the tension between these worldviews need not be experienced as overt conflict, as residents value and draw upon both *sheria* and *mila* within the context of everyday life. For example, all Chole residents that I knew viewed being Muslim as a highly positive form of identity (although residents were more lax in their practice than religious leaders on the island might like), while, at the same time, the core of daily life was inextricably bound up in the beliefs, rituals, and practices of *mila.*

Since kinship arrangements have strong implications for gender and generational relationships, tensions between the values associated with *mila* and *sheria* emerge most clearly in terms of contestation over hierarchy within families. For example, debates over appropriate behavior for women and men were a constant source of good-natured teasing as well as real tension in the home of Bi Sharifa and Mzee Bakari, as the following anecdote illustrates. One afternoon, I had stopped by their home on the way to meet a mutual friend, Hadija, who had asked me to accompany her to gather firewood near the ruins at Kua on Juani. Although Bi Sharifa was preparing to cook, when she heard of the excursion she told me that she would come along as well. Throwing a clean *kanga* around herself, she informed her husband who was sitting on the porch that she was going out. "Oh," he cajoled, "Don't go! Stay home and cook for me—Krisi won't mind." "No," she answered amiably but decisively, "I'm going!" As she entered the house to give cooking instructions to her younger daughters, Mzee Bakari laughed good-naturedly and said to me, "See how it is, Krisi? Women don't listen to men these days. I tell her to stay home and she goes out anyway. What can I do?"

As we sat at Kua squatting among the ruins, Bi Sharifa jokingly pulled her *kanga* over her face to mimic a veil. "Krisi, would you agree to cover your face like this?" she asked. Without waiting for a reply, she added proudly, "For me, no! I could never do that." As she glanced for support to Hadija and Rukia, another married woman who had joined us, she went on to tell how her husband, Mzee Bakari, had many years earlier once beaten his first wife. Although I expressed surprise that her good-humored husband would do such a thing, I was also aware that for an earlier generation a beating could be interpreted as the appropriate and responsible action of the head of a household if a wife or child "misbehaved." Laughing quietly as she spoke, Bi Sharifa informed me that Mzee Bakari would never dare hit her because he knew she would leave immediately and go back to her father's home in

Baleni. Hadija and Rukia offered this as an example of how male elders generally lacked the power to be as strict as they were in the past. To support this point, Hadija reminded me how even Maryamu, Mzee Bakari and Bi Sharifa's five-year-old daughter, merely laughed at her father's threats to discipline her.

Although Rukia and Hadija quietly supported Bi Sharifa's outright challenge to the gender (and generational) hierarchies of an earlier era, not all women on Chole agreed. A few older women mildly lamented what they perceived as a loss of "respectability" in the current period. In the past, the wearing of long black veils or *buibui* had constituted an outward sign of a stricter adherence to Arab cultural norms. Perhaps even more importantly, the *buibui* symbolized upward social mobility for poorer women, since slaves had been forbidden from veiling before abolition (Fair 1994). In the late 1990s, women on Chole, unlike those in Zanzibar Town and other urban areas along the coast, almost never wore the *buibui* unless traveling to distant places. Yet, as previously mentioned, during the course of videotaping historical narratives on Chole, several elderly women brought out their *buibui*s and displayed the garments as artifacts for the camera. They also used the occasion to laughingly chide the unrepentant young women around them for the immodesty of the present era. Perhaps the most outspoken proponent of the stricter values associated with *sheria* was Bi Safiya, an older, heavy-set woman who was of the few remaining Chole residents who could claim descent from Arabs. One afternoon as we sat in her courtyard, she lectured me on the superiority of an earlier period on Mafia when young girls were married off before they reached puberty (presumably to ensure their virginity). This view, however, like those on veiling, did not go uncontested. Her young daughter-in-law, Hadija, who sat cutting onions nearby, safely outside of Bi Safiya's vision, responded by rolling her eyes in silent derision.[13]

Over the centuries, the relative strength of *sheria* and *mila* has waxed and waned along the coast, a dynamic linked to broader historical, social and political processes (Caplan 1982). I would argue that in recent decades the balance on Mafia has once again shifted towards *mila* or "custom." Although *sheria* still holds the greatest social status on these islands, the political and social pressures that encouraged stricter adherence to Islamic law have, in many cases, dissipated (although this is not true in neighboring Zanzibar).[14] In a related process, the power-laden relationships of gender and generation have, as most Chole residents agree, become more relaxed. This is not only due to the waning influence of Arab social norms on Mafia and the reascendency of the logic of *mila*, but because of the demise of European colonialism. As many scholars have noted, British indirect rule worked through, and consolidated the authority of, older men (for example, Hodgson 2001). As Yusuf, the adult son of the village chairman explained, the greater respect accorded to elder men or *wazee* in the past was partially due to the fact that they were officially granted the right to punish and beat people by the British, an authority that buttressed their position over both women and the young.

In general, contemporary life on Chole has been characterized by widespread social bonds based on kinship that work to create a particular type of "community." However, unlike assumptions of community that draw attention away from power relationships, such ties are bound up in hierarchies based on gender and generation (if no longer of social class), even as these hierarchies have become more attenuated. Just as community cannot be understood apart from power relationships, so too it cannot be understood as simply the result of "local" processes. Indeed, kinship dynamics on Mafia have been strongly shaped by influences originating in such geographically distant places as Arabia and England. Consequently, in order to understand "community," it becomes necessary to look outward as well as inward—a reality equally relevant to understanding the social drama of the contemporary marine park.

Consensus and Jealousy

Social bonds were strong on Mafia, and residents placed considerable emphasis upon the importance of consensus among *wenyeji*. Nevertheless, I was struck by the prominence of jealousy in daily relationships and the tensions that this invariably caused. The value accorded to consensus was perhaps most apparent in the context of meetings. At the 1995 Ecotourism Seminar sponsored by WWF and described in the introduction to this book, park "stakeholders" including village representatives, were divided into groups and asked to list their goals for the marine park. I myself was asked to moderate a group of village representatives. Worried that the venue of an expensive tourist hotel and an organizational agenda that was established by international donors would inhibit discussion, I attempted to explain to the village representatives the task required of them. I had barely begun, however, when I was politely interrupted by an elderly man from a village on the main island who expertly assumed the role of moderator. In what seemed to be an astonishingly brief period of time, opinions were floored and consensus positions reached, and I was told by the group what to write in English on the posterboards provided for the purpose. The village representatives then sat expectantly, waiting while the European tour operators, government officials, NGO representatives, and others taking part in the seminar continued to argue within their own groups. I was struck, as I had been at many meetings on Chole, by the skill and efficiency of island residents at a form of hands-on democracy that Euro-Americans, among others, often found difficult.[15]

In village meetings on Chole, consensus was equally valued, although potentially more difficult to achieve than at the Ecotourism Seminar where opinions about the park were widely shared. Theoretically, everyone was allowed to attend village meetings and to speak their minds. However, Caplan noted in the 1960s and 1970s that women rarely attended meetings in northern Mafia (1982:34). Presumably, this was because government meetings had been viewed as a male preserve under European colonialism, and because norms of appropriate behavior during the preceding Omani period would also have encouraged men to represent women in public. During the course of my fieldwork, residents on Chole nonetheless generally concurred that women *should* be present at meetings, perhaps because this readily accorded with the logic of bilaterality and of complementary spheres for men and women implicit in *mila*. Although women often did attend meetings, customary standards of politeness made it immodest for both women and young people to speak publicly in front of older men. As a result, such meetings were largely dominated by middle-aged and older men. (In many villages, however, women were often elected as secretaries of village committees, including marine park committees, thereby holding positions of responsibility that did not entail extensive public speaking.) After opinions were solicited at such meetings, the perspective that seemed most persuasive to the greatest number present was informally accepted as the consensus position. Those in disagreement were neither asked nor expected to change their minds, although it was assumed that all residents should theoretically support such decisions. Ultimately, however, village residents had few means of enforcing such support. Like village elders who relied upon the respect conferred to them to mediate disputes, Chole residents relied upon a respect for consensus.

The value placed on consensus also supported the view that island residents as *wenyeji*, or the "proprietors" of a place, should present a cohesive front to *wageni* or "guests." People on Chole considered it to be shameful when this was not the case. For example, after island residents were collectively asked for permission to be filmed by a European film crew, one elder expressed his concern when opinions were divided on the island. "Is this not shameful," he asked, "for the island to be divided in this manner? Either we should all agree or we should all refuse." In general, Chole residents hesitated to air "dirty laundry" to others and suggested that the good name of the island was one shared by all. At the same time, however, the ideal of consensus on Chole, much like the mythic ideal of "community" in English, was inevitably tainted by realities of social division and conflict.

On Chole, the most common form of conflict within daily life centered upon jealousy. I was introduced to this reality through my own peculiar social location on the island. As both an *mzungu* and a "teacher," I was in some sense a public person on Chole. This public status was reinforced by my residence within the emerging tourist camp. Had I stayed with a particular family, the social networks of my hosts would have been expected to dominate my own social interactions. However, as an individual who was not aligned with any of the diffuse kin groups on Chole, residents paid close and sometimes competitive attention to noticing which houses I stopped at to say hello as I walked around the island. Consequently, in order to avoid inadvertently giving offense, I found my walks taking longer and longer. Although at a brisk pace, one could walk the length of Chole in about twenty minutes, by the time I finished my fieldwork it often took me an hour or more as I stopped at more and more homes for a leisurely greeting. At social gatherings and celebrations, people on Chole also took note of where I sat. Although initially I was often seated near male elders who generally assumed the duty of welcoming guests onto Chole, both women and men approved as I gradually became more incorporated into social networks and insisted, as was proper on Chole, on sitting with other women. However, this change also meant a heightened awareness among residents of which groups of women had adopted me and which women I sought out. Through a growing understanding of the spoken and unspoken pressures exerted on my social interactions, I became painfully aware of the broader dynamics of jealous competitiveness on Chole.

Eventually, I learned to negotiate this ever present potential for jealousy through a variety of means. When in a hurry, I traveled along less populated side paths to avoid insulting anyone by failing to visit. I learned to pass money in crumpled wads slipped discretely from covered hand to covered hand, and to give treats of sweet *halua* for an elderly friend in such a manner that it could be quickly whisked under the folds of her *kanga*. I learned to be secretive not only about what I gave, but about what I received as well. These strategies were not my own, but ones I had observed Chole residents using in their interactions with others on the island, actions that underscored the centrality of jealousy, and the fear of provoking it, that shaped their social relationships in myriad ways.

On Chole, this concern with jealousy took many forms. Friends who opened tiny stalls or *genge* to sell matches, soap, and tea out of their homes would first commission a *mganga* or local healer to conduct a rite to ward off potential evil-wishers. Parents would hang old coins around the necks of their babies to protect their health from the envious. Gifts were kept covered and passed at discrete moments to avoid the jealousy of others, in contrast to the practice of public gift-giving with which I was familiar from the United States. In February of 1997, I attended the launching of a *jahazi*, the largest variety of wooden sailboat made along the coast. Although the owner was from another part of Mafia (no one on Chole had possessed sufficient means to own or build a *jahazi* for many years), the boat had been built in Chole's boatyard and the owner had sponsored a well-attended *maulidi* or Quranic reading the night before to celebrate the launching. As men pulled the boat from the beach towards the water with ropes, women joined in the festivities by singing. Some, however, also took mud and smeared it over the bodies of the boat owner's protesting female relatives—a ritual expression both of jealousy and a reminder for the families of the prosperous to temper their pride.

In general, nearly all conflicts on Mafia were attributed by residents to *wivu* (jealousy), while some argued that Swahili people were distinguished by their peculiarly jealous nature. Within polygynous households (a minority of those on the island), jealousy was a common source of tension, as wives worried not only about a potential loss of affection but of material support. Sexual jealousy was also common among both men and women who feared (often not unrealistically) that their spouses were taking clandestine lovers.[16] Some men argued that husbands on Chole did not dare leave on extended fishing trips because they were "jealous" of their wives' behavior (i.e., they were worried that the women would take other men as lovers), and many disapproved of their wives working at or even entering the tourist camp for similar reasons. Women expressed parallel concerns. When I distributed several photos I had taken of camp staff, the wife of one night watchman assumed that the pictures depicting her husband and other male workers alongside the camp's cook meant that this woman was having an affair with her husband. She promptly destroyed the photos by cutting the offending woman out of the pictures.

One of the central ways in which jealousy was expressed on Chole was through fear of witchcraft. As previously mentioned, spiritual beliefs on Mafia include not only beliefs in Islam but also in spirits, spirit possession and witchcraft (Caplan 1997; see also Giles 1987; Middleton 1992). Although some spirit beliefs are recognized within Islam, others are associated with the low status realm of *mila* or are simply perceived as being anti-Islamic. Such realities led to conflicting opinions regarding spirit beliefs (similar to those surrounding kinship). For example, some residents who were initially dismissive to me of spirit and witchcraft beliefs, later acknowledged that they themselves were believers. While some spirits in which residents commonly believed were viewed as dangerous, others were not. For example, Fuadi, a gardener in the camp, was regularly possessed by a category of spirit thought to provide aid and advice (see also Caplan 1997). However, witchcraft that was sent by particular individuals to deliberately injure others was necessarily perceived as malevolent. Because it was widely believed that witches were provoked by jealousy, it behooved individuals to avoid causing jealousy. As a result, fear of jealousy was strongly linked to fear of witchcraft. In general, those individuals on Chole who managed to find a wage labor job or who achieved some other form of economic gain constantly expressed their fear of the jealousy of others. Employees in the tourist camp, for example, complained that other island residents commonly spread malicious gossip and plotted against them because they were jealous of their jobs, implying that such jealousy might take a more dangerous turn. When I suffered a serious injury to my foot that forced me to leave Chole for six months for medical treatment, I later discovered that many residents attributed this event to witchcraft sent by two older men on the island whom other residents claimed wanted to stop English classes to prevent them from gaining *maendeleo* ("development"). Not only was jealousy (or the fear of it) expressed whenever anyone had the potential to do well in relation to their peers on Chole, jealousy was also commonly perceived as the underlying motivation for the actions of those off the island as well. For example, Chole residents attributed the corruption of government officials and their lack of concern with Mafia's well-being to their being "jealous" and not wanting regions such as Mafia to gain "development" (*maendeleo*), a topic that will be further discussed in chapter 7.

While jealousy is obviously a common human emotion, it takes on different meanings within particular social and historical contexts. I would argue, in fact, that the significance of jealousy has shifted over time on Mafia. Historically, jealousy had been widely remarked upon along the Swahili coast. For example, some scholars have commented upon the history of jealous competition in dance or *ngoma* societies or in relation to weddings (Ranger 1975; Fair 1994). Chole residents themselves talked about the jealousy of *waungwana* or elites in the past that allegedly caused them to cut off the hands of slave artisans to prevent them from building other homes as elaborate as their own. However, jealousy in such cases was linked to the negotiation of status within a hierarchical, yet dynamic, social world. Taking on the accouterments of higher status offered individuals a route to upward social mobility that included such practices as former slave women taking on the veil and Zanzibaris adopting *taarab*, the former court music of the sultan (Strobel 1979; Fair 1994). However, the jealousy found on Chole in the present is of a different nature. It is a brand of jealousy that instead emerges when social relationships are relatively unstratified. In such instances, jealousy stems from the worry that when a few move ahead, they will leave their former peers behind. This form of jealousy attempts to level impending inequalities and to enforce egalitarianism, if only through ill will. On Chole, such jealousy exists in tension with the value placed on consensus, continually threatening to disrupt this ideal as well as the social bonds that underlay it. Thus, if "community" exists on Mafia, it is not in romantic, homeostatic images of people bound by primordial bonds of sociality. Rather, community on Mafia, as elsewhere, is forged in lived worlds marked by conflict and tension as well as by shared viewpoints.

COMMUNITY AND PARTICIPATORY PROJECTS

The Chole Kisiwani Enterprise

During the mid-1990s, the social impact of the Mafia Island Marine Park on Chole was still largely a matter of conjecture. However, the dynamics surrounding another "community"-based endeavor, the budding tourism initiative, were already becoming apparent. Indeed, the establishment of the Chole Kisiwani Conservation and Development Company constituted its own mini–social drama. Although the company brought in resources and encouraged new forms of community organization desired by residents, it also increased the potential for conflict. Here, I examine a particular instance of conflict within the tourism camp and consider what this event suggests about social relationships on Chole as well as the potentially contradictory social impact that community-based organizations and projects can have more generally.

The Chole Kisiwani company was conceived at the same time as the Mafia Island Marine Park. Although not overtly associated with the marine park, its developers were friendly with the British expatriate who was one of the authors of the park's General Management Plan, and consciously designed the tourism company to coincide with its participatory ideals. Like the marine park, the Chole Kisiwani initiative was conceived as a cutting-edge example of a conservation and development project at a time in which free market agendas had gained ascendency. It was premised on the idea that private investment could be done in a way that would foster real benefits to both communities and to the environment, representing, in some sense, the privatization of development. Because the Chole Kisiwani project was a profit-oriented enterprise rather than the work of international organizations and government bureaucracies, it was organized in a very different manner than the marine park, although it drew upon similar ideological frameworks and sought partnerships with international donors.

The Chole Kisiwani Conservation and Development Company was the creation of three tour developers of Euro-American backgrounds (a hotel owner from the United States, a South African former doctor turned diving instructor and, eventually, the wife of the latter, a British development worker raised in Kenya), all of whom were residents of Zanzibar during the mid-1990s. Not only did the Chole Kisiwani initiative pose a contrast to institutionalized "development" efforts, it also differed radically from other tourism enterprises along the East African coast. It included elaborate plans for the participation of area residents, and it offered assistance in building a new school and health clinic on Chole as well as other development activities. When I first arrived on Mafia in 1994, Mafia's tiny expatriate community of tour developers and environmentalists harbored considerable animosity toward the project, believing either that it would "damage the environment" or that it would create unrealistically high expectations for tourism among Mafia residents. Although the Chole enterprise advertised that it would bring benefits to residents, it was also clearly an endeavor from which the developers hoped to benefit as well. Residents would receive considerable assistance with development initiatives and a percentage of the profit for each tourist who stayed on the island, while the developers themselves stood to benefit from greatly reduced capital costs. Chole's village council rented land along the waterfront to the developers for a nominal sum. Local committees elected to liaise with the company helped to oversee it during the early years of construction, forestalling the need to hire managerial staff. In addition, the island committees helped moderate relationships with other residents, as well as with camp workers and with the "social problems" associated with tourism more broadly.[17] Finally, the "development" aspect of the initiative was used by the tour operators to attract donor funds from NGOs as well as the volunteered or nominally paid services of visiting professionals from which the tourism camp also benefited.

Chole Kisiwani, although widely supported during the time I lived on the island, nevertheless, had opponents. When the developers originally met with Chole residents to discuss their proposal in 1992, some residents expressed skepticism, worrying that *wazungu* (Europeans) desired to *tawala* or "rule" again on Chole as had occurred under colonialism. If the developers were allotted part of the island for tourism development, these critics asked, would they seek to expand their holdings on tiny Chole, disenfranchising residents in the process? By the time I arrived on Chole in 1994, most people had come to support the tourism project, hoping to benefit not only from the school and the clinic, but also from the possibility of jobs that tourism might bring. Nevertheless, a small contingent of residents (estimates ranged from 12 to 30 adults) maintained their opposition to the enterprise. Out of a sense of good manners and the importance of consensus among *wenyeji*, those people who supported the Chole Kisiwani company never mentioned the names of those who opposed it. However, supporters periodically complained about the critics and invariably attributed their motivations to *wivu* (jealousy). They argued that opponents of the project were generally middle-aged to slightly older men who, as owners of homes, boats, and trees, were in a relatively strong economic position on Chole. Supporters complained, at times bitterly, that opponents did not want younger or poorer residents to improve their lives through the opportunities the tourism initiative might bring (hence, decreasing the relative position of strength held by these men on the island).

At the same time, however, some of the strongest supporters of Chole Kisiwani were themselves relatively well-off *wazee* or elders who hoped that the project would create new economic opportunities to aid their increasingly disenfranchised children, making it economically viable for them to remain on Mafia. Thus, this conflict partially reflected tensions between what might be called "progressive" and "conservative" factions of adult men and elders on Chole.[18] When I asked whether it was not legitimate to worry about the potential future dominance of *wazungu* (Europeans) on the island, one of the night watchmen at the camp dismissed the idea saying that times had changed. He argued that the fact that he and I ate together, something that would not have occurred under European colonialism, demonstrated that *wazungu* in the present were not capable of doing what they had done in the past. Others on the island, perhaps, were less sure.

During the time I stayed on Chole, the Chole Kisiwani Conservation and Development Company *did* create new opportunities for residents to work together as a "community." The two elected committees, the Chole Economic Development Society and the Chole Social Development Society, which drew upon residents' adroitness in face-to-face meetings, served to represent the island in such matters as supervising the building of the school, the clinic, and other developments. The committees were also consulted, if superficially, on a variety of matters including the grants being written to donors in their name, on the designs for the new school and clinic, and on the involvement of various visiting professionals. Most crucially, the committees held responsibility for the community development fund deposited at the bank in Kilindoni.[19] During the time I stayed on Chole, the committees kept close watch over this funding, as well as the construction of the new school and health clinic. Many mornings I would leave my tent to see Mzee Ramadhani and Bi Safiya, the chairs of the two committees when I last left Chole, surveying the cement blocks made the previous day that would be used to build a house for the future clinic doctor, or carefully examining the cargo of building materials being unloaded from a packed *mashua* and heatedly haggling over prices. Although the committees were intended only to supervise the community aspects of the enterprise, the committees and island elders also helped mediate disputes among employees and offered assistance with various problems in the camp. At this stage, there was an overall sense on Chole that residents were an integral part of the tourism initiative, and discussions of camp politics and the functioning of the project's committees were widespread on the island. Many residents seemed proud of the project and took its appearance as a sign that Chole was once again improving its status in the world.

At the same time, however, the Chole Kisiwani initiative also served to exacerbate existing tensions on both Chole and southern Mafia more generally. The project had originally faced considerable opposition at the district level, a reality which Chole residents attributed to the *wivu* (jealousy) of those in Kilindoni "who wanted all good things for themselves." In addition, residents of other villages periodically demanded to know why this project should be located on Chole and not in their own village. Tensions, not surprisingly, were also apparent on Chole. Although all Chole residents could theoretically benefit from the school and health clinic, only a handful of residents found ongoing employment in the tourist camp, while a dozen or so more found periodic work as day laborers (*vibarua*) during periods of construction. The scarcity of employment opportunities was a prominent source of tension, and those who worked in the camp (two residents during my first stay on Chole in 1994 and seven by 1997) worried continuously about the jealousy of other island residents. Employees complained that their neighbors carefully watched their behavior, searching for opportunities to gossip about their work performance or trustworthiness, not only to each other but to the developers when they periodically visited Chole. Employees feared that other residents talked about them behind their backs, and underneath this worry lay the fear that such ill will could easily lead to witchcraft.

Conflict in Camp

The story of one young man, who was one of the two original guards hired by the tourism project developers, offers some sense of the texture of conflicts that periodically erupted in the Chole camp. This young man, who was nicknamed *Mzira* or "Barracuda," had the rare reputation on Chole for being a "bad boy." Although village elders had advised against his being hired, one of the developers had attributed such advice to prejudice against the young man's family and insisted on employing Mzira to guard the camp (a place where valuable building materials were kept, as well as the belongings of visiting volunteers and, in later years, tourists). Although occasional small items, particularly food, would periodically "go missing" around the camp, the situation worked well until the camp began to expand and more employees were hired. The ensuing tensions suggested common lines of conflict on Mafia as well as how such conflict intersects with outside projects and enterprises.

Bickering among the two original guards (both of whom were considered contentious by other island residents) soon drew in the newer employees. Tensions were also heightened by the hiring of a new camp manager named Salim, a younger cousin of Mzira. Despite Salim's good nature, conflict quickly ensued as other camp employees, many of whom were older than Salim, resented being told what to do by a younger person. While some employees accused Mzira of siding with Salim because they were cousins, Salim complained bitterly that Mzira ignored his authority because he was his *mdogo* or younger relative. As conflict escalated in the camp, Mzira would periodically seek me out to complain about the behavior of his fellow employees. While at the time I resented his behavior, perceiving such complaints as an attempt to sow discord, such actions could also be interpreted in terms of the customary practice of seeking "outsiders" to act as mediators in internal disputes.

After a string of complaints about his behavior, Mzira was fired from the camp after he was caught stealing a tip left for another employee by a visiting European in 1995. When one of the developers, intending to set a stern example, threatened to turn Mzira over to the police, Mzee Maarufu and other elders pleaded on his behalf, saying that Mzira's family relied upon his economic support. The firing, however, caused a stir on Chole and was the subject of much gossip. Other residents who were jealous of camp employees gleefully spread rumors of the episode. The reality that he had lost his job also radically changed Mzira's social position on the island. While many residents had long been convinced that Mzira was a petty thief, the issue before had been merely a matter of whispered rumors and distrust. Now, however, Mzira had turned into Chole's only publicly acknowledged "thief."

Although Mzira was the first person to be caught stealing in the camp, he was not the only person fired for the offense during the time I stayed on Chole. He was, however, particularly bitter about his situation, implying that he had been judged more harshly than later employees would be. In the ensuing months, another theft of far more dramatic dimensions would also occur on the island. During the night, someone entered the tent of two German men who were helping with the construction of Chole's new school. As they slept, several thousand dollars in traveler's checks and German marks were stolen. The theft left the camp and much of the island in an uproar. Whereas the previous thefts had occurred between camp employees or from camp operating expenses, this theft involved an *mgeni* or guest and, hence, for Chole's *wenyeji,* who felt responsible for the treatment of visitors, it was a matter of public shame (*aibu*). When I visited Mzee Bakari that afternoon he expressed his outrage in dramatic terms. He maintained that it would have been far better for something to have been stolen from himself than from a guest. As he put it, the news of Chole's shame "would now travel all the way to Europe!" Around the island and on the ferry that day, residents could speak of little other than the theft. One elderly man, Mzee Mwalimu, spent an entire ferry ride lecturing his fellow ferry passengers on the shame that had befallen the island—Chole, he warned, would be known in the future as the home of thieves.

Committee members and village elders quickly met to take charge of the situation since the developers were residing in Zanzibar at the time. Island elders asked that the word be spread that if the money were returned by that evening, the thief would not prosecuted; if not, the matter would be turned over to the police. Later in the day, Fuadi the camp gardener, during the course of watering plants, came upon some of the traveler's checks, which had been thrown on the ground at the camp's edge. Only half of the amount stolen was recovered, however, and the deadline set by the elders and committees passed. In the meantime, speculation over who the thief might be was rampant. Almost everyone—camp employees, committee members and other island residents—expressed the opinion that the thief could only be Mzira. One person had seen Mzira walking near the camp before the checks had been strewn on the ground; others had seen him looking nervous and sweating. For most people on Chole this circumstantial evidence, combined with the fact that Mzira was now publicly recognized as a thief, constituted sufficient proof of his guilt. Camp employees in particular were convinced that Mzira, motivated by "jealousy," had used his knowledge of the camp to commit the act. They were convinced he wanted to make other camp employees look bad because he was himself angry at having been fired. The new camp watchguards were particularly nervous. Not only did they worry that they would be fired for allowing the theft (a standard practice in Tanzania), but they knew that the police often took watchguards in for questioning on the assumption that they were either operating in conjunction with thieves or had been delinquent in their jobs. I did not fully understand the depths of their worry until they revealed that "questioning" often involved torture (*kutesa*) and that the police commonly beat "confessions" out of suspects (a situation of which most residents approved). Fuadi, the gardener who had found the money, was so overcome with fear that he became physically ill and took to his bed for several days. When I expressed astonishment that Fuadi felt he might be accused, other camp employees explained that he had "enemies" on the island. These enemies, led by the husband of one of his many lovers, were spreading rumors that because Fuadi found the money, he himself must be the thief.

The following morning Mzira himself came to my tent pleading his innocence and hoping for my support (despite the fact that I had no influence in the matter). He assured me he had not stolen the money and resentfully complained that, since being fired from the camp, any item that went missing on the island was blamed on him. He bitterly described his life as one of increasing social isolation, arguing that he was being scapegoated for being an *mgeni* or "outsider" (his parents had moved to the island from Songo Songo near Kilwa). He also lamented that he and his new wife had nowhere to go to begin a new life. Ultimately, however, the case against Mzira was dropped. Although committee members and elders had hoped to have Mzira arrested—this time feeling that a harsh example was truly necessary—the German man whose money had been stolen refused to pursue the matter, not wanting to be responsible for having a man sent into what he knew to be a harsh penal system. Although the matter was thereby closed, the shame, nevertheless, persisted. When I visited Utende or other villages in the ensuing months, people would grill me with questions about the theft, apparently eager for malicious gossip. Chole was a den of thieves, they warned; clearly the tourism project should have been located in their own village instead!

After this second episode, Mzira was almost entirely ostracized, and his growing bitterness led him to increasingly disregard customary standards of behavior on the island. When I returned to Chole in 1997, I was told that Mzira had been caught with stolen pieces of cloth belonging to Mzee Maarufu and that he had also been selling coconuts stolen from Chole on Juani. Entering the family compound of a friend one afternoon, I found Fatuma and her siblings angrily discussing the coconuts that had been taken during the night from their trees. Together, they planned to obtain magic that would cause the thief—Mzira, they were convinced—to fall while stealing nuts. By this point, Mzira had been fully transformed from a "bad boy" within the fold of local social relationships to a person on the outside, a thief not only by virtue of actions but public labeling, and a man who, in his own bitterness, increasingly scorned the social networks on which all depended. Mzira had truly become what everyone was convinced he was—a thief.

This example of the tensions generated during the establishment of the Chole Kisiwani tourism initiative can not be labeled simply as the "fault" of the project nor a failure of "community" on Chole, but instead represented the perhaps inevitable conflict that accompanies the introduction of new re-sources into a situation of widespread scarcity. While the Chole Kisiwani Conservation and Development Company did create benefits from which all residents stood to gain, such as the clinic and school, it inevitably also worked to increase inequality in a context of shared poverty as some resi-dents, and not others, benefited from jobs and from access to the compara-tively wealthy outsiders that the project was bringing to the island. Despite such inequalities, most residents during the mid-1990s did not oppose the project for this reason, instead gambling, in a context of few other alterna-tives, that they would be among those residents who would benefit from the resources it created.

Seeing beyond Community

While the concept of "community" directs attention toward internal dy-namics, the Chole Kisiwani initiative also makes clear the necessity of look-ing outward. Although the conflict surrounding Mzira highlighted relation-ships among Chole residents, the most important relationship in determining whether or not Chole residents would benefit from the tourism initiative existed between island residents and the Euro-American developers. Al-though the Chole Kisiwani company was couched in a language of partner-ship, the relationship between the two groups was inevitably a hierarchical one. Unlike Chole residents, the developers had access to capital and financing and possessed the educational and professional background necessary to negotiate with national bureaucracies, interface with donor organizations and create a viable international tourism business. Chole residents did exercise influence in a number of ways: by their vote to allow the company onto the island; by their participation within the various committees established in relation to it; by the power of gossip and social pressure; and by holding out the ability to either assist or to make life miserable for both the developers and tourists. Nevertheless, this relationship is most accurately conceived, not as a partnership, but as a variant of the patron–client relationships long familiar along the coast.

Chole residents' perception of the developers as patrons was not simply a hangover from a more "traditional" era, but rather a reasonable assessment in a context in which the relative influence of residents and developers was highly imbalanced. On the one hand, residents sought to gain leverage over the developers by treating them as patrons who were bound to them by relations of reciprocity, however unequal. On the other hand, such inequalities meant that they had little control over the relationship, and I regularly observed residents or committee members hesitating to raise unpopular issues for fear that the developers would pull the enterprise from Chole or cease to act as patrons. Even as many Chole residents perceived the developers as patrons, some powerful outsiders found this role to be an attractive one. The developer who spent the most time on Chole while I was there was a man with a larger-than-life personality who spoke KiSwahili, cultivated strong relationships on Chole, and enjoyed playing the role of patron in the coastal style of an earlier era. Referred to as *babu* or "grandfather" by people on Chole (a term of respect), he would sit at a long table in the tourism camp during his visits, wearing a *kofia* and a colorful cloth wrapped around his waist, as residents came to pay their respects and seek his assistance. Thus, this relationship born of a cutting-edge community-based project was at another level a variation on a much older theme. Chole residents themselves seemed far more comfortable with the accessibility of this style than with the more distant modes of wielding power often found among Euro-American tour operators, many of whom sought to minimize their social contacts with residents altogether.

In general, many of the forces which helped create "community" on Chole had regional, national and international origins. For example, the social dynamics on Chole previously described were shaped to varying degrees by the historical role of Shirazi sultans, Arab slave owners, Islamic law, British legal conceptions of "tradition," slave culture from Central Africa, and mainland government ideas of *ujamaa*. In contrast to assumptions found in commonplace narratives of globalization, the channels through which power came to be expressed in this contemporary international project—one overtly concerned with "community"—were not new. Rather, this project represented the intersection of historical dynamics with contemporary trends. In this context, the concept of *wenyeji,* the role of patron–client relationships, and the reality of "modern" institutions within Tanzania were all being reworked in a post–Cold War context in which long-standing models of development and conservation were being transformed according to a free market model.

If, by contrast, we follow the direction in which the term "community" points, namely toward internal social dynamics, what do we learn? We have seen that those social relationships that might be called community on Chole were based on an ideal of consensus and egalitarianism, as well as a reality of pervasive jealousy. This jealousy, however, was not the kind presumed by Western free market models that held that someone who "got ahead" would be admired and emulated by others, leading to an ideal of constructive competition. Rather jealousy in this context sought to cut down those who "got ahead," presuming that they profited unfairly or at the expense of others. International projects that brought in resources that benefitted some and not others, thus, risked being remembered more for exacerbating jealousy and heightening social tensions than for offering assistance.

Given that the Mafia Island Marine Park was still in an early stage of implementation, its impact on day-to-day social relationships on Mafia was less explicit than that of the Chole Kisiwani initiative. It was, nevertheless, clear that the park held a similar power to encourage residents to work together in support of their interests, while also possessing the ability to generate contestation among residents. Such contradictory dynamics were apparent, for example, in relation to the 1995 Ecotourism Seminar in which residents came together as a group to argue for their interests, a consensus that was later undermined as individual leaders were "bought off" by park officials. At the same time, it was also clear that marine park plans had paid far less attention to social relationships within the park than the Chole Kisiwani initiative had for Chole. Despite the experience that some park planners had on Mafia, the broader framework for the marine park was generated by those in national and international offices who knew little about Mafia and who were institutionally invested in a generic concept of "community" that would be applicable to other projects worldwide. Although planners clearly hoped that the marine park would bring benefits to the "community" by stopping the dynamiting and by helping to conserve fish populations, they failed to acknowledge that the jobs and access to resources that the park would bring would only be available to some and would simultaneously underscore who had "gotten ahead"and who had been "left behind."

While it seems inevitable that such dynamics will encourage conflict among Mafia residents in the future, it is important to keep in mind that during the mid-1990s most Mafia residents *desired* the marine park (just as

Chole residents supported the Chole Kisiwani initiative) precisely because they hoped it could act as a source of resources and assistance. In a context of severe economic hardship, any influx of resources was deemed welcome, while each individual hoped that his or her family might be the one to benefit. Although an influx of resources would presumably cause tensions, the degree of conflict would also depend upon how well international projects understood "community" on Mafia and served to support ideals of consensus rather than to provoke jealousy. In short, the reality of "community" on Chole is very different from the static and harmonious image conjured by the term in English, by the ideal views of Nyerere's socialism, or the presumed egalitarianism of all nations in an "international community." Rather it exists in terms of social dynamics that are characterized by tensions and conflict as well as cross-cutting social bonds. Because communities harbor both tendencies, community-based projects can work in either direction. Such projects might draw people together by encouraging them to act as "communities," or they can create situations and newer forms of hierarchy that pull people apart.

CHAPTER FOUR

Where There Is No Nature

★CONTEMPORARY IDEAS OF participatory conservation and sustainable development found among international organizations are based upon particular assumptions about the relationship between rural residents in poor regions, such as Mafia, and the environments in which they live. Historically, there has long been a tendency to portray rural residents of the so-called Third World as degraders of the environment who are in need of regulation, a tendency built upon colonial-era assumptions (see chapter 5). In more recent years, however, a counter viewpoint with an equally lengthy genealogy in European romantic traditions has gained greater ascendency. This viewpoint focuses attention on what are now called "indigenous" communities and presumes generally harmonious relations between such groups and the natural environment. Both sets of viewpoints form part of international discourses around the environment and can be found in the policies and literature of contemporary international organizations. However, in order to understand the relationship between people, such as those on Mafia, and international projects like the Mafia Island Marine Park, it is necessary to delve into both sets of assumptions to consider the complex socioeconomic and environmental forces at work.

This chapter begins by examining ideas of "nature" and asking whether a concept of nature similar to that found within Euro-American traditions can also be found on Chole. It then explores the history of fishing and marine resource use on Mafia and argues that such practices fail to accord easily with conceptions of the "indigenous" or "traditional." Instead, fishing techniques and other uses of the natural environment are historically malleable and drawn from diverse origins. In addition, contemporary Chole residents mix subsistence and market practices in complex ways, not because subsistence practices are a hold-out from a "traditional" past that have not yet succumbed to the "modern" world, but because both sets of practices allow Mafia residents to cobble together an existence that allows them to survive in the contemporary era. Such "hybrid" realities are not simply functional, however, but rather represent a reality in which day-to-day life in both "First" and "Third" World countries consists of a patchwork of ideas and practices of mixed origins. Finally, this chapter explores the worries that Chole's fishers expressed about the marine park during the mid-1990s. Although it was unclear at that time how marine park regulations would affect Mafia islanders, the concerns expressed by Chole residents offer a sense of their previous experience with regulatory regimes, their own difficult economic situation, and a willingness to discuss conservation alternatives despite a lack of interlocuters within what was intended to have been a "participatory" marine park.

Searching for Nature

One March day late in my fieldwork, I accompanied a woman from Chole to visit a relative who was staying in a town on Mafia's main island. Like other Chole residents, we depended for transportation on the one wooden sailboat that served as a ferry and landed in the main island village of Utende. The most crowded ferry generally left Chole at dawn, laden with passengers hurrying to meet the broken-down minitruck that traveled once daily from Utende into Kilindoni. By the time we began our journey, however, it was midmorning and the only would-be passengers on this trip were myself, Mwanajuma, my traveling companion, and Rukia, a thoughtful, capable woman who was the daughter-in-law of Bi Rehema Hassani. Although unusual at this late hour, an early morning calm was still apparent on the water. Not a breath of wind could be felt, and the bay lay as still as a sheet of glass. As was common when the tide was going out, we hiked up our skirts and, carrying plastic bags and handwoven baskets either in arms or on our heads, we waded waist deep into the water to meet the incoming ferry. The ferry captain, Mzee Hamisi, a tall, gangly man, who enjoyed entertaining his passengers with his acerbic wit (often at their expense), kept the sailboat from beaching on the sand by maneuvering it with a long pole as the water receded around us. After hauling ourselves over the side of the *mashua* sailboat, Mzee Hamisi again hoisted the sail. With the sail hanging limply on the mangrove pole mast, we began drifting, rather than sailing, toward Utende on the outgoing tide.

Rukia and I, as relatively young adults, offered Mzee Hamisi the respectful greeting *shikamoo* (I clasp your feet), a term which had originated during slavery but had evolved into the customary greeting for all persons older than oneself. In response to our inquires about his health, Mzee Hamisi responded philosophically that his state was much the same as it was every day: The world merely passed by around him as he sailed back and forth on the ferry. Rukia asked playfully what he could see of the world from his vantage point on the boat. Perhaps recognizing that there were too few passengers to provide an adequate audience for his wit, his reply came with uncustomary tolerance, and he waxed eloquent about the unchanging state of the world. Then, reclining in the back of the boat with his hand casually placed upon the tiller, he began quietly describing a conflict over land involving one of his wives, a story intended to elicit the moral support of his passengers as well as to pass the time.

Out of politeness, Rukia periodically offered noncommital responses to Mzee Hamisi's story; her attention, however, was directed over the side of the boat. Much of the channel between Chole and Utende was shallow at low tide and the glasslike stillness of the water afforded a crystal clear view of the world beneath us. Small schools of brightly colored fish swam below the boat, hovering over outcroppings of coral rock and passing through fields of sea grass swaying with the tide. Now and again, Rukia would pull at my arm, pointing out some particularly interesting phenomenon—a large aqua blue parrotfish or *pono* swimming serenely beneath the boat, a school of tiny black and white *viambuzi* fish darting about the coral, a large crab marching past sea urchins and anemones. Women on Chole knew the beaches and tidal flats well (these were the places where they hunted for octopus and shells or buried coconut fiber in the sand to soften in order to make rope), but they had few dealings with deeper water, and most did not know how to swim. Nevertheless, Rukia was clearly fascinated by this underwater world populated by what some women referred to in shorthand terms as the *vijidudu* or "thingies" of the sea.[1] After drifting halfway to Utende, Mzee Hamisi roused himself and, interrupting our reverie on this underwater world, exhorted us to take up the wooden paddles lying in the bottom of the boat and begin rowing for shore. An outrigger canoe passed nearby heading toward the mouth of the bay and the fishermen shouted encouragement at the unusual sight of women wielding the paddles, a job generally assumed by men. Mwanajuma called back jokingly that this was the "women's boat" and we continued our course toward Utende.

Rukia's curiosity about the underwater life beneath the ferry suggests a central question for an ethnography concerned with the environment: What do the people living in a place like Mafia think about the natural world which surrounds them? After switching my research focus to the marine park and exploring scholarship on the origins and meanings of Western conceptions of nature (Williams 1973; Merchant 1980; Worster 1994), examining what "nature" might signify to people on Mafia became a central goal for my research. What, I wondered, did Chole residents think about the sea and marine life, not only as fishers and octopus hunters, but also as people, like Rukia, simply going about their daily lives?[2]

The task of discovering what Mafia residents believe about "nature" was, however, more difficult than I had anticipated. In KiSwahili, the word most commonly translated as nature or the environment is *mazingira*, a term which implies general surroundings and carries none of the connotations of *nature* in English. Not surprisingly, my first awkward attempts to ask people on Chole about their feelings about *mazingira* met with blank or quizzical looks. In fact, people on Chole almost never used *mazingira* in the sense in which English-speakers use *nature*. This was not the case, however, with all Tanzanians. With the increased emphasis on conservation within development circles, government officials, academics, and other Tanzanians associated with aid or development organizations did, in fact, increasingly rely on the language of environmentalism. Indeed, in a country, like many in the so-called Third World, where public discourse is shaped in myriad ways by development institutions, the language of the environment has rapidly gained in importance. In Tanzania, *mazingira* has become a popular topic in recent decades, particularly among educated elites in Dar es Salaam, as well as in national newspapers and school curriculums. This concept, while rapidly becoming part of the world view of some Tanzanians, nonetheless, gained its impetus from outside the country. Consequently, it bore little relationship to the way people in "remote" regions like Chole talked and thought in the course of their daily lives (although projects like the marine park could easily change this dynamic).[3]

Nevertheless, I continued to assume that there must be some "indigenous" conception of nature along the coast distinct from the First World–inspired language of *mazingira*, and I sought a variety of means to uncover such a conception of the marine environment. On occasion, I participated in marine-related activities like octopus hunting at low tide with groups of young women from Chole. Experts at spotting the tips of octopus tentacles in holes in the coral, these women would prod the creatures with long, sharpened sticks until the animals left their hiding holes and, in a peculiar form of attack, aggressively wrapped themselves around the sticks. In the case of a particularly recalcitrant octopus, a woman would pull the fighting creature from its hole with her hand as it attached its gelatinous body with suction cups to her arm. Pulling away the ink-spewing octopus, she would flip the animal, quickly cutting off its dangerous beak, and then throw the catch into a dripping plastic bag. There was plenty to do on such trips, and although I became proficient at gathering and cutting the mollusks known as *mapanga*, I squeamishly avoided octopus hunting (friends would good-naturedly present me with an octopus at the end of such trips to spare me the presumed embarrassment of going back to camp empty-handed). We conversed about numerous topics on such outings; however, little of our talk focused on the sea itself.

When I asked men on Chole to tell me about the marine environment (almost all of them having been fishers at some point in their lives), most volunteered detailed descriptions of fishing gear, of wind directions, and types of fish—practical knowledge that once again did not easily convert into a conception of "nature." Frustrated that both direct questioning and simple observation were not bearing fruit, I decided to try another tack. I reasoned that fishing yarns were probably common among coastal peoples who make their living from the sea; perhaps gathering stories about the marine environment would provide greater insight into how people on Chole conceived of nature? Consequently, I asked various men I knew to tell me "stories" about the sea. Once again, however, I met perplexed looks. By way of offering an example, I related that *wazungu* (Euro-Americans) sometimes tell fantastic tales about mermaids and other sea creatures. However, in conveying this idea, I was forced to translate the English term *mermaid* into KiSwahili as *nguva*, a word used by coastal people to describe the manatee, a large ocean mammal remarked upon along the coast, as it is in other parts of the world, for its resemblance to humans. With a glimmer of recognition, Saidi Abdallah responded, "Yes. I once saw a manatee when I was fishing." Drawing a picture in the wet sand, he elaborated, "It had a face like a cow and teats like a woman and from a distance you thought it could be a person." Hoping he had been helpful, he asked if this was the kind of story I had meant. "Sort of," I responded, unsure of what I wanted. Hemedi Salum, a carpenter in the camp then offered a tale, a wonderful story about a princess who turned into a sea creature. Like much of the storytelling along the coast, it reflected the strong influence of Arab tales of princes and horses, but had relatively little to say about Chole residents' experiences of "nature." Mzira later volunteered that he knew of a man from Jibondo who had gone out fishing in a canoe alone at night. His hook had apparently gotten caught on a *tanga* (giant manta ray) and he was pulled around the islands until the line finally broke loose and he was set free; was this a suitable story? Over time, I stopped asking such questions, unclear what exactly I was searching for and why none of these things added up to a concept of "nature."

One night, as I looked over my notes, I wondered whether to continue this line of inquiry. My closest friend Fatuma, a young widow who worked as a cook in the camp, sat nearby knitting a sweater for her baby daughter. Throughout my research I often relied on Fatuma's incisive, analytical mind for insight into social dynamics on Chole, and, at a loss how to proceed, I once again turned to her for help. Unsure how to describe what I had been looking for on Chole, I sought to sketch for her common ideas of "nature" in Euro-American thought. Somehow, I ended up outlining anthropological arguments about nature and culture in the Lévi-Straussian tradition, as well as how some feminists had posited that women were universally devalued in relation to men due to their association with nature (Lévi-Strauss 1969; Ortner 1974). These were difficult arguments to convey, in part because the concept of "culture" is as elusive in KiSwahili as "nature," but Fatuma listened intently and then, needles flashing, explained that she thought such theories held little relevance for the coast. "Women are not as devalued as all that here," she added summarily.

This conversation represented a turning point in my thinking, not so much because of the details of our discussion, but because it affirmed my sense that I was looking for "nature" in the wrong way. Perhaps nature was not a category of thought in the way I expected? After all, is it reasonable to assume that people with vastly different histories necessarily shared a concept of nature? The word *nature* in English is itself a heavily loaded term that has taken on its current symbolic meanings in the context of, and largely in opposition to, the rise of capitalism and "modernity" in Europe and the United States (Williams 1973). Even within European thought, the conception of nature which arose in the nineteenth century differed significantly from beliefs in earlier periods (Merchant 1980; Pepper 1984; Williams 1973; Worster 1994). Was the problem I had on Chole a result of attempting to construct a universal category from a historically specific concept (even if that category was conceived as a general one to be filled in with different cultural particulars)? While obviously all people have relationships with, and ideas about, the environment, since it is the medium in which we live and which sustains us as human beings, must we all possess a common view of nature that bounds our perceptions of the environment in similar ways and sees it as distinct from other phenomena?[4] Although much academic thought particularly in its French variants has rested upon a symbolic distinction between nature and culture, is such a distinction, as Descola and Palsson (1996) also ask, truly universal? Need there be a concept of nature at all?

Certainly there were aspects of cultural and social life on Mafia which *could* be viewed in terms of a concept of "nature." Mzee Maarufu, the chairman of the village, described to me how monkeys had once been like people but assumed their current form because they were being punished by God— a view that measures humanity in terms of its distance from animals, a conception common in other parts of the Islamic world. The spirit possession practices that form part of *mila* along the coast also incorporate beliefs in land and sea spirits (Caplan 1997; Giles 1987). Heidi Glaesel notes that fishers on the Kenyan coast offer *sadaka* (offerings) to sea spirits (1997), a practice that also occurs on Mafia although fishers argue that it has become less common due to increasing poverty. In addition, malevolent spirits (*masheitani*) are thought to live in and be attracted to the "bush." Yet, there was nothing that could easily be equated with the symbolic concept of "nature" in English.

Like many environmentalists, Glaesel views Swahili coastal beliefs in sea spirits as "eco-cosmological" and implies they have a determinative effect on human behavior (1997). Such analyses are common and draw upon environmentalist representations of non-Western people as having primarily spiritual connections with nature. At the same time, however, such tendencies bear a disturbing likeness to those of nineteenth century social theorists like Levy-Bruhl who viewed "savages" as in a state of mystic participation with nature. During an era of European colonialism, such presumptions, which implied that "natives" were a part of nature in a way that presumably modern people were not, underwrote the tendency to treat non-Westerners as children rather than intelligent and capable social actors. Even the more respectful contemporary accounts in this vein, leave little room for the pragmatic, everyday ways that all people deal with their environments.

Suggesting that there is no symbolic equivalent to "nature" on Mafia does not, however, mean that Chole residents lacked curiosity or appreciation for the natural environment. Many people I knew, for example, were adept at mimicking birdcalls and well versed in the habits of the small creatures that inhabited the island. People were not only knowledgeable but curious and, at times, moved by the beauty of what Euro-Americans would call "nature." While Rukia's fascination with the underwater world beneath the ferry offers one example, the trip with Mzee Bakari to visit Bi Sharifa in Baleni offered another. On that day, the boat, filled with Mzee Bakari's grandsons, as well as friends and neighbors, returned at dusk. After the orange streaks of the sunset gradually faded, the water became silvery in the light of a full moon. Mohammed, Mzee Bakari's vivacious youngest grandson, began singing verses he had learned at the Quranic school in an attempt to entertain the other passengers. As he sang, a school of dolphin surfaced nearby and began swimming and jumping alongside the boat. All the passengers watched this display with delight, ohhing and ahhing with each jump of the dolphins.

These same people, nevertheless, saw no contradiction in throwing rocks at hawks that ate their baby chickens, complaining about the large fruit bats that ate the oranges on their trees, or breathing a sigh of relief that the wild pigs and monkeys that destroyed the crops of relatives on Juani had been eradicated on Chole. People were puzzled by the penchant of *wazungu* (Euro-American) visitors to Mafia to go to "deserted" places and to prize photographs of peopleless landscapes (invariably, they politely ignored such scenic shots, focusing their attention on the photographs that were important to them—those of people). As in an earlier period in European and U.S. history in which rural life and farming still predominated, "nature" signified both something more and something less than it does for contemporary Euro-American urban dwellers. It offered them the means by which they could live, yet also continuously threatened them with disaster by withholding its fruits and through storms, droughts, and dangerous pests. In short, people on Mafia did not share the romance for "nature" found among those who seek refuge from "modernity" in the natural environment.

THE PATCHWORK QUALITY OF DAILY LIFE: MIXING THE "TRADITIONAL" AND THE "MODERN"

Fishing on Mafia

The aspect of Mafia residents' relationship to nature that most concerned Mafia Island Marine Park planners was their relation to fish and the marine environment. Indeed, the expansion of "participatory" projects like the marine park in recent years has meant a growing interest in "indigenous" or non-Western conservation and environmental practices, including those relating to the marine environment (see chapter 6). Fishing practices on Mafia, as well as along the Swahili coast in general, have a very long history. Yet, such practices do not easily accord with concepts of either the "traditional" *indigenous* or its contemporary variant, the "indigenous," which is increasingly being applied to rural African populations (see also Hodgson 2002). Both terms imply an unchanging historical continuity and homogeneity of beliefs and practices among clearly defined ethnic populations (Gupta 1998; A. Agrawal 1995; Ellen 1986; Walley 2002).

In contrast to assumptions about "traditional" or "indigenous" practices, fishing on Mafia has been a product of continual historical transformation as well as influence from a wide range of geographic regions. In addition, its economic meanings have differed sharply over time. Along the East African coast, for example, the relative dependence of residents upon fishing has varied considerably. While the economies of urban coastal areas, such as Zanzibar Town or Mombasa, have historically centered around the more high-status occupations of mercantilism and trading, rural areas of the coast (apart from former plantation regions) have depended more upon a combination of fishing and farming. Geography also plays a significant role, as the situation on Mafia makes clear. Residents from the interior of the main island, such as those living in "Minazini" where Pat Caplan (1975) did her research, rely heavily on farming and livestock rearing. In contrast, in the waterfront villages and smaller islands of Chole, Jibondo and Juani, most men focus their energies on fishing (Jibondo being the most extreme case in which residents rely almost entirely upon the sea).

Despite the fact that fishing on Mafia draws upon a long history of "Swahili" maritime culture along the East African coast (Prins 1965; Glaesel 1997), fishing practices have meant very different things at different times and have occasionally been subject to abrupt transformations. For example, oral accounts relate that tiny Chole once served as a home to fishers and as a farm region for Shirazi elites on Juani in the days before Kua's demise. Yet, the rise of Chole as Mafia's urban center in the nineteenth century meant that fishing took on a very different role. Residents of Chole Town were then stratified into plantation owners, merchants, wage laborers, artisans, and slaves, in contrast to the free farmers and fishers that populated the villages of much of the coast. Although some slaves and free individuals presumably fished, it was only with the end of the plantation economy and the ensuing disintegration of Chole Town that this tiny island was once again poised to become an island of fishers and farmers.

Elderly men on Chole can recall the particular point at which fishing reappeared on the island in the years following independence. Mzee Bakari, one of a handful of people who had lived on Chole since he was a child, described this process in detail. He argued that while in the heady days after independence some young men preferred the adventure of working on *dhows* that sailed up and down the coast, he and a half dozen other male residents, including his close friend, Mzee Maarufu, cleared land and planted trees across much of Chole, thereby establishing the basis for their relative prosperity in later years. Once that work was finished (and given that tree crops require little attention), he described how he and a few other industrious men began to direct their attention to fishing and deliberately set out to learn the necessary skills. Intriguingly, these men learned to fish, not only from "Swahili" men living on Juani Island, but also from Makonde immigrants from southern Tanzania who had settled in Utende—a reality that contradicts assumptions that "traditional" environmental knowledge is invariably bounded by, and passed on within, particular cultural groups.

Although fish have long been sold in the past on Mafia, their commodification has greatly intensified in recent years. During his visit in 1895, German geographer Oscar Baumann documented a substantial trade in *ng'onda* (fish that have been sliced and dried in the sun), with local merchants exporting the dried fish from Mafia to Dar es Salaam and Zanzibar. A sizeable trade in shark meat between the Arabian Gulf and Zanzibar has also been documented as part of the Indian Ocean trading world of previous centuries (Gilbert, 2003). Nonetheless, fish were a relatively unimportant commodity on Mafia in the more recent past. Idi Hassan noted that men of previous generations fished primarily for food (*kitoweo*), perhaps selling a few fish on the side for cash. He also described such fishing as being like "a game" (*mchezo*), rather than the serious occupation it is now. In recounting Chole's history, Bi Rehema Hassani noted that when she was growing up fish were both abundant and "had no price" (*samaki hana bei*), that is, held no value as a commodity.[5] This situation poses a striking contrast to today, when most men, particularly younger men who lack access to sufficient land or trees, generally sell fish to obtain cash.

The relative lack of commodification of fish in the more recent past, however, does not mean that a cash economy was a distant reality on Mafia. Instead, economic attention on Mafia over the last one hundred years was directed primarily toward the production of dried coconut or copra (*mbata*). Destined for international markets, copra was used to make oils and soaps and served as the motivating factor for the rise of Mafia's coconut plantations in the late nineteenth century. Although cashew nuts, woven mats, and coconut fiber rope (the latter two items made by women) in addition to dried fish (Baumann 1896), had historically been exported from Mafia, coconuts were the most important cash crop during the Omani, German, and British colonial periods. From 1890 to World War I, Mafia was the largest supplier of copra among Germany's East African colonies, and, after the demise of slavery, coconuts continued to be widely cultivated as a cash crop by individuals. Eventually, however, coconut oil was replaced by other products in international markets, leading to the collapse of *mbata* prices. According to Chole residents, the *mbata* trade had largely ceased on Mafia by the 1970s, although residents continued to sell coconuts in Dar es Salaam for the production of cooking oil for local markets.[6]

While Mafia residents in general relied upon coconuts as their primary source of cash, Chole residents also sold oranges from the high-quality trees that had been imported to their island by Arabs. (Although Chole's soil never produced the enormous coconuts found on the main island, the island was well known for its sweet oranges). However, the collapse of the international copra market was accompanied by a series of other problems that make selling agricultural crops difficult in general. Transporting crops to market in Dar es Salaam is both difficult and expensive (tellingly, many oranges are simply left to rot on trees on Chole). Residents also complain that Chole's soil is "tired," its fertility having been depleted from long use. Perhaps most crucially, land shortage on this tiny island has meant that many people now lack access to land for trees as well as subsistence farming. As a result of these combined factors, there has been a pronounced shift on Chole in recent years from reliance upon tree crops as a source of cash to dependency on fishing. Although the prices of many agricultural crops have decreased in recent decades, the price of fish has increased, presumably due to the depletion of fish along other parts of the coast as well as increased international demand.

The plummeting of international agricultural prices has been a leading cause of the downward economic spiral that has widely affected the African continent in recent years, a trend that has led many Mafia residents to characterize the contemporary period as *maisha magumu* or "the tough life." Other changes with origins in distant regions have also had a profound impact upon their livelihoods. Although Tanzania's economy was already in tatters prior to the period of structural adjustment (a result of the oil shock of the 1970s, Tanzania's war with Idi Amin, growing debt, and declining productivity), the free market reforms of the IMF-backed Structural Adjustment programme that began to be implemented during the late 1980s have also generated widespread hardship. In response to currency devaluations and rising inflation, Chole residents during the mid-1990s commonly remarked that money "no longer had any value" (*hamna thamani*) (see also Caplan 1992). Although residents noted that money was difficult to come by in "the past," they argued that it carried far greater purchasing power than at present. Free market reforms have increased the availability of consumer goods within Tanzania (although to a still limited extent on Mafia itself), but most Mafia residents lack the money to be able to purchase such goods. Free market reforms have also meant a drastic reduction in social services. During the socialist period, medicines and doctors were scarce; however, access to both was ostensibly free.[7] In the 1990s, medicines were increasingly available in the new pharmacies and private clinics on the mainland, but were priced well out of the range of most Mafia residents. In addition, already beleaguered Mafia residents were now required to pay school fees for primary education (even as teachers in urban areas like Zanzibar and Dar es Salaam combined ill-paying jobs in government schools with more lucrative employment as private tutors). Thus, in general, the "tough life" has meant a growing need for cash—a need that has been increasingly met through fish.

The growing tendency to turn fish into commodities to earn cash, also means that people on Chole eat less well than they had in the past. Many Chole residents complain that they no longer have access to fish, and many mothers worry about the diet of their children. Fishers now only bring home an occasional fish for their own immediate families, selling the rest off the island. Several Europeans expressed surprise to me that contemporary Mafia residents would rather sell fish than use their catch to feed their families. Yet, the cash earned from selling fish can feed far more mouths than the fish itself would have. Families can subsist without *kitoweo* or "relishes" like fish; however, they cannot exist without grain. Although historical accounts suggest that Mafia has rarely been self-sufficient in food production, most people try not to spend scarce cash for such basic foodstuffs. However, for those who lack sufficient access to land or for many people during the lean periods between harvests, store-bought grains may offer the only means for survival (see also Caplan 1975).

The increasing tendency to convert fish into commodities is also linked to technological changes. Refrigeration has had a profound effect on residents' ability to turn fish into cash. In recent years, residents have begun selling, not simply dried *ng'onda*, but fresh fish to Dar es Salaam "ice boats" (wooden *mashua* powered by engines and carrying ice chests), which make periodic appearances in Mafia's waters. In 1997, a dried fish would only bring 15 to a few hundred shillings depending on size (600 shs for a very large fish), but a *tenga* or woven basket of fresh fish could sell for 30,000 shillings (approximately US$37) to an ice boat. Although the ice boat might not wish to buy the largest fish (they reportedly preferred smaller fish that could be sold to individual buyers in Dar es Salaam's market), the ice boat would also purchase fish that was unsuitable for *ng'onda* (for example, unicornfish, mullet, and surgeonfish, which are too oily to be properly dried, or wrasses, parrotfish, and grouper, which are likely to rot during the rainy season). In addition, a Greek-owned seafood export company bought large numbers of octopus on Mafia during the 1990s, particularly from an octopus-hunting collective that was formed by women on Jibondo.[8]

Other technological changes include transformations in types of fishing gear. In the more distant past, Chole residents primarily fished with handmade fence traps (*wando*), box traps (*madema* and *ming'onyo*) and handlines (*mishipi*). After independence, however, the socialist government, following the modernizing logic of the late colonial period, emphasized the extractive uses of natural resources and the need to increase production. Consequently, at the same time that fishers from southern Tanganyika were bringing more extractive fishing methods to Mafia, the state was encouraging fishers to invest in "modern" (*ya kisasa*) fishing gear, especially nylon seine and shark nets. This policy paralleled the efforts of the post-independence government to transform agriculture through the use of "modern" technologies such as plows and tractors.[9] Ironically for Mafia residents, it is this "improved" gear that is currently being criticized by international environmentalists for its destructive impact on the marine environment. Seine nets drag on the bottom, breaking coral, while shark nets may inadvertently catch turtles (Horrill and Mayers 1992). Although the ability of Mafia residents to intensify fishing remains limited by their nonmechanized gear and boats (paling in comparison to the heavily mechanized fleets including trawlers used by "First World" countries [McEvoy 1986; McGoodwin 1990]), nevertheless, nylon nets have radically increased the extractive potential of small-scale fishers, contributing to decreasing fish populations, as Glaesel notes for the Kenyan coast (1997).

In general, however, at the same time that Mafia residents have become increasingly dependent upon fishing as a source of cash, their ability to catch fish has become ever more precarious. In contrast to modernist narratives of continually advancing technological progress, the types of fishing gear being used on Mafia have not continued to undergo a process of "modernization." In fact, there appears to be a trend toward reversion to more "traditional" types of fishing gear in response to current economic hardship. During the 1990s, the cost of fishing gear in Tanzania radically increased at the same time that currency devaluations were making money, in the words of Chole residents, increasingly "worthless." According to residents, between 1975 and 1996, the price of nylon used for making nets had skyrocketed from 150 shillings to 20,000 shillings—a remarkable increase even given inflation. In addition, during the mid-1990s many people on Chole could no longer afford to build or even repair their wooden sailboats and the number of boats on Chole was decreasing.[9] Thus, the high cost of gear also meant that some men lacked the means to fish or found it more difficult to find a boat on which they could work for a share of the catch. Consequently, there has been a tendency to revert to more "traditional" modes of fishing that require less capital investment. For example, fishers reported that there was an increase in fishing with handlines from small canoes (*ngalawa*), setting box and fence traps by hand, or fishing while swimming.[10] For others, the increased cost of fishing equipment has meant that it is necessary to harvest more fish in order to cover the amount of money they had already invested, creating an added incentive to intensify fishing (for example, in contrast to the past, men have begun to fish during the long rainy season). In general, the result of such trends has been an incongruous mix of added difficulty in being able to fish and an increasing pressure to overfish.

Still other changes, however, have contributed to making fishing a more precarious economic option. Dwindling fish populations present a daunting challenge in addition to the high cost of gear or difficulties in marketing catches. Although compared to other areas along the coast, fishing was still rich around Mafia during the mid-1990s, the decrease in the number of fish is striking to residents who offer detailed accounts of past catches in contrast to those of the present.[11] Many fishers today complain that when they go out fishing they have no assurances of what they will catch, and one man described fishing at present as a "lottery" (*bahati nasibu*). Rather than considering the intensification of fishing to be a cause of decreased fish populations more generally, residents tended to focus their attention on dynamiting. And, indeed, Chole residents offered detailed descriptions of the destruction caused by this practice around Mafia, particularly to Tutia reef, Miewi, Kifinge, and Jambe on Juani. They described sea bottoms converted to *jangwa* (desert), unharmed fish fleeing from the impact, sound and smell of dynamiting, and the reluctance of the fish to return to their destroyed coral "homes" (*nyumba*).

Increased difficulties in fishing and decreasing fish populations, however, do not stem solely from "local" phenomena. Just as the role of fishing in Mafia's past was linked to regional and transregional dynamics including those of the Indian Ocean trading world, contemporary pressures on Mafia's reefs and waters also relate to broader national and international dynamics. As Horrill and Mayers noted, the number of fishers from outside Mafia District who sought permits to fish in Mafia's waters (excluding a potentially large number of unlicenced fishers) increased ten-fold during a six-year period while the number of resident fishers remained largely the same (1992: 11). This growing presence reflects many of the changes already mentioned: the destruction of other marine areas along the coast (attributable in part to dynamiting), an increase in fish prices in both national and international markets, and a growing ability to "commodify" fresh fish given the advancement of refrigeration technology. Mafia's marine environment has also been affected by less visible forces originating in other parts of Tanzania or internationally. Silting from the nearby Rufiji River delta (a product of soil erosion and farming practices inland as well as chemical run-off from increased use of fertilizers and pesticides) has had an as yet unspecified impact on the ability of coastal waters to support marine life, while large ocean-going ships have generated pollution by dumping waste into coastal waters (resulting, for example, in skin rashes and other irritations among Mafia fishers who came in contact with the water after such discharges). In addition, Semesi and Ngoile (1995) note that the main transportation artery for oil from the Mid-

dle East to Europe and the United States passes along the East African coast.
It is estimated that 644 ships cruise the East African region on a given day,
spilling approximately 33,250 metric tons of oil into the Indian Ocean every
year (Semesi and Ngoile 1995:301).

In short, it is impossible to understand the fishing practices of Mafia's
residents in terms of a "traditional" or subsistence-based economy. Nor can
fishing be discussed solely in terms of "local" dynamics. On the contrary,
Mafia's fishers, like other fishers worldwide, are operating in contexts
shaped in myriad ways by national and international forces beyond the control of area residents. Yet, there are profound differences in how different
categories of actors relate to localized marine environments. Because poverty on Chole imposes limits on the types of fishing gear that residents can
use (thus affecting their extractive abilities), there are constraints on the fishing practices of area residents that do not necessarily apply to actors from
off the islands. Although Mafia residents may participate in overfishing or
other forms of environmental degradation, they are also the same actors who
are most dependent on such resources for their survival and who suffer the
most profound consequences of this degradation. National and international
actors, on the contrary, possess far more freedom to escape the damage that
they create.

Fish and Land as Partial Commodities

As economic circumstances have become increasingly difficult on Mafia,
Chole residents rely ever more intensely upon particular day-to-day social
practices regarding land and marine environments which allow them to "get
by." Understanding such practices is crucial to making sense of how residents
conceptualize their economic life and utilize natural resources, as well as how
they relate to the policies and goals of the Mafia Island Marine Park. On
Chole, people manage to get by, not only by selling fish, but also through
long-standing practices that mix market and nonmarket dynamics and that
create social safety networks upon which they can draw when cash is not
available. Yet, such nonmarket practices should not be conceptualized as
simply hangovers from a more "traditional" past or, alternately, as "local"
dynamics destined to succumb to, or be reconfigured by, the logic of expanding global capitalism. Indeed, J. K. Gibson-Graham (1996) reminds us that in
spite of the totalizing language in which capitalism is often discussed, capitalist practices in all societies inevitably coexist with a range of nonmarket
social practices (including those relating to family and kinship, as many
feminist scholars suggest) (see also Mitchell 1998). On Mafia, this mixing of
market and nonmarket relationships takes on its own unique configuration.

The role of private property emerges at the heart of many contemporary
debates over the relationship between conservation and development and,

*Theory &
environment* [handwritten marginalia]

indeed, about the role of free market reforms in the so-called Third World more generally. Social theorists of both environmentalism and capitalism have long debated its significance. Economic theorists have commonly viewed the transformation of natural resources, such as land, into commodities that can be bought and sold as a defining feature of capitalism with profound implications for socioeconomic relationships (Marx 1995; Polanyi 1994). Environmentalists have also participated in such debates by considering the role that private property plays in contrast to "the commons" and what this has meant for natural resource use. For example, Garret Hardin in an influential 1968 article entitled "The Tragedy of the Commons" presented a variation on the classical argument that the enclosure of the commons in England offered a more productive system of land use. He postulated that private property was also more environmentally viable since communal land use is more likely to lead to degradation as individuals follow their own best interests, extracting as much as they can from common resources. Ironically, the rise of capitalism pushed the regulation of marine environments in the opposite direction, bringing with it the doctrine of "freedom of the seas," which was intended to allow open transport for commercial ships (McGoodwin 1990). More recently, as the seas have become less important for transport and more valued as a source of marine resources, arguments have also been made for the privatization of marine environments. Such arguments are based on the assumption that marine environments become degraded because of collective use (Carr 1998). In contrast, social scientists have contested the assumption that collective use inevitably leads to degradation and have stressed the difference between open access systems of land/marine use and common property regimes. Many note that the latter are governed in many parts of the world by customary rights and restrictions that serve as a form of environmental management (B. Agrawal 1992; McCay and Acheson 1990; Johannes 1981). Some scholars have offered excellent in-depth discussions of changing tenurial regimes for land or sea, the implications of differing understandings of "ownership," and the impact of changing technology and forms of economic organization for particular environments (B. Agrawal 1992; Cronon 1983, 1991; McEvoy 1986; Peters 1994).

The goal here, however, is to direct the analytical debates over the "commons" versus private property in a way that highlights the social implications of the coexistence of market and nonmarket practices on Mafia. Even in a country like the United States, which is perceived as the foremost proponent of free market perspectives, natural resources are not solely viewed as commodities or private property. Indeed, the national and state park systems in the United States, as well as the alternate use values for "nature" championed by environmentalists and others, makes this clear. On Mafia, the situation is even more complex. In this region, ideas of "ownership" are a complicated mix of cultural beliefs and practices associated with the historical Indian Ocean trading world, *mila* (i.e., historical coastal practices), Arab colonists, contemporary capitalism, and colonial and post-independence states. This mixture once again demonstrates the inadequacy of ideas of the "traditional" or "indigenous" to make sense of natural resource use (see also Gupta 1998). Furthermore, the ongoing vitality of non-market economic relationships challenges a view of globalization that depicts capitalism as an expanding, inevitable, and all powerful force, a language that is also used to justify an explanation of environmental and socioeconomic relations solely in free market terms (Gibson-Graham 1996; Mitchell 1998). Indeed, "property" and "ownership" mean something very different on Mafia than free market advocates suggest.

Although the Mafia Island Marine Park focuses on the marine environment, Mafia residents view the "ownership" and use of both land and sea in related terms and fail to make an artificial distinction between the two. Indeed, on tiny Chole island where land is both relatively fertile and extremely scarce, terrestrial and marine activities are largely viewed as complementary. When I asked Mzee Bakari to assess the relative value of work on land versus sea, he summed up a common perspective by explaining that farming and fishing do not "quarrel" but rather complement each other, just as men's and women's work do. On Chole, both women and men "farm" (*kulima*) land as well as the sea, albeit to differing degrees.[12] Men fish from boats or with other gear, but also help to clear land for farming, tend their tree crops, and perform such tasks as picking coconuts. Although women most commonly work on land and do most of the planting, weeding, and harvesting of subsistence crops (in addition to tending the smaller number of trees they inherit), they also hunt for octopus, shells, and mollusks in the tidal shallows at low tide. Although fish are currently the primary source of cash on Chole, the crops grown by women both on and off the island, which include potatoes, corn, millet, cassava, rice, beans, squash, cucumbers, and peas, supply much of the basic food needs for their families. This interrelationship between land and sea is also apparent in the life cycles of individuals. For example, younger able-bodied men tend to engage more often in fishing, while older and more prosperous men depend more often upon income brought in by coconut and orange trees.

Like fishing practices, ideas about access to land on Mafia are the result of a complex range of influences. Such influences include ideas of "proprietorship" based on the concept of *wenyeji*, precedents set by Arab plantations, German and British colonial policies, and the transformations associated with the post-independence socialist government. As already mentioned, land in the nonplantation areas of Mafia has historically been held communally by bilateral descent groups or *ukoo*. In the late nineteenth century, the communal tenure of land, which was held by kinship groups that allocated usage rights to members, was challenged in some regions of Mafia by the

Arab-based plantation system. As Fair (2001:121) suggests for neighboring Zanzibar, individuals could own trees, which allowed usufruct rights to the land below the trees, despite the belief that the land itself belonged to God. British colonialism brought a new conception of land that emphasized, not the extraction of tribute as had the Omani state or the wealth of plantation tree crops as had Arab planters, but the idea of sovereignty over the land itself. While the relationship between the colonial authorities and land tenure shifted over time, communally held land was readily appropriated as Crown lands to be held in "trusteeship" for the "natives," who were granted rights of occupancy at the discretion of the colonial government (and with the assumption that land tenure would eventually "develop" toward a private property system (Shivji 1998:2–7). In the post-independence period, the new nation-state, following in the footsteps of the colonial government, similarly claimed jurisdiction over the land for itself. President Nyerere abolished freehold property, that is, the private ownership of land, and claimed all land for the state on behalf of the people, arguing that such actions took their precedent from historic practices of communal land tenure in Africa (1966). As during the period of Omani overlordship, residents, however, could continue to buy and sell trees as private property, giving them usufruct rights to the land below. Although Chole's current residents benefited profoundly from the new land laws of the socialist government, which allowed them to claim rights to the land of Chole's now absentee former owners by clearing and planting crops, such provisions had other impacts as well. Ironically, it attenuated the rights of *ukoo* or kinship groups in other parts of Mafia to communally "own" land, and also undermined their ability to allocate land use or allow the soil to recover by allowing it to remain fallow rather than keeping land in constant use (Caplan 1992).

Other nonmarket dynamics also determined who would gain access to natural resources on Chole. Despite vague assertions by residents on Chole that land could be "bought" or "sold," during the time of my fieldwork, access to land was largely controlled through kin-based or affinal networks. Although land on Chole is not currently allocated by corporate *ukoo* units, some Chole residents suggest that the present situation is similar in that individuals inherit trees through parents and gain the right to use or "borrow" land from them or other relatives. If a person wishes to sell "land" (i.e., by selling trees), members of that person's kin group who live in the adjacent area have first claim in contrast to outsiders. Based on anecdotal evidence, it appeared that selling to outsiders also required the agreement of island elders. For example, a well-liked Zanzibari man who worked doing construction in Chole's camp in the mid-1990s, was informed by Chole's *wazee* (elders) that they would offer him a piece of land if he wished to move to the island with his family. The only people I knew of who actually "bought" trees and hence land on Chole were men who had married women from Chole and had come to live on the island.

Many people on Chole who lacked sufficient land could also appeal to the nonmarket mechanism of "begging" (*kuomba*) land from both relatives and nonrelatives. Given the paucity of land for subsistence crops on Chole, many women commonly "begged" land in Utende, which they used for growing potatoes. During the planting season, such women could often be seen entering the ferry with hoes (*jembe*) in one hand and potato vines in the other. These women were not charged rent for this land, nor, they contended, were their hosts inconvenienced since their potatoes did not interfere with the owners' rice crops grown at other points during the year. Such practices were discussed in terms of mutual assistance and appeared to draw upon a long history of lending and borrowing land as part of patron–client relationships along the coast (Cooper 1980). These practices also held parallels to ideas found in other parts of Tanzania that all persons should have access to land (Feierman 1991). Within such contexts, those who extended aid would not only establish a reputation for generosity—an important component of being a "big person" along the coast—but could also expect reciprocal assistance in the future.

Mafia residents did not believe that land could be used in any way that "owners" saw fit, as more commoditized perspectives might suggest. For example, when I asked one man who worked in Chole's tourism camp whether an "owner" could prevent others from crossing his or her property, he offered a look of disbelief and quickly responded, "That is impossible." He described how, according to "custom" or *mila*, even if an owner blocked a customary footpath, it was necessary for that person to substitute an alternate footpath in order not to cause undue hardship to others. The disparity between this view of "ownership" and more commoditized perspectives also came into play at the Ecotourism Seminar in 1995. There, village representatives protested that the *mzungu* (European) owner of Utende's new hotel had barred residents from access to the property (which he had acquired through an extended lease from the government). However, he had not substituted alternate pathways and had prohibited the use of the beachfront down the bluff from the hotel (despite historical usage in which beaches are always open for landing boats). These worries underscored those expressed by Chole residents in the initial planning stages of Chole Kisiwani tourism enterprise that *wazungu* might desire to "rule" (*tawala*) the island once again and could potentially force them from their land.

Such conceptions of land "ownership" also hold relevance for Chole residents' views of the marine environment. Just as Chole residents sometimes describe the work they do on both land and sea as "farming," there also exists an idea that the communal "proprietorship" of *wenyeji* over the land extends to the sea as well. Whereas marine management officials tend to view the sea as an open access commons, which requires regulation through science and state policies, some scholars have suggested that "traditional" tenurial rights over marine environments offer important means of conservation management for small-scale fishers, thereby decreasing pressure on fish populations and discouraging the competition to overfish (Johannes 1981; McGoodwin 1990; McCay and Acheson 1987; Ruddle and Johannes 1985). Indeed, there are strong ideas of tenurial rights over near-shore waters in many parts of the Pacific and among some other non-Western fishing peoples. However, the situation on Mafia is not so clear-cut. The waters around Mafia are not conceived as an open access environment; however, the concept of being *wenyeji* suggests "proprietorship"—not ownership—of the region. There are no historical norms on Mafia for barring "outside" fishers from Mafia's waters and, according to Chole residents, fishers from other coastal regions such as Kilwa have been freely allowed to fish in Mafia's waters in the past. However, there has been an ideal that "outside" fishers should follow the same norms of appropriate behavior, including the same types of fishing gear, as residents. Indeed, it would seem more accurate to view regional waters, not as a common property resource, but as a "commons" defined and governed by appropriate social behavior. Given the rising number of "outside" fishers, the failure of many of these fishers to comply with such norms or to use legal fishing gear, has presented a disturbing trend for Mafia residents (see also Glaesel 1997). Since residents possess few sanctions other than social pressure, those fishers who exist on the fringes of island social relationships, or outside of such relationships altogether, are effectively beyond "local" social control. It is precisely for this reason that Mafia residents turned to the park for help in managing the marine environment.

At the same time, this "commons" of appropriate social behavior *has* served in the past to help regulate fishing practices in Mafia's waters. As previously mentioned, there have been ongoing efforts by Mafia's elders to control the use of a plant-derived poison, *mtupatupa*, that kills fish but also damages coral reefs. One well-known fisher, Suleimani Rajabu, offered the following account:

> The use of poison for fishing has been considered undesirable for a very long time. Although some people have, nevertheless, used it, there has never been permission for it. It's not only the government that has forbidden it, but villagers themselves have fought very hard to keep fishers from using poison. . . . [Poison] has been forbidden from long ago, and if you were caught with it by the *wazee* [elders], you know, the elders of the past could be very harsh. You could be called before them and beaten with a cane.

Suleimani attributed decreased control over *mtupatupa* in recent years to changing relationships between young and old. He continued:

> But these days, you know, people are more disrespectful. We younger people, there are some of us who are living badly, and we don't listen to our elders. We don't have proper respect for our parents. [The young people] say, "These are things of the past." They are scornful. They go and [use poison] anyway and feel that their lives have improved. Because if they go out to fish with nets, what do they come back with? Nothing! . . . . So some of them do it, but we view fishing by such methods as stealing. They do it when the moon is bright [i.e., clandestinely]. In our traditions, this kind of fishing is not permitted.

As Suleimani suggests, these customary restrictions later came to be overlaid by state measures to control destructive fishing in the post-independence era. For example, the government attempted to enforce marine conservation regulations (with limited effect) by requiring outside fishers to notify village governments and to obtain permits through district government offices.

This "commons" of appropriate social behavior has also placed limits on the degree to which fish can be commodified. For example, Suleimani Rajabu also argued that, historically, one of the few quarrels among fishers concerned *choyo* (greed). He elaborated:

> For example, if you're from Bwejuu or Jibondo, and you're fishing here [near Chole] and you get a lot of fish and, say, that you're at the beach and there are old people and children there who ask you for a fish for their dinner. If you deny them that fish, that is *choyo*. And if you do that, maybe they'll have a meeting and chase you away and not allow you to stay on Chole. They will say that even though you were welcomed here [on Chole], and you caught fish with which to feed your children, you, nevertheless, refused when people here asked you for something to eat. Or perhaps you might try to make them pay for the fish, then again you would be denying them. You will be chased away for that *choyo*.

Like land, fish can also be "begged." During the time I lived on Mafia, it was a common sight to see a fisherman landing on the beach with a canoe full of fish and being instantly mobbed by a dozen or more running women, men, and children, all hoping to obtain a fish. Initially, I simply assumed that people were buying the fish, but I later learned that many people were simply "begging" (*kuomba*) for fish, requests that were difficult for fishers to refuse given the thick layer of kinship and social networks that bound together village residents. Suleimani also explained that many fishers attempted to avoid requests for fish by selling their catch at sea to the iceboat or, alternately, quickly slicing fish into *ng'onda* either in deserted beach areas or on their boats. While dried fish were recognized as commodities intended for market sale (and hence inappropriate objects for such requests), fresh fish were not perceived as fully commodified and hence were subject to norms of gift-giving and generosity.[13]

In general, noncommodified norms of resource use created spaces in which people without access to cash could lay claim to such resources, although not without contestation as Suleimani's account suggests. Such dynamics were not only evident in relation to land and fish, but also surfaced in a refusal to pay for other kinds of goods and services. For example, Mzee Hamisi, the ferry boat captain, often complained that passengers failed to pay the few shillings required for the ride to Utende. Once, sitting amidst a boat full of passengers that he clearly intended to shame, he loudly informed me that he had christened the ferry the "*Hamna Upenzi*," (literally "there is no love") to suggest to passengers, including neighbors and relatives, that everyone was expected to pay his or her own fare. Few, however, took Mzee Hamisi's ill-tempered witticism seriously, a testimony to the recognition that in a context in which all are highly dependent on social networks, few dare to jeopardize such ties by shows of "selfishness" or refusal to help others.

Contestation over market and nonmarket norms of behavior also surfaced in relation to the profits made by merchants. Such norms not only placed limits on the extent to which fish could be commodified, but also on the amount of profit that could be made. One afternoon, a group of workers in Chole's tourism camp, all of whom were former fishers, described how it was often difficult to sell fish both because of the erratic appearances of the Dar es Salaam "ice boat" and because many Chole residents who had sold dried fish or *ng'onda* in Dar es Salaam had since gone bankrupt (*wal-ifilisika*). When I asked why, I was told that they had been punished by God (Mungu). In response to my puzzled look, they elaborated that those residents who had acted as fish merchants paid fishers low prices and then kept secret the selling prices of *ng'onda* in Dar es Salaam. One man, who admitted that he himself was one of the bankrupt fish sellers, agreed with his companions that such hardship was God's punishment for making unseemly profits at the expense of fellow residents.

Thus, we see that for Chole residents, partial commodification works as a social safety net in a context in which none other is available. It is through the ability to "beg" land, fish, ferry rides, and assistance of other kinds that residents survive periods of hardship. Although all residents depend upon such networks, poorer residents (including a disproportionate number of divorced or widowed women) rely upon them most (see also Feierman 1991). In contrast to common neoliberal viewpoints, the contemporary period is not only generating an expansion of the market "sector" but a countersurge of social claims by cash-poor residents in which natural resources are not depicted as commodities, but rather as common resources which can be "begged" and borrowed. In this context, the lack of "nature" as a symbolic construct does not mean a lack of struggle over access to natural resources, although the terms of this struggle may not be easily recognized by Euro-American market supporters or environmentalists.

THE PROBLEMS WITH FISHING AND WORRIES OVER THE PARK

It was in this context of "tough times" or *maisha magumu*, that residents expressed both high hopes and profound worries about the new Mafia Island Marine Park. But what exactly were their hopes and worries, and how did such concerns relate to these broader economic realities? In general, residents' growing dependence upon fishing, and their nervousness about its viability, profoundly shaped their interests in the incipient Mafia Island Marine Park. Fishers hoped that the marine park would buttress their rights as *wenyeji* or the "proprietors" of the area in a context in which they were losing influence over fishing practices in regional waters. At the same time, however, they were aware that management could be a double-edged sword. Although it offered possibilities for greater control over "outside" fishers as well as funding through donor organizations, it also meant the potential for increased regulation of residents themselves—fears fueled by the history of preservationist parks in other parts of Tanzania. Despite promises of "participation," residents were well aware that their claims as *wenyeji* historically meant little in relation to the authority of both colonial and independent states to appropriate natural resources in the name of a paternalistic government.

The hopes and tensions felt by many of Mafia's fishers during the mid-1990s are illustrated by the following incident. On a February day in 1997 toward the end of my stay on Mafia, I served as a translator on a fishing expedition that included both Mafia residents and David Holston, the WWF technical adviser. Holston was interested (as I was) in observing local fishing practices, and Suleimani Rajabu agreed to take him out fishing. As an anthropologist, I assumed that it would be a simple affair—we would tag along in the *mashua* and try to offer as little distraction as possible while the men fished. The logic of getting things done in anthropology, however, differs from that common among donor agencies, and actual events were considerably more dramatic. In the days preceding the expedition, I was asked to translate Holston's request that he be allowed to bring along an underwater camera to film the action of the nets on the sea floor. Suleimani hesitated: he cautiously related that other fishers on Chole had already told him that he was foolish to take Holston on his boat. It was common knowledge that *wazungu* (European) environmentalists opposed the use of seine nets and shark nets (*nyavu ndogo* and *nyavu kubwa* or *jarife*), and they warned that Suleimani could get into trouble. Suleimani added that he had personally been berated by a European tourist on a diving holiday who loudly insisted that he was "destroying the environment" by using such nets. When Holston gave assurances that the fishing trip would not be used against him and expressed his opinion that tourists had no right to lecture residents, Suleimani agreed while subtly making it clear that he was acting on trust.

Suleimani's relative openness stemmed from several factors. He had previously worked assisting the divers of the British Frontier group during their stay on Chole, and he was comfortable with environmentalists and the language of conservation (a familiarity that also allowed him to feel "enlightened" in relation to coresidents). Furthermore, Suleimani was one of the men whose wages for conducting survey work had been embezzled during the early stages of the park's implementation, and he appreciated Holston's efforts to compensate them. Perhaps most crucially, however, Suleimani had an ambitious dream of opening a small tourism establishment on Chole for which he hoped he could apply to the park for funds for small-scale community development, an endeavor in which he hoped Holston would prove an important connection.

On the appointed day, Holston brought with him not only diving equipment and an underwater camera but the glistening *Ukombozi* crewed by two boat hands, and he suggested that, after fishing, Suleimani and the other men might enjoy a ride in the sleek speedboat. Although everyone seemed excited by the possibility of riding in the *Ukombozi*, I also noticed that Suleimani and his crew, which consisted of two nephews and two other companions, grew unusually quiet. Next to the gleaming hull and high tech equipment of the Boston Whaler, the old wooden sailboat which Suleimani and his siblings had inherited seemed suddenly shabby, and I wondered whether I detected a fleeting expression on Suleimani's face indicating embarrassment. He merely noted, however, that due to the lack of wind (it was the end of the *Kaskazi* or northern monsoon season), they had set their *jarife* nets within the bay rather than in the deeper waters where they preferred to use such wide-mesh nets. With the wind barely fluttering the sail of the *mashua*, the fishers settled back in the boat, preparing for a slow trip to the middle of the bay to haul in the nets. However, Holston called for a line to be thrown over and the powerful *Ukombozi* quickly towed the *mashua* to the place where the nets had been set, an ease that further underscored the daily transportation difficulties which Chole residents took for granted.

As Suleimani and his companions began hauling in the *jarife* nets from the water, Holston zipped himself into a diving suit and dove overboard with the expensive underwater camera in hand. As they pulled the nets on board, the crew plucked bits of branching corals that had broken off into the net and tossed them back into the sea, coming only occasionally upon a fish—a stingray, a baby shark, a small grouper. Suleimani related that although *jarife* nets could catch more fish outside the bay, within the bay a standard catch

consisted of only about ten fish. On this day, it was a disappointingly average catch. Perched on the prow of the *Ukombozi*, I translated Suleimani's
commentary to Holston when he surfaced periodically between dives. Holston, more accustomed to the language of activism and science than open-
ended inquiry, asked the skeptical questions that plagued many Euro-Americans: Given the small catch, why did people on Mafia continue to fish? Why
did fishers sell their fish and not simply rely on their catch for food? Even as
I translated for Suleimani and watched him struggle to explain, I was struck
by the difficulties of conveying in a few sentences what fishing meant to
people on Chole. While the trip demonstrated why residents were so concerned about the state of fishing on Mafia, these unspoken tensions also
suggested the worries fishers had about the marine park itself.

Such worries suggest the degree to which marine regulations are not
merely a matter of figuring out how best to do it—a technocentric understanding that fails to convey the economic situation experienced by residents
or the politics that lie at the heart of the park. To communicate a sense of
these worries, I draw upon a range of interviews conducted with fishers on
Chole during the course of my fieldwork. In these interviews, fishers described their hope that the marine park would be able to halt dynamiting
around Mafia. At the same time, they also expressed the vague desire that
the marine park buttress the rights and claims of area fishers as it sought to
bring "development," including jobs in the tourism industry, to Mafia. Worries and fears, however, were expressed almost as quickly as hopes.

From the point in the late 1980s, when the idea for a park first emerged
through its early planning stages in the early 1990s, only limited dialogue
occurred between Mafia residents and marine park planners. During this
time, marine biologists from the Institute of Marine Sciences, including the
authors of the park's original General Management Plan as well as several
Maritime officials, did conduct preliminary discussions with Mafia residents.
The coupling of new community participation ideals with a legacy of regulatory zeal common to both preservationist and conservationist models resulted in an ambivalence among environmental scientists and donor organizations that fueled both residents' hopes and their fears. Marine biologists
expressed concern with environmental degradation caused by coral mining
and shark and seine nets, and they envisioned solutions based on zoning (the
seasonal closing of particular areas to fishing), as well as the regulation of
fishing gear, possibilities that created worries among Mafia residents.

The actual regulations that the marine park would impose, however, remained unclarified, and, indeed, contested during the entire period of my
fieldwork. Although the General Management Plan suggested potential regulations of the marine environment (bargaining that benefits to residents could
be used to gain support for unpopular measures), the WWF technical adviser

who was subsequently installed, David Holston, instead insisted that all regulations would be generated by the villagers themselves who would thus control the restrictions they faced within the park. Holston emphasized to residents that, "The park isn't here to 'forbid' anything but rather to work with residents towards their own goals." However, the acting warden of the marine park, Pius Mseka, placed far greater stress upon the enforcement of regulations among Mafia residents. During the period of the park's implementation, questions over park regulations and their potential effect on islanders instead took a back seat to struggles between the WWF-Mafia staff and the acting warden and his supporters. The resulting void left considerable space for worry among Mafia's residents. As one fisher, Saidi Abdallah, told me early on during the park's implementation, "To tell you the truth, we don't yet know how exactly [the park] will help people, because we don't yet know its real purpose or how it will be brought about."

In general, the fishers with whom I spoke on Chole during this period expressed complex opinions about the marine park and potential regulations. They stressed that people on Chole and the surrounding islands and villages survived by fishing, and they worried that restrictions on fishing would damage their ability, and that of their children, to simply survive. As Mzee Bakari stated, "For those of us here on Chole, because we haven't been able to "study" or get inside the thoughts of those people who started the marine park, of course, we must have doubts. Because, here, we are very dependent on fishing, this is how we feed our children and our people. . . . In our lives, this is central." Some, however, supported the general aims of conservation, arguing that if the number of fish increased people on Mafia would benefit. Abdallah Suleimani, for example, noted:

> The marine park can help because [even] if it is forbidden to fish in certain areas on Mafia . . . after a period, people will again be permitted to fish in that area of the marine park. Places where the number of fish have decreased will be put aside, and that area will be "funga"-ed [i.e, "husbanded"]. This can help us because the fish will again become plentiful in those areas where they used to be in the past. [The park] is able to help by increasing the number of fish.

Mzee Bakari, who had once sold shark teeth in Mombasa and had heard first-hand accounts of coastal marine parks in Kenya also stated that:

> The benefit of a marine park is, for example, what has happened in one area of Kenya which I visited that is on the border with Tanzania. If you fish with handlines (*mishipi*) there, you are arrested. There are real patrols there. The fishermen who live there have a special area to fish where they make their catch. But there is another area where there is no fishing, the fish there are being bred (*kufunga*) and, indeed, those fish are reproducing in large numbers. During the year there are certain special days when they tell fishers that they can go fish there, not with

No connection to the people → [handwritten marginal note]

dynamite but with lines, with nets of both the *nyavu* and *jarife* varieties [i.e., seine nets and shark nets] and so on, and they get a lot of fish which they sell. So they themselves are profiting from this.

The lack of information concerning what regulations might be imposed by the marine park was particularly troubling to residents, since it could mean the difference between being fatally damaged by the park or being helped by it. In interviews, many fishers launched into detailed arguments about regional fishing methods as well as the potential impact of regulations on their activities. Again, their responses were complex: in some cases, they agreed that certain fishing practices were destructive and should be banned; in other cases, they acknowledged potential environmental damage, but argued that restrictions would cause widespread economic hardship; and in still other cases, they argued that assumptions that certain practices were destructive were based on erroneous information.

Mafia's fishers themselves supported restrictions on some fishing practices found among island residents. As previously mentioned, some Mafia residents had historically resorted to the use of the poison *mtupatupa* to kill fish, a practice that had been opposed by island elders for generations. Restrictions on this practice continued to be widely supported by Mafia residents who viewed fish gained by poisoning—much like dynamiting—as the "theft" of natural resources from other residents. Some residents acknowledged that other fishing methods were destructive as well. For example, Suleimani Rajabu, described a fishing technique conducted on foot on an outgoing tide in which fish congregating among the mangroves in shallow water are scared into nets by banging on the coral. Other fishers appeared to oppose this practice as well.

There were widespread worries among Chole residents, however, about potential restrictions on net fishing. Many readily acknowledged that protected species such as turtles might be unintentionally caught in their nets and that nets dragging on the sea floor could break off bits of coral, outcomes over which many environmentalists have expressed concern. Whether or not residents agreed with such assessments, they were widely aware of such impacts. They worried greatly, however, that restrictions on net fishing would pose serious economic hardship. Many noted that fishers specialized in the use of particular gear, whether it was the more recently introduced nylon seine and shark nets (*nyavu ndogo, jarife*) or more "traditional" gear such as handlines (*mishipi*), fence traps (*wando*), and box traps (*madema, ming'onyo*). They argued that requiring fishers to switch their specialization and their type of equipment would pose considerable difficulties and they viewed such restrictions as viable only if adequate replacements could be found which would not entail greatly increased financial expenditures for already economically precarious islanders.

In other cases, however, residents contested potential restrictions because they perceived "outside" views of such practices to be inaccurate. For example, Mzee Bakari argued that coral mining for use on Mafia was less destructive than claimed by park planners because the coral used was usually dead coral rock located near shore rather than live coral from the sea. Indeed, in recent years, an escalation in the mining of live coral, which generates a higher grade of white coral limestone, has resulted, not from the use of island residents, but in response to a government contract to renovate Kilindoni's airstrip, which called for 200 tons of high-grade coral limestone (Andrews 1998). Although the remarkably destructive impact of the airport contract was recognized and criticized within the park's General Management Plan, there was little attempt to recognize more broadly that the "local" dynamics among Mafia's communities were widely affected by national and international events.

In general, I was struck by the willingness, even eagerness, with which Chole's fishers sought to discuss and debate such issues. Mzee Bakari seemed eager to debate whether the idea of imposing fishing seasons was made redundant by the limitations already posed by monsoon winds (during *Kusi*, or the southerly winds, residents were unable to fish outside the bay). Others pondered the potential for miscommunication. Saidi Abdallah wondered whether, if areas were restricted, boats that were simply passing over these areas to other fishing grounds would be harassed. Ibrahim Hassani described to me how he had been stopped by Natural Resource officers and the difficulties he had in explaining fishing methods to officers who were ignorant of coastal fishing practices and unaware of the variety of ways in which particular gears might be used. In short, within this willingness to talk, there appeared ample room for negotiation among residents, who themselves debated these issues and suggested potential compromises.

What was lacking, however, was anyone with whom to discuss these opinions. According to some residents, initial planning visits by IMS and Maritime officials were too short and did not involve talking with villagers in the "customary" way (*kwa kawaida*) that coastal residents saw as important in making public decisions. Mzee Bakari complained that the men from Chole who accompanied planners on their fishing trips were too young and eager to please, and that speaking with elders with more authority would have been more appropriate. In general, the claims that the marine park would work with residents in a "participatory" manner in order to address conservation issues were put on hold as district, national, and international institutions struggled over the nature of the incipient park. In short, residents were, ironically, forced to offer their support for the park as a package deal without knowing what the contents of that package would be.

While the contents of future regulations were a primary concern for residents living within the Mafia Island Marine Park, they also worried about the politics of the marine park itself. Such issues direct the discussion away from the technocentric terrain of regulations and their effectiveness to questions of power—who would be determining and enforcing such regulations within the park and at whose expense? While Mafia residents hoped that the marine park could help end dynamiting, they also worried that Maritime officers associated with the marine park would prove to be the unlikely instruments for such ends. For residents, the issue was not whether Maritime and Natural Resource Officers possessed the "capacity" to halt dynamiting (the reason given for the continuation of dynamiting by both the government and international organizations), but whether such officials possessed the will to do so. When I asked Abdallah Suleimani in the days before the *Ukombozi* arrived on Mafia whether residents had faith that District Natural Resource officers (of which "Maritime" is a subdivision) could stop dynamiting, he explained:

AS: [Residents] don't really have faith because they [Natural Resources officers] are "cooperating" [*wanashirikiana*] with those who are doing the destruction. People from Maritime and the illegal fishers are cooperating together, and the reason I'm saying this is because they are in communication. They understand each other. Whenever the dynamiters come, they always go to a different area. They stay on this island or that island. When [Maritime] goes on patrol, they are able to see them. They understand each other. They talk a little, some money is left, and then the patrol goes to another area. Indeed, this is the issue that is causing problems in trying to halt dynamite fishing, because they are operating together with those from Maritime.

CW: I've heard others say the same things. If you think this sort of thing is happening, do you think that the marine park will be able to go well in the future? Or will there be problems?

AS: This isn't an easy question. Because the people from Maritime are the same as those from the marine park. They understand each other, they talk to each other, they are in agreement with each other. So concerning the issue of illegal fishing, it isn't easy for them to try to do something about this.

Mzee Bakari, in an interview conducted during the same period, also expressed worries about marine park leadership. He noted bitterly that those who were supposed to be "protecting the fish" on Mafia would instead:

stay inside their nice houses, taking naps after they have received their salaries, [while] those who intend to dynamite come and steal the fish and then go on their way. The news is brought to them [the Maritime Division] that the fish are being stolen, but by that time the dynamiters have already left. There is no protection. However, if there were real patrols, then they could catch them right away and there would be no problem at all. What we say among ourselves is that maybe this kind of thing is a result of the "big people" themselves, if you understand what I mean. Those boats that are coming to do the dynamiting, maybe they are operating in conjunction with the "big people" themselves, [such as] those who are getting the money and profiting [like] those at "Mali Asili" [the Natural Resources Department]. However, they do so by secret means. Indeed, those who are coming to do such things [as dynamiting] are "feeding" them [i.e., bribing the "big people"].

Regarding the marine park he had learned about in Kenya, he noted with some wonder that: "Nothing at all [illegal] gets into that marine park—I don't know what the government people are getting that makes them do their work like this [so well]. But this is the way it is." He finished this account with a worried comparison to Mafia's situation, speaking at length about what he perceived as government Natural Resources officers' complicity in dynamiting, which could undermine any attempts at conservation. He, nevertheless, ended on a positive note: "If this state of things [i.e., corruption] is overcome, and if there are patrols and [the dynamiters] are truly being caught, then there will be no problem. We ourselves will profit because there will be fish which we will be able to procure ourselves."

Thus, in the face of an increasingly grave economic situation, the Mafia Island Marine Park promised regulations that residents both wished for and feared. Recalling the social drama of the marine park outlined in Chapter One, Chole residents hoped that the marine park would halt the practice of dynamite fishing, even as they expressed concerns about those who were leading such endeavors. Yet, they also feared future park regulations. Indeed, such concerns foreshadow the controversies that would envelop the park in later years, as the epilogue to this book attests. More generally, the worries regarding the marine park expressed by Mafia's fishers point to the necessity of understanding regulatory regimes in relation to broader economic, social and political contexts. Indeed, it is only in relation to such broader contexts, as the preceding chapters suggest, that the full meaning of the social drama of the marine park becomes clear.

PART THREE

Establishing Experts: Conservation and Development from Colonialism to Independence

IN AN EFFORT to provide the context necessary to understand the social drama of the Mafia Island Marine Park from the point of view of island residents, previous chapters have discussed the historical narratives told by Chole residents, considered sources of "community" ties as well as social discord, and examined residents' ideas and practices regarding "nature" and natural resources. It is also necessary however, to explore in greater depth the relationship between island residents and the marine park itself. In essence, the marine park is a bureaucratic entity that has been built upon—and is understood in terms of—a long history of natural areas, conservation policies, development initiatives, and ideas about knowledge within East Africa. Consequently, the current chapter considers the history of national parks and conservation and development policies within Tanzania, while subsequent chapters will explore the social dynamics and knowledge production associated with park bureaucracy, as well as the economic implications of the park's focus on ecotourism as a "development" strategy. In short, part 3 of this book makes it possible to further understand the social drama of the Mafia Island Marine Park by offering a sociological exploration of the park itself.

An examination of the history of national parks and conservation and development within Tanzania offers insight into how and why the Mafia Island Marine Park came to be experienced, understood, supported, and reacted against in particular ways by Mafia residents, national government officials and Euro-American representatives of environmental NGOs. This history also demonstrates that geographic links between widely separated regions have been central to conservation and development policies in East Africa since their inception. While mainstream globalization narratives imply that the realities of power operating across vast distances is a phenomenon uniquely pervasive in the contemporary period (as epitomized, for example, by the swelling numbers of international organizations and multinational corporations), this history reminds us that power-at-a-distance was even more crucial during the period of European colonialism and has always been an integral part of conservation and development policies in this region. Once again, the point of documenting such history is not simply to force a recognition that "global" dynamics existed in the past (clearly such dynamics did exist if we define the term in any meaningful kind of way). Rather, its importance lies in documenting some of the historical institutions, ideas and relationships that have shaped the contemporary social drama of the Mafia Island Marine Park—whether through ongoing institutional structures or still-influential beliefs or, alternately, as a form of reaction against this legacy. In sum, rather than epitomizing the "newness" of a global era, this drama demands an exploration of the past.

A History of Conservation and Development in Tanzania

Preservationism and the Rise of African Game Reserves

In contemporary Tanzania, approximately one-quarter of the land surface is under some form of nature protection and 14 percent has been formally declared either national parks or reserves, an extraordinarily high figure in contrast to many other countries (Neumann 1998:4). As already mentioned, the Mafia archipelago was itself the site of "paper" marine reserves established in the 1970s. It is also situated opposite the mainland's Selous Game Reserve, which constitutes the largest protected natural area on the entire African continent and which rivals Switzerland in size (Neumann 1998:145). Thus, it is hardly surprising that contestation over parks and reserves in other parts of Tanzania, both in the past and in the present, formed a backdrop to the worries expressed by Chole residents about Mafia's marine park. Historically, Tanzania's national parks and colonial-era game reserves had their origins in European conceptions of nature (albeit conceptions that had in turn been shaped by European images of the non-Western world).[1] Such understandings reflect socially stratified natural resource use in European societies historically dominated by aristocracies, as well as the impact of changing understandings of "nature" in the nineteenth and early twentieth century as capitalist social relationships transformed the metropole. As expressed in Tanganyika's game reserves and natural areas, both of these perspectives on nature worked to expropriate rural Africans from rights to natural resources—a legacy that the Mafia Island Marine Park has both inherited and sought to critique.

Game reserves were first established in mainland Tanganyika by the Germans in the late nineteenth century and were later expanded by the British after Great Britain assumed Tanganyika as a League of Nation's trusteeship territory in the post–World War I era. The fascinating history of colonial-era reserves in East Africa has been explored by such scholars as John MacKenzie (1987, 1988) and Roderick Neumann (1992, 1996, 1998, 2000). This history suggests that such reserves cannot be fully understood apart from the historical role that hunting, poaching, and game laws played in Europe. Indeed, hunting privileges and the depiction of nonelites as "poachers" were primary fault lines along which social hierarchies played out in Europe, a history that was transferred in racialized form to the colonies (Hay et al. 1975; Thompson 1975; MacKenzie 1988; Neumann 1996). In England, the enclosure of common land and its transformation into private property owned in large measure by aristocrats and other elites emerged as a central conflict accompanying the rise of capitalism (Thompson 1975; Polanyi 1944; Humphries 1990). The commons had included, not only rights to farm and graze, but also to hunt. As part of the broader process of curtailing villagers' customary rights, aristocrats during this period sought to expand their hunting privileges as well as those game areas reserved for their exclusive use. Tellingly, it was precisely at the point when the enfranchisement of the masses in the nineteenth century began to challenge aristocratic prerogatives that poaching and game laws from England and other European countries were transferred to their colonies (Neumann 1996; MacKenzie 1988). Within this context, East Africa and Asia emerged as the new hunting grounds for the privileged, while ritualized aspects of what MacKenzie refers to as "The Hunt" were reinvented as important cultural markers of social status, masculinity, and alleged racial superiority in a colonial world (1987, 1988).

Like the Swahili coastal caravan trade, the earliest European hunting in East Africa centered around a lucrative ivory market and was conducted for reasons of economic gain and, later, to provide meat for soldiers. The rise of the region's game reserves, however, was also linked to the establishment of white, and particularly aristocratic, privilege (MacKenzie 1988, 1987). The formal establishment of European colonies in Africa in the late nineteenth century offered the wealthy access to exotic forms of wildlife and, beginning in the 1890s, elites from France, Germany, Austria, Britain, and the United States regularly traveled to Kenya to hunt. Many colonial officials were themselves hunters and viewed hunting as important for maintaining morale and instilling the sense of superiority and mission they felt necessary for colonial officers. As MacKenzie argues, in the nineteenth century, hunting become a crucial aspect of imperial culture: "An imperial and largely masculine elite attempted to reserve for itself access to hunting, adopted and transformed the concept of the Hunt as a ritual of prestige and dominance, and set about the separation of the human and animal worlds to promote 'preservation' (later 'conservation') as a continuing justification of its monopoly" (MacKenzie 1988:22).

The expansion of elite European hunting inevitably meant the marginalization of Africans living in affected regions and varying degrees of exclusion from rights to natural resources. Rural Africans were systematically denied rights to hunt either by outright prohibition or by game laws designed to exclude them (for example, through requirements that necessitated expensive hunting licenses or that game be shot with a gun) (MacKenzie 1988; Neumann 1998). Accusations that Africans were abusive of animals and im-

[handwritten margin note: like the fishers on Mafia]

provident with nature also offered widespread justification for their exclusion and for the need for colonial regulation. For example, African hunting methods were depicted as "cruel," while the idea of hunting for food rather than sport was perceived as base by elite Europeans (MacKenzie 1987; Adams and McShane 1992). In short, those Africans who hunted as part of their livelihood came to be systematically redefined as "poachers." Although this situation mirrored the exclusion of Europe's lower classes from hunting privileges at home, the racialized logic of the colonial encounter meant that the situation in Africa was taken to far greater extremes. Indeed, in a few cases, the boundaries between animals and those human beings deemed "primitives" by Europeans were entirely erased. MacKenzie notes, for example, that one of the earliest aristocratic hunters in Kenya, the German Count Teleki boasted that he had "shot 35 elephants and 300 niggers" (1988:161), while Sir Claude Champion Crespigny wrote of stalking humans and of killing one hundred Africans (cited in Adams and McShane 1992:28).

Although the ritual logic of "The Hunt" was based on aristocratic European precedents, ideas of nature were also being transformed by the expanding logic of capitalism. In England, like many other European countries, nature over the course of the nineteenth and twentieth centuries came to be increasingly seen as something separate from people and as symbolically opposed to the "modern" world (Williams 1973). Dominant viewpoints maintained that nature must be "tamed" or exploited in order to promote capitalistic progress (provoking reactions from others who sought to redefine nature in spiritual terms as "wilderness" or as a threatened domain that required paternalistic protection [Cronon 1996]). While the Hunt was based on ideals of sportsmanlike behavior in which men proved their masculinity in "fair" contests with animals, such elite ideals were often supplanted by an emphasis on firepower and a profligate attitude toward nature, which formed one cultural thread of European and North American economic and political expansion. For example, tales of the mass slaughter of animals by Euro-Americans, not only on hunting safaris in the "bush," but also from the safety and comfort of moving trains are common (MacKenzie 1988; Adams and McShane 1992). Former U.S. president Teddy Roosevelt, who traveled to East Africa in 1909 with his son Kermit, offers a telling example. Game regulations were waived for this "hunter-naturalist" and Roosevelt and his son shot 512 head of large game (including nine white rhinoceros), a carnage that disturbed even his hunting guide (MacKenzie 1988:162; Adams and McShane 1992:27). Yet, in an ironic twist, European hunters often blamed Africans for the rapid decrease in game animals (MacKenzie 1988). In 1929, for example, Lord Cranworth argued before the British House of Lords that:

> More animals have been killed [in Africa] to fill the native stomach than have been killed from the previous cause [white sport hunting] without any doubt. . . . the

native is perfectly capable of eating 14 to 16 pounds and even 20 pounds of meat straight on end. . . . No doubt eating with the native becomes almost a craze (cited in Neumann 1996:17).

European hunter Frederick Selous also claimed that 997 of every thousand elephants were killed by Africans (Adams and MacShane 1992:46). Although it is unclear from these accounts how the expansion of international ivory markets affected the frequency of African hunting,[2] such accounts ignore the role, either direct or indirect, which Europeans played in such transformations.

Over time, the rationale for the exclusion of Africans from the reserves shifted from ideas of aristocratic and racial privilege to a concern with the preservation of nature couched in scientific terms (even Teddy Roosevelt's East African hunting trip was ostensibly a mission to collect specimens on behalf of the Smithsonian Institution). In general, as the numbers of animals in Africa dwindled, European calls for preservation greatly expanded. Beginning in the 1920s, such calls began to take the shape of demands for an East African national parks system that would be partially modeled upon Yellowstone National Park in the United States. Some elite former hunters also moved to the forefront of the preservationist movement. For example, Neumann documents the history of what was arguably the first international wildlife organization, the Society for the Preservation of the Fauna of the Empire (SPFE) nicknamed by British skeptics the "Penitent Butcher's Club" (1996). (Interestingly, Neumann also notes that several elite leaders of the SPFE were instrumental in the creation of the IUCN (then IUPN), from which WWF would emerge as an offshoot [Neumann 1996: ftn.17].) The SPFE would prove to be a powerful and well-connected organization that would have a strong impact on colonial policy in Tanganyika. In 1933, the SPFE in London brokered an agreement designed to encourage the establishment of national parks in British colonies, and the Serengeti was declared to be Tanganyika's first national park in 1948.

Whereas restrictions had been common since the earliest game reserves, the shift to national parks meant increasing exclusion for rural residents. Indeed, many colonial officials in Tanganyika themselves opposed the establishment of national parks fearing it would create large-scale economic hardship and lead to political instability (Neumann 2000). However, pressure from groups like the SPFE and colonial offices in London, ultimately, prevailed. Although the SPFE opposed human settlement in East Africa's parks, it did concede that residents then living within proposed park boundaries would be allowed to stay, provided they remained in their "primitive" state (with the trustees of the Serengeti in the early 1950s going so far as to describe the pastoralist Maasai as "fauna" within the park [Neumann 2000: 125]).[3] However, park regulations would become progressively stricter over time and the rights legally retained by Africans would in practice often be denied by park officials (Neumann 1998, 2000). Even the Maasai were eventually ejected from Serengeti national park in 1959 and only permitted within the reconstituted conservation area at Ngorongoro. In the end, large numbers of rural residents faced mass evictions, the denial of both customary and legal rights, and systematic harassment, thereby setting the stage for conflicts that would continue until the present day (Neumann 1992, 1998, 2000; Adams and McShane 1992; MacKenzie 1988; Hodgson 2001; Honey 1999).

Yet, the expansion of national parks and protected areas—as well as the forced relocation of rural residents—would continue after Tanganyika gained its independence in 1961 as wildlife tourism became a lucrative source of foreign exchange for the financially strapped new country (Neumann 1992).[4] Three months before the country's independence in 1961, Julius Nyerere, then prime minister of Tanganyika, delivered the Arusha Manifesto at a conference hosted by WWF-IUCN in support of conservation in new African nation-states.[5] In this talk, which was enthusiastically received by environmental organizations, Nyerere declared: "In accepting trusteeship of our wildlife we solemnly declare that we will do everything in our power to make sure that our children's grandchildren will be able to enjoy this rich and precious inheritance" (as cited in Neumann 1998:140). He then called on international organizations to aid in such efforts. Although this statement is still cited as an example of Third World commitment to preservationism, in actuality this speech was written by leaders of WWF-International (Neumann 1998:140; Honey 1999:225). Nyerere himself made clear that the importance of preservation in Tanzania's game parks was as a source of foreign exchange for the incipient nation-state. He stated, "I personally am not very interested in animals. I do not want to spend my holidays watching crocodiles. Nevertheless, I am entirely in favor of their survival. I believe that after diamonds and sisal, wild animals will provide Tanganyika with its greatest source of income. Thousands of Americans and Europeans have the strange urge to see these animals" (Neumann 1998:144, quoting Nash 1982:342).

The shift to tourism within East Africa's wildlife reserves emerged during the 1920s through 1940s as mass tourism began to appear in other parts of the world. Indeed, over the course of the twentieth century, middle-class Euro-Americans would increasingly seek refuge from the stresses of "modern" urban life in communion with nature and wildlife. In contrast to earlier elite European hunters who had traveled to East Africa in search of animal heads as safari trophies, later Euro-Americans began visiting the wildlife reserves with cameras rather than guns in hand (see Sontag 1973; Haraway 1989). However, Tanzania's national parks and nature areas hold a very different meaning for its citizens than national parks in countries like the United States. The latter have largely been middle-class phenomena offering recreational spaces for a broad mass of the population with access to cars and cameras. The overwhelming majority of Tanzanians, however, continue to be rural rather than urban dwellers and lack the disposable income required for recreational tourism. They may also not necessarily perceive "nature" as something exotic and deserving of special visits (on the contrary, those living in close proximity to national parks may be most concerned with the dangers presented by wild animals). In short, Tanzania's parks exist overwhelmingly for the enjoyment of wealthy tourists from Europe and the United States and are popularly associated by East Africans with the alienation of land and natural resources. While some "poachers" within East Africa's parks and reserves are currently backed by business and political elites or international rings, other "poachers" are rural residents either hunting on lands from which they have been dispossessed or violently resisting restrictions on their herds (Neumann 1998; Adams and McShane 1992).

In recent years, the dynamics associated with parks and reserves have once again begun to shift as the history of such areas comes under increasing international criticism for what are now considered to be human rights abuses. In response, environmental NGOs, in partnership with government bodies, have begun to push for "community-based" conservation (Neumann 2000). There have also been widespread calls to make parks and reserves "pay," not simply for governments, but for communities that live in or near natural areas and which deal with the day-to-day dangers posed by close proximity to wildlife (Adams and McShane 1992). It is also important to recognize, however, that while nature reserves and national parks have historically been associated with the dispossession of rural Tanzanians, these natural areas are also currently under siege by businesses and wealthy individuals seeking their own advancement. For instance, Shivji offers the example of an Irish company that was given approval to occupy land in the midst of a wildebeest migration path in 1991. The intent of the company was to slaughter the animals as they crossed the property in order to procure red meat for distribution to Europeans (Shivji 1998:34–36). In short, the important issue in trying to understand the environmental politics surrounding natural areas is not the existence of national parks per se, but rather the underlying power relationships at work that determine who controls, gains access to, and benefits from natural resources. Although the contemporary period is one in which national parks and reserves are in flux—a changing climate that is apparent in the rationale for the Mafia Island Marine Park—it is, as yet, unclear what the impact of such reforms will be for rural Africans, including those living on Mafia.

The Relationship between Conservation and
  Development in Tanganyika

While the language of preservation that emerged around wildlife reserves in East Africa emphasized the need to maintain rigid distinctions between nature and human beings (and would remain an ongoing preoccupation of Europeans in the metropole), the realities of colonial administration in the region inevitably meant dealing with the large numbers of people who lived there. For colonial officials, day-to-day policies regarding "nature" from the 1930s until independence were largely concerned, not with preservation, but with conservation or the regulation of the economic relationship between Africans and their environment. Unlike preservation, which stressed the segregation of humans from "nature," conservation policies sought to husband natural resources in a way that ensured their economic productivity. While preservation was largely the domain of game wardens, naturalists, and former hunters, conservation would be the province of bureaucrats and agricultural experts. MacKenzie suggests that the rising importance of conservation policies in African colonies can also be associated with a demographic shift in the backgrounds of colonial officials. Although many of the colonial officials who had strongly emphasized "The Hunt" had been aristocratic elites, those interested in conservation often had more diverse political and economic backgrounds and concerns, marking what he refers to as a shift from aristocrats to "progressives" (MacKenzie 1988).

In popular discussions today, conservation and development are often conceived in opposing terms—creating a tension that the language of "sustainable development" presents itself as surmounting. However, from the 1920s onward, the framework of conservation was strongly linked to incipient ideas of "development" in British colonial Africa and was based on ideas that the "rational" use of natural resources would lead to economic well-being (see also Hodgson 2001). Historically, links between what would now be called conservation and development were not, in fact, unusual, as nineteenth century French and German forestry policies (which had a strong effect in the United States through the conservationist Gifford Pinchot) as well as the "wise use" movement makes clear (McCormick 1989). Although British colonial policy oscillated between the demand for greater economic productivity and the worry that cash cropping and markets corrupted the "traditional" lifeways of Africans and led to famine (Illife 1979; Spear 1996; Vaughan 1987), various historical factors contributed to the growing emphasis on economic productivity and the "rational" use of natural resources in the colonies. One of these factors was the financial difficulty faced by the metropole itself as a result of the 1930s world depression, the high costs of World War II, and postwar efforts to rebuild. Despite the terms of the trusteeship mandate, which stipulated that Tanganyika territory was to be held in trust for, and for the benefit of, its people, the British responded to this situation not only by containing spending (a long-standing policy in Tanganyika), but by economically squeezing the region (Illife 1979; Shivji 1998:4; Hodgson 2001).

At the same time, budding independence movements, particularly in the post–World War II era, mounted serious challenges to colonial governments. Although in some cases such challenges were met by force (as was the case with the Mau Mau movement in neighboring Kenya), in general there was an attempt to counter such movements by emphasizing the role that colonial paternalism could play in improving African lives and economic well-being through "development" and "nation-building" policies (Cooper and Packard 1997; Hodgson 2001). The ideas of "development" that emerged from such policies were also strongly shaped by the ascendency of Keynesian economics from the 1930s through the 1950s, which envisioned "national economies" as bounded objects that could be made to "grow," not by external expansion (such as adding new territory), but by policies internal to a particular region (Mitchell 1995, 1998). Since most Africans in Tanganyika lived by farming or herding, colonial efforts to increase economic productivity and "development" were inextricably linked to conservation policies and included widespread efforts to control soil erosion and to maintain cattle herds (Maddox et al. 1996; Anderson and Grove 1987; Hodgson 2001).

Africa's needs

Although the language of "development" was rapidly coopted by African independence leaders and became a rallying cry for greater economic equality in a postcolonial world (Cooper and Packard 1997), conservation measures often provoked resistance and anger in Tanganyika and elsewhere and helped to foster the growing anticolonial movements (Maack 1996; Maddox et al. 1996; Anderson and Grove 1987; Hodgson 2001). This section explores why this might have been the case and considers how conservation and development policies were not only linked by a common focus on economic productivity but also by a common faith in scientized and managerial models premised on expert opinion and centralized authorities. Mirroring European stereotypes of things "modern" as opposed to "traditional," such models emphasized the importance of expert opinions based on Western-oriented science and downplayed the popular knowledge of rural residents regarding the environment (a topic that will be further explored in the following chapter). These models also opened up a space for both the colonial and postcolonial states to extend regulation of residents' relationships with the environment in the name of providing utilitarian benefits.

According to Chole residents, the office of Agricultural Officer (or Bwana Shamba in KiSwahili) first appeared on Mafia during the German colonial period. This official was described as a person largely preoccupied with measuring land plots for the German coconut plantations that gradually superceded Arab ones on Mafia's main island. Mzee Bakari recalled how the plantation of an older female relative of his had been alienated at that time in order to allow a German plantation to obtain the neat, straight boundaries so craved by Europeans. In general, however, contemporary discussions of colonial agricultural policies focused on the post–World War I British period, which lasted until independence. During this period, colonial officials demanded that Mafia residents weed their coconut plantations and stop clearing land with fire (along with other directly economic policies such as the injunction to grow "famine" crops like cassava). Chole residents also describe being forced to make *mabiwi* or piles of leaves and branches, which were used as mulch, as well as *matuta* or dirt mounds in which they planted crops such as cassava. Mzee Bakari argued along with Fatuma Fadhili that many residents abandoned constructing *matuta* because this practice attracted pests such as "wild" rats (*buku, panya mwitu*), lizards, millipedes, snails, and guinea-fowls (*kanga*) which destroyed their crops. He also noted that British agricultural officers insisted that residents dip cattle (ostensibly to fight livestock diseases and parasites), a policy that many Mafia residents also resisted. Mzee Bakari contended that cattle were sent into the dip in an erratic and dangerous manner that could cause pregnant cows to give birth and others to become injured. Consequently, he suggested that if a person had ten cows, he or she might send only two to the dip and hide or refuse to send the rest.

Numerous scholars have described the often highly unpopular conservation measures of the British colonial era, which largely focused on soil conservation and cattle policies (for example, Feierman 1990; Maack 1996; Spear 1996; Hodgson 2001). In the post-1930s era in particular, colonial policy exhibited a pronounced emphasis on antisoil erosion measures that some argued had less to do with the particular realities of Tanganyika than with the influence of the "Dust Bowl" phenomenon in the United States on European policymakers (Beinart 1987:17). Colonial officials themselves often preferred to ignore the role that land appropriation for European settlers played in creating erosion by forcing too many people on smaller and often unsuitable areas of land (Hodgson 2001). Instead, officials focused on a range of causes attributable to Africans including the following: too many animals in limited areas, shifting cultivation, the burning of bush and trash, the cultivation of slopes, and the failure to construct erosion barriers (Illife 1979:473). Consequently, colonial policy sought to encourage such measures as constructing tie ridges and terraces to prevent erosion in agricultural areas and the dipping and culling of cattle herds (Maack 1996, Feierman 1990).

In many areas, including Mafia, rural residents resisted such measures, not because environmental issues were not a cause for concern, but because the policies being advocated were considered to be ill advised or counter-productive. In general, agricultural advice was based on generic models that did not necessarily conform to the geographical requirements of particular regions and that was often inaccurate. For example, resistance to cattle dipping has been widely acknowledged throughout colonial Tanganyika. Andrew Coulson noted that some pastoralists resisted efforts to force them to dip their cows, arguing that dipping decreased their herds—a realistic appraisal given that irregularly dipped cattle possess a greater susceptibility to disease

(1982:54). James Scott has also noted that ridging as a soil erosion measure is not economically or ecologically sound in all contexts. For example, on sandy soils ridging is unstable, leading to erosion gullies in the rainy season and causing the soil to dry out more quickly in the dry season (Scott 1998:227). Coulson notes that in Uluguru, terraced land was found to be sterile and that rice yields were often better on unterraced lands (Coulson 1982:54). Thomas Spear describes how British Agricultural Officers argued up until the early 1950s that coffee and bananas should be grown separately in the northeastern highlands, despite residents' (accurate) appraisal that intercropping resulted in higher yields and that customary farming methods offered comparable protection against erosion to the laboriously constructed terraces advocated by policymakers (Spear 1996:228–9).

In addition, conservation policies at times had unintended social implications that scientifically based models proved incapable of recognizing. For example, Steven Feierman detailed the unacknowledged social impact of soil erosion policies in the Shambaa region (1990). In Shambaa, the work required to construct ridges to prevent erosion radically increased the work load of farmers, particularly women. It also redefined ridged land as "improved" land, which was generally reserved for cash crops grown by men. Women and poor men who lacked sufficient land had in the past been able to borrow farmland from neighbors rent-free. The owners of ridged land, however, became increasingly reluctant to lend such valuable land. Forced requirements to construct ridges meant that if a poor person borrowed land, he or she would have to build tie ridges, investing in another person's land, while also ensuring that this now improved land would be taken out of circulation for lending in the future (Feierman 1990:182–3). Consequently, women and the poor offered the loudest opposition to soil conservation measures since such policies heightened their own marginalization and meant an increasingly precarious economic existence.

Such dynamics raise an obvious question: Why did colonial officers fail to recognize such outcomes? Clearly, some colonial officials were aware of such problems and the idea of relying upon "experts" as a panacea had been challenged beginning in the preceding German colonial administration. For example, the German governor, Albrecht von Rechenberg, was said to have despised agricultural experts whom he felt knew far less about "peasant" farming than those they were supposed to instruct (Illife 1969:70). In a debate over whether the salvation of African farming lay in the introduction of iron plows to replace hoes (a scheme Rechenberg thought utopian since most farmers could not afford animals to pull the plows even in areas where the absence of tsetse fly allowed for herd animals), he was told that the solution lay with increasing the number of veterinary officers. His response: "Are the vets to pull the ploughs?" (Illife 1969:70). Similarly, some colonial officials in the British era, often district officials with long histories in particular regions, did recognize the contradictions posed by colonial conservation policies (Spear 1996; Hodgson 2001). For example, in a colonial file labeled "community development" (which tellingly was largely concerned with "conservation" policies), a 1952 report from Mbulu District suggests the reasons that agricultural policies were unpopular. The British author of the report reminded his superiors that government policy had been to insist upon strip cultivation in which 50 percent (later 30%) of the land would remain fallow. However, he noted that the results of a government-run experimental farm confirmed the criticisms of residents, namely that this form of cultivation made it "extraordinarily difficult" to protect against damage from birds and that the fallow areas served to introduce "undesirable" grasses and weeds, which made rebreaking the land extremely difficult.[6] In general, however, such officials remained subordinate to the decisions of policymakers in Dar es Salaam and London who themselves had little or no knowledge of specific locations and who might have political stakes in advocating particular policies regardless of their actual efficacy in these regions.

In addition, the technocentric frameworks in which conservation and development policies were couched also served to obscure social relationships and to downplay the popular knowledge of rural residents while buttressing the opinions of formally trained experts. According to Feierman, British colonial officials viewed erosion as a technical problem, denying its social and political origins in scarcities of land and labor (Feierman 1990:163; Hodgson 2001). Generalizable rules and managerial solutions common to such frameworks also implied a reliance upon generic solutions. For example, much like contemporary development and conservation projects, colonial conservation policies were often based on events happening in other colonies or regions that had captured the interest of policymakers (for example, the "Dust Bowl" in the United States). In addition, technocentric models intersected with a particular narrative of modernity that depicted Africans as traditional and conservative and that viewed "modern" (i.e., European) practices as inherently superior and progressive. For example, colonial records routinely depict Africans as hindered from "progress" by a lack of knowledge, by conservative predispositions and by laziness. Colonial records from 1950s Tanganyika assert that development and conservation schemes require "the gradual conquest of popular opposition, conservatism and plain laziness" and a "changed mental attitude among the people."[7] Thus, in the words of a prominent agriculturalist, "the African must be compelled to help himself" (as cited in Illife 1979:473).

To a surprising degree, such viewpoints were equally apparent in the post-independence era after 1961. Despite the new celebratory language associated with independence, colonial agricultural policies largely remained in force (including policies that had been protested as part of the anticolonial movement). At the same time, the emphasis on productivity through "hard work" increased since it was seen as the only way a poor nation could realistically gain "development." For example, a letter to the Mafia District Development Committee from the new (African) Regional Commissioner in June of 1962 noted:

> these committees [District and Village Development Committees] have already been formed and have started embarking upon different important projects which will help in raising up the lives of the people of Tanganyika. Such projects are indispensable for a new nation such as Tanganyika. It is evident, and the whole world knows that Tanganyika attained its UHURU [freedom] only in December last year after being a SLAVE for 75 years.
>
> Our most important task now is to encourage productivity. So in my Regional Development Committee of 7th July, 1962, we all agreed on early planting and stressed that steps should be taken to see that every farmer prepares his shamba [fields] before the rains and is ready to grow cash-crops as well as food-crops as soon as the rains start. This applies not only to people in shamba but also to the people living in towns especially those who have no proper occupations. I therefore order that every body, man and woman, should grow the following cash crops: [Here acreage of crops such as cotton are listed for various regions]
>
> Every farmer in Kisarawe, Bagamoyo, Mafia and Rufiji areas should start weeding their coconut plantations and cutting down the old unproductive trees replacing them with new ones. This must be done by following the agricultural officers advice. They must also do the same with cashew trees.
>
> With regard to people living in the valleys [presumably including Mafia's main island] each one of them must grow at least one acre of rice.

The commissioner then ordered district authorities to take steps against "lazy and idle" people, "indisorderly" fellows and drunkards.[8]

Such policy statements capture both the excitement and high expectations of the independence era as well as the continuation of authoritarian measures from the colonial era, which assumed that rural residents must be compelled to be "good" farmers. According to Coulson, policies from this era continued to be "justified by an appeal to modernization theory. The view that peasants are primitive, backward, stupid—and generally inferior human beings . . . provides ideological support for an otherwise insecure class of the educated, causing them to believe that they, rather than workers or peasants, have the answers to the problems of development" (1982:161). This analysis is not meant to suggest that "experts" never offered useful advice or to take the romanticized position that rural residents had perfect knowledge about their environments (see chapter 6). However, this analysis does suggest that for both the colonial and postcolonial governments, the focus on technocentric and managerial solutions to conservation and development intersected with highly centralized and authoritarian state structures and served to discredit and render invisible the popular knowledge possessed by rural Africans.

Although both preservation and conservation policies in Tanganyika focused on the environment, the conflicts between the two sets of policies are clearly visible in the historical record. For example, in colonial-era archival documents pertaining to Mafia, day-to-day tensions among officials were readily apparent in relation to the archipelago's small wildlife population, which in some areas included monkeys, wild pigs, a tiny species of antelope, and an apparent sub-species of miniature hippos.[9] These documents record an ongoing debate during the 1940s and 1950s between colonial game rangers in Morogoro on the mainland and Mafia's district commissioners concerning policies toward these animals.[10] According to official policy, animals designated as "game" required "preservation" and could not be killed without a permit, as opposed to "vermin" that could. In the 1950s, there was a spirited interchange about whether hippos found in the wet interior regions of Mafia's main island should be classified as game or vermin.

While Mafia's district commissioner (like his predecessors) emphasized the destruction of crops by hippos and desired that hippo remain classified as vermin, the game ranger (echoing his own predecessors) suggested that "it would be a pity to wipe out the hippo population completely, and I gather there are probably some areas (i.e. some swamps or pools) which are not in close proximity to damageable crops." The district commissioner bluntly responded:

> I really cannot see what is the point of preserving them here and in fact there are no swamps at any distance from cultivation; they do no good whatever and they do a great deal of damage physical and psychological. People who want to see hippo in their natural surroundings have only to cross to the Rufiji! The political effects of clearing them out of Mafia would be most valuable quite apart from the increase in food crops. I should therefore, like you to put the question of posting a Game Scout here [to shoot the animals] for one or two months . . . even if you and de la Fontaine [the owner of the Mafia Island Fishing Lodge] do not support it.[11]

During the course of this debate, the Morogoro game ranger also asked about a species of pygmy antelopes (Mozambique Blue Duiker and Mount Meru Suni; known as *chesi* on Mafia). While he acknowledged the population was too small for a full set of "Local Game Rules, Native Authority licences, etc.," he asked the district commissioner to restrict their killing. The district commissioner agreed that the animals were "delightful little things." However, he also noted that the animals were occasionally hunted for food and given that "the deficiencies of the Mafia African's diet are notorious" he argued against placing restrictions on the animals.[12] The district commissioner did, however, promise to ensure that shotgun owners [mainly Europeans] would pay for bird licences since "I'm less worried about the diet of shotgun owners than that of their poorer neighbors!"

While an exclusive focus on wildlife sidesteps issues of environmental damage caused by other colonial-era policies (such as reserving forests for commercial concessions and mining and drilling operations), this interchange does underscore the real tensions that exist between maintaining wildlife populations and meeting the economic needs of agriculturalists. However, what emerges most forcefully in such encounters is the government monopoly on power to address such issues. Although the district commissioner did recognize and attempt to address residents' complaints, the rights to decision making lay entirely with government officials and entailed no public discussion or debate. Elaborate bureaucratic procedures such as obtaining costly permits also constituted a commonplace tactic in regulating residents' relationship with the environment regardless of longstanding customary rights. Yet, at the same time, the power of colonial officials in these situations should not be exaggerated. As the district commissioner himself remarked to the game ranger regarding restrictions on hunting *chesi*: "as you are well aware effective prevention [of hunting] is impossible. The only thing I can do—issuing threatening tangazos [orders]—would I am afraid be more likely to encourage trapping than stop it. While attempts to control it by licences would have no effect other than putting a few shillings into the Native Treasury and probably a few more into other hands."[13] The limitations on government directives are also underscored by the fact that during the seven-month period between October 1953 and April 1954 documented in government files, the requested game scout succeeded in killing only one hippo.[14]

Although agriculture and pastoralism constituted important conservation concerns in the minds of colonial officials, marine environments did not. According to Chole residents, British agricultural officers did control the cutting of mangroves as part of forestry regulations, permitting the cutting of three types of mangroves while prohibiting the cutting of three others (although colonial records are unclear on this point, there is some suggestion that this was not done simply for reasons of "conservation" but to protect trees which might be of future interest to commercial concessions). Although the archival record is scanty, fish and other sea creatures appear to have been largely ignored by policymakers. Chole residents themselves suggested that government regulation of marine resources did not emerge until after independence. Although British colonial documents do make mention of regulatory efforts, the discrepancy between the official record and residents' memories is easily understandable. According to archival records, the "Maritime" division became a subdivision of the Department of Agriculture in the early 1950s and, at that time, included only four officers for the entire territory of Tanganyika—three working on inland lake fishing and only one on maritime matters.[15]

The efforts of the early Maritime Division centered on increasing economic productivity, echoed in the 1954 development plan for Mafia district that called for the "further development of commercial fisheries." The colonial documents I have been able to obtain, however, suggest little serious effort. Records do note a scheme to encourage fish ponds and the culturing of oysters, efforts apparently attempted by a handful of European settlers.[16] However, the only maritime activity of note appeared to be the purchase of a used 50 ft motorized fishing vessel, the *Patoni*, from a European living in Zanzibar.[17] The boat was equipped with a refrigerated fish room and an echo sounder for locating shoals of fish and was intended to help establish a deepsea trawler fishing industry. However, the boat only made three expeditions in three years due to engine problems and in 1955 was sold at a substantial loss to R. de la Fontaine, the European owner of Mafia's colonial era fishing lodge, for use as a house boat. After this fiasco, expenditure on offshore fishing investigations was largely halted.

This scanty material on fisheries, however, does suggest a broader shift in "development" policies. Although development was originally assumed to emanate from those at the economic vanguard of "progress" (i.e., European settlers and businesses as well as the state, as evidenced by their involvement in fish ponds and ocean trawling), we see the beginnings of a shift in the terminology of "development" to focus on the broader populace. After selling the *Patoni*, colonial officials suggested that two small motorized fishing boats be purchased to demonstrate mechanized fishing to Africans since "experience suggests that attempts to improve fishing methods are likely to be more effective if based on close contact with local fishermen."[18] This shift in thinking among colonial officials serves as a portent of the worldwide intensification of fishing in the ensuing decades that has more recently become a source of concern to environmentalists (McEvoy 1986; McGoodwin 1990). It also suggests the gradual shift in the focus of "development" interventions away from elite actors and toward "poverty alleviation" among poorer individuals (see also Finnemore 1997).

Technocentrism and Centralized Governments:
The Case of the "Forced Villagization" Program

What is perhaps most striking about the post-independence period is not its ruptures with the colonial past but its continuities. Crawford Young (1994) suggests that this stems from the late stage at which European colonialism occurred in Africa in contrast to other regions and the highly centralized and authoritarian forms of government it brought. Post-independence governments did not so much replace this highly centralized colonial state as perpetuate the inherited system in new ways. Although there may have been relatively few European settlers in Tanganyika in comparison to other colonies like Kenya, the powerful impact of colonialism is widely felt through the institutions and incipient class relationships that it left behind. These institutions were not free markets or constitutional governments—what is often presented as the legacy of the West to the rest of the world—but rather centralized and authoritarian bureaucratic structures that would have a far reaching impact. The tenacity of colonial bureaucratic institutions in contemporary Tanzania is evident in myriad ways, from how government memos are written, to the details of agricultural policies, to the importance of "experts" assisting supposedly ignorant "peasants" on the road to development. For example, the speech of a high-ranking national government official, who visited Mafia in 1997, closely mirrored the lectures of colonial officials, chastising Mafia residents for allegedly failing to weed their coconut plantations, for clearing their land by burning, and for failing to send their children to school (see also Haugerud 1993).

The linkages between authoritarian state structures and preservation and conservation policies in both the colonial and post-colonial eras are drawn into stark relief by the reliance upon forced relocations as a policy technique. For example, the region that now constitutes the Selous Game Reserve (named after a famous European hunter killed during the East African campaign of World War I who was buried within its boundaries) offers a prime example. The WaNgindo, one of the peoples who lived in the region, have already been mentioned in this book as a group that suffered heavily from the slave trade and which had numerous members brought to Mafia as captives. However, WaNgindo peoples not only suffered dislocations from slavery, but also from preservationist, conservationist, and "forced villagization" policies as well.

During World War I, numerous WaNgindo were displaced due to the military campaigns that moved through the region. In 1945, at the end of yet another world war, the British removed several thousand WaNgindo from what is now the eastern part of the Selous, ostensibly for reasons of tsetse fly control (Rodgers 1976). The forced relocation of populations to stem the spread of tsetse fly, which can infect and kill cattle and lead to sleeping sickness in humans, was a pervasive policy during the colonial period and appeared to stem from what is now recognized as a faulty understanding of the relationship between the disease, wildlife populations and human settlements (for more detailed discussions, see MacKenzie 1988; Kjekshus 1977). In later years, however, in order to keep the WaNgindo and other residents from returning to "undesirable" areas, the game reserve itself was expanded (Matzke 1976). Some observers estimate that a total of 40,000 WaNgindo and other residents were dislocated for the expanding Selous reserve (Neumann 1998:146; Matzke 1976). After independence, rural residents nevertheless continued to be excluded from protected areas because such policies corresponded with a new government initiative that reached its peak during the mid-1970s—the effort to move Tanzanians into nucleated "*ujamaa*" villages (Coulson 1982; Scott 1998; Matzke 1976; Shivji 1998; von Freyhold 1979). In all these instances, the colonial and postcolonial governments shared a common policy of forcibly relocating populations in pursuit of the ostensible goals of nature preservation, disease control, and "development."

The impact of the post-independence "forced villagization" programs is still vividly etched into the memories of many contemporary Tanzanians. The stated goal of such policies was to create nucleated villages that could jump-start "development" in this newly formed nation by encouraging the collective labor of villagers, by allowing them to leave behind "traditional" methods in order to utilize "higher" forms of technology such as tractors, and by creating the possibility of more concentrated government assistance and access to "expert" advice.[19] Not coincidentally, scholars also noted that such villages allowed for greatly increased administrative and political control by the state (Coulson 1982; Scott 1998; Matzke 1976; Shivji 1998). I was introduced to talk about forced villagization policies on Mafia one afternoon as I sat around the table in the tourist camp talking with Idi, Juma, and Mzee Salim. The conversation turned to the troubles of the past and the men described how even residents of tiny Chole Island, less than one half of a square mile in size, had been forced to "villagize" and how houses had been knocked down and property lost.

They described the villagization program as a *donda* (wound) that would not heal, adding that they could never forgive or forget what had happened to them. Mzee Salim described his sense of betrayal that the post-independence government could do something worse to its citizens than had even occurred during the colonial era. Juma Omari related in quiet, pensive tones how, after his family was compelled to relocate when he was only a child, he had been forced, sick and miserable, to sleep outside with his siblings during the rainy season while his family built a new shelter. Mzee Salim described residents burying possessions they could not take with them, hoping to recover them in the future. Such stories were echoed by others at different times on Chole, including Mzee Bakari who bitterly described how he was told by a government official that the coral and limestone house he had inherited from his forebears needed to be "moved." Although it was sufficiently close to the planned village "center," it was considered to be improperly aligned and government officials demanded that it be "moved" to form a straight line with other houses along the main path of the island. "Can a house be 'moved'"? Mzee Bakari asked me rhetorically, still filled with anger although the offense had occurred decades earlier.

Talk around the camp table that afternoon, however, also suggested occasional acts of resistance. Idi described an old man who refused the order to move and waited with a *panga* (machete) behind a door for those sent to relocate him. Juma mentioned another elder who had dared to challenge

Nyerere publicly when he arrived on Mafia for a state visit. They acknowledged that most people, however, simply threw up their hands in despair, believing there was nothing they could do. Others counted themselves lucky that their losses were less than many mainlanders who had been forced to move further, who suffered not only from exposure but from wild animals, and who had no fish to tide them over in the period before new crops could be planted.

Overall, the decision to create centralized *ujamaa* villages in Tanzania resulted in the forced relocation of approximately 5 million people, mostly in the years between 1973 and 1976 (Scott 1998:223). The idea for villagization had origins spanning several continents. Precedents had been set, not only by the tsetse fly resettlement schemes of the colonial era such as that in the Selous, but also by a 1960 World Bank report commissioned just before Tanganyika gained its independence that recommended the creation of nucleated villages to speed "development." In addition, Nyerere believed that collectivized villages would also allow for the creation of *ujamaa* socialism and such policies had obvious parallels with more extreme developments in China and the Soviet Union. These policies, however, contradict other images of Nyerere who, in the post-independence era, was a relatively benign leader compared to many on the African continent. Indeed, Nyerere was morally sincere as well as a widely respected intellectual and an inspiration for many throughout the world for his peculiar brand of "African" socialism and his position of non-alignment during the Cold War. However, Nyerere was also the product of a highly centralized and authoritarian colonial system in which education and technical expertise were widely depicted as giving an educated elite the authority to direct the masses "for their own good." Recognizing that in a country overwhelmingly populated by farmers, "development" would not easily come through industrialization, he argued that Tanzanians could only achieve material prosperity through hard work and increasing agricultural productivity under the guidance of experts. It was his hope that *ujamaa* villages would provide the impetus for such transformations. Despite his populist language, however, policies during the Nyerere era mimicked those of the colonial government, which assumed that rural residents lacked the ability to make valid decisions about their own lives and had to be compelled to act in their own best interests.

As was suggested by the men in Chole's camp that afternoon, the results of the villagization program were, ultimately, disastrous. Nyerere initially emphasized that relocation would be voluntary (and, indeed, the first *ujamaa* villages in the 1960s had been spontaneous phenomena). However, coercion was widespread after 1973 as Nyerere became frustrated with the slow pace of villagization and as bureaucrats interested in meeting quotas used force to overcome the resistance of rural residents to abandoning their homes. Not only were such policies implemented by force, they were remarkably distant from the realities of everyday life and led to devastating consequences. People suffered as they were forced to abandon homes and property (in some cases, homes were burned to keep people from returning to them), and many people were simply packed into trucks by officials and the military and dropped in designated areas with no housing, water, or other amenities.

Bureaucratic considerations rather than practical realities led to the siting of new villages; it was estimated, for example, that 60 percent of the new villages were located on semiarid land that did not allow for permanent cultivation (Scott 1998:239). State officials also ignored the fact that dispersed settlements allowed rural residents to be closer to, and better tend, their crops. The removal of residents from their fields into nucleated settlements resulted, not in greater productivity, but the widespread loss of crops and disastrous decreases in food supplies. Ensuing famine caused the need for massive food imports between 1973 and 1975 (Scott 1998:23). Ultimately, the socialist veneer on post-independence policies (as was true for capitalist policies in Kenya) proved less important to understanding these policies than the fact that post-independence governments were built almost entirely upon the authoritarian precedent set by the colonial state—a legacy that has also served to unite preservationist and conservationist policies in Tanzania.

While the merging of conservation and development to form the philosophy of "sustainable development" is often portrayed as a relatively recent phenomenon, the history presented in this chapter suggests otherwise. The Mafia Island Marine Park, as an institution and a joint initiative between national and international organizations, has both built upon—and, in some instances, sought to challenge—a much older history in which conservation and development ideas and policies have long been intertwined. This history suggests the basis for the worries about the marine park expressed by Chole fishers in the previous chapter. While some of the policies outlined in this chapter (such as the preservationist policies of the early nature reserves) were overtly intended to "regulate" rural Africans, many others were ostensibly meant to help rural residents and to generate a greater social "good" (whether through tsetse fly control or ujamaa villages). Yet, even in such instances, the knowledge of rural Africans remained widely devalued in relation to "experts," rural communities were excluded from input into decision making, and dictatorial policies served to work against rural Africans in ways that affected both their lives and livelihoods.

In contrast to the sense of "newness" common in many discussions of the "global," this chapter has explored a long history of power relationships operating across wide geographic reaches. Indeed, the era of European colonialism created many of the bureaucratic pathways, networks, and structures through which contemporary power relationships continue to unfold, albeit with different players. In some cases, the tensions evident in these colonial-era transregional linkages are also evident in the present. For example, just as district officials who were historically more cognizant of local realities often came into conflict with colonial officials in metropolitan offices, tensions similarly appear in contemporary international organizations such as WWF. Indeed, contemporary decision makers in Gland, Switzerland, Washington, D.C., or Dar es Salaam may know relatively little about the particular circumstances of a place like Mafia. This is not to suggest that local decision making is always better (as the social drama of the marine park also demonstrates, some "local" officials may be interested in using their knowledge to extend their own authority or to extract resources within particular locales). Such tensions, however, do suggest the particular channels by which power-at-a-distance operates and the impact that such geographic and social disjunctures might have upon particular communities.

Yet, the primary issue of concern in this history is not geography, but power. Who ultimately has the authority to make decisions, whether near or far, and who does not? As outlined in this chapter, conservation and development policies in both the colonial and postcolonial eras in Tanzania were largely based upon the assumption that decision making must and should lie with "experts" or elite political cadres. Indeed, the most clear-cut departure that the contemporary Mafia Island Marine Park makes from this history is the expansion of the rhetoric of "participatory" decision making. Yet, given that the marine park of the mid-1990s constituted a peculiar form of national bureaucracy with transnational linkages, what did this mean at a day-to-day level? This is the topic to which we now turn.

Pushing Paper and Power: Bureaucracy and Knowledge within a National Marine Park

THIS BOOK HAS CENTERED around the struggles over the Mafia Island Marine Park, but what sort of entity, exactly, is a national park? In some ways it is easy to conceive of the marine park as an object despite the fact that its boundaries, invisible across Mafia's land and waterscapes, exist most firmly on the paper maps of policymakers. In contrast to something as seemingly amorphous as ecological or social dynamics (which alternately might have been viewed as the focus of this international project), the apparent "thing-ness" of a park has particular social implications. For example, for tour operators, a "park" creates an attraction through which nature and conservation can be advertised, packaged and sold. For Tanzanian government officials, national parks generate foreign exchange via admission fees and taxes, while also garnering contributions from international donors.[1] Environmental and donor organizations can direct funding towards a park while publicizing it as part of a portfolio of projects in international fund-raising efforts. For Mafia residents, the park is an entity that can attract resources, repel dynamiters and also take away rights.

Despite the tendency to represent the marine park as a "thing," this analysis treats the Mafia Island Marine Park as a constellation of social processes organized in and around bureaucracies. Although current discussions of "globalization" tend to focus on the workings of capitalism, the rapid expansion of international organizations in the contemporary world suggests the need to take seriously the kind of social entities such organizations represent, namely, a particular kind of transnational bureaucracy. Clearly, such structures are not new. The colonial bureaucracies described in the previous chapter, as well as many historical activist movements such as those associated with women's suffrage and the abolition of slavery (Keck and Sikkink 1998), were also organizational structures that spanned wide geographic reaches. Yet, the particular terrain being created by contemporary NGOs, as viewed from the vantage point of a place like Mafia, also requires ethnographic exploration and can point to both continuities with the past and areas of transformation in the present.

After outlining the managerial structure of the park, this chapter examines two broad sets of processes. First, it considers bureaucracy itself as a terrain for social struggle. Rather than assuming that bureaucratic institutions possess an inherent political valence (whether for good or ill), this analysis recognizes that bureaucracy can be used *either* to institutionalize rights or to enact and further entrench particular kinds of hierarchy. Thus, it is necessary to explore the contested nature of bureaucracy and how this form of organization comes to be used for particular ends. An exploration of these issues in day-to-day life within the marine park allows us to see how Chole residents come to be excluded by bureaucracy, as well as how various officials and representatives utilize park bureaucracy as part of their internal struggle to determine the future of the marine park. The second half of this chapter examines social interactions around knowledge. It recognizes that bureaucratic institutions can only assimilate particular forms of knowledge, a reality that serves to privilege certain groups within the marine park and marginalize others. It also suggests that evaluations of knowledge form one of the most basic ways in which existing social hierarchies are reproduced on a day-to-day basis on Mafia, despite the park's official emphasis on "participation."

ORGANIZING A MARINE PARK

The question of whether international organizations can mandate "participation," and, thus, implicitly encourage greater democratic accountability, calls into question the relationship between international bureaucracies—for this is what donors and projects essentially are—and democracy (however that might be defined). This question is one with a long genealogy. Nearly a century ago, Max Weber astutely noted the tensions between bureaucracy and democracy, suggesting a skepticism about "modern" liberal institutions that would prefigure the influential analyses of social theorist Michel Foucault. Weber argued that while democracy calls bureaucracy into being as a way to institutionalize meritocracy and equality before the law, bureaucracy simultaneously creates an elite of educated experts who are not subject to the control of the masses (Weber 1958:196–244). Foucault instead emphasized the disciplinary techniques of modern institutions, the generation of modern subjectivities which internalized such disciplining, the formation of new modes of governmentality, and the role that modern knowledge production plays in imposing particular power-laden viewpoints as regimes of "truth" (Foucault 1972, 1977, 1978, 1994). The critical perspectives of both these theorists contrast sharply with the hopeful outlook of those who work with international organizations and presume that such bureaucracies can enforce rights, encourage participation, protect natural resources and, generally, work toward a greater social and environmental good.

Although the following analysis is a critical one that draws upon elements of both Weber and Foucault, I believe that it is important not to lose sight of the reality that bureaucracies *can* institutionalize "rights" that serve to counter or reform existing power relationships (providing there are functioning legal or institutional mechanisms to support such rights). If this were not the case, it would be difficult to make sense of the social drama of Mafia's marine park and why particular officials struggled so assiduously to derail attempts at institutionalizing "participation" in an effort to maintain their own authority. However, it is also necessary to explain how and why Mafia residents' viewpoints would come to have so little impact upon decision making within park bureaucracy, as evident in the "social drama" outlined in chapter 1. In order to fully understand the marginalization of island residents, we must turn to the social workings of the marine park as a particular kind of bureaucracy linked to other national and international institutions. In contrast to both Weber and Foucault, however, I would argue that the social dynamics of bureaucracies do not suggest something intrinsic about the nature or practices of "modernity." One of the most profound impacts of park bureaucracy has not been rationalization, as presumed by Weber, or even a particular form of "global" governmentality, as adherents of Foucault might suggest, but rather the calling into existence of a presumably older form of social interaction—patron–client relationships.

In exploring the bureaucratic workings of the marine park, it is necessary to consider how the language of "participation" obscured a profoundly hierarchical managerial structure that excluded Mafia residents from any real decision-making power. In general, the organization of the marine park is a generic one. Like other forms of managerial bureaucracy based upon generalizable principles, the structure of the marine park did not emanate from the particular realities of Mafia, or of Tanzania, or even of the African continent. The organization of the Mafia Island Marine Park was instead generalized from IUCN guidelines drawn from the management structure of the Great Barrier Reef National Marine Park in Australia (Andrews 1998). Its broader conservation and development goals also formed part of a generic framework and strategy that, during this period, had gained ascendancy within WWF as well as in numerous other conservation and development organizations around the world. This formula centered around the creation of "participatory" projects that sought to produce sustainable development through ecotourism and that focused on the need to generate "alternative income" sources for the Third World poor who were presumed to be overexploiting the environment. To offer but one example, in 1998 the "Hall of Biodiversity" in the Museum of Natural History in New York City highlighted a WWF forestry project in the Central African Republic that almost exactly mirrored the calls for "ecotourism" and "alternative income sources" found on Mafia. Indeed, the goals of the Mafia Island Marine Park can be found almost verbatim in WWF literature and projects from around the world (Kempf 1993). This act of creating general frameworks for projects which can then be replicated in a range of countries, regardless of differing economic, social, political and historical contexts, is a strategy that conservation organizations such as WWF broadly share with development institutions (Ferguson 1994; Ake 1996). The growing prevalence of the language of the "global" has also supported and given a contemporary veneer to such generalizing tendencies by identifying "global" problems that need to be addressed through "global" solutions.

The structure of the Mafia Island Marine Park is not only generic, it is also remarkably hierarchical for a project labeled as "participatory." This hierarchy poses a stark contrast to the ideals embodied in the preamble for the park's initial General Management Plan, which expressed the hope that the Mafia Island Marine Park would serve as "a true model of a park created and run 'for the people and by the people'" (GMP 1993:iv). Indeed, it was this ideal that Mafia's residents enthusiastically supported and to which village representatives agreed when the decision to create a marine park was formally adopted at the 1991 Planning Workshop. As previously mentioned, the idea of popular participation had already made an appearance in Tanzania during the Nyerere years; however, the participatory goals of Mafia's marine park were deemed radical enough to warrant entirely new legislation. Paralleling the structure outlined in the Mafia Island Marine Park's preliminary General Management Plan, the Marine Parks and Reserves Act of 1994 legally mandated the involvement of area residents, not only within Mafia's park, but within all existing marine reserves and future parks in Tanzania.[2] This participatory language, however, concealed the reality that Mafia residents were only given legal rights to *offer opinions* rather than to directly affect decision making within the marine park.

As spelled out in the Marine Parks and Reserves Act (a document to which Mafia residents only gained access in 1997), the organizational structure of the marine park, much like that of older preservationist national parks, was to center around an appointed warden holding an extraordinary degree of power (a position to which Pius Mseka's post of acting warden would serve as a precursor).[3] According to the legislation, the warden was to be selected by a board of trustees appointed by the minister for Tourism, Natural Resources, and the Environment and would be accountable solely to that body.[4] All positions on the board of trustees were reserved for individuals involved in national and international institutions with no place allotted for a local representative. In reaction to criticism concerning this lack of local representation, national government officials (with the agreement of the WWF Country representative) argued that appointing a Mafia resident as a member of the board of trustees would be inappropriate given that the body was to oversee all existing and future marine parks and reserves within Tanzania. (Interestingly, however, this argument ignored the fact that a "representative from a private business with interests in a marine park" *was* allotted a space on the Board of Trustees, even though most businesspeople would similarly have interests in particular localities.)

According to the legislation, the warden would be accountable only to the board of trustees, although he or she would be assisted by an advisory committee particular to each park. However, the advisory committee would hold no direct authority over the warden and would serve, as the title suggests, only to "advise." This advisory committee was to include positions for two local representatives out of a total of between ten and thirteen members.[5] Yet, all members of the advisory committee were to be appointed by the principal secretary of the Ministry for Tourism, Natural Resources, and the Environment in Dar es Salaam. In other words, area residents were not allowed to elect their own representatives to the advisory committee, meaning that there was no legal requirement that "local" appointees either be popular choices or representative of local interests. Indeed, after the first meeting of the board of trustees in November 1996, Pius Mseka himself appointed the "local representatives" for the advisory committee (presumably after officials in Dar es Salaam delegated this responsibility). After protests by the WWF-Mafia staff, two of Mseka's choices were eventually changed under pressure from the principal secretary of the Ministry for Tourism, Natural Resources, and the Environment. Nevertheless, the WWF technical adviser, David Holston, continued to contest these newer appointments, arguing that Mseka had chosen representatives compatible with his own interests rather than those of Mafia residents.[6] Two subsequent external reviews of the project criticized the hierarchical nature of the planned organization for the marine park and also argued for the necessity of increased village representation on the advisory committee and board of trustees.[7]

By law, each village within the marine park was also required to elect a village council (known as a "marine park committee" on Mafia). The village councils were required to send their written opinion on specified park matters to the advisory committee and were ostensibly entitled to "participate fully in all aspects of the development or any amendment of the regulations, zoning and general management plan for the Marine Park" (legislation, 1994). However, once again the councils were given no actual decision-making power nor any means for ensuring that their opinions would be considered, much less implemented. In short, for a "participatory" park, there existed an extraordinary lack of checks or balances on authority within its governing structure. According to the General Management Plan, not only did village councils and representatives *not* hold decision-making power in any capacity in contrast to a legally omnipotent warden, they were expected to use the warden to "liaise" with the board of trustees and, thus, had no independent channels for making their opinions known to other actors operating within national and international institutions. In addition, village councils were required by law to invite the warden to all meetings relating to marine park matters, thereby guaranteeing that there would be no independent space for village action given an unpopular warden.

In sum, the legal and bureaucratic structure of the marine park glossed over the various meanings given to "participation." As previously discussed, conflicting interpretations of participation were widely evident among various actors involved in the marine park, and even within WWF as a single organization. For example, WWF employees in offices in Dar es Salaam and Washington, D.C., stressed that it was crucial to gain the "participation" of all "stakeholders" in the park, or as one employee put it, "of getting everyone on board," a reference to government officials as well as other donors. In contrast, WWF field staff on Mafia and some other individuals involved in the early formation of the park stressed participation as the "empowerment" of local residents in decision making. Masked by the ability of "participation" to refer to anything from simple consultation with residents to actual decision-making authority, the Mafia Island Marine Park ultimately embodied a weak form of consultation while using the rhetoric of empowerment. The conflation of these meanings of participation held the potential to deceive Mafia residents, who lacked access to most project documents. Inundated with oral pronouncements stressing their empowerment, islanders were encouraged to support a project that ultimately denied them any real decision-making authority.

The conceptual framework of "stakeholders," which has gained widespread currency not only on Mafia but within a range of international institutions and projects in recent years, also carries important implications. On Mafia, stakeholders were conceived of as users of the marine environment who had legitimate interests within, and a right to participate in, the park. Although this concept suggests a broadly democratic ideal, it is important to examine how the concept of stakeholders worked in practice. By presuming positions of theoretical equality between widely disparate actors, the idea of stakeholders served to obscure existing power relationships on Mafia. Much like economists' generic views of how abstracted individuals operate in the marketplace, the concept of stakeholders suggested an equivalence among such diverse park actors as government officials, conservation and development professionals, commercial businesses, and Mafia residents.

One of the most remarkable realignments created by the use of this term was the depiction of government actors as mere "stakeholders." On the one hand, this move suggested the downgrading of national governments within international discourses, allowing governments to be represented as simply one "interest group" among many (rather than as the embodiment of a people or nation as is common in nationalist accounts). On the other hand, this terminology implied that Mafia residents should be able to act on par with government officials as fellow stakeholders, thus obscuring the power and authority wielded by such governmental bodies as the military, police, and various national government agencies. This language also obscured the very different social, educational, and economic backgrounds possessed by various stakeholders which affected their ability to interact with others and press for their interests.

Finally, the language of stakeholders downplayed the qualitatively different interests that different actors held in Mafia's environment. Commercial enterprises, for example, were depicted as "stakeholders" in Mafia's marine park, just as were the approximately 15,000 residents living with marine park boundaries. Commercial enterprises also held a seat on the board of trustees (unlike residents) and two seats on Mafia's advisory committee (one for tour operators and one for extractive industries), making their representation on these bodies equivalent to or greater than that of island residents. However, the *only* formal extractive marine-based enterprise on Mafia during the time I was there (as opposed to the numerous small and informal local enterprises), was a small Greek-owned seafood extracting and processing company. This company was overseen by one expatriate, employed a handful of Mafia residents and bought octopus and crayfish from some of the women and men in the area. Thus, at least on paper, the interests of one small foreign-owned company were equated with the interests of the entire population living within the marine park who were directly dependent on Mafia's marine environment for their survival. In short, the populist image suggested by park rhetoric obscured the fact that the "participants" within the Mafia Island Marine Park included, not only village residents, but a range of powerful internal and external actors. Although park documents would occasionally acknowledge the slippage that characterized the uses of the term *participation*, the vagueness of this concept and the generic nature of the category of "stakeholder" allowed planners to promote the park as a democraticizing influence despite a far more ambiguous reality.

BUREAUCRACY AS A SITE FOR SOCIAL STRUGGLE

Although bureaucracies constitute entities that may potentially serve as sites for institutionalizing rights, bureaucracies can also work to marginalize particular groups in relation to others. Such dynamics are not straightforward, however, but are the result of negotiation. In short, bureaucracies form sites of social struggle. Here, I offer a brief overview of the beginnings of a women's group on Chole as well as interactions between Chole residents and district bureaucrats in relation to the nascent ecotourism initiative. I consider how, even as Chole residents desire external assistance and seek to negotiate its terms, they find themselves marginalized by bureaucratic procedures. Bureaucracy, however, also forms a terrain for struggle within the marine park itself, as the ensuing account of conflict among government officials and WWF representatives suggests.

Bureaucracy and the Politics of Exclusion on Chole

One afternoon, I ran into Rukia, who was conversing with several other women near Bi Sharifa's house, and we began talking about the new women's group that she, like many other women on Chole, had joined. The concept of forming a women's group had originated with the Chole Kisiwani Conservation and Development Company, the community-based ecotourism initiative, but had quickly taken on a life of its own. At the suggestion of the developers, Margaret, a British volunteer funded by a service organization in England, arrived on Chole in 1997 to spend several weeks forming a hand-icrafts group. Although Margaret could not speak KiSwahili, she had brought cloth and sewing materials, and about twenty women began to regu-larly meet with her. Sitting upon stone blocks at the clinic construction site, the women would sew and converse. When I returned to the island after a trip to the United States in February of 1997, Margaret asked if I would serve as her translator. Although she had assumed that the women were gossiping while they sewed (and, indeed, the meetings had become enjoy-able social occasions), it turned out that the women were also discussing such difficult issues as how to find markets for future handicrafts, how to maintain access to sewing materials once Margaret had left, and how the group could be turned into a formal organization that would help the women generate the cash they so desperately needed. Shortly thereafter, an organiza-tional meeting was called to formally elect officers for the women's group. Since the group was planning to appeal to WWF for funding to purchase sewing machines, the WWF Community Development assistant, Rashidi He-medi, attended the meeting along with myself and Margaret's husband (who appeared in her stead because she was ill). In contrast to the easy, informal nature of the gatherings up until this point, this meeting was noticeably awk-ward. At this more formal occasion and with men in attendance, the women seemed suddenly embarrassed and sat in silence, unsure what to do. Finally, Rashidi agreed to help facilitate the elections and officers were duly chosen. In the next few weeks, he and the Community Development officer, Charles Mtui, would meet again with the women's group, asking what the women described as "harsh" (*kali*) questions about the group's rationale and their potential handling of funding from WWF (an attitude prompted by worries on the part of the park's technical adviser that the group was not a "true" grassroots organization because it had been encouraged by "outsiders.")

On the afternoon of that later meeting, I joined the group of women who were sitting on a woven mat in front of Bi Sharifa's house. Rukia imme-diately asked for my assistance. She related that even though she had been elected vice chair of the women's group, she and most of the other women did not know what such positions entailed, what their responsibilities would be, or how they were to go about setting up this organization. Indeed, she seemed acutely embarrassed by their lack of knowledge of the proper protocol for formal meetings (parliamentary procedures being one of the British colonial legacies that continued to have widespread salience within Tanzania). The other women agreed and revealed that they were unclear what an institution like WWF expected from them and what they needed to do in order to gain development funds. They began talking about meetings in general, lacing their embarrassment with defiance. They claimed that they were now constantly exhorted to speak up at meetings, but that they preferred not to since it was pointless given that the "big people" and particularly men never listened to them anyway. Nevertheless, they did ask me whether I could help them with the organization of the women's group. Unfamiliar with parliamentary procedures myself, I attempted to help in another way. At the next meeting of the women's group, I audiotaped its members discussing their hopes and concerns for the women's group, the particular problems that women on the island faced in earning cash, their need for money for themselves and for their children, and the detailed worries and questions they had about setting up a cooperative business. Later, I jotted down a summary of these issues that included debates over membership rules for the group, the division of profits, potential taxes, the cost of raw materials, the need for new markets, and the cost of transportation to these markets. I brought the summary to the Community Development staff at the WWF office the next time I passed through Utende.

Surprised by the complexity of the issues the women had raised, the WWF community officers agreed to come to another meeting of the women's group for further discussion. However, once again, on the appointed day, there was a painful silence. The women, wrapped in their colorful *kangas*, simply stared at the ground and refused to speak, while the WWF staff looked vaguely put out. In an attempt to break the ice, I raised one of the topics that the women had described on the audiotape. As some of the women began to speak, the tone of the meeting slowly shifted as well. Rather than speaking to the women as if they were errant schoolchildren needing to be coaxed, the community development staff now began conferring with the women as adults. At the end of the meeting, one of the women exclaimed, "Finally. This is exactly the kind of conversation we had hoped for. Before we felt like children and were afraid of making a mistake." Others acknowledged that they had been afraid to speak for fear of "looking stupid."

The initial difficulties experienced by this women's group illustrate the different degrees of familiarity individuals may have with the workings of formal organizations, as well as the difficulties that those who have long been accustomed to bureaucratic exclusion have in surmounting such obstacles. In Tanzania, such barriers are particularly high for rural women with little education. In international development circles as well as among Tanzania's elite, such difficulties are often attributed to gender inequalities that are presumed to be a product of "tradition" or "culture," particularly in the case of Muslim women. Such assumptions, however, ignore the reality that coastal women often have greater rights to inheritance and other sources of control than many of the more educated "modern" African women from patrilineally organized ethnic groups on the mainland. Even more importantly, the tendency to blame "culture" for the contemporary marginalization of women on Mafia ignores the role that the historical exclusion of women within colonial and postcolonial bureaucracies played (both directly and indirectly) in generating such dynamics (see also Caplan 1992).

Although marginalization may have been particularly extreme for women on Mafia, both men and women on the island were often discomforted by their encounters with both bureaucrats and bureaucracies. Because institutional bureaucracies possessed a long postcolonial as well as colonial history within Tanzania, such tensions were widely apparent in relationships among Tanzanians, as well as between Tanzanians and Euro-Americans.[8] These tensions are aptly illustrated by a controversy that erupted in the mid-1990s over monies collected from tourists for Chole's community development fund. In 1994, Chole's village government, as well as the village committees elected as part of the Chole Kisiwani Conservation and Development Company initiative, instituted a plan based on advice from the Euro-American tourism developers. They decided to charge a small fee to tourists who visited Chole (nearly all of whom were staying at hotels in Utende).[9] The fees for these "tickets" entered a community development fund along with a percentage of the profit made on each tourist who actually stayed in the Chole camp. Such monies, along with funding grants from such organizations as the British Council, were to be used to build a new school, a dispensary, and other community projects.[10] In June of 1996, the ward and divisional secretaries—low-level district officials appointed by the District Council—appeared on Chole and demanded that a percentage of the money earned on each ticket be turned over to the district authorities. Chole's intimidated committee members, believing this to be an *amri* (order) of the government, reluctantly agreed to the demands.

The next meeting of the Chole village committees was attended by the American developer as well as Rashidi Hemedi, who had served as the manager of the Chole Kisiwani tourism enterprise before he became the Community Development assistant for the marine park. When the developer learned that Chole's committees had agreed to give a portion of the money from the tickets to the district government, he angrily protested the legality of the move and left the meeting. Rashidi Hemedi immediately stood up and harangued Chole's committee members. He argued passionately that this change threatened the integrity of the entire project and protested that the few committee members present at the last meeting could not change an agreement entered into by the entire village. When the embarrassed and puzzled committee members protested that they had been "ordered" to do this, Rashidi argued that this could not have been an official order without the written authorization of the district commissioner (Rashidi had himself served as a low-level government official and he was able to specify the exact form that would have been required). When Rashidi attempted to ascertain whether there had been a legal quorum at the committee meeting when the decision was made, the Katibu Kata (the ward secretary and a resident of a neighboring island who had a rather unsavory reputation) told Rashidi that the minutes of the last meeting were "lost," and a heated exchange ensued between the two.

While Rashidi Hemedi clearly felt that there had been an illegal attempt to extort money from the committees, chagrined committee members seemed mystified by such bureaucratic complexities. One committee member, after embarrassedly admitting that they had made a "mistake" (*kosa*), suggested that without Rashidi and his knowledge of bureaucratic procedures they did not know how to handle such situations. The situation seemed to epitomize residents' self-characterization as *sisi tusisoma*, "we, the uneducated" in comparison to educated bureaucrats. Indeed, it was Rashidi Hemedi's educational background and his familiarity with government bureaucracy that prompted Mzee Maarufu, the village chairman, to stress to me the great loss that the village committees had suffered when Rashidi left as the manager of the tourism enterprise.

This attempt to extort money from the village committees was eventually remedied through the intervention of one of the tour developers, demonstrating the importance of "patrons" in political battles fought on bureaucratic terrains. The American developer addressed the situation by strategically inviting the new district commissioner to an elaborate luncheon in the Chole camp to be held in his honor and by making sure that village elders and committee members would be present. Although Mzee Maarufu, the village chairman, was clearly worried that there would be repercussions if the village did not hand over the money, the developer, in the midst of this public occasion, urged the intimidated chairman to address the matter with the district commissioner. In a self-conscious display of public magnanimity, the district commissioner assured Mzee Maarufu and the other island residents in attendance that he was giving his personal assurance as the leading official in the district government that there was no cause for worry: the ticket money would enter the community fund as had been planned. This political stratagem saved the day and Mzee Maarufu and other committee members went home looking visibly relieved. In short, this incident illustrates the reality that Mafia residents were often unable to interact with bureaucracies as individuals who possessed rights and were instead forced to rely upon powerful or well-educated patrons to act on their behalf. In the social drama of the marine park outlined in chapter 1, residents were similarly denied direct influence and forced to rely upon patrons.

Naming the 'Ukombozi': Battles over Bureaucracy

Although Mafia residents were largely excluded from the bureaucratic contestation within the marine park itself, significant and ongoing battles occurred during this period between (and among) Tanzanian government officials and Euro-American WWF employees.[11] In such instances, bureaucracy itself constituted the terrain for struggle. One common way in which bureaucracy could be used to fight larger political battles entailed the strategic use of language to draw in, exclude, or harass particular park actors as well as to control information. For example, the acting warden of the marine park, Pius Mseka, opposed the translation of the Marine Parks and Reserves Act into KiSwahili as well as efforts by WWF fieldstaff to make this information publicly available to Mafia residents. Indeed, permission to translate the Marine Parks and Reserves Act came only after protracted struggle and the intercession of an independent review panel over the marine park. An article by T. R. Young on the legal framework of the Mafia Island Marine Park suggests that such efforts reflect broader political and institutional realities:

> Tanzania's legal system is analogous to the soviet model, in that legislation and other government actions are not subject to the level of publicity, public dissemination and public scrutiny that is found in civil and common law traditions. Even within government, the dissemination of legislative documents and presidential orders is haphazard and few agencies possess copies of even the most basic Tanzanian laws. Laws that prohibit or mandate activities of government officials or members of the public are often futile, since the overwhelming majority of persons so prohibited or mandated will never see or hear of the law (1993:164).

Extrapolating from Ferguson (1994), I would argue that the issue of informing—or not informing—citizens of a country's laws is not simply a matter of attempting to gain the greatest degree of compliance possible. Rather the apparent "inefficiency" of failing to publicize laws, ultimately, relates to issues of control. The refusal to publicize laws not only denies residents knowledge of their rights and responsibilities, but makes the law itself much more ambiguous, thereby expanding the personal power and potential for accumulation through bribery on the part of those who hold the responsibility for enforcing such laws.

The selective use of either English or KiSwahili was also regularly used to exclude or include particular park actors. The following minidrama, which erupted over an attempt to define a meeting with villagers as "illegal," draws attention to such dynamics. In January of 1997, a flurry of correspondence circulated among the WWF-Mafia office in Utende, the marine park head-quarters in Kilindoni, a range of district offices on Mafia, and the WWF country office in Dar es Salaam. The ostensible reason for this heated circu-lation of paper was a proposed meeting called by the WWF-Mafia staff to assemble the leaders of each of the village marine park committees. The purpose of the meeting was to provide information about the recently trans-lated KiSwahili version of the marine park legislation and to select a name for the new antidynamiting patrol boat that had recently arrived on the island (see chapter 1).

On January 14, David Holston, the WWF technical advisor, delivered a memo to the acting warden, Pius Mseka, informing him that a meeting with village representatives had been scheduled for January 22. Utilizing informa-tion provided by the acting warden, the district executive director, as the second highest government official at the district level in Kilindoni, sent a memo to Holston the following day declaring the meeting to be illegal. De-spite the fact that Mseka and other high-ranking government officials like the district executive director had a reasonable command of English, and even though it was well known that Holston spoke only English, the memo was written in KiSwahili. While Mseka and his supporters in Kilindoni often strategically used KiSwahili in memos and meetings to isolate Holston, the WWF-Mafia staff in Utende also used language choice to make their own political points. For example, the WWF-Mafia staff insisted upon using the KiSwahili name for the marine park *Hifadhi ya Bahari* rather than the En-glish name, Mafia Island Marine Park (or MIMP), which was preferred by Mseka as well as by those in national and international offices. In a region where elites often used English to denote their high status, their ties to more prosperous regions of the world, and their authority over residents who lacked access to English, the continued usage of the KiSwahili name of the park suggested a challenge to such practices as well as support for the partic-ipation of Mafia residents.

At the center of this interchange was the ability to define the legality of meetings. The technique of declaring meetings illegal due to a presumed failure to follow bureaucratic protocol or to notify the proper authorities was a weapon often wielded by bureaucrats in Tanzania and one with striking parallels in the colonial era as well as in nearby Kenya (Haugerud 1993). The memo sent by the district executive director to David Holston stated that Pius Mseka, the Mafia District Council, and village governments within the park had not been officially informed of the proposed meeting and that it was therefore illegal. It concluded that since "the Technical Advisor is not a citizen of this nation, he is not permitted to call any type of official meeting without the permission of District Authorities or MIMP [i.e., Mseka]" and that this situation "poses a danger to the security of the nation."[12] Copies of the letter were also sent by the district executive director to Mafia's district commissioner, the chair of the district council, the acting warden of the park, Mafia's member of Parliament, and the district security officer. Such tactics paralleled efforts previously made by the acting warden to halt the 1995 Ecotourism Seminar to which village representatives had also been invited.

Upon receipt of this memo in the WWF Utende office, Charles Mtui, the Community Development officer, faxed a copy to Holston who was temporarily in Dar es Salaam. Delayed by the need to request a translation, Holston responded in a memo dated January 21 that was addressed to Mafia's district executive director. It declared that no illegal actions had been taken and that Mseka had been duly informed of the meeting. Challenging the amorphous use of "illegality" to halt the meeting, the memo asked with presumed irony, "Could you please provide me with a copy of the law that states that all meetings must inform the District Council so I can follow the correct procedure for the future." The memo then concluded that due to the "serious nature of the allegations" it would be necessary to ask the WWF country representative in Dar es Salaam to look into the matter with the overseeing Ministry of Tourism, Natural Resources, and the Environment. Copies of this letter were sent to the same officials who had received the original memo in addition to the WWF country representative in Dar es Salaam.

The strategy of sending (or not sending) copies of memos to select individuals in distant offices was a potent one with the potential to draw in—or exclude—more powerful actors. In this instance, the threat to take this matter to the WWF country office and to the overseeing ministry of the project, thereby demanding accountability at the national level, brought a quick response. The following day, a brief memo was sent to Holston from the district executive director's office on Mafia tersely stating that there was no longer opposition to the meeting. No copies, however, were sent to the other individuals who had received copies of the original memo. Holston then directed a new letter to the district executive director's office (cc'ed to all recipients of the January 21 correspondence) asking that copies of the memo retracting the illegality of the meeting be sent to the various offices "to set the record straight" and "clearing WWF of any wrong doing." On February 7, a considerably more apologetic note retracting the original memo that had declared the meeting illegal was sent from the district executive director's office to all the offices that had been involved. This technique of strategically using copies of official correspondence to control information about the struggles over the marine park was a subtle but effective means of attempting to shape the image of this project to actors beyond Mafia.

The struggle over this meeting demonstrates the ways in which bureaucracy itself became a site of struggle between the two marine park factions at the core of the social drama as described in chapter 1. In contrast to many social analytical accounts that obscure the impact of individuals, we see in this instance the crucial importance of individual personalities in determining how such bureaucratic structures would be used. Although the issue at stake was access to, and communication with, Mafia's residents (backhandedly suggesting their importance by the need to maintain their exclusion), island residents were prevented from direct participation in these sorts of regularly occurring bureaucratic battles due to the hierarchical managerial structure of the park and their lack of formal education. As was also true in the contestation over the ticket money on Chole, Mafia residents were forced to rely upon more powerful others, in this case the WWF-Mafia fieldstaff, to struggle on their behalf and to obtain their supposed "right" to participate. Such dynamics once again closely resemble patron–client relationships, as also suggested by Mzee Mohammedi's request that David Holston fight on their behalf as described in chapter 1. Such dynamics are not limited to so-called Third World countries but also appear in places like the United States in situations in which hierarchical bureaucratic structures come to be dominated by a few powerful persons in a context in which a majority of individuals are dispossessed.[13] In general, these kinds of relationships point to the ability of "modern" bureaucratic institutions to call into existence patron–client relationships, rather than the rationalization of rights and responsibilities predicted by commonplace narratives of modernity.

BUREAUCRACY AND KNOWLEDGE

Mafia residents were excluded from direct influence upon the marine park bureaucracy, not only because they lacked the proper educational credentials to achieve formal positions of power within the bureaucracy, but also because of widespread assumptions about the kind of knowledge they possessed. The participatory ideals of the marine park, which specified that residents would offer input into the functioning of the park, also served to draw attention to the knowledge of Mafia residents since their "participation" would presumably be based on this knowledge. Indeed, the growing interest in "participatory" frameworks among contemporary international organizations has been broadly paralleled by an increased attention to "indigenous" or "local" knowledge (A. Agrawal 1995; Brokensha et al. 1980; Brush and Stabinsky 1996; Gupta 1998; Johannes 1981; Peters 2000; Ruddle and Johannes 1985; Shiva 1988; Walley 2002).

Although bureaucracies like the Mafia Island Marine Park now include "participation" as part of their mandate, such institutions are also constructed to assimilate literate, managerial, and technical forms of knowledge and often prove unable or unwilling to "read" or incorporate the popular knowledge of groups like Mafia's residents. In general, knowledge within the Mafia Island Marine Park circulated along two distinct tracks. Scientific and technical knowledge traveled among national and international offices via bureaucratic channels, while popular knowledge circulated in a far more circumscribed fashion. As we shall see, this was the case even in instances in which park representatives attempted to solicit the popular knowledge of residents. At the same time, in day-to-day knowledge interactions within the marine park scientific forms of knowledge continued to be coded as high status and "modern" in contrast to the popular knowledge of Mafia residents, which was often perceived as "backward," unsubstantiated, or of low status. Such evaluations served to reinforce the existing stratification of social groups and to exclude residents from informal as well as formal influence. The remainder of this chapter explores day-to-day knowledge encounters among Euro-American NGO representatives or researchers, national government officials, and Chole residents, as well as the ways that particular kinds of knowledge circulated—or failed to circulate—within the marine park.

The Status of Science

Within the Mafia Island Marine Park, many Euro-American and Tanzanian NGO representatives, government officials, researchers, and visitors offered scientific frameworks as the basis for their knowledge about Mafia's environment. Although some of these individuals were intrigued by and open to what I shall refer to as *popular knowledge*,[14] for many, science continued to be perceived as the only legitimate means for generating knowledge and was often viewed in antithetical terms to the knowledge of island residents. Intersecting with the longstanding historical emphasis on conservation and development "expertise" within Tanganyika, as described in the previous chapter, such viewpoints served to reinforce assumptions found among many national and international elites that rural Africans generally lacked knowledge.

The following incident recorded in 1994 suggests the perceived gap between scientific and popular knowledge on Mafia. On this particular evening, I was visiting the camp of the British divers from the Frontier project, who were gathering baseline scientific information to aid in the implementation of the marine park. I found myself sitting between an older Austrian scientist, Karl, who was assisting in the work, and Rajabu Issa, a young man from Chole. A large book of colored photographs of fish found in the Indian Ocean lay on a nearby table. As I curiously fingered the volume, the Austrian scientist eagerly pulled me aside to explain the photographs. Rajabu, however, was also interested in talking about the pictures and two conversations simultaneously ensued, one in English, the other in KiSwahili, each oblivious to the other. Karl would point to a particular fish, informing me of its scientific name, its range, and the beauty of its colors as observed underwater with diving equipment. Rajabu, who fished for a livelihood, would point to the same fish and describe whether such fish were found around Mafia, any idiosyncracies in the fishes' behavior, and how they tasted. Rajabu pointed out one fish in particular as having unusually large and sharp teeth and showed me the white scars on his hand where he had once been bitten. Discomforted by the lack of communication between the two men, I translated to Karl that these fish had big teeth, hoping this might lead to a more inclusive conversation. The Austrian scientist, however, frowned skeptically and, pointedly ignoring Rajabu, peered at the photo's caption to validate or invalidate this particular piece of information. Not finding the answer, he went on to the next page and continued his scientific monologue.

While this incident suggests the awkwardness with which some trained in the sciences perceived the knowledge of island residents, numerous other encounters recorded in my fieldnotes suggested a more thorough suspicion. To offer another example, a Danish marine scientist, Johan, arrived in 1997 for a five-week research project on corals within the marine park. My first conversation with this scientist occurred one afternoon when Johan was heading to Chole to check on repairs to a wooden sailboat that he had rented from a man there. As we boarded the decrepit sailboat that served as a ferry to Chole, Johan politely asked me about my research and we began conversing in English from opposite ends of the boat (while curious Chole residents, heads turning back and forth, watched this exchange in a language they did not know). As I began talking about the marine park and residents' concerns about dynamiting, his manner took on what had by this time become a familiar skepticism. He asserted in definitive tones that he did not believe dynamiting to be a real problem on Mafia. In light of his work on corals in the area near Jibondo Island, he saw no evidence that dynamiting was having a significant impact on corals or fish populations in the region. Unable to counter his arguments in a scientific manner, I relied upon Chole residents' accounts of dynamiting, their observations of the ways it affected corals and marine life, and their assessments of how it had impacted fishing over the last decade or more. His look of skepticism now turned to one of open derision. But, he protested, "People here don't even know the coral is alive. How could they possibly know the impact of dynamiting on marine life?!!"

After reaching Chole's tourism camp, I related the incident to Idi Ibrahim, Mzee Salim, and Juma Hassani, who were all working in the camp. While Juma responded with an uncustomary flash of anger, maintaining that Mafia's *wenyeji* (inhabitants) knew far more than *wageni* (visitors), Idi carefully drew a picture on a scrap piece of paper torn from my notebook. Drawing a picture of the Mafia region, he marked with x's the places that had been bombed by dynamiters and then circled a part of Tutia reef referred to as "Ufungo." Although this scientist, like many expatriates, knew little about residents, Mafia's residents had, through observation and gossip, gleaned considerable information about the scientist. Idi knew whose boat this man had rented as well as the exact location of his research. He does not see damage from dynamiting, Idi tolerantly explained, because "Ufungo" has not yet been dynamited and he has not examined other reefs. Juma angrily added that he would be glad to take Johan out in a boat himself to show him the dynamite craters.

The kinds of assumptions evident in these encounters should not be viewed as reflective of "science" per se. Rather, such assumptions form part of a broader historical framework in which particular ethnic and racial groups have come to be associated with various kinds of knowledge labeled as either "modern"or "traditional," with science deemed to be characteristic of Western thought in general, while "tradition" or even "superstition" have been assumed to epitomize the mindsets of formerly colonized peoples. (This is not to deny that there are real differences in how science and popular knowledge come to be validated and framed; however, the assumption that these forms of knowledge are inherently antithetical are equally problematic [see Walley 2002; A. Agrawal 1995]). As documented in the previous chapter, the intersection of status distinctions with particular kinds of knowledge has a long history in Tanzania as well as in other parts of the world. In particular, "modern" and especially scientific forms of knowledge (in contrast to faulty or nonexistent kinds of knowledge based on "traditional" conservatism presumed to be found among rural residents) have long been held up as the key to development and conservation in sub-Saharan Africa.

Although such perspectives grew out of a modernist discourse generated in the colonial era, the belief that rural Africans fundamentally lack knowledge remains salient in many international circles and forms the basis against which "indigenous knowledge" advocates have been struggling. Within the Mafia Island Marine Park, however, such dynamics were not limited to encounters between Euro-Americans and rural Africans. During the course of my fieldwork, some of the most vociferous proponents of the authority of science and the lack of knowledge of rural residents were Tanzanian government bureaucrats and other educated elites, a group that has been largely ignored in international discussions of "indigenous knowledge" (however, see Pigg 1997). For those well-educated Tanzanians living on Mafia (individuals who almost always hailed from the mainland), the emphasis on literacy, formal education, and science as markers of social status, authority, and individual worth was extremely strong. Indeed, the patronizing tone that government officials regularly adopted with Mafia residents (a didacticism fostered by the post-independence socialist government that encouraged cadres to "teach" the people what development required of them) points to the fundamental social divide between the "educated" and the "uneducated" within Tanzania.

On Chole, residents referenced this division when they referred to themselves in self-deprecating terms as "sisi tusiosoma" or "we the uneducated" (despite the fact that many younger women and men had benefited from the expansion of primary school education in the post-independence era and knew how to read and write).[15] The tensions between the "educated" and "uneducated," as well as the links between formal education and social worth, were evident in numerous ways in daily life on Chole. For example, at a meeting called by a nonprofit Christian organization to determine possibilities for funding social projects on the island (projects that never happened), I was struck by the actions of one of the educated Tanzanian visitors who rudely interrupted Chole residents as they were speaking to correct their grammar. He did so until the Scandinavian leader of the missionary group pointedly asked him to stop. Although this act held the potential to be doubly offensive along the coast (KiSwahili is the first language of coastal residents and the second language of many mainland groups from which educated elites are usually drawn), Chole residents, although perhaps somewhat annoyed, had clearly experienced such treatment before and appeared unsurprised.

In another instance, a university-educated mainlander from Dar es Salaam, Peter, who temporarily worked in Chole's tourist camp, developed the habit of himself answering questions directed toward Chole residents. One afternoon, I asked Mzira, who was working in the camp that day, whether women on Chole kept their own names upon marriage (this being the case in many other Muslim regions) or changed them to their husband's last names as is common in the United States. Peter, a Christian, intervened and patronizingly explained that when women married they naturally took the names of their husbands and became "Mrs. so-and-so." Although this was untrue (Muslim women along the coast do not change their names upon marriage), Mzira was too embarrassed to correct so formidable a personage and merely stared awkwardly at his hands. The depth of the barrier between the educated and the uneducated, however, was illustrated most vividly to me by the comments of Mzee Maarufu, one of the most respected elders on Chole. At one point, Mzee Maarufu related that although Pius Mseka, the acting warden of the marine park, treated him in a friendly manner in public, he knew "in his heart" that Mseka thought of Chole residents as being as lowly as "little bugs in the bush" (*vijidudu maporini*). On yet another occasion, Mzee Maarufu offered the disturbing suggestion that while educated Tanzanians placed their trust in each other, "the uneducated" were more trusting of *wazungu* (Euro-Americans) because "we have already seen that fellow Africans can be more contemptuous of us than Europeans."

In general, the valorization of scientific knowledge and formal education, both internationally and within Tanzania, served as an important marker of class status as well as upward social mobility, realities which run counter to the growing interest in "indigenous knowledge" and "participation" expressed by international organizations (Pigg 1997). Within East Africa, Euro-American backgrounds in particular were symbolically coded as of higher status, as more "modern" and, often, as linked to "science" (as I discovered as a high school teacher in Kenya during the late 1980s when I was told that I was qualified to teach chemistry because I was white). Many Tanzanian elites, who were not afforded such a priori status, appeared to instead rely heavily upon scientific knowledge and other elite cultural markers to buttress their social position in relation to rural villagers. Overall, the disdain for popular knowledge expressed by both Euro-American and Tanzanian experts within the park offered possibilities for reproducing status hierarchies that carried both national and international dimensions.[16]

Bureaucracy and the Exclusion of Popular Knowledge

Although scornful attitudes toward popular knowledge were widespread within the park, there *were* a minority of Euro-Americans and Tanzanian elites who expressed interest in "local knowledge" and the reformist efforts that were gaining ground within international organizations. Even in such instances, however, institutional dynamics often continued to marginalize the popular knowledge of Mafia residents. For example, two marine scientists, one Tanzanian and one British, both of whom held positions of authority within Tanzania's Institute of Marine Sciences and had been crucial figures in the establishment of the marine park, were advocates of "community participation" as well as attention to "local knowledge." In addition, the WWF technical adviser, David Holston, who was similarly trained in the marine sciences, fought endless political battles to actively include island residents in decision-making processes and to make the reality of "participation" more than mere rhetoric. In interviews conducted with two of these men, both expressed the desire to be out in boats with Mafia's fishers rather than bound to offices, and both appeared motivated by a pragmatic respect for the experience of those who had spent a considerable part of their lives in boats and on the water. In general, these scientists did not display the romanticized fascination with the "indigenous" expressed by some tourists and environmentalists, or (with the possible exception of Holston) the more radical desire to have residents define the parameters of the park from the ground up. Rather, these individuals were largely interested in the pragmatic goal of using such knowledge to further the internationally defined goals of conservationists and to rationally manage marine resources.

In the end, however, the interest these men expressed towards the popular knowledge of Mafia residents would remain largely unexplored, as would their desire to spend more time in boats. Ironically for a park conceptualized in terms of "participation," the bureaucratic organization of the marine park left almost no room for such endeavors. Indeed, the knowledge that Mafia residents possessed about the marine environment was largely deemed extraneous to the bureaucratic organization of the park as conceived by international organizations. Although in the park's planning stages, the British and

Tanzanian marine biologists *did* go out in boats with Mafia residents to help determine the boundaries of the proposed marine park, such efforts were brief (too brief, as residents complained) and were often part of formal excursions with government officials, a situation that made it difficult for Mafia residents to freely express their views.

When attempts *were* made to incorporate popular knowledge, such knowledge was reduced to information to be slotted into preexisting bureaucratic frameworks. For example, in the years following the establishment of the park, efforts were made to solicit "local knowledge" through Participatory Rural Appraisal (or PRAs), a survey technique commonly used by international organizations engaged in "participatory" work with rural people in the so-called Third World. Indeed, WWF had allotted funding for its community development staff to gather baseline information about the ten (later twelve) villages within the park. Although the Village Holistic Study (WWF 1996) was a large, KiSwahili language volume, it consisted mainly of bullet lists of the official "needs" and "problems" of various villages (from the desire for new schools to anger over dynamite fishing) with little in-depth discussion of either residents' viewpoints or their knowledge. In general, the information that was gathered was intended to fit within the predetermined park organization and was not designed to aid in the formation of the marine park itself. Indeed, this study was only completed several years *after* the official gazetting of the marine park and only a small portion of it would be translated into English (making it unlikely that its findings would circulate off the island). In short, the knowledge of Mafia residents would play almost no role in the actual formation of the marine park, an organizational structure which emerged full-blown from the national and international institutions that had conceived of the park.

In the end, whether or not the popular knowledge of residents would be incorporated within the Mafia Island Marine Park was not simply determined by the individual proclivities of NGO representatives, the stated policies of organizations like WWF, or even the accuracy or usefulness of particular pieces of information. A key factor proved to be whether information was accessible in a format easily recognizable and digestible by scientifically and managerially oriented bureaucracies. Such formats required, not only advanced educational credentials for legitimate publication, but also the use of English, the international lingua franca, which would allow such knowledge to circulate in the international development and conservation world. As one of the community development officers complained to me, even after the compilation of information from hundreds of Mafia's fishers, it was difficult to get anyone in national and international offices to recognize such knowledge since it was "not based on citations" (see also Latour 1987).

It perhaps comes as no surprise that not all of the scientific information compiled for the park was "good." Indeed, academics recognize as a matter of course that some scholarship is better than others, just as Chole residents make distinctions about who possesses more reliable knowledge about fishing or the history of the region. Indeed, many of the reports that had been written about Mafia were undertaken by educationally credentialed researchers and consultants who had visited Mafia only briefly (in some cases only weeks) and which were, as the WWF technical adviser complained, frequently riddled with inaccuracies. Despite potential problems, however, reports and articles generated by credentialed professionals had the power to circulate in WWF and government offices as well as in other national and international venues in ways in which the knowledge possessed by Mafia's fishers, even those who have fished for most of their adult lives and have formidable practical experience of Mafia's waters, did not (see also Latour 1987).

The ability of such institutionalized knowledge to circulate also meant that it had the capacity to take on a life of its own (see also Weber 1958). To offer one example, a British warship mapped the coastal waters around Mafia in the early 1800s (Baumann 1957[1896]), marking an uninhabited island near the mouth of Chole Bay as "Jina Island." This island, however, is popularly known on Mafia as "Miewi."[17] Nevertheless, subsequent maps of the region, from the colonial to the postcolonial era, as well as some reports on the marine environment written by Europeans (again inaccessible to residents) continue to refer to the island as Jina. As I sat reading one such report in Chole's camp, I puzzled over this tendency to refer to Miewi as "Jina." Juma Hassani, who had worked in the past for the British divers doing research on the marine environment, gave a laugh of recognition. He revealed that the divers had often asked him about an island called "Jina" of which he had never heard. He smiled, noting that they must have thought him a fool for denying any knowledge of an island that was only a short distance from Chole and well known to all fishers on Mafia.

In short, knowledge about Mafia largely circulated along distinct tracks. Knowledge documented on paper and produced and recorded by those with official positions or proper educational credentials readily circulated in national and international offices. In particular, those documents written in English and that followed the conventions of international bureaucracies or of scientific scholarship (regardless of their potential accuracy or depth) had the ability to circulate freely among international conservation and development organizations. In contrast, the popular knowledge of those living on Mafia traveled along different routes. Built upon long experience in the region and linking coastal residents largely (but not exclusively) by word of mouth, this knowledge circulated in ways that were generally excluded from, and unrecognizable by, bureaucratic institutions and that were easily dismissed as merely "local" or "traditional" by national and international elites.

The power-laden implications of this distinct tracking of knowledge, however, cannot be reduced to the presumed superiority of literacy in contrast to orality.[18] Indeed, the oral pronouncements and gossip of those who worked within national and international institutions had a profound impact upon park decision making, while the written requests of village marine park committees concerning such vital matters as the location of the park's temporary headquarters ended up relegated to file cabinets in Kilindoni. Nonetheless, the framing of knowledge within—or outside of—such prescribed formats had a powerful effect on the ways in which knowledge circulated, or failed to circulate, both on Mafia and beyond. Thus, in the end, it was more than the disdainful attitudes of experts like Johan that served to marginalize popular knowledge within the Mafia Island Marine Park. There was also the unspoken reality of a bureaucratic structure premised on advanced education that allowed the formally trained to both influence park decisions and to reproduce their own status. Ironically, the bureaucratic structure of the park, which was intended to institutionalize the rights of residents to "participation," worked to marginalize and exclude the very people it claimed to incorporate.

"Sisi tusiosoma": "We the Uneducated"

Yet, how did Mafia residents themselves view and evaluate the kinds of knowledge they possessed? First, it must be acknowledged that in contrast to popular assumptions about "indigenous" knowledge, the knowledge that Chole residents possessed about the marine and terrestrial environment was eclectic in origin (as is presumably true in most cases, see also Gupta 1998). In addition to drawing heavily upon personal experience (experiences that differed widely among individuals as well as by gender), residents' knowledge also drew upon shared as well as unevenly transmitted cultural information from such diverse sources as coastal maritime traditions, the seafaring practices of Arabs, Portuguese, and Indonesians, and the science-based knowledge conveyed through colonial and post-independence government officials and visiting researchers. As described in chapter 4, many men on the island, most of whom had fished at some point in their lives, could offer detailed information about the types of fish in Mafia's waters, the particular habits of various species, the types of fish caught by different fishing gear, the impact of seasonal changes in rains and monsoon winds on fish populations, and the increasing rarity of certain fish species in Mafia's waters (see also Walley 2002).

It should also be recognized, however, that while fishing has a long history in the region, it has been less culturally valued than trading which formed the highest status occupation in historical urban centers along the coast. Thus, fishing was not the same kind of central cultural preoccupation on Chole that it is (or was) among some artisanal or small-scale fishers in other parts of the world, and residents' knowledge—although extensive—reflects this reality. This point was underscored for me one afternoon as I sat in camp reading an article about historical fishing practices in Polynesia. Idi Ibrahim sat down next to me and pointed to a black and white photo of an elderly Polynesian man next to a dug-out canoe. He asked who these people were, commenting that they resembled WaGunya from the northern part of the Kenyan coast. I explained that the article described how village fishers in this region have complex knowledge about the sea, including the ability to navigate by the stars, to time runs of particular fish, and to place ritual prohibitions on fishing to conserve fish populations. I asked Idi if people on Chole possessed similar kinds of knowledge. No, he admitted, suggesting that the difference lay in the fact that for the people depicted in the photo, fishing was their *asili* or "origin" in contrast to those on Mafia. Such comments warn against the tendency to generalize and romanticize concepts of "indigenous" knowledge or to try to isolate environmental knowledge from the broader social dynamics of which it is a part.

Although many Chole residents privately displayed considerable assurance in their own environmental knowledge, few would publicly contradict elites whom residents clearly expected to lecture rather than converse with them. Yet the underlying tensions surrounding the worth of residents' knowledge appeared in accounts such as the one told by Mzee Bakari regarding a fishing school that he had attended as a young man along with other Mafia residents. The school, located in Mtwara, was led by educated mainlanders who themselves did not come from fishing backgrounds. According to Mzee Bakari, he had encouraged the instructor to teach by doing rather than from books, protesting that the men from Mafia already knew what was contained in the texts. The teacher, however, ignored his suggestion. Near the end of the course, the class went on a field trip to the ocean and the instructor demonstrated the laying of a fish trap. Mzee Bakari protested that the winds were wrong and that the trap would not catch any fish. The next day, in accordance with his prediction, there was nothing in the trap except a single small fish. Mzee Bakari, who had been chosen leader (*mwenyekiti*) of his group, triumphantly related how he then set a trap himself drawing upon his own knowledge as a fisherman and brought in a large haul the following day. Clearly, this story was intended to underscore the value of residents' (and his own) knowledge in contrast to that of book-educated "experts."

In other instances, however, Chole residents demonstrated an ambivalent attitude toward the "expert" knowledge which they were assumed to lack, whether in relation to national elites or to Euro-Americans. The hopes for development that had flowered on Mafia in the post-independence period, as well as across the so-called Third World more generally, nonetheless, also meant taking on assumptions about the importance of "modern" education in contrast to the presumed lack of knowledge and "backwardness" of rural villagers like themselves. Such attitudes presumably led to the tendency of some Chole residents to express exaggerated understandings of "modern" book-learning as well as respect for the technical knowledge associated in their minds with *wazungu* (Europeans). For example, the elderly Bi Rehema Hassani informed fellow anthropologist Rachel Eide, that *wazungu* "knew everything." When Rachel protested, Bi Rehema countered, "Tell me, is it true that *wazungu* sent people to the moon"? When Rachel acknowledged this was true, Bi Rehema responded, "*Bas*" meaning "enough" or "no more need be said."

Nevertheless, others were more skeptical. Idi Ibrahim also asked me whether it was true that *wazungu* had sent people to visit the moon, but this time implying that such a story might have been circulated to mock the presumed gullibility of Africans. My affirmative answer did nothing to alter his skeptical expression. On another occasion, I was looking over a picture book about dinosaurs procured for Chole's primary school through a U.S.-based non-governmental organization. As Fatuma Fadhili examined photographs of an archeological dig in which crews were uncovering enormous bones, she smiled and announced in a tone conveying both admiration and bemusement that *wazungu* were very "naughty" (*watundu*) for digging up the remains of the past. The ambivalence in this comment captures both a respect for the technological endeavors associated with Euro-Americans and a perplexity over their motivations that equated Euro-Americans with precocious but naughty children. Thus, while Chole residents at times expressed the denigrating viewpoints espoused by elites, at others times they explicitly countered such assumptions in ways that supported the validity of their own knowledge.

Although many Euro-American and Tanzanian professionals who visited Mafia assumed rigid boundaries between scientific and popular knowledge, it should be noted that more constructive interactions occasionally occurred. For example, I witnessed a mutually satisfying sharing of information on several occasions on Chole as I translated for visiting Euro-American professionals who were working as part of the community-based tourism initiative. To offer one telling experience of this kind, I translated for a British naturalist, Geoffrey Owens, who spent several months on Chole creating a nature trail and an accompanying booklet for tourists. Geoffrey first gathered scattered information about Chole's natural life from conversations with residents who were working or passing through the camp. He constructed the rest of the trail on his own, however, drawing on his prior knowledge as a science teacher. Once the trail was completed, Geoffrey again asked me to translate as he offered two guided tours of the trail: one, with children from Chole's primary school; the second, with members of one of Chole's village committees who were involved in the ecotourism project.

What emerged, to Geoffrey's good-natured chagrin, was less a "tour" than the give-and-take of a learning session in which he was more often the recipient of information than the teacher. The schoolchildren already knew most of the information that the trail was designed to teach. For example, when Geoffrey tried to stump them by asking whether the large fruit bats on the island were birds or animals, the children readily responded that the creatures were animals "because they suckle their young." However, the children *were* intrigued to learn information to which they did not have access—the word for "mangrove" in English, the territorial range of the fruit bats, and the migratory patterns of birds that traveled from Mafia to as far as South Africa and Europe. The tour also created the impression among the schoolchildren that the trail was not simply for foreign tourists but also for them, and I later spied children taking their younger siblings, generally easily captive toddlers, on the tour and explaining to them in worldly tones what was to be learned at each station of the trail. Later that day, the adult women and men of Chole's committee even more clearly emerged as Geoffrey's teachers, correcting information and themselves explaining the role of bats in pollinating the baobab trees, the types of mangroves found around Mafia, the ways to differentiate among types of termites as well as their idiosyncratic behaviors, and the nature of parasitic "strangler fig" trees and why such trees grew on the tops of the stone ruins that littered the island (the answer: birds who had eaten their seed excreted them on the roof tops). However, they were again fascinated by occasional new bits of information and, when Geoffrey brought out his beautiful ink drawings of the plants, birds, and wildlife of the island, they were particularly thrilled and one elderly woman proclaimed him truly an "expert" (*mtaalamu*). Unfortunately, such scattered moments of shared knowledge were remarkably few within the marine park despite its promotion as a "participatory" project.

Although this analysis has stressed the role that "expertise" played in generating social hierarchy on Mafia, this does not mean that Chole residents have no use for "experts." Indeed, Chole residents were often annoyed with "experts," not because their knowledge was superfluous, but because government officials and various other "experts" *did not help them enough.* The critical accounts of Suleimani Rajabu, Mzee Bakari, Juma Hassani, and other fishers often focused, not so much on what experts did, but on the perceived reality that government technical staff such as those at the Maritime Division "did nothing." Their goal was to cajole officials and development workers to offer greater assistance with the problems residents were having such as identifying the diseases that attacked their tree crops or helping them obtain fishing gear that would allow them to fish further out at sea. Although it took some time for me to recognize the particular nature of their critique, it seems obvious in retrospect that their position was one that was heavily conditioned, not simply by a faith in technical assistance or the power of education, but by the realities of escalating poverty. It is not surprising that in a context of pervasive need residents desired to be assisted—not ignored—and their resentment was directed most intensely at their perceived neglect. The "help" residents seemed to hope for, yet never receive, however, was conceived according to their own priorities and understandings of their situation. In other words, the problem of expertise for Chole residents was not a product of knowledge per se, but of the broader power relationships in which such expertise was embedded and the problematic relationship between the "educated" and the "uneducated."

The "social drama" of the Mafia Island Marine Park, as previously described, demonstrates how Mafia residents were marginalized within this ostensibly "participatory" project. This chapter has explored some of the means by which such exclusion has occurred, focusing both on the managerial structure of the park and the ongoing marginalization of the popular knowledge of island residents. Although bureaucracies may serve to institutionalize rights, such organizations also work to exclude and dominate—outcomes which are not predetermined, but rather the result of struggle. Because Mafia residents were excluded from direct participation within the bureaucratic battles over the marine park, they were forced to rely upon more powerful others to struggle on their behalf. Thus, I have argued that, in contrast to commonplace narratives of modernity, bureaucracy itself can call patron–client relationships into being. In a context of expanding numbers of international organizations, some theorists suggest that transnational bureaucracies constitute a new form of governmentality in a "global" era (Leve 2001; Hardt and Negri 2000; Gupta and Ferguson 2002). Yet such transformations are not simply "new" phenomena, but are building upon and reworking older dynamics, including patron–client relationships and the institutional processes put into place by colonial and post-colonial bureaucracies. Thus, our attempts to understand contemporary transformations require that we look to the past as much as to the future. Although the participation of Mafia residents was to have been institutionalized through park bureaucracy, the goal of the marine park was also to produce development. It is to this effort which we now turn.

CHAPTER SEVEN

Tourist Encounters: Alternative Readings of Nature and "Development"

THE MAFIA ISLAND Marine Park differs from previous national parks in Tanzania in that it promises more than the preservation of nature. In addition to pledging participation for residents living within the park, it also explicitly seeks to encourage development. This development, however, is of a particular kind. In an effort to foster "sustainability" rather than the environmental destructiveness associated with many mainstream development initiatives, planners for the Mafia Island Marine Park and similar projects worldwide have attempted to foster tourism or, in some cases, environmentally friendly forms of "ecotourism." Although tourism on Mafia remained at relatively low levels during the mid-1990s (in contrast to the sharp surge in tourism in the neighboring island of Zanzibar), the construction of several new lodges catering to wealthy international tourists underscored the possibility that tourism might become an increasingly dominant economic force on Mafia.

Despite the academic tendency to debate development in terms of technical policy issues or in Manichaean terms as either a source of economic salvation for the world's poor or a source of ongoing oppression, the analysis offered here starts from another place. It begins by considering the multiple meanings given to "development" by Chole residents, Tanzanian government officials, and Euro-American tourists and expatriates, as well as how such meanings relate to their own social positioning within the Mafia Island Marine Park. It also considers the types of social interactions that emerged among tourists and coastal residents of both Mafia and Zanzibar during the early-to-mid 1990s and, ultimately, asks whether tourism has the capability to offer the kind of *maendeleo* or "development" that Mafia residents desire.

EXPLORING DEVELOPMENT ON MAFIA

Maendeleo: The Meanings of Development for Chole Residents

For those people whom I knew on Chole, development or *maendeleo*[1] formed a continuing preoccupation. Indeed, their desire for "development" was at the core of residents' support for the Mafia Island Marine Park and tourism-oriented Chole Kisiwani Conservation and Development Company. Residents' desires, however, were also intimately connected to the stark sense of marginalization they felt from "development" both within Tanzania and in relation to other parts of the world. Given the relational connotations of the concept, it is perhaps not surprising that discussions of development invariably led Chole residents to compare themselves with others. They were acutely aware of their low-ranking position on an imagined ladder of development conceptualized in both international and national terms, and they regularly contrasted their situation with that of more "developed" regions, such as Europe and the United States, as well as other areas within Tanzania and even other villages on Mafia. In the mid-1990s, people on Chole regularly complained that they had "no development at all" (*hatuna maendeleo yo yote*), citing their lack of access to schooling, health care, or dependable transportation to the main island. Residents found this situation particularly galling given the previously documented history of Chole as a prosperous nineteenth-century port town with a market, paved roads, and candle-lit streetlamps. Chole residents also expressed embarrassment that "outsiders" (*wageni*) might perceive them as lacking development.

Although Euro-American tourists to Mafia were primarily interested in activities that emphasized "getting away" from the "developed" world, Chole residents considered those sites that suggested development on Mafia as those most worth seeing. This became particularly apparent to me one afternoon when I joined one of the workers from Chole's tourist camp, Idi Ibrahim, on an excursion to Jibondo, the most distant island in the government ward (*kata*) that also encompasses Chole and Juani. In the *mashua* sailing boat that Idi had inherited in conjunction with his brothers and sisters, we were joined by Idi's wife, Maryamu, and their youngest daughter, Sharifa, as well as Hadija, Ally Ahmadi, and a few others. As we sailed across the peaceful bay, Idi carefully negotiated the boat past the jagged coral outcroppings beneath the water's surface. In the distance, Jibondo lay white and glaring in the sun. It was a dry coral rock island with few wells and little of the greenery that made Chole appear so hospitable; nevertheless, the houses were well built and prosperous looking. Indeed, Chole residents often claimed that Jibondo possessed greater "development," the result, some ventured, of rising fish prices and the expert abilities of Jibondo's fishers given their almost total dependence upon the sea.[2]

Once upon land, my hosts took me sight-seeing. Interspersed with side-stops to visit with friends, relatives, and acquaintances, we visited Jibondo's small medical clinic (unfortunately, sorely bereft of supplies), the primary school surrounded by boisterous students in tattered but brightly colored uniforms, the concrete office of the ruling political party Chama Cha Mapinduzi, and, finally, the tin-roof-covered cistern used to collect water on this dry island. On virtually all of my trips to Mafia's other islands and villages that were accompanied by Chole residents, I was taken to a similar set of places considered by my hosts to be the relevant sites to visit. This is not to say that Mafia residents never expanded their repertoire of what was worth visiting (after the tent in which I stayed in Chole's camp was built into a tree house, it became something of a tourist site for Swahili visitors who joked that it resembled *dungu* or the raised homes common in the flood-prone Rufiji area of the mainland). In general, however, those sites that were deemed worth visiting on Mafia were ones that signaled "development" to residents in one form or another.

Although donor organizations and residents might agree that Mafia lacked development in comparison to other places, the connotations of "development" among Chole residents both paralleled and differed from those meanings commonly proffered by international organizations and government elites. When asked in the abstract how they defined "development" or what kind of "development" they would like to see on Mafia, people on Chole mentioned many of the things that Euro-Americans also equated with development. They emphasized their desires for electricity, improved transportation (particularly a motorized ferry for travel between Chole and Mafia's main island), better roads, additional schooling, and "modern" boats and fishing equipment. In other words, they hoped for the infrastructure and technology commonly associated with "developed" countries that could make their lives easier and serve as potential sources of upward mobility.

However, in day-to-day usage, many Chole residents used the word *maendeleo* in a variety of ways that differed from international discourses. Rather than considering development in terms of the transformation of societies as a whole (a historical vestige of the concept's nineteenth-century origins in European evolutionary thought), development was commonly used by Chole residents to refer to individuals getting ahead economically in highly specific ways. Thus, a person who desired a job or some money could speak of the need for a "a little *maendeleo*." This perspective was evident in the practice of naming the small-scale entrepreneurial activities residents commonly engaged in, such as selling bread or sweets, raising chickens, or collecting shells, as *miradi* or "projects"—the same word used for development projects organized by international donors (see also Tripp 1997). Such usages also applied to noneconomic aspects of *maendeleo* such as education. For example, one afternoon when I was teaching English to adults on Chole, an elderly woman in the class joked with curious passers-by that she was "busy getting a little development." Spoken in a simultaneously proud yet self-deprecating tone, this comment was perceived as humorous because it recognized something of which Mafia residents were acutely aware—their own marginalization from the institutionalized education that was taken as a marker of "development." At the same time, her remark suggested that development could be most dependably gleaned by individual initiative.[3]

In other instances, *maendeleo* came to be mapped onto prior historical understandings of wealth. For example, as noted in chapter 2, Mzee Maarufu drew upon ideas of children as wealth when he described the "*maendeleo ya kuzaa*" or "the 'development' of giving birth" on Chole. He recalled how, after the demise of Chole as an urban area when he was a child, the island had become radically depopulated. Happily, he noted, the few remaining members of the younger generation had borne children and now their children had repopulated the island. This usage clearly offers a distinct departure from the discourse of contemporary international organizations, which equates development with having fewer rather than more children. Other usages of development were even more unusual to my American ears. For example, Mzee Bakari once told me that the *wazee,* or former generations of people on Chole, used to "bury their *maendeleo* in the ground." This usage was so dissonant with my own cultural preconceptions of the term *development* that I simply assumed at the time that I had misunderstood his KiSwahili. However, upon repeatedly replaying a tape of our conversation after I returned to the United States, I realized there had been no mistake. Here, *maendeleo* was used to stand in for money—the hoped-for object of "getting ahead." Instead of putting their money in the bank, Mzee Bakari described how previous generations had secretly buried their money in holes dug in the ground (noting that, in the case of sudden death, such practices could result in the unfortunate outcome that the heirs of the deceased would be unable to locate their inheritance).[4]

In general, historically based understandings of wealth or *maendeleo* on Chole posed a sharp contrast to commonplace narratives of modernity. In the accounts of Chole residents, no divide necessarily existed between the modern and the traditional, nor was there an assumption of inevitable "progress" as time passes. From this perspective, residents' ancestors also had access to *maendeleo*, contradicting modernist narratives of history that presuppose earlier periods to be characterized precisely by their lack of development. I later continued my conversation with Mzee Bakari and asked him what term Chole residents had used before *maendeleo* gained ascendency in the period around Tanganyika's independence in 1961. He immediately answered "*uchumi*," referring to the business activities that he himself had engaged in as a younger man and that had a long history along the East African coast. When I asked whether he saw any differences between the two, he quickly stated there was none and demonstrated his surprise that I would ask.

In other cases, individuals (often younger ones) did reference presumed differences between "traditional" and "modern" forms of wealth, but played with such dichotomies in ways that have no equivalent in English. For example, Fatuma Fadhili sarcastically remarked to anthropologist Rachel Eide that the only *maendeleo* occurring on Mafia these days involved men using the cash they had earned to take second wives. As in Mzee Maarufu's comment, Fatuma's witticism drew upon the historical value of people as wealth (spouses as well as children) which she playfully contrasted with contempo-

rary "development" based on cash and procured through wage labor or selling fish. In doing so, she suggested that Chole residents continue to be marginalized from "real" development, while simultaneously offering a gendered
critique that hinted that the only "development" occurring on Chole hark-
ened back to older models that benefited men more than (and potentially at
the expense of) women.

In sum, the use of the term *maendeleo* on Mafia contrasted with Euro-
American understandings in a number of ways: it was commonly used to
refer to individuals rather than societies; it referred not to a general state of
"progress" and societal uplift but very concretely to financial well-being
(cash as well as social status); and it did not necessarily assume that the
present was more evolved or qualitatively different from the past. Although
the idea of "development" in Euro-American usages is predicated on a modernist view in which time progresses and moves forward, on Mafia such
understandings competed with alternative understandings of time. For example, some older Chole residents, including Mzee Bakari, relied upon millennial Islamic ideas of the "coming end of the world" or *aheri zamani*. According to such ideas, the world was gradually falling apart, contemporary
life was a degradation of the life led by one's ancestors, and time was slow-
ing down rather than speeding up. For Mzee Bakari, the growing worthless-
ness of money due to currency devaluations, the flimsy nature of contemporary goods made in China and India, the decreasing fertility of the soil and
the seas, and the growing impoverishment of Mafia's residents in an era of
Structural Adjustment Programs were understood, not as a failure of "development," but a manifestation of *aheri zamani*. Not everyone agreed with
these views (for example, Bi Sharifa, Mzee Bakari's wife, vociferously challenged her husband's ideas that the presumed lack of control men held over
women in the contemporary era was a sign of the coming end of the world).
Nevertheless, this concept proved better able to explain the economic hardships that residents were experiencing than modernist notions of "development" or "progress."

Development and National Elites

National government officials, whether assigned to the marine park or Mafia's district government offices, offered a considerably different view of
development. These views alternately resonated and conflicted with those of
Mafia residents and Euro-American NGO workers and tourists. In general,
government officials agreed with Mafia residents that such things as better
roads, improved houses, electricity, a motorized ferry, and the other "modern" accouterments that Mafia residents desired, would all constitute "development." Like residents, they also considered development in explicitly relational terms, operating from the uncomfortable position in which Tanzania

was defined internationally in terms of what it was perceived to lack. The tensions of this position surfaced, for example, in debates between donors and government officials over the new Mafia Island Marine Park headquarters. When government officials commissioned elaborate architectural plans for a state-of-the-art office, donors were angered by what they saw as extravagant and wasteful planning, which was both out of proportion to the project and which contravened its populist goals. Donor representatives privately suggested that such actions were indicative of government officials' refusal to acknowledge more progressive views of development that stressed basic needs and community participation. The wish for an opulent headquarters, however, might alternately be "read" as a desire for international recognition and prestige by a national elite which felt itself to be marginalized on a world stage.

At the same time, government officials offered a far more state-centered view of development than either Mafia residents or park donors. In contrast to Chole residents' focus on individuals "getting ahead" or NGOs' interests in reforming development through an emphasis on environmental sustainability and community participation, national officials continued to support the state-oriented views of development that had first gained international prominence in the immediate post-World War II era (Finnemore 1997). Like their colonial predecessors, government officials in the post-independence socialist period commonly attributed Mafia's lack of development to residents' ignorance, to their stubborn and irrational devotion to "tradition," or to a refusal to work hard (see also Caplan 1992; Snyder 2001). In a context in which money was largely lacking for development initiatives (or in which donor funds routinely disappeared for such projects as paving the road between Utende and Kilindoni or tarmac-ing the tiny sand-covered airstrip in Kilindoni), it was also easier to offer lectures about development rather than substantial action. As previously mentioned, government officials regularly chastised Mafia residents for such activities as clearing land with fire, failing to weed coconut trees, and keeping children out of school to help with chores—activities that they, like their colonial predecessors, viewed as impediments to "development" or signs of regional "backwardness."

In contrast to Mafia residents, government officials also shared the evolutionary assumptions of development common in international discourses that posited societies as in a process of progressive social transformation. Within Tanzania, this meant not only that different countries could be characterized as more or less developed, but that particular people and regions within the nation-state were perceived as more "developed" than others. For example, many officials implied to me that they viewed themselves as more "developed" than Mafia residents. Some made a point of stressing to me how "undeveloped" Mafia was, asking how I could stand to live in such a place.

Others hinted, some more subtly than others, at the apparent backwardness, laziness, and lack of interest in education they found among coastal Muslims, explicitly contrasting this situation with regions like Kilimanjaro which they deemed much more "developed." In addition, those few who had studied abroad were quick to point out this fact to me, aligning their sensibilities as closer to my own as a citizen of a "developed" country, while simultaneously distancing themselves from Mafia residents. Although government officials clearly believed that development should be directed by the nation, officials were also quick to assert that the citizenry unjustly expected the government to do "everything" and that the people needed to "learn" that their own hard labor was required. In short, much like international discourses, the language of national elites was readily able to attribute internal differences in "development" to hard work and the proper attitudes toward development rather than to social marginalization or varying class positions.

While government officials often attributed the lack of development on Mafia to the ignorance of residents themselves, those living on Chole instead ascribed this condition to marginalization and neglect by these very same officials. Residents argued that officials from more developed regions such as Kilimanjaro were "jealous" (*wanaona wivu*) of other regions gaining development and hence sought to block Mafia residents from obtaining *maendeleo*. As evidence of this tendency, they pointed to the opposition of some officials to the new tourism camp on Chole and later efforts to "eat" the tourist entrance fees that were intended for community coffers. In short, while for government officials the language of development was a modernist one that focused on the necessity of further education and hard work to attain new levels of "development," for Chole residents, development was a language of social access and exclusion.

From Alternative Development to Discourses of Ruin:
Euro-Americans within the Marine Park

While "development" was highly valued by both Chole residents and government officials, Euro-Americans within the park were markedly ambivalent. To understand this situation, it is necessary to consider how conflicting views of development among Euro-Americans stem from longstanding tensions within European thought. Beginning in the late colonial period, development gained ascendency as the reformist idea of bringing planned "progress" to the non-Western world (Cooper and Packard 1997; Cowen and Shenton 1996; Crush 1995). Such assumptions centered around encouraging particular economic arrangements (namely, capitalism or, in some cases, socialism), the use of the sciences to achieve social transformation (as described in previous chapters), and the entrenchment of other "modern" political and social institutions. This perspective, based on discourses rooted in nineteenth-century Europe and the United States which presumed the superiority of "modern" life, symbolically underscored European dominance and naturalized international economic and political inequality (Escobar 1995). At the same time, however, "development" could also be appropriated as a language of rights and entitlement by formerly colonized peoples (Cooper and Packard 1997; Peters 2000). Today, developmentalist perspectives clearly remain common among many Euro-Americans, both in popular discussions and in the policies and viewpoints of numerous international organizations, even as mainstream development projects and institutions are transformed to varying degrees by such concepts as "participation" and "sustainability."

Yet, there has also been a long counter-history of antimodernist discourses within Euro-American symbolic traditions as discussed at various points in this book (indeed, reform efforts stem in part from such discourses). Arising in reaction to modernist conceptions of the world, antimodernist discourses have been promulgated by critics from across the political spectrum and form a powerful strand in Euro-American thought. Such discourses focus on arenas perceived to be outside modernity, such as nature and the "traditional" cultures of non-Western peoples, and seek to preserve sites and ways of life viewed as "pristine" or "authentic" by virtue of their supposed distance from modernity. Such discourses are widely apparent within the tourism industry. Indeed, advertisements for lodges within the Mafia Island Marine Park, which promise, for example, that "Mafia is little changed from ancient times and retains a traditional, friendly culture,"[5] are premised upon such ideas, promising visitors an escape from the development of the modern world at the same time that the park ironically promises Mafia residents its exact opposite.

Differing perspectives on "development" at times resulted in a mutual sense of bewilderment between Chole residents and Euro-Americans on Mafia. When visiting the islands, Euro-American tourists did not seek out the schools, office buildings, and water collection tanks that I have suggested that Mafia residents considered important sites to visit. Rather, tourists were attracted to the region's abundant reefs and marine life, its beaches and coral atolls, and the stone ruins on Chole or at Kua—all sites which signaled valued forms of nature and culture within Euro-American symbolic traditions. In addition, those things which Mafia residents associated with poverty (for example, thatched rather than tin roofs, cloth sails rather than outboard engines, and the toys that children fashioned from palm leaves and twigs in contrast to the store-bought motorcars carried by tourist children), were instead perceived as valuable forms of "tradition" by many visitors, attractive precisely because of their difference from "modern development."

Occasionally, on Mafia, I was peppered with questions regarding the seemingly odd habits of Euro-American tourists. For example, Bi Sharifa wanted to know why light-skinned Europeans would want to lie in the sun and make their skins dark, while people on Mafia themselves wished for lighter skin (a legacy of both Arab and European prejudices). Why, Idi Mohammed asked, do Europeans always want things to be quiet? Don't they like music? An elderly woman near Mlola forest on Mafia's main island quizzed me as to why *wazungu* (Europeans) would want to hike out to the rocky, windy coastline where there are no people, a place where she admitted that she found no beauty. And, why, Ibrahim Abdallah asked, did two young German men camp on Chole's shores several years back and stay there for a week—living completely naked? According to Ibrahim, they even went to fetch water at the main well next to the mosque, right in the middle of a cluster of houses, without wearing any clothes. In such instances, I tried to explain as best I could why so many Euro-Americans, myself included, might be tired of urban noise and environmental pollution at home and instead seek nature, quiet, and peacefulness in places like Mafia. Even though I was aware that many Chole residents experienced the island's "peacefulness" as boredom, such explanations were politely received (indeed, many Chole residents were themselves ambivalent about urban spaces such as Dar es Salaam). Yet, trying to explain the presumed desire of the German nudists to be "natural" with the "natives" proved more embarrassing and, in the end, I simply left Ibrahim to his presumption that these individuals were simply not right in the head.

Conflicting conceptions of development among Chole residents and Euro-Americans emerged most clearly, however, in ideals for Mafia's future. During my stays in 1994 and 1995, for example, it became clear that the transformations happening in Chole's growing tourism camp were causing consternation among Mafia's tiny Euro-American expatriate population, all of whom were either conservationists or involved in Utende's tourism industry. During this time, camp workers on Chole had carefully lined the expanding network of footpaths linking the camp to the waterfront with coral rock, painted brilliantly white with limestone. Some of the Euro-American expatriates vocally expressed their dissatisfaction to me, complaining that the rocks (a cliche of hotel development along the Tanzanian coast) were "tasteless," and they derided the aesthetic sensibilities of Chole's *wazungu* developers for failing to adopt the low-key sensibilities suitable for "ecotourism." I later learned, however, that the white rocks, like the flowers planted along the paths near the waterfront, were not the design of Chole's absentee tour operators, but had been undertaken for very different reasons by Chole residents involved in the camp. One camp worker, Fuadi Hassani, commented cheerfully to me one morning, as he painted even more rocks brilliantly white, that they were once again creating a *barabara* (avenue) on Chole. Indeed, the sandy path from the waterfront to the camp lay upon the remains of the coral stone boulevard built by the ambitious Arab administrator who had been derided for his "modernist" pretensions by German geographer Oscar Baumann in the 1890s. For Chole residents in the contemporary period, the coral-lined footpaths of the camp, as ephemeral as these paths were, signaled their hopes for a revival of prosperity and *maendeleo* on Mafia.

Beneath such aesthetic differences lay still other tensions, as became clear in a conversation I had with Rashidi Hemedi in 1994, a period in which he was still camp manager for the Chole Kisiwani Conservation and Development company. This conversation occurred shortly after one of the tourism developers had decided to build a "tree house" or wooden platform upon which my tent would be relocated. When one of the British divers from Frontier heard this news as he walked through the camp one afternoon, he commented sarcastically under his breath, "What next? A Jack-In-The-Box?" I was well aware that the Frontier leaders opposed the idea of tourism development on Chole for fear that it would destroy "nature" (I admit that I was also disturbed by the thought of the tangled vines, civet cats, and multi-colored birds that dominated the overgrown ruins being shortly replaced by a café and a plethora of tourists). The Frontier divers, however, sought to buttress their perspective by arguing that "people" on Chole opposed the tourism initiative, suggesting that the school and clinic were a trick used by the developers to impose their will on the island. (I would spend my first few months on Chole attempting to determine whether or not this was true, and discovered that most Chole residents in fact supported the tourism project, despite contestation in some quarters as described in chapter 3). The potential insult in such easy assumptions became clear to me in my conversation with Rashidi Hemedi.

On this particular evening, Rashidi was figuring the account books by lantern light, while I finished my dinner at the camp table. He cautiously asked me if I knew what the Frontier divers thought of the Chole development (and by extension of myself since I was living in its camp). I understood what Rashidi was implying. I told him that I was aware that they, like many Europeans, feared that tourism and the Chole Kisiwani enterprise would "ruin" Chole. Although Rashidi began this conversation cautiously, he soon launched into an impassioned monologue:

We debated long and hard among ourselves whether to accept this project. I am a smart man and can tell the difference between one project and the next. Do they think we are fools and would agree to anything? We know that this is a business for the developers and that they have their own interests, but we also know that the government has never helped us fix even a single well on this island. How else could we get those things [i.e., the school and clinic]? They [the divers] don't know how we make a living here. They just sleep and do their research and greet people. They don't know our financial problems or how we are feeding our children. If they want us to protect the environment, fine, then they should help us to make a living so that we can feed our children so that we can protect the environment!

As Rashidi's impassioned plea suggests, there was an insult implicit in the assumption that Chole residents were simply pawns, whether of the tour operators or, I would add, international organizations or even "global" forces. Such viewpoints failed to acknowledge that Mafia residents possessed their own perspectives on development, not simply as its recipients, but as social actors and commentators in their own right. Indeed, Euro-Americans, who often perceived themselves as more "modern" than Mafia residents, were quick to presume that they knew best the benefits—as well as the pitfalls—of development.

In the end, the differing ideas of development offered by Chole residents, government officials, and Euro-American tourists and expatriates suggest something important about international projects. In general, the language of development found among international and national institutions tends to be abstracted from the social realities of particular locales and is often couched in technocentric terms that reduce complex socioeconomic and political issues to rationalized policy directives and generic solutions. In contrast, I would argue that the situation on Mafia suggests that the "meaning" of development cannot be separated from the particular desires and social positions of those who either plan or are the target of such projects. Indeed, the complex social relationships that various individuals and groups had with each other on Mafia points to the broader social hierarchies at work both within countries and between them. Yet, the particular kind of development proposed for the Mafia Island Marine Park—tourism—would also have important implications for all park actors, including Mafia's residents.

TOURISM: A STRATEGY FOR SUSTAINABLE DEVELOPMENT?

It was widely asserted in international circles during the 1980s and 1990s that tourism offered an important route to development, a claim found, not only within planning documents for the Mafia Island Marine Park, but in many similar projects worldwide. During this period, international organizations ranging from the World Bank to environmental NGOs stressed the importance of tourism as an industry that could wield together conservation and development into a "sustainable development" strategy for poorer countries. But what does tourism development mean in the context of Mafia's marine park? In order to answer this question, we will consider the history of tourism within Tanzania, the transformations in social relationships generated by tourism both on Zanzibar and Mafia, and, finally, whether tourism development might be able to provide the kind of *maendeleo* that Mafia residents themselves desire.

The History of Tourism in Tanzania

Although the celebration of "ecotourism" as a form of sustainable development is a relatively recent phenomenon which has gained momentum over the last two decades (Boo 1990; Honey 1999), tourism itself has long been conceptualized as a development strategy. Shortly after the first passenger jet service was instituted in 1958, tourism was touted as a premier development strategy for so-called Third World countries (Brohman 1996; Crick 1989; de Kadt 1978; Smith and Eadington 1992; Honey 1999). As Crick notes, in the 1960s international tourism was portrayed as "manna from heaven," an economic panacea for Third World countries that was promoted by the Organization for Economic Cooperation and Development (OECD), the World Bank, and the United Nations (1989:314–5). Supporters viewed tourism as a way to diversify the economies of former colonies, which had centered around a few agricultural or raw material exports, and argued that warm climates and natural settings offered many tropical Third World countries a "comparative advantage" in the tourism industry (Brohman 1996). Although such perspectives suggest numerous parallels with contemporary ones, ideas of development have also been transformed in the intervening period. Whereas more contemporary perspectives on development have focused on poverty alleviation among the poor, "development" in the immediate post–World War II era was largely conceptualized in terms of states (Finnemore 1997). Tourism fit this state-centered perspective by offering important opportunities for newly independent countries to generate much-needed foreign exchange.

The interest in tourism as a development strategy in Tanzania was presaged by British colonial efforts to foster tourism in the postwar period of the 1940s and 1950s. For example, archival records document the formation of the East African Tourist Travel Association in 1948, which united the efforts of the colonial governments of Kenya, Tanganyika, Uganda and Zanzibar to expand their tourism industries (by 1959, tourism would be ranked the fourth top economic earner in East Africa).[6] After independence in 1961, the fledgling mainland government also took an active interest in tourism, utilizing colonial-era game reserves and recently formed national parks to generate foreign exchange (Curry 1990; Neumann 1992). Like most post-independence African states plagued with a lack of private capital, the Tanzanian government took on the role of leading investor. Thus, tourism, in essence, became state tourism. In the late 1960s and early 1970s, the government parastatal, the Tanzanian Tourist Commission, built hotels in Dar es

Salaam and the northern game parks, as well as the Mafia Island Lodge, in an effort to create two tourist circuits in Tanzania, one in the north of the country and one in the south (Curry 1990:138). Mafia's lodge, built near the site of a former European-owned fishing lodge, formed one part of the southern tourism circuit. Given the region's relative inaccessibility, however, it would see only sporadic handfuls of tourists in the ensuing decades. During this period, the revolutionary government of Zanzibar, which had joined with Tanganyika to form the federal state of Tanzania in 1964, used East German development aid to build several tourist hotels despite the severe restrictions its government placed on travelers. On both the mainland and Zanzibar, hotels were often designed in a monumental modernist architectural style intended to signal the "modernity" of the fledgling nation-state. (Ironically, the Mafia Island Lodge and Zanzibar's state-owned hotels would prove unpopular with later Euro-American tourists precisely because of the dated architecture and, during the 1980s and 1990s, such hotels were the butt of widespread jokes among travelers).

Despite its initial popularity, it was not long before tourism as a development strategy came under widespread attack in international circles. Critics noted that tourism was associated with increasing disparities in wealth, the overseas "leakage" of profits, and detrimental environmental and cultural effects (Crick 1989). Within Tanzania, intellectuals debated the appropriateness of international tourism for a state committed to socialism and economic self-reliance (Curry 1990; Shivji 1973). In addition, the closure of the border with neighboring Kenya in 1977 cut off a primary entry point for tourists into Tanzania. Although tourism within the country was floundering by the late 1970s, this situation would once again radically change only a decade later.

Heavily indebted and with a deeply troubled economy, the Tanzanian government agreed to an IMF-backed economic restructuring program in 1986. This and subsequent structural adjustment programs (SAPs) were intended to implement the free market reforms called for by international donors. This was also a period, however, in which greater attention was being paid to environmental issues and there were increasing calls that development be made "sustainable." International tourism seemed capable of addressing both sets of concerns. Replacing direct state involvement with market incentives, tourism was now heralded as a free market approach, which would "open up" regions like Tanzania to the "global" economy. At the same time, tourism's heavy reliance upon the natural environment in poorer countries suggested a way to make nature "pay." If more environmentally and culturally sensitive forms of tourism could be found, why could not tourism become the centerpiece of sustainable development efforts? Some activists pushed further, calling for "ecotourism" or a type of tourism that was consciously designed to be sensitive to the environment and, in some cases, to explicitly benefit the communities in which tourist establishments were located (Boo 1990; Honey 1999). The visions found in the planning documents for both the Mafia Island Marine Park and the Chole Kisiwani Conservation and Development Company were direct responses to such trends.

As the Tanzanian state began to loosen restrictive policies that had previously discouraged foreign visitors, tourism took a sharp upturn in the 1990s. Between 1990 and 1991, for example, tourist arrivals increased from 130,000 to 187,000, while earnings from tourism expanded from $40 million to $95 million (Reuters 8/28/92). By 1992, tourism was Tanzania's leading earner of foreign exchange and, by 1993, Tanzania had the second most rapidly growing tourism industry on the continent (Honey 1999:234). In 1994, the World Bank and other donors approved plans for a $900 million project to further this transformation by developing tourism infrastructure on both the mainland and Zanzibar (T.I.P. 1995; Honey 1999:235). At the behest of international donors, the Tanzania Tourist Commission also sought to "privatize" its state-owned hotels, although the state continued to play a crucial role in subsidizing the industry through policy initiatives and the creation of expensive infrastructure. With the state no longer serving as the primary economic support for tourism, capital-rich foreign investors hailing from such regions as Europe, South Africa, and the Middle East became increasingly prominent within the tourism industry. During the 1980s and 1990s, economic policy papers and management plans for mainland Tanzania and Zanzibar emphasized the need to make tourism attentive to environmental and cultural concerns and to incorporate benefits for the regions' residents. For example, the Tourism Infrastructure Project report that was written for the Zanzibari Commission for Tourism and funded by the World Bank noted that "tourism must be culturally responsible, ecologically friendly and environmentally sustainable," while also stipulating that "[t]ourism development should provide opportunities for indigenous Tanzanians to become stakeholders" (T.I.P. 1995). However, it remained largely unclear how such goals were to be achieved, contributing to what would prove to be a wide gap between rhetoric and reality on Zanzibar in the ensuing years. On Mafia, such trends were clearly apparent in the formation of the Mafia Island Marine Park, which sought to link tourism development to nature conservation and which encouraged the construction of several high-end new tourism establishments (even as the state-owned Mafia Island Lodge became increasingly decrepit and was readied for transfer to private management).

In the hands of planners, tourism as a sustainable development strategy promised a great deal, including the means to achieve conservation goals for international donors, the opportunity for states to accrue foreign exchange from tourism taxes and park entry fees, and the possibility of alternative income sources and the conservation of natural resources for residents. Discussions of tourism planning, however, also tended to be abstract and based upon generalized assumptions. Indeed, the policy statements found within Tanzania are virtually identical to those found in a range of other projects and initiatives around the world (see, for example, Stonich 2000). But both abstracted policy statements and the aforementioned statistics provide only a distant perspective on tourism in Tanzania. To counter such tendencies, it is necessary to consider the day-to-day meanings of tourism for those who live along the Tanzanian coast.

Tourist Encounters: From Discourses of "Ruin" to Day-to-Day Sociality

It is a much-discussed irony of the tourism trade that tourism itself is thought to bring about the "overdevelopment" which so many Euro-American tourists proclaim they are trying to escape. Indeed, debates within the marine park over whether tourism development should be viewed as a harbinger of progress, or as a source of cultural and environmental "ruin," were commonplace among Euro-Americans tourists, NGO workers, and even tour operators who stood to benefit from the industry. The concept of "ruin" itself is linked to the antimodernist discourses previously described in which non-Western cultures and presumably "traditional" peoples and practices come to be viewed in symbolic opposition to a modernity that holds the power to contaminate or spoil. However, the ideas of "ruin" expressed by many Euro-Americans also served as a gloss to refer to social dynamics associated with tourism that followed very different logics from those suggested by antimodernist discourses. Consequently, it is helpful to consider how Euro-American discourses of "ruin" accorded—or failed to accord—with those of Mafia residents as well as how such discourses related to broader social processes.

Mafia's tiny expatriate community and tour operators often looked to the more heavily touristed neighboring island of Zanzibar for images of Mafia's future, whether in positive terms or as a future they wished to avoid. Although tourism was still a relatively young industry on Mafia, there had been a dramatic transformation on Zanzibar, a place where I frequently stayed during the five-year period between when I first studied KiSwahili there in 1992 and the end of my fieldwork in 1997. From my own initial fieldwork experiences as a researcher of tourism on Zanzibar, I was aware that many visiting Euro-Americans were worried about the possibility that the region would become "ruined." Such concerns were succinctly captured in an exit survey of international tourists on Zanzibar conducted in 1995.[7] Many of these tourists revealed that they came to Zanzibar (a region with numerous sociocultural and historical parallels to Mafia) because it was "unspoilt" and "exotic," and they expressed their concerns that the region would become "overdeveloped." The following were typical comments:

The quintessential attraction of Zanzibar to current visitors is unique and unspoilt way of life and environment. It would be a tragedy if this were spoil [sic] by uncontrolled mass tourist development.

Too much beach tourism being constructed; Zanzibar should not become a mass tourist destination.

Protect your environment.

Don't let tourism destroy your people.

Care needs to be taken not to overdevelop tourism or the thing that makes Zanzibar special will be lost.

Slowly, slowly—you have a unique environment, protect your heritage, culture and wildlife—it's what makes you special.

We would advise to be careful not to change too much, your way of life only reason for tourism.

Should be carefully planned and monitored to preserve the habitats and customs.

Please conserve! Do not overdevelop just to cater for Western tourism.

Take care of the environment, folklore, friendliness, etc.

We really hope that the island will keep its authenticity and wildness.

Try to develop tourism in accordance with the principle of sustainable tourism.

Please don't let it get too touristy. Don't build big hotels, etc. Try to keep it sweet and simple.

In contrast to other types of tourism that emphasized the "hyperreality" of obviously created tourist destinations like Disneyland or Las Vegas (Eco 1986; Zukin 1991), many international tourists who traveled to East Africa were attracted by ideas of the authentic, the natural, and the unique.

Over the course of the 1990s, the expanding tourism trade on Zanzibar generated economic as well as other kinds of social transformations. The winding maze of streets, homes, and kiosks in Zanzibar's historic Stonetown began to be transformed from a state of decrepit shabbiness to an increasingly revitalized series of shops geared toward international visitors. Although this trend suggested growing prosperity, it was also potentially deceptive. As many Zanzibaris were themselves quick to point out, those who stood to benefit most from tourism were the "rich" (whether Zanzibar's own political elite, capital-rich emigres from the island's pre-revolutionary days who were increasingly returning as investors, or European and South African expatriates). At the same time, day-to-day encounters between Euro-Americans and Zanzibaris also began to shift as tourism increasingly became the template for social interactions between these groups. Indeed, many long-term *wazungu* residents of Zanzibar, including development workers, researchers or individuals seeking to "escape" Western society, were quick to point out the changing nature of such relationships. Many noted that the friendly customary greetings that had been a ubiquitous part of life in Zanzibar's Stonetown were now often intermixed with pleas for money, with the catcalls of young men seeking to "befriend" tourist women, with would-be guides seeking to show visitors the town, and by the occasional rude insult (generally by individuals who assumed that their targets would not understand KiSwahili). Although such transformations were sometimes described by Euro-Americans in terms of a discourse of "ruin," this shift needs to be considered in terms of the particular social dynamics encouraged by the tourism industry on Zanzibar.

In general, tourists visiting Zanzibar tended to stay for short periods, usually a few days (Honey 1999:267). An increasing number of visitors were also coming to the island directly from Europe for what was advertised as a beach holiday or as an add-on to safari vacations on the mainland (in contrast to many early visitors who were vacationing development workers and expatriates from other regions of Africa). The brevity of tourist encounters served to contribute to a proliferation of racial and cultural stereotypes, which in many instances became the medium through which social interactions were negotiated. For example, in their interactions with tourists, Zanzibaris who worked the tourist trade often relied upon stereotypical images of the habits and personalities of British, Italian, German, American, and other visitors, and some offered satiric imitations of the various ethnic groups they encountered (see also Crick 1994). Indeed, in my own trips back and forth between Zanzibar and Mafia, I was constantly struck by the degree to which I felt myself to be more of an "individual" on Mafia and more of a "type" on Zanzibar (a sensation that increased as Zanzibar's tourism trade expanded). Physical genotypes also came to be increasingly used as economic social markers, with white skin coding as wealth, and darker skin as poverty (conveniently ignoring the reality that many wealthy—and generally dark-skinned—Middle Eastern relatives of Zanzibaris were returning to the island, while also leading to puzzled discussions among Zanzibaris as to why Euro-American "backpackers" would wish to act "poor"). The use of a racial shorthand to draw attention to vast disparities in economic and social circumstances is clearly a widespread phenomenon (and one that took on its own particular dimensions during Zanzibar's colonial period). However, over the course of the 1990s such racialized "readings" appeared to intensify as Zanzibaris increasingly came to rub elbows with well-heeled tourists on a daily basis.

Tourist encounters were also strongly shaped by the fact that such interactions were largely negotiated upon an economic terrain. Although some tourists expressed a desire to deemphasize the commodified aspect of such encounters,[8] in general, the relationships that Euro-American tourists most commonly participated in with coastal residents were economic ones in which tourists bought the services of guides, waiters, cooks, street vendors, taxi drivers, and other tourism service workers. Not surprisingly, coastal residents also perceived tourism—widely touted by the state as well as international organizations as the new official route to "development"—through a largely economic lens. However, in contrast to wealthy, often foreign, investors who built hotels, restaurants and other tourism infrastructure, many coastal residents felt they lacked sufficient opportunity to benefit from tourism and sought a range of formal and informal means to convert the presence of rich foreigners in their midst into personal *maendeleo* or development for themselves and their families. Tourists, perceived as potential sources of resources, often found themselves to be the focal objects of zealous shopkeepers' interest, of "touts" who sought to earn money by "helping" tourists, of young men who sought to "befriend" them, and of children who quickly learned to assume a sad expression and call to tourists *Nipe shilingi* (give me money).

The shifting and contested line between the overtly economic and less economic aspects of such relationships appeared most clearly in the emergence of a "romance industry" on Zanzibar.[9] The "romances" that were occurring with increasing frequency between tourist women and young Zanzibari men were also linked to the rise of a "beach boy" subculture that had appeared in response to the tourism trade. "Beach boys," who were disapprovingly labeled *mapapasi* (ticks) by other Zanzibaris, were generally poorly educated young men who had few opportunities to gain formal employment in the tourism industry (in contrast to better-educated young Zanzibari men and women who spoke some English and could potentially find jobs as hotel staff, waiters, and cashiers). Many of these young men, some of whom had previously been fishers, sought to make a living in the informal economy by acting as guides, taking backpackers out snorkeling, socializing with tourists, and, in some cases, sexually "befriending" tourist women and, occasionally, men. The "beach boy" subculture was also associated with the appropriation of, and participation in, high-status tourist lifestyles as well as what were considered to be countercultural elements on Zanzibar, such as Rasta dread locks, sunglasses, reggae music, drinking alcohol, and drug use (for similar dynamics along other parts of the coast, see Beckerleg 1995; Peake 1989). As in the Jamaican tourist industry (Pruitt and LaFont 1995), tourist women who participated in sexual encounters with Zanzibaris often described such relationships as "romances," downplaying the economic component (a tendency heightened by the presumed lack of awareness that public "dating" was not a part of social life along the coast). On Zanzibar, such relationships were extremely fluid, resulting in outright prostitution in some cases and committed marriages in still others. In general, however, such encounters might perhaps be best understood as a form of sexual patron–client relationship, which involved presents of food, alcohol, clothing, money, and other gifts, occasionally including plane tickets to Europe or the United States paid for by overseas lovers.

The negotiation of economic and other social disparities within the context of tourist encounters at times led to tensions on Zanzibar. For some Euro-American visitors, the possibility that the residents who had "befriended" them during their vacation might have instrumental desires could result in disappointment and even cynical resentment (presumably because such realities contradicted images of what an "authentic" experience should be, as well as the desire to escape from the commodification associated with "modern" lifestyles). However, for those Zanzibaris, including many "beach boys," who did have economic interests in establishing relationships with tourists, the anger that such motives generated at times seemed perplexing. Along the coast, social relationships were not viewed in terms of a symbolic separation between public and private in which the private realm of family and friendships was to be qualitatively different from the instrumentality of the public. Rather, in the context of coastal society, social relationships *were* the terrain across which economic support was to be negotiated.

The conjunction of these conflicting desires and assumptions with stark economic disparities in wealth contributed in some instances to a downward spiral in relationships between tourists and Zanzibaris. For example, such dynamics led some Euro-American visitors to Zanzibar to presume that island residents were *always* acting in calculating ways, occasionally leading tourists to engage in insulting behavior toward well-meaning residents and, in turn, contributing to resentment against tourists. To offer a commonplace example, several young Zanzibari men once vented their anger to me that when they saw a tourist who was clearly lost in Zanzibar Stonetown's winding maze of streets and tried to offer him or her assistance, the tourist would often brusquely refuse. But as someone regularly assumed to be a tourist, I was aware that those tourists might fear that "help" would ultimately entail a request for money. Nevertheless, despite such tensions, most Zanzibaris with whom I spoke continued to emphasize the importance of tourism in generating *maendeleo,* even if many had not personally benefited in the ways that they had hoped.

In contrast to Zanzibar, tourist arrivals on Mafia were still relatively small in number. Nevertheless, many Euro-American expatriates and visitors worried that Mafia would experience that shift in social relationships, which signaled to many visitors that a place had become "spoiled." Indeed, marine park planners strongly emphasized the need to ameliorate the "cultural" and environment impacts of tourism on Mafia. Like Zanzibar's tourism policymakers, who over the course of the 1990s sought to steer the tourism market away from young European "backpackers," Mafia's park planners similarly endeavored to promote environmental and cultural preservation by encouraging a high-end tourism industry that would maximize the number of dollars spent while decreasing the number of tourist arrivals (presumably curtailing the impact that tourists would have in the process). Although such policies suggested a desire to prevent the region from becoming "spoiled," such assumptions proved to be strikingly different from the concerns that Mafia residents expressed regarding tourism.

Although some Zanzibaris did fear a certain kind of moral "ruin" relating to tourism or, more specifically, to the growing sex trade, the discourse of "ruin" utilized by Euro-Americans, which was associated with antimodernist sentiments and an ambivalence about "development," proved strikingly foreign along the coast. Indeed, it was extremely difficult to convey to friends on Mafia why Euro-American tourists feared that tourism development might "ruin" the region. I once attempted to broach this topic with Mzee Bakari; yet, it was daunting to even find the words to begin this conversation. The concept of "culture" is as difficult to translate into KiSwahili as "nature" (I used an awkward litany of concepts [i.e. *mila, desturi,* and *utamaduni*] to signify "culture," none of which carry similar symbolic connotations to the term in English). Mzee Bakari was clearly puzzled by the suggestion that Mafia's "culture" could be spoiled by tourism and argued that this was clearly incorrect. Although the historically cosmopolitan outlook of the coast might have made the idea that cultural contact could generate ruin seem particularly far-fetched, he suggested an even more basic consideration. In his view, "development" (*maendeleo*) clearly enhanced "culture" rather than spoiled it. This was so because greater material prosperity allowed people to decorate their homes and to perform ritual ceremonies in closer accordance with *mila* (or "custom") in ways which were becoming increasingly rare because of growing poverty on Chole.

During the course of my fieldwork, Chole residents, like many others along the coast, proved remarkably hospitable and friendly toward visitors. However, the few tensions with tourists that had appeared—tensions that were also common in Zanzibar and throughout the region—are suggestive of the broader social relationships at work.[10] Mafia residents, for example, were surprised by the failure of some Euro-American visitors to greet others, a perplexing act of rudeness to Mafia residents given the importance of elaborate greetings along the coast. Even more seriously, many tourists tended to dress in ways that were widely considered to be inappropriate in the region. For example, the handful of Euro-American tourists who had begun to reach Mafia for beach and snorkeling holidays would often walk in villages or visit the ruins at Chole or Kua wearing only string bikinis and swimming trunks, or what Chole residents considered to be *chupi* (underwear). In a place where men and women covered up in public (although men wore shorts while fishing and women often wore only a *kanga* cloth around their torsos at home) for visitors to walk around "naked" in public areas was taken as a sign of disrespect, particularly in the presence of the elderly.

The tendency of tourists to take photographs of residents without permission was another issue that at times sparked angry words. Tourists generally came to Mafia with cameras in hand, seeking to document their visits by taking photographs (MacCannell 1976; Sontag 1973). For tourists, such practices were presumably viewed as a natural extension of the free use of photography among friends and relatives or in public spaces at home. However, these actions were interpreted very differently along the coast. Vast disparities in wealth meant that picture-taking was not a reciprocal action, but one in which one group, the tourists, were almost invariably engaged in taking pictures of the other, that is, residents. Almost all Chole residents I knew enjoyed being photographed in contexts in which the relationships at work were clearly understood, for example, when they paid an entrepreneur to take a snapshot (a relatively common small industry or *mradi* for those who owned cameras in Tanzania), or when the photographer was a Euro-American friend or acquaintance who could be trusted to send copies as keepsakes. Yet, the dynamics of tourist photographs presented a different kind of encounter. Susan Sontag has described the potential for social aggressiveness involved in photography, which is encapsulated in its terminology; film, for example, is "loaded," cameras are "aimed" and "shot," and images "captured" (1973:14–15). Such language takes on a heightened significance when it is remembered that the European interest in hunting wild animals within East Africa's game parks was eventually supplanted by the idea of "shooting" them with cameras (see also MacKenzie 1988).

On Mafia, there was a strong sense that tourist photographs were something "done" to residents and such acts were often perceived as hostile or at least asocial. I recall one incident in particular in which an Italian tourist in a speedo bathing suit disembarked from a speedboat near Chole's Boma and walked up to a fisher sitting on the pavement repairing his net. Without greeting him, the tourist came within a few feet of the man and pointed an enormous black zoom lens in the face of this obviously upset individual—a clearly dehumanizing act. While this was a particularly egregious example, such incidents were not uncommon in the mid-1990s and I often heard Mafia residents angrily protest when tourists pointed cameras in their direction. One of the first sentences I was asked to teach in English classes on Chole was "please, do not take my photograph."

The tensions over photography point, not so much to "cultural" differences, but to the profound economic and social inequalities that existed between Mafia residents and Euro-American visitors. Indeed, Chole residents commonly expressed worries that tourist photographs would be paraded in Europe as embarrassing proof of the poverty of Africans. Others subscribed to conspiracy theories that held that Europeans made large amounts of money from such photos, presumably selling them for postcards and coffee table books (theories that occasionally came true). Residents' belief that their images remained their own (rather than becoming the legal property of photographers who are presumed to be the "authors" of photos taken in public spaces in places like the United States), further contributed to their discomfort in being photographed. In an effort to make such interactions more reciprocal, many coastal residents demanded that tourists pay them to take their photographs, a move that occasionally offended tourists through its perceived lack of "hospitality."

Although such tensions were readily apparent on Mafia, residents did not perceive these dynamics as bringing about social "ruin" in the sense so often assumed by Euro-American visitors. Indeed, many Chole residents pragmatically recognized that some tensions stemmed from visitors not understanding KiSwahili or appropriate norms of social behavior in the region. (These tensions were also ameliorated over the course of the 1990s by educational materials supplied by the Chole Kisiwani Conservation and Development Company and other hotels). However, the most serious aspect of these tensions stemmed, not from "culture contact" or the presumed fragility of traditional lifeways in the face of an expanding "modern" world, but from vast disparities in wealth. Such inequalities were an inescapable part of such interactions and were constantly apparent in terms of who had the ability to travel internationally, to own cameras, or to possess the money to buy souvenirs or offer a tip. Although tourism had not created these economic and social faultlines, it nevertheless brought such inequalities into stark relief. Coastal residents were clearly the disadvantaged party in tourist interactions; yet, Chole residents did not depict such tensions as generating "ruin." Indeed, discourses of "ruin" could serve to disguise Mafia residents' own hopes for *maendeleo* or "development." The more crucial question for residents was whether tourism was, in fact, capable of bringing about the kind of *maendeleo* that they desired.

Tourism as a Development Strategy

Although Chole residents generally viewed the expansion of tourism with hope, this did not mean that there were no dissenting voices. Some residents, for example, expressed worries about the tourism industry, particularly the fear that *wazungu* (Euro-Americans) desired to "rule" (*tawala*) Mafia once again. Others were concerned that they would end up pushed off their land or disenfranchised from the use of natural resources by encroaching tourism operators. In general, however, the prevailing sense of economic hardship meant that tourism, as well as any other possibilities for "development," were viewed as promising. Residents hoped that tourists would buy their produce or crafts, that the tourist industry would encourage investment in infrastructure such as roads and transportation, and, most importantly, that tourism would bring jobs. In addition, the Chole Kisiwani Conservation and Development Company had made the unusual move of helping build a new school and clinic and supporting other community projects on Chole, activities which not only heartened Chole residents but others on Mafia as well.

Despite their relative openness towards tourism, Chole residents continued to center their attention around fish during the mid-1990s. For example, at the WWF-sponsored Ecotourism Seminar held in 1995, village representatives persistently steered the discussion away from tourism in order to focus on the politics of fish and the marine park. On Chole, marine park matters were debated in village meetings with far greater fervor than those associated with tourism, despite the high visibility and community involvement of the Chole Kisiwani Conservation and Development Company. For instance, Mzee Maarufu prefaced the elections for representatives to the village marine park committee by stating that this vote could be the most crucial decision that residents would make. Indeed, the realization that area residents were far more passionate about fish than about tourism, ultimately, led me to shift my research topic from tourism to the politics of the marine park itself.

Such priorities raise questions regarding the perceived role of tourism as a development strategy within the Mafia Island Marine Park and, perhaps, in similar projects elsewhere. The assumptions made by many international organizations regarding tourism as a sustainable development strategy follow a similar logic. Because environmental degradation is thought to stem from the poverty of local residents leading them to overexploit natural resources, tourism is thought to have the potential to alleviate this situation and to provide development by offering residents "alternative income sources." The availability of economic alternatives is assumed to decrease pressure on natural resources (in this case, the marine environment) leading to enhanced conservation. Since the tourism industry is itself dependent upon a healthy environment, it is believed that a feedback loop can be established from which all major stakeholders will benefit. Although this scenario appears eminently reasonable at first glance, I would argue that this analysis ignores important social and economic realities.

The reasons for the ongoing preoccupation with fish on Chole are, in fact, not difficult to discover. Although the tourism industry does offer possibilities for wage labor in a region in which formal employment has been virtually nonexistent, many residents were aware that such jobs offered only limited possibilities for *maendeleo*. First, only a relatively small percentage of individuals would be able to find jobs within the nascent hotel industry, with jobs going disproportionately to young and middle-aged men. Second, tourist industry investors were not only attracted to Mafia's "pristine" environment, but also to the possibility of paying low wages. This reality is perhaps particularly critical for foreign investors on Mafia since low wages help offset the expense of obtaining supplies as well as the other difficulties posed by operating in a relatively inaccessible region. Indeed, as both critics and supporters of "globalization" acknowledge, low wages are one of the strongest incentives to foreign investment in poorer countries like Tanzania. During the time I spent on Mafia, a monthly wage of 20,000 to 30,000 shs. (between US$30 and $50) was common for six or even seven days of labor per week (and even this was difficult to guarantee given the seasonal nature of the tourism industry and the even more temporary nature of construction work). Although such salaries were "high" given that annual per capita income on the Tanzanian mainland was US$90 per year in 1993 (Tordoff 1997:xx), the prices for store-bought commodities on Mafia were far higher. Due to the difficulties of shipping to Mafia, prices could in fact exceed those of urban centers like Dar es Salaam and Zanzibar Town. If one lived solely off purchased goods and services (something which no one did), the cost of living might approach that of Europe and the United States.

As is true in many so-called Third World countries, however, wage labor on Mafia was not expected to allow people to meet their economic needs and those of their families (as would generally be expected in Europe or the United States). Indeed, the aforementioned wage scale on Mafia could buy little more on a daily basis than a kilo of flour and a handful of tomatoes. Instead, wage labor served to *supplement* the subsistence activities engaged in by other family members or by the laborers themselves. Although family members and friends might look to wage laborers for the cash needed to buy medicines, clothing, school fees, and, during some seasons, food, wage laborers were in turn dependent upon spouses, children, other family members and friends to engage in subsistence farming, to fish, to cook, to build and repair lodging, and to perform childcare and other forms of housework. Indeed, no wage earner on Mafia expected to support himself or herself as an individual on wages alone, much less members of their immediate family or kin group. In short, while jobs in the tourism industry might help certain individuals and potentially their families, it was widely recognized that the vast majority of people on Chole—including the wage laborers themselves—would continue to depend directly and indirectly upon fishing as well as other forms of "subsistence" labor. It was for this reason that people on Chole viewed fish and marine park matters as far more serious to their collective well-being than the tourism industry.

The failure on the part of planners to adequately acknowledge these issues calls into question the relationship between development and planning more broadly. The depiction of tourism as a development strategy presumes a particular outcome. Yet, tourism—both planned and unplanned—has had a long history of unintended consequences in Tanzania and elsewhere. Some of these consequences have long been pointed out by critics. Not only is tourism a notoriously fickle industry that is highly sensitive to economic fluctuations in other regions, it has also been widely linked to expanding disparities in wealth. While foreign investors and businesses often reap much of the profit, those Tanzanians who most clearly benefit are those few who possess capital or political connections (as Zanzibari residents were quick to point out). The tourism industry may offer helpful, if low-paying, employment for some; however, all residents are also subject to the inflation and real estate speculation that so often accompanies tourism development. And, finally, while some environmentalists link tourism to the conservation of the environment, others point to its ability to degrade natural resources, particularly in island communities where such resources as fresh water are in limited supply. It is important to acknowledge that other industries, such as manufacturing, can potentially generate even more intractable problems; however, such cautionary accounts point to the need for a more careful consideration of the nature of the tourism industry than the current international emphasis on tourism would suggest. Despite the importance of an alternative path for tourism, as argued for by ecotourism advocates, there are, unfortunately, no guarantees that tourism development will take the road less traveled.

On Mafia, the deleterious consequences of tourism were ostensibly to be controlled by the Mafia Island Marine Park; yet, it remained unclear whether this would in fact be the case. The technical adviser, David Holston, warned that the park, in fact, had relatively little control over tourism development (indeed, all of the new lodges on Mafia had begun construction before the marine park was gazetted, thereby avoiding the requirement to submit environmental impact assessments). The dynamics of dynamiting in the region also made clear that, even when official regulation was available, it could easily be subverted toward other ends. Once again, the unintended consequences of tourism on Zanzibar underscore such possibilities.[11] Although donor plans for Zanzibar in the early 1990s emphasized the need to create an environmentally and culturally "appropriate" tourism industry that would not make the mistakes of "overdevelopment" found in many other regions of the globe (Koth 1990), the ensuing situation was, in fact, quite different. As a World Bank consultant within Zanzibar's Commission for Tourism acknowledged, a number of rural Zanzibaris in the east and north of the island had been dispossessed or threatened with the dispossession of land for tourism development. Controversy was particularly intense over a proposed 350-bed hotel development that would have displaced large numbers of local residents in the Nungwi region (Griffiths 1998). This consultant described how she had sought to meet with a high-level government official to protest this particular development only to find a model of the hotel sitting on the official's desk. She soon discovered that some of the islands' most influential political elite were investors in, and stood to personally benefit from the proposed hotel (personal communication, September 8, 1994).

Such disturbing realities suggest the need to consider not only the "formal" economy, but also the existence of "informal" activities that could have a profound impact on the day-to-day realities of tourism development. For example, on Zanzibar during the mid-1990s, there was widespread speculation that some of the island's east coast hotels had been infiltrated by international crime syndicates for the purpose of money laundering and drug trafficking (see also Greenberger 1996). On Mafia, worries that similar dynamics might appear surfaced in a persistent rumor heard among both expatriates and residents during 1995. This rumor suggested that the island of Juani was going to be "given" for tourism development to an Irish arms dealer to whom Tanzanian national officials "owed a favor" for supplying weapons during Tanzania's war with Uganda's Idi Amin in the 1970s. Although such stories were mere speculation (and nothing to that effect actually happened), such concerns suggest the extent to which those living and working in the region felt that the actual outcome of "development" initiatives might be very different from those promised by planners.

In sum, the potential problems associated with the tourism industry along the coast stem less from its propensity to generate cultural "ruin," than from the tensions and economic logics set into effect by an industry built upon vast social and economic inequalities at international and national levels. Given such tendencies, can tourism bring about the "development" that Mafia residents crave? In trying to better understand what Chole residents desired as *maendeleo*, I once asked Mzee Bakari what he believed constituted "real" development. After briefly pondering the issue, he replied that "true" development was something that endured. In making this statement, he drew upon the previously mentioned distinction made on Mafia between wealth (*mali*) and money (*pesa*). While boats, animals, land, trees and houses were forms of wealth that endured and allowed for the social reproduction of life, *pesa* or cash was noted for its ephemeral qualities given inflation, currency devaluations, and the many demands placed upon it. Due to the unstable nature of both work and wages in the tourism industry, it seems unlikely that tourism employment can translate into "true" development in Mzee Bakari's sense. In addition, the reality that tourism employment will only benefit a relatively small number of people points to the possibility of widening social inequality and the sorts of jealous contention described in chapter 3.

This is not meant to suggest that tourism can not offer economic benefits, and it was clear that Mafia residents themselves did not wish tourism to go away. When I left Mafia in 1997, it was also too early to tell whether the Chole Kisiwani Conservation and Development Company (which at that point was still not officially open for tourism) would be able to create a new model for tourism and for tourist relationships in the area. This unusual company clearly offered far greater benefits to residents than is usually the case (and, hopefully, will be emulated in other regions). Nonetheless, it is difficult to imagine a situation in which tourism, in this case as well as other less socially conscious ones, could transcend the vast inequalities in wealth (and the patron–client relationships built upon such inequities) that would allow it to forge the kinds of egalitarian relationships that "participatory" development suggests. The emphasis that Chole residents instead placed upon fishing as a source of *maendeleo* points to an economic activity from which a far broader spectrum of island residents could benefit. Yet, can a declining fish population provide the kind of lasting "development" for which Mzee Bakari hoped? Thus, the question of development brings us back once again to the question of fish and the social drama of the marine park. Does the Mafia Island Marine Park hold out the possibility of a true "husbanding" of marine resources in a way that could benefit island residents in the future? To answer this question we must now turn back to the twists and turns that the social drama of the Mafia Island Marine Park had taken by the year 2000.

Participating in the Twenty-first Century

THE SOCIAL DRAMA of the Mafia Island Marine Park, a description of which began this book, offers some important insights into how we might think—or perhaps should not think—about the contemporary world. In what is depicted as a "globalizing" era, it points to the importance of looking at the socially grounded pathways through which contemporary interactions and power relationships occur. This internationally sponsored marine park, which holds numerous parallels with projects in other parts of the world, was designed to mix conservation and development in a "new" way. Yet throughout this social drama we have seen the centrality of older structures of power and the importance of history and cultural context—not the revolutionary break promised by modernist narratives of the "global." Although some argue that a new form of governmentality is appearing in the world that is centered around international or "global" institutions, this account suggests that the reality that many, if not most, international organizations are premised upon and organized through nation-states—and thus, national elites—has a crucial impact in day-to-day life. Rather than "global" dynamics simply undermining the nation-state, we see the growing influence of international organizations serving both to reshape nation-states and to buttress the national elites that represent them.

More pragmatically, this account suggests that in order to understand environmental degradation or social and economic inequality—the "target" problems of myriad conservation and development projects—it is necessary to move far beyond the scientized and managerial concepts in which both are generally conceived. Until recently, environmentalists have sought to counter the growing degradation of natural environments through the formation of national parks, maintaining a preservationist ethic that was premised upon the separation of nature and people. However, within both parks and environmental organizations, preservationism is giving way to a revamped version of conservation that emphasizes people's relationships with the environment and the importance of economic activity, particularly for residents of poorer countries like Tanzania.

Yet, conservation in so-called Third World countries, much like the development paradigm with which it is increasingly integrated, relies heavily upon a scientific and managerial language that depicts the complex relationships between people and the environment as reducible to such concepts as carrying capacity, population density, or subsistence practices. Although some conservationists, including those involved in the Mafia Island Marine Park, *are* attempting to incorporate "communities" and "participation" into their planning, these concepts are easily conceived as generic slots to be fit into preordained projects while the socioeconomic and political processes at work are left unexplored. Thus, despite the seeming promise of "participation," the institutional frameworks in which participation is embedded easily leaves existing social inequalities unchanged. Indeed, within the Mafia Island Marine Park, environmental degradation and poverty continue to be depicted as issues separate from politics; the targeted "problems" continue to be conceived as difficulties that are specific to rural regions of poor countries rather than as part of national and international political landscapes; and the "solutions"are still conceived in technical or managerial terms rather than as social or political endeavors.

In contrast, this book has offered a very different analysis of the dynamics at the core of the Mafia Island Marine Park, dynamics that perhaps have parallels in other parts of the world (for example, Lowe 2000). It has focused, not on abstractions, but on the everyday realities of a complex "social drama," including as its primary actors representatives of development and conservation organizations, national government officials, and, most centrally, island residents. It has argued that in order to understand how this drama has played out on Mafia it is necessary to consider the geographically intertwined histories of places and peoples as well as the social and economic processes by which people interact with the environment and with each other. Yet, the social drama of the Mafia Island Marine Park is a continuing one, and there is no easy conclusion to the "story" contained in this book. Indeed, this epilogue underscores this reality by considering the transformations that occurred within the marine park between 1997 and 2000—transformations that reveal unexpected as well as historically familiar patterns. Ultimately, this new chapter in the "social drama" of the marine park suggests that, as long as potential conflict lies at the heart of the park, this drama will be an ongoing one.

REVISITING THE PARK

In July of 2000, I returned to Tanzania for a one month follow-up visit that would allow me to ascertain any transformations that might have occurred in the marine park "drama" since my last trip to the region. Upon arriving in Dar es Salaam, I was immediately struck by the changes in this city since 1997. After a period of increased foreign investment (including investment drawn from the former Indian Ocean trading world), internet cafes had sprung up on virtually every corner in the downtown area along with shiny new stores and office complexes. In other quarters, however, there appeared to be growing poverty, and escalating crime rates reflected the tensions of an increasingly unequal social terrain. In contrast, life on Mafia seemed deceptively similar. Despite early predictions that throngs of tourists would begin visiting the new marine park, this group of islands had remained quiet and isolated, and visitors were still relatively few and far between.[1] The sand, coconut trees, and ragged sail of Chole's lone ferry as viewed from Utende were all much as I remembered.

When I arrived on Chole, however, it became apparent that changes had, indeed, been afoot. The Chole Kisiwani tourism camp, although not the full-fledged hotel envisioned years earlier, had continued to grow. Luxury tree houses now dotted the baobabs at the water's edge and an expatriate couple, the business partners of the American tour operator in Zanzibar, were now in residence on the island along with their two young children. Although the relationship between the camp and island residents was complex, including no small measure of tension and frustration on both sides, it was also one of constructive collaboration. The women's group, still in an embryonic stage when I had left in 1997, had been renamed the Chole Society for Women's Development and now counted many of the women on the island as members. Supported by the financial backing of a Norwegian women's group, as well as the organizational assistance of the Chole Kisiwani developers, the women had built a nursery school as well as a waterfront market to sell their handicrafts (the women proudly informed me that the market had been partially built with their own labor despite the initial skepticism of men in the community). Although neither of these buildings were yet functional, and despite apprehension within the group that some might reap more benefits than others, I was excited to see the women highly energized and increasingly self-confident.

The most impressive change, however, was the new health clinic that had opened on Chole after I left the island. Funded by European non-governmental organizations approached by the tour operators, the clinic had opened under the directorship of an Australian husband and wife medical team, with a governing board drawn from island residents. Over time, its day-to-day operations had been transferred to medical staff from Mafia, while the former directors continued to monitor it from Dar es Salaam. The clinic was cheerful and well-organized, and it was also supplied with donated medicines and equipment that otherwise would have been far beyond the economic reach of residents. Given that in previous years even rudimentary health care had been unavailable, everyone I encountered was understandably thrilled with the clinic, and, much to the pride of Chole residents, its good reputation had begun to attract patients from as far away as Kilwa and the Rufiji Delta.

Not all changes, however, were so positive. The day-to-day trials of life in this poor region continued to exact their toll. Although numerous babies had been born on Chole, many other individuals had died. In the United States, I had secretly dreaded receiving letters from Chole since they often told of the death of yet another friend, many of whom have formed a central presence in this book and whose absence now left gaping holes in the social fabric of the island. Some had been respected elders, others were still young like Abdallah Ally who had eventually succumbed to injuries sustained after falling from a coconut tree and, most painful to me, Bi Sharifa, whose household I had counted as a second home and who had died of an unknown illness shortly before my return.

Other changes reflected, not the cyclical rounds of life and death (as distorted by poverty as they were), but still wider transformations. Ironically, at the same time that projects like the health clinic and women's group were providing much needed assistance and making Chole the envy of other islands in Mafia district, there was widespread consensus that times had become even more difficult. Even as a few wage laborers in the tourism industry flaunted shiny new possessions, most people were noticeably poorer, thinner, and more worried than I remembered only a few years earlier. As in previous years, people noted that land on Chole was increasingly scarce and its soil ever more tired. At the same time, the market value of coconuts in Dar es Salaam continued to drop, and I overheard people on the ferry and in courtyards discussing the futility of trying to sell their produce. However, for the most part, residents' worries continued to center on the sea, and on the ongoing difficulties that fishing presented.

These difficulties would form the backdrop for a very different "social drama" within the marine park than the one I had left in 1997. Over the course of three years, dramatic transformations had taken place, far more substantial than the appearance of new boundary markers and colorful tourist brochures which signaled the park's solidifying status. Some changes were positive, such as the fact that dynamiting, which had been eradicated in Mafia's waters in 1997, continued to be held at bay and was no longer a major source of concern to residents. Other developments were more complex. For example, personnel changes within the park had a strong impact in both positive and negative terms. The biggest change, however, concerned residents' attitudes toward the park. When I had last been on Mafia in 1997, residents had still been strongly supportive of the park (or at least WWF) and had praised it for stopping dynamiting and supporting their interests. Yet, in 2000, people claimed to hate the park, declaring bitterly that it was out to "kill" island residents and that it was waging a "war" against them and their livelihoods. For that group of actors who were the least powerful protagonists in the park, participation had brought not "rights" but rather oppression. In this epilogue, I chart these transformations, asking what such changes can tell us about the nature of both environmental conflict and social inequality in what many refer to as a "globalizing" world.

THE CHANGING HIERARCHY OF THE PARK

Shortly after my arrival on Chole, it became strikingly clear that people were talking about the park in very different ways than when I had left. In chapter 1, I describe a 1995 meeting in which a Chole resident angrily informed his fellow villagers that the "big people" had "not yet understood that the park is ours." What had struck me at the time was how residents conceived of (or at least wished to conceive of) the marine park as their own. Yet, only a few years later, residents no longer referred to the park as "ours" but rather as an alien and hostile "they" which they feared threatened their very existence. It became apparent that people now believed that the park intended, not to encourage "participation," but to impose its decisions upon residents for the benefit of park officials or rich tourists, demonstrating in their view a callous disregard for residents' well-being. One fisherman expressed widespread sentiments when he told me in slow and emphatic tones that "The marine park is no good! It is going to kill us through hunger." Another fisherman suggested that there was now a common assessment on the island that promises of "participation" had been merely a hoax designed to gain acquiescence to the park; now that the park was in place, he surmised, park staff felt free to do as they pleased.

The growing disillusionment with the park seems to have begun shortly after I left Mafia. As described in chapter 1, an evaluation of the marine park conducted by NORAD in 1997 had recommended that both Technical Adviser David Holston and Acting Warden Pius Mseka be replaced. In the end, the acting warden did leave the marine park, returning to the Maritime Division (although in 2000, in a rather remarkable turnaround, I was told he had been promoted to head of the newly formed Marine Parks and Reserves Unit, which was responsible for all marine parks in Tanzania). Several months later, Holston resigned as technical adviser and returned to Australia. One of the final acts of the acting warden before he left Mafia had been to enforce a ban on coral mining (*chokaa*, or coral limestone, was used to plaster homes). However, the enforcement of the ban in 1997 occurred only after government bodies, with the tacit approval of the marine park, had purchased 200 tons of locally produced lime for improvements to the Mafia airport (Andrews 1999, Horrill and Ngoile 1991:34).[2] Hence the ban pointedly targeted small-scale users, while ignoring the reality that much of the most destructive coral mining had been generated by government bodies themselves. Although laws prohibiting any form of coral mining had long been on the books, this was the first time such regulations had been enforced, and the sudden implementation in ways that selectively hurt island residents contradicted earlier assurances that changes would not be imposed without consultation. Such precipitous action—taken without any serious effort to develop or locate viable building alternatives[3]—also suggested to residents that their interests were meaningless in the eyes of marine park officials.

It has been difficult to reconstruct the power relations that existed within the park for the period following the departure of the acting warden and the technical adviser. The acting warden and his allies were no longer in a position to shift park dynamics to suit their personal interests, but there was also no one willing to actively fight for a more inclusive interpretation of "participation." Although a new acting warden was appointed and the WWF Community Development officer assumed the role of acting technical adviser, it is unclear where real decision-making power lay during this time. Nevertheless, it is clear that the park gained a reputation for an increasingly authoritarian stance.

In January 1998, the new acting warden was officially appointed warden for the Mafia Island Marine Park. Although he was also an official in the government's Maritime Division, the new warden nonetheless established a very different reputation on Mafia from his predecessor. In 2000, Euro-American expatriates and tour operators described the new warden as an unassuming man who refused to pay kickbacks to superiors (or extort bribes from those below him). Chole residents described him as someone who spoke "well" and did not act furtively "in the corners" (*pembeni*), as had been suggested of the previous acting warden. Despite the tendency of social theorists to reify states, the differences between these men reveal the obvious but often overlooked reality that governments are not monolithic entities and suggest the importance of individual personalities. Indeed, in Tanzania as elsewhere it might be more useful to conceive of governments as competing networks of departments and individuals that represented a range of interests and positions (Moore 1993; Mitchell 1990; Gupta 1995).[4]

Despite such differences, state actors were nonetheless bound up in a common set of institutions and a shared national context. Indeed, the actions of individuals like the warden simultaneously suggested the influence of particular personalities and the broader institutional dynamics in which government actors were embedded. In an interview in July 2000, the new warden ruefully acknowledged that many government officials were not always supportive of conservation and that his commitment to the environment occasionally put him at odds with the Maritime Division, a body historically concerned with the extraction rather than conservation of natural resources. More pointedly, tour operators on Mafia speculated that the new park warden faced difficulties acquiring fiscal and logistical support from the Maritime

Division precisely because of his personally ethical stance. Yet, although some of the warden's positions put him at odds with other governmental bodies, his perspectives also reflected the prejudices common among government officials as well as educated mainlanders. Much like the previous acting warden, he emphasized the lack of education or "awareness" on Mafia as the following quote (from the original English) suggests:

> Now the main problem [in the marine park] is awareness, lack of awareness, especially the local people. . . . [T]here were a lot of expectations that they were going to benefit quite a lot in terms of economical [*sic*] benefits. They are not ready to give away, to sacrifice, especially when if comes to zoning, [and] that now we have to advance the mechanism so that we can control and regulate the resource[s] of the park. . . . The local people of Mafia they have not fully grasped the idea of conservation, you see. They think that conservation is just to keep on spoiling the resources. They don't think about the so-called regulating or wise-use of the resources, that's why when we come to use some of the so-called alternative activities it becomes very difficult, people are so much [attached] to their traditional way of life. . . . We have to try to make them aware [of] the concept of conservation before they come to terms with the so-called objectives of the park.

Although the warden emphasized that the general "poverty" and economic dependence of Mafia residents on marine resources was the central constraint on the marine park, this recognition was coupled with suggestions that cultural differences might be partly to explain for this poverty. Offering a view common among educated elites from the mainland, the Warden remarked:

> There are people here who have not gone to the mainland since they were born. So they don't have the so-called standard [by] which to compare their life and other people's lives on the mainland. . . . They are satisfied with their way of life, but you as a foreigner or somebody like me who comes from other regions where people are actually. . . . [pause] I find these people really somehow a bit slavish. Now, this is contributing to their poverty.

Thus, despite the new warden's efforts to remove the marine park from the "in the corners" orientation of his predecessor, the general tenor of mainland attitudes towards uneducated coastal residents supported the tendency to downplay the rights of Mafia residents in deference to conservationist goals determined elsewhere.

In October 1999, the warden was joined by a new WWF technical adviser, a British expatriate who had earlier spent time on Mafia with the Frontier program. Like the warden, the new technical adviser found himself thrown into a preexisting political quagmire and it is unclear how much either of them understood of the situation that had preceded their arrival. Nevertheless, both the warden and the new technical adviser were committed to placing the tensions and "personality conflict" of the Mseka/Holston era behind them. The new technical adviser joined the American director of the WWF regional office in Dar es Salaam in asserting that WWF was there solely to assist the government and should actively subordinate itself to Tanzanian government bodies. Thus, the popular perception that the marine park had two very different "heads," one associated with WWF and one linked with the Maritime division effectively ended. However, as the "park" became an increasingly unified entity in the minds of Mafia residents, WWF simultaneously lost residents' trust that it was willing to represent their interests.

The new WWF technical adviser was clearly troubled by the tensions he found between the park and Mafia residents upon his arrival. Recognizing the centrality of economic issues to the park, he sought to shift attention to alternative economic activities for residents. In commenting on the ambitious scope of a new Five Year Funding Plan, he noted:

> [with this plan] you're suddenly getting into a whole big area of rural development which is not the basic expertise of the park. It's not what a lot of people imagine a marine park or a conservation area as doing, I mean you don't fund the Serengeti to engage in rural development programs although they do a little bit of community stuff. And yet here you have to do that in order to make the basic conservation objectives even feasible and so the whole task of Mafia and the marine park is huge.

Although the technical advisor's comments emphasized the importance of economic issues, such comments also suggest an almost wistful desire for the simpler goals of preservation. Indeed, the new technical adviser, much like his predecessor, worried that directly engaging in "development" was beyond the scope of a national park. Such tensions reveal the fissures in the concept of development itself. While planners viewed "development" largely through the free market mechanism of encouraging tourism and through relatively minor attempts at creating "alternative income sources," residents sought more substantial actions that would help them withstand an increasingly precarious economic existence.

Yet, the meanings of "participation" also appeared to shift during this period. Although the new technical adviser worked hard to ameliorate tensions with residents through greater emphasis on consultation with villagers, "participation" during this phase of the park stressed getting residents to further environmentalist goals rather than being seen as an inherent "democratic" value in and of itself. This change is evident in the new version of the general management plan. Although the new technical adviser crafted a very well-researched and impressively detailed new management plan (GMP 2000) (the first park document to reveal complex knowledge of Mafia as a particular place rather than a generic entity), the management plan also subtly shifted the focus of the park toward issues of regulation and away from "participation." For example, key references to the Mafia Island Marine Park being "a true model of a park created and run 'for the people and by the people'" as well as one that would work toward the social goal of "political empowerment" (GMP 1995:iv) were eliminated from the final version. This transformation reflects the reality that differences of opinion regarding the meaning of "participation" (as well as disagreements over the relative emphasis to be placed on conservation versus development) may be rife within international organizations like WWF (as other NGO workers were also quick to inform me). In short, the transformation in high-level personnel within the park revealed that institutions like WWF and government bodies are not monolithic, but rather are internally differentiated and, potentially, contested.

From an institutional viewpoint, however, the Mafia Island Marine Park appeared quite calm during this period. Indeed, park documents, officials, and NGO representatives (particularly those positioned away from Mafia) suggested that the park was now functioning well and that most preexisting problems had been rectified. Yet it is deeply ironic (and disturbing) that during the time in which official organs were asserting that the park was functioning at its best, Mafia residents, whose voices would remain unheard in national and international offices, were declaring their hostility toward the park and insisting that it was waging a "war" against them.

The high level of distrust and anger that was apparent in comments heard from residents of Juani, Jibondo, and other fishing communities as well as Chole, became strikingly apparent one afternoon at Chole's boatyard. On that day, Rajabu Issa, the young man whose observations on fishing had been ignored by the Austrian scientist in a previous chapter, had agreed to a taped interview along with a few of his friends. I found to my surprise that he had taken it upon himself to gather a group of 25 fishers, both young and old (simultaneously apologizing that more were unable to attend because they were out at sea). Asking me to convey their words to the distant offices and decision makers who held so much power over their lives, these angry men spoke not only to me but to my tape recorder.[5] In this instance, my role shifted to that of being a simple messenger. Here are some of the views I was asked to convey:

> SM: We say that the marine park is no good. The marine park is totally unacceptable! . . . [T]he marine park has refused to cooperate with us and this is a problem for us. If they wanted to meet with us fishers, we could agree: in what areas should we preserve the fish [literally, "rear" or "husband"]? What areas should we leave them [the marine park] for their activities [i.e., for tourism]? Right away we could cooperate with them. Because we're the ones who know the landscape here, not those people from the marine park. . . . [But] if you tell me not to fish here, where will I fish? What kind of work will you give me today so I can

continue my life?. . . . It has to be today, not tomorrow. If it takes six or seven months before I get food, what am I going to do right now? What will my family eat? What will they wear? And if my children want to go to school, what will I do? . . . The marine park is killing us. It is totally unacceptable!! It is killing us now. It's goal is to make us Tanzanians, us people from Mafia, to die from hunger. . . . to reduce us to the worse kind of poverty.

YG: It brings thievery. We have no work. . . . .How do you think, Mama Kris, that thievery comes about? It can come about because of hunger!

Another argued:

BM: They want us not to fish, but they're not going to give us money if they tell us not to fish in there [the bay]. And if we don't fish there, we or our children will die! We will have to organize ourselves together and go to the government offices [to protest]. . . . we will take this to court, although we also don't know what would happen there [in court]. . . . If I can't go to sea, I'm already dead. I don't have any money in my pocket I can use. My only money is what I get when I return from sea with maybe a thousand shillings that I use to buy rice. . . . [If we have no money] and we go to the store, if we're able to borrow money, then we eat. If we are not able to borrow, then we, along with our children, don't eat, ... Now today, if they tell us not to fish in there [the Bay], what kind of work will we do? They say that the marine park is to prevent us from causing damage by not fishing. Their attitude is that they're already educated [i.e., they have already advanced personally and are unconcerned with the livelihoods of others]. But, if they tell us not to fish, there will be a fight. There will be a war. Can I agree if someone says you can't take your net and fish there [in the bay]? Am I supposed to die along with my children? What are you supposed to do? . . . We won't agree to not fish in any part of the bay. We will fight with knives there, we will fight there [in the bay]. We don't have guns, but if we had them, we would fight with guns. We are ready to fight and we will fight.

Understanding the Anger: Residents' Views of the Marine Park

Clearly, the anger Chole residents directed toward the marine park stemmed from what they perceived as the increasingly dictatorial attitude of the park and its apparent disregard for the ability of residents to feed themselves or their families—a shift that seemed particularly egregious after widespread assurances that this would be a "people's park" based on local "participation." This shift was aptly symbolized by the transformation in residents' ·perspectives of the *Ukombozi* patrol boat; rather than being their "liberator," Chole residents now joked it had become their oppressor. As one fisher noted, "If we're minding our own business and simply going along with our fishing, right away [we hear] Innnnn! [the sound of the park's patrol boat engine], and the boat is there. . . . This kind of punishment really has harmful effects and it doesn't accord with the customs of our mothers!" Yet, what exactly were the park policies being enforced and how did they relate to both social and environmental dynamics on the islands? Here, I will address these questions by considering points of contestation between residents and the marine park in July 2000, touching upon such issues as coral mining, fishing permits, park zoning, and the regulation of fishing gear.

In order to understand the acrimonious nature of residents' relationship to the marine park in 2000, it is first necessary to consider the broader economic climate in which residents found themselves. Not only had falling coconut prices continued to marginalize farming as a livelihood on Chole, but fishing had become increasingly difficult as well. Despite the end of dynamiting, both residents and conservationists agreed that fish populations and the health of the area's coral reefs were continuing to decline. The reasons for this were complex and not completely understood. In general, fish populations worldwide had plummeted in recent decades due to overfishing and marine pollution, drawing increasing attention to the plight of marine environments (Safina 1999; Thorne-Miller 1999; McGoodwin 1990). However, it also appeared that the El Nino weather system of 1997–1998 had a major impact on Mafia, killing coral through rising water temperatures. Indeed, some researchers estimated that 50–70 percent of corals had been killed in the Tanzanian region of the Indian Ocean (Wilkinson 1998; Muhando 1998).

Changing social dynamics on Mafia, however, were also playing a role. As discussed in chapter 4, the escalating cost of fishing gear, and the need to extract ever more fish to pay for these rising costs, had been a growing trend. Such transformations were now reaping a grim reward. Many of Mafia's fishers, unable to pay the exorbitant cost for fishing gear, were resorting to the use of borrowed nets supplied by Dar es Salaam businessmen working out of Kilindoni. These entrepreneurs offered residents the free use of nets if fishers agreed to sell their catches back to the businessmen at low prearranged prices. In some cases, the entrepreneurs encouraged the use of destructive gear such as small mesh nets and *mtando* surround nets. Although Mafia residents had used small mesh nets in the past to catch sardines (*dagaa*), they were now being encouraged to use these nets in new and destructive ways that captured high numbers of juvenile reef fish. Although the use of small mesh nets had occurred among Kilindoni fishermen in 1997, village residents, particularly older ones, had been highly critical of such practices and had hoped that such usages would be controlled by the marine park. Now, however, these practices had spread throughout the islands. While some (particularly, economically vulnerable young men) defended the new fishing techniques, others publicly, or more often privately, acknowledged that these new methods were highly destructive. However, given the economic difficulties that were widely faced by residents as well as the pervasive anger and distrust directed at the marine park, older men who might have supported the park's position on regulating these nets found themselves increasingly hesitant to express their views. Thus, at the same time that economic difficulties were transforming residents' interactions with the environment, creating new social faultlines in the process, these tensions were being papered over by the common front of anger directed at the marine park.

Given the increasingly difficult environmental and economic climate just described, the park's attempts to regulate residents (rather than "outside" fishers as had been the case with dynamiting) was clearly at the core of this anger. Yet, as I would quickly discover, the nature of these regulations was shrouded in a veil of confusion that extended even to marine park officials. Equally frustrating to residents, the basis of such restrictions was not always clear. The extent of this confusion first became apparent to me as I attempted to piece together an understanding of restrictions on coral mining. On Chole one afternoon, I mentioned the coral mining ban to Ibrahim Abdallah with whom I had conducted long interviews about fishing in the past. Stating that he had something he wished to show me, he arranged for us to meet at his house a few days later.

When I arrived at his home, Ibrahim laid out on his mud front porch several samples of coral rock that he wanted me to inspect. Pointing to a rock composed of a hard land-based coral known as *kongwa*, he noted that the marine park was encouraging the use of this kind of coral in making limestone. However, Ibrahim elaborated, this kind of rock is extremely hard. In order to generate the heat required to convert it into limestone, it is necessary to cut far more firewood from mangrove trees than would have been needed before—an activity opposed by the marine park. He then pointed to a piece of another kind of coral known as *"matumbawe ya bahari,"* a soft coral mined live from the sea. He acknowledged that it was destructive to mine this kind of coral given that it provides a "home" for the fish (*nyumba ya samaki*). As I already knew, this soft coral was also the most difficult to obtain and provided the highest quality limestone used by the "rich" (*watajiri*), as well as by government building projects and tour operators. Finally, Ibrahim pointed to a third type of coral rock *"matumbawe ya kufukua chini,"* a dead yet soft coral, which residents obtained from digging in the shallow, sandy strait separating Chole and Juani Islands. It was this kind of coral that residents commonly used in household limestone production.

Leading me to the beach near his home, Ibrahim then began showing me the shallow holes in the sand where he and others had dug for *matumbawe ya kufukua chini* in the past. He also pointed to the nearby mangrove trees, demonstrating how individual branches had been cut for firewood leaving the tree to regenerate as was customary. He grimly noted that firing hard coral like *kongwa* would instead require cutting down entire trees. Since the coral under the sand in the strait was clearly dead coral and not the "home of the fish," he challenged me to explain why he and other Mafia residents should be banned from using this type of coral. This would either force them to break regulations on cutting mangroves or would leave them without plaster for their houses. Since it was plaster that differentiated temporary mud huts from a "real" house along the coast, the only conclusion that he and many others could draw was that the marine park did not want them to "get ahead" in life but to keep them impoverished, since only tour operators and other "wealthy" people could afford to use cement as an alternative building material.

Puzzled myself as to why the marine park would enforce such a policy, I began asking various people about coral mining restrictions. The answers revealed a high level of confusion, even among park officials. On Chole, residents like Ibrahim asserted that the mining of all types of coral had been banned. The Community Development assistant for the marine park disagreed, however, maintaining that the mining of *matumbawe ya kufukua chini* or buried coral had not been banned. He added that the park was also attempting to soften its earlier position in order to address community opposition and that individuals were now allowed a permit to mine coral for their own homes (although most people in the villages were as yet unaware of this exception). It was all too clear, however, that even this concession would prove problematic since it assumed that the economy of coral mining on Mafia was subsistence based when in actuality limestone has historically been prepared by a handful of specialists who then sell it to fellow villagers.

The next day, I spoke with the marine park warden in Kilindoni who informed me that all types of coral mining had indeed been banned within the marine park including that of soft buried coral. The hotel developers on Chole also stated their belief that all kinds of coral had been banned. Although they personally disagreed with the ban on *matumbawe ya kufukua chini*, they related that it had been instituted due to the fear that digging buried beach coral could potentially change water currents. Given the lack of building alternatives and the seemingly esoteric nature of this claim to residents who had long mined buried coral in the strait, this position could only be perceived as antagonistic. Although confusion over park regulations stemmed partially from the transitory nature of the regulations and from a very uneven dissemination of information, it might also have been exacerbated by what one Utende hotel developer described as a tendency to "unofficially" ban activities that were technically allowed. The tendency to impose a more authoritarian version of regulations than had legally been mandated had been common in Tanzania's mainland national parks beginning in the colonial period. Such realities formed one means by which rural residents who retained legal rights within natural areas became increasingly disenfranchised (Neumann 1998). Either way, such confusion points to the need to understand the role of regulations, not on paper, but in terms of how they are understood and implemented (or not, as the case may be) in daily life.

The uncertainty surrounding marine park regulations was also important in sociological terms because of the spaces it potentially opened up for the repressive control of residents by both park officials and, in some cases, fellow residents. Such possibilities, for example, began to surface in the confusion resulting from the marine park's new permit system, a system originally intended to differentiate between residents and nonresident users. The implementation of a permit system was in fact widely supported by Mafia residents, who viewed it as a means to control the destructive fishing practices of outside fishers within Mafia's waters. At the beginning stages of its implementation in mid-2000, however, the permit system was generating widespread frustration and anger. Although the procedures for obtaining permits had been designed by village-based marine park committees, the system was highly bureaucraticized and ponderous, making it difficult for residents to obtain permits. In the view of the park's new technical adviser, the system had been designed by the village committees to retain power in their own hands rather than to ensure the efficient distribution of permits. Such results suggest the possibility that "participation," if organized without careful attention to existing social dynamics, can easily lead to the establishment of new hierarchies in which some residents gain authority (legitimate or otherwise) over fellow residents. By July, even though many residents had still not received their permits, the *Ukombozi* patrol boat led by the new park security forces located in Kilindoni had begun stopping boats and confiscating the vessels and gear of those without permits. As the technical adviser himself ruefully acknowledged, the permit system, which had been designed to help island residents, was instead being used to harass them.

While such difficulties might be viewed as simply the temporary result of poor implementation, there were portents of more disturbing tendencies. Several fishers on Chole complained to me that the patrols had asked both fishers and ice boat operators to pay "fines" and then failed to provide receipts, suggesting to these men that their money was being "snatched" (*kunyang'anya*) by those on patrol. Given the reality that vague and ambiguous regulations provide fertile ground for harassment and the extortion of bribes, the complex permit system that the park outlined for the future (with a series of user zones and special permits for general marine use, coral mining, and mangrove cutting, among other activities) offers considerable ground for worry that park regulations will be used, not to help the environment, but rather against island residents.

The core of most residents' anger, however, concerned zoning. In the early 1990s, the initial General Management Plan had specified that the park would be divided into designated core, user and buffer zones, a model based on Australia's Great Barrier Reef park. (Core zones represented sensitive areas in which no human activities would be allowed; user zones would allow specified activities, and buffer zones, a still broader range of activities). Although the zoning for Mafia's park had ostensibly been conducted with the participation of Mafia's residents, from the time I first arrived on Chole in 1994 through my visit in 2000, islanders consistently complained that the original zoning had been based on discussions with too few individuals and not on consultation with residents as a whole.[6]

This discomfort turned to anger in 1999 after a visiting expert proposed broad changes to the zoning after a brief stay on Mafia. These unilateral changes to the zoning plan appeared in a draft of the new General Management Plan (GMP) for the park and were only later discussed at village meetings. Infuriated residents not only resented being excluded from the decision-making process, but feared that the zoning changes would make historically crucial fishing grounds inaccessible and destroy their ability to generate a livelihood. It was these fears that prompted the angry comments by Chole fishers previously quoted. Some hotel developers also expressed dissatisfaction with the plan, arguing that the new zoning failed to isolate those regions under the greatest environmental threat or of the most ecological importance. In the end, the ensuing outcry *did* result in the scrapping of the draft of the new GMP and its extensive reworking by the new technical adviser. Although park officials like the Community Development officer maintained that the new GMP had simply been a "draft," it is significant that residents had not been consulted in its making. Even more to the point, although the new version did modify the zoning plan from the consultant's proposal in order to give greater latitude to Mafia's fishers (this fact was not yet popularly known when I left Mafia at the end of July 2000), it nonetheless still added additional areas to the "core" zone that had not been part of the original management plan agreed to by village representatives in the mid-1990s.

Thus, between 1997 and 2000 important transformations had occurred in the "social drama" of the Mafia Island Marine Park that continued to raise crucial questions about the nature of "participation." Although Mafia residents had been led to believe that "participation" meant the right to share in decision making within the park, it had become clear that "participation" could be ignored entirely by park officials or reduced to the mere solicitation of opinions. The organization of national parks in Tanzania, as in many other countries, has historically been structured almost on a model of small fiefdoms under the highly centralized leadership of a warden. However, the reality that people now live within such parks means that such autocratic structures are particularly worrisome. Despite the language of "participation," will the inclusion of area residents within a national park such as Mafia's lead further away from democratic accountability rather than toward it?

Indeed, many of those I spoke with on Mafia admitted that they were angry and worried not only over what had actually been forbidden by the park, but by what they *feared* would be forbidden in the future. Thus, residents' worries about the park were taking on heightened dimensions, extending beyond the actual regulations being discussed (as important as those were) to incorporate residents' knowledge of exclusion within other national parks in Tanzania, as well as their own prior historical encounters. The initial hopes many residents held for the park had been shaped by the relatively egalitarian coastal heritage embodied in the concept of being *wenyeji* or the "owners" of a place, a discourse that had allowed residents to appropriate and assert rights of "participation" on their own terms, but these hopes were rapidly disappearing. In their place, residents had resurrected fears that stemmed from a long counter-legacy of hierarchy spanning the precolonial, colonial, and postcolonial eras. Despite their initial hopes, residents increasingly seemed to feel that their relationship with the park would not be any less authoritarian than these other relationships from the past, and numerous residents pointed out to me that the new regulations were even more onerous than those of the colonial era.

Perhaps most disturbing of all was the fact that central economic activities were being prohibited in contexts in which viable alternatives had not been established. At best, this was thoughtless, backward planning; at worst, it was the kind of blatant disregard that residents had experienced under colonialism as well as the forced "villagization" campaign of the postcolonial era. At the same time, declining numbers of fish and the increasing conversion of Mafia's fishers into wage laborers dependent on borrowed gear meant that residents had begun to be inextricably caught in the downward spiral of having to resort to increasingly destructive practices simply to survive. Alternative sources of income had now become crucial, but still largely existed only on the planning table. When I went out sailing with Issa Hamisi and his younger cousin, for example, they described how they would like to use their family boat to take tourists out snorkeling. Yet, they wondered, how would they go about setting up such a business and making contact with tourists given the language barriers? In addition, the Chole Kisiwani developers seemed irritated with such ideas, viewing it as competition with their own business. Before I left Mafia, Issa informed me that he had given up his plans for starting a business and had gone to work in one of the tourist hotels in Utende. However, only a week earlier, Issa and his cousin had characterized such work as not being "real" employment. Given the low wages, erratic tenure, and lack of benefits in the tourism industry, Issa had described those who did such work as merely being *vibarua* or "day laborers" or doing what his cousin scornfully referred to as "donkey work." Yet, I also knew that Issa was glad to have found any source of income at all.

Although the newly arrived technical adviser had begun shifting attention toward community initiatives, he also expressed reservations about this role, arguing that the park was not a "development" organization. Yet, without primary attention being paid to economic issues, it is becoming increasingly clear that the marine park can only serve to oppress residents. If residents cannot survive without breaking park regulations and being subject to harassment, than residents are correct in their assessment that this supposed "people's park" is waging a "war" (*vita*) against them. By 2000, it appeared that the divisions might have become too deep to surmount. While in previous years residents had expressed a willingness to discuss the difficult issue of controlling their own practices, the hostility engendered by the "war" against them now meant that their own position had hardened. Some men on Mafia had become unwilling to acknowledge the questionable nature of any of their practices; at the same time, those who did were increasingly hesitant to do so in public. Ironically, destructive fishing methods that had long been ethically questionable on Chole were, in the end, valorized by the perceived aggression of the marine park against residents. Thus, the "war" had served, not to shift public opinion against those who engage in such questionable practices but to undermine the moral authority of their internal critics. One of the most disturbing elements in all of this is the palpable sense of missed opportunity. Residents themselves feared their inability to regulate marine resource use, as the case of dynamiting makes clear. Indeed, it was support for such regulation that initially won residents' approval for the marine park. If difficult issues such as the use of nets had been negotiated earlier, when popular support and trust in the park was strong and economic circumstances less dire, these issues might have been resolved to the ultimate benefit of all. However, as residents in 2000 expressed it, the reality was that the park did not "go with" the people.

Although the explanations offered in this epilogue have been mainly economic in nature, the ongoing social drama of the marine park may also be understood in terms of the role that modern education plays as a social and cultural marker of status and class both nationally and internationally. The angry fishers at the boatyard, as well as others on Mafia, drew attention to this point. One fisher argued in relation to park zoning that officials had unilaterally changed the boundaries and ignored earlier zoning efforts in which at least some residents had participated. "They changed things [the zoning]! If we tell them that we don't want something, they write down that we want it anyway. Is this any way to proceed?" Another man argued that once a person is a salaried (hence, educated) employee, that person is no longer concerned with others. He argued that if those from the marine park would meet regularly with residents so that they would "go with the people" there would be no problem. But he noted, "They stay in their big offices in Kilindoni and just concern themselves with their salaries. If we enter there, they treat us like goats. It is there in their offices that they make the decisions by themselves, saying 'people shouldn't fish, ok, they won't fish.' They treat us like insects." The language of such comments pointedly parallels that used to describe the degradation of slaves from an earlier historical era (see chapter 1), suggesting in both cases the dispossession and dehumanization of the marginalized.

Once again, Mzee Bakari, was an articulate observer of such dynamics. His long days at home were now made even lonelier by the loss of his wife and he welcomed the chance to ponder these issues at length. One afternoon, as I sat in his home, neighbors heatedly discussed their anger at the marine park. The next day, Mzee Bakari called me aside to say that he had spent the night thinking about the park and that he had something important to convey for my work. Mzee Bakari warned against the potential oppression that lay in the relationship between the educated and the uneducated. He argued:

> Those people [from the marine park] shouldn't be snatching all the decision-making power to themselves to do with as they please. It shouldn't be so. . . . If the fishers could meet together with those from the Maritime Division and if those [from Maritime] would listen, they could reach an agreement. And then, in my view, there wouldn't be any argument. But those people [from the marine park] oppose this and are [instead] robbing us of our birthright. They have already studied and received their education, and indeed they are "stealing" their education for themselves [i.e. using it for personal advancement rather than to help others]. [But] people here [on Mafia] have their own education [i.e., knowledge]. In other words, they are people from here, their origins and their lineages are from here, and they have been making their living here. Things have turned out as they have [i.e., badly] because [marine park officials] are robbing these people of their livelihoods which have been given to them by God and simply because [people here] are uneducated.

Mzee Bakari elaborated upon the power dynamics at work by noting that the educated assume that their own minds (*ubongo*) "work well," while denigrating the thought processes of the uneducated. He countered this view with a proverb which translates into standard KiSwahili as "*Mjinga akierevuka, mwerevu iko mashakani*" or "When the fool becomes clever, the clever has doubts." Its meaning, according to Mzee Bakari, is that when an ignorant person acquires knowledge through experience or long-term residence in a place, the clever become agitated. Since their authority over the "ignorant" is based on the lack of education of the latter, when the formerly ignorant acquire or possess knowledge, the clever then have a "problem" (*matatizo*). He concluded by explicitly linking the meaning of this proverb to the situation within the marine park.

> Those people [from the marine park] are the clever ones and the fishers here are the ignorant ones. But even in their ignorance they [the fishers] understand the

situation. . . . The [park officials] continue with their work but it's apparent that [the knowledge] is just in their heads. Just in their heads. [They simply say] "Things should be done this way," and so they make decisions for us. Basically, I'm saying we should be accorded more worth, but [as things stand] this is impossible, it complicates things [for them]. It would be better for the ignorant and the clever to sit down together and come to an agreement. It's better than this [what is now happening with the marine park], better than robbing a person and then saying don't mention your hunger or don't eat—a person can't agree to that! . . . Indeed our life is based on this [using natural resources in the area]. Now for those who are coming here with their education and forbidding these things, what are they doing? Have they thought about these things?

CONCLUSION

It is strikingly clear, as it has been for more than a century, that capitalism and the other offshoot of "modernity," socialism, have exacted a heavy toll on the environment with their logic of ever increasing productivity and natural resource extraction. Holding this position does not require romanticizing other supposedly more "traditional" ways of organizing social and economic life as being inherently kind to the environment. However, it does mean recognizing the impact of contemporary economic logics upon the environment. Although at present the entire globe is enmeshed in capitalist (or socialist) economic relations, this is not an even process. In poorer countries like Tanzania, many residents, due more to poverty than to "tradition," cobble together an existence that relies upon cash markets (whether regional, national, or international), wage labor, and subsistence practices. The ability to consume is also a highly uneven one, and it must be acknowledged that those living in richer countries with vastly higher rates of consumption generally cause far more environmental degradation than people in poorer countries like Tanzania. The reality of environmental deterioration in the marine environment has become widely apparent in recent decades, the result of a wide range of pollutants being released into coastal waters as well overfishing (often on a "factory trawler" scale intended not only for human consumption but to feed farm animals in wealthy countries). Given the (literally) fluid nature of marine environments, such dynamics affect people in all parts of the world, but the consequences are greatest in places like Mafia where people depend directly upon the environment for their daily existence.

It is not enough, however, to simply call attention to the reality of environmental degradation; it is necessary to understand how such degradation relates to human social relationships. Although the environment undergoes its own transformations apart from human interventions, many of the disturbing changes of the last 150 years are a direct product of human activity, and it is only by understanding the nature of such activities that we can hope to transform them. Yet, much environmental literature pays scant attention to people. Or, when it does so, it is through a scientized or technocentric discourse valued among conservation and development organizations as well as policymakers, but which distorts human-environmental interactions by reducing the complexities of human life to such reductionist ideas as "carrying capacity" or "population density" or to the equally technocentric managerialism common to development paradigms.

The insistence on environmental "management" has often been based on a naive technocentrism that presumes that the mere formulation of management plans and international regulations readily translate into action in the world. I do not wish to suggest that management or the creation of parks cannot serve important functions; indeed, Mafia residents themselves had high hopes for both, believing that outside assistance and mediation could help control fishing practices that they themselves could not. However, it is clear that management is not a merely "technical" endeavor but a highly politicized one, embedded in both the politics of national governments and international organizations, as well as complex class relationships with both national and international dimensions. In reality, "management," as translated through such powerful institutions, can easily lead to outcomes antithetical to those officially intended (Ferguson 1994; Lowe 2000). I would argue that "management," even when conscientiously directed toward the needs of the poor, needs to remain subordinated to, rather than serve as a substitute for, analysis of broader social processes—how and why do people relate to each other and to the environment as they do? It is with these goals in mind that I have sought to understand the "social drama" of the Mafia Island Marine Park, considering how Mafia residents, national officials, and representatives of international organizations are embedded in a range of social, economic, and historical relationships with each other as well as the environment.

Like other qualitative social scientists, anthropologists have sometimes gone to the opposite extreme of such people-less analyses, ignoring the nonhuman environment in their concentrated focus on social and cultural processes. Clearly, however, an understanding of environmental dynamics would benefit from analyses that could combine both perspectives, and call attention to the complex ways in which people, organisms, and environments are all interlinked in a politically charged and historically changing world. Although I do not consider this book as having reached this ideal, it is my hope that it can serve as a stepping stone to this kind of dialogue.[7]

The Mafia Island Marine Park can teach us other lessons as well. Analyses of the contemporary era rely heavily upon the concept of "globalization." While this concept is often viewed as synonymous with expanding free market capitalism, it has also been used to reference the recent and dramatic increase in international organizations, which have been associated in turn with the merging of conservation and development discourses. Yet, the "social drama" of the Mafia Island Marine Park does not support, but rather challenges, contemporary narratives of "globalization." Although the concept of the "global" has been useful in pointing to interconnections across space and to the changing nature of capitalism itself, the concept of "globalization" also has the ability to distort those social processes at work on both Mafia and a wider world stage. The narrative of globalization downplays the importance of national dynamics, failing to adequately address the symbiotic relationship between national and international institutions and elites. It obscures the complex nature of power relationships that do not always operate in top-down fashion. And it downplays the importance of history, despite the reality that nearly all those dynamics conceptualized as "new" about the Mafia Island Marine Park, including the merging of conservation and development agendas, the isolation of ecotourism as a development strategy, and the role of participation and transnational bureaucracies, are not ruptures, but rather build upon and work through existing and historical institutional structures and power relationships. As a narrative for understanding the contemporary world, the concept of the "global" itself emerges as a new packaging for older narratives of the "modern," leading us back to many of the same constricting analytical spaces from which the "global" was intended to help us escape.

Finally, in order to do justice to the "social drama" of the Mafia Island Marine Park, and the many similar "dramas" happening in other parts of the world, I would argue that we must actively embrace rather than shy away from a recognition of the "patchwork" complexity of human experience as well as human-environmental relations. In arguing for greater acknowledgment of complexity, I do not naively assume that such recognition can cause the power relationships that appear in this book to disappear (they will not). Nor do I assume that some new "narrative" for thinking about the world can fully incorporate such complexities or remain outside of existing power relationships (indeed, our narratives for understanding the world will always carry omissions and distortions and will be embedded within broader power relationships). Yet, I would argue that the *search* is an important one. The goal of acknowledging and addressing such complexity, and the attendant refusal to reduce the world to the technocentric equivalent of "sound bites," can be a politically powerful one. Acknowledging complexity as a platform for political action can help create forms of social action that are more astute about the power dynamics at work in the world and can encourage dialogues in spaces where it was not previously recognized they were required. It is my hope that this analysis of the complexity of the "social drama" of the Mafia Island Marine Park leads, not to disillusionment among those interested in social and political action, but to new efforts at grassroots organizing that will be based on more substantial partnerships than the chimera of "participation" as currently conceived. In the end, this work pleads for a new exploration of the social and economic inequality to be found at the core of contemporary environmental conflicts.

Notes

1. From the Arabic, *sahel*, meaning "coastal."

2. For histories of the East African coast, see Cooper (1997, 1980), Glassman (1995), Gray (1962), Nicholls (1971), Sheriff (1987), Strobel (1979), and Trimingham (1964), among others.

3. In an 1890 Anglo-German agreement, the British, who had established a protectorate over Zanzibar and ruled through the sultan, "traded" Mafia to the Germans, who controlled the mainland. In return, they received Stephenson Road between Lake Nyasa and Lake Tanganyika (Baumann 1896/1957).

4. In the mid-1990s, the marine park encompassed approximately 15,000 of Mafia's 40,000 or so residents.

5. In 1998, average per capita income in Tanzania was US$173 and the country was ranked third poorest in the world in terms of GDP (Redfern 2000:5).

6. According to Honey (1999:9), tourism was the world's number one employer during the 1990s, accounting for ten percent of jobs globally, and it vied with oil as the world's largest legitimate business. In 1995, spending on travel totaled $3.4 trillion.

7. Frustration with mainland national parks stemmed from the reality that many people had been displaced from the land for game reserves for aristocratic Europeans or natural areas under colonialism. The independent government, which viewed the parks as sources of foreign exchange, continued to prohibit the use of natural resources for residents and maintained national parks as sites for the enjoyment of foreign tourists. See chapter 5 as well as Neumann 1998 and Adams and McShane 1992.

8. For example, Keck and Sikkink (1998) (who eschew the term "global" in favor of "transnational") focus on the progressive political possibilities of non-governmental organizations. The emerging literature on governmentality, which draws upon Foucault, encompasses a range of viewpoints. Hardt and Negri (2000) see a new supranational or "global" juridical apparatus emerging from international organizations ranging from the United Nations to NGOs. They see this apparatus as constituting a new form of "empire" that rules in terms of police actions, even as they identify progressive possibilities in globalization more generally. Leve (2001), building upon Cruikshank (1999), suggests that the "empowerment" models offered by international NGOs generate new and politically problematic forms of subjectivity. Gupta and Ferguson (2002) offer an interesting and helpful discussion of transnational governmentality that focuses on the role that NGOs play in "privatizing" state functions. Most crucially, they call attention to the possibility that nonstate oganizations are serving as "horizontal contemporaries of the organs of the state," which variously act as rivals, servants, watchdogs, and parasites (2002:994).

9. While Keck and Sikkink (1998), for example, focus on the progressive political

possibilities of non-governmental organizations, Hardt and Negri (2000) view international institutions ranging from the United Nations, the World Trade Organizations, G7 countries and NGOs as constituting a new form of governmentality—or "sovereignty" in their terminology—suggestive of a new kind of "empire." See also Leve (2001). See previous endnote for additional information.

10. See also Tsing 2001, Rouse 1999, Cooper 2001, Ong 1999 for useful discussions of the concept of the "global."

11. Discussions of "global" dynamics have precursors in world-systems theory that attempted to understand the impact of capitalism on the relationship between Europe and others parts of the world (for example, Wallerstein 1974). Others attempted to offer a less Eurocentric viewpoint. For example, Abu Lughod (1989) described the Indian Ocean world system in the thirteenth century, Wolf (1982) offered insight into the impact of capitalism and colonialism from the perspective of colonized regions and, more recently, Frank (1998) revised his previous ideas to suggest that Asia was initially the center of world systems and will likely become so again. In the 1980s and 1990s, other theorists on the left attempted to understand the changing nature of capitalism, most expertly Harvey (1989), as well as phenomena such as deindustrialization in the First World, the spread of multinational corporate factories in the Third World, and the expansion of an Internet economy and service industries (Logan and Molotch 1987; Ong 1987; Nash 1989; Castells 1996; Sassen 1992).

12. For example, such influential theorists as Anthony Giddens (2000) and Pierre Bourdieu (1998) have weighed in on the topic, with Bourdieu being critical of the concept and the dynamics associated with it and Giddens viewing it in a more positive light. Other scholars who have engaged with such debates include Castells (1996), Hardt and Negri (2000), Appadurai (1996), Ong (1999), and Held and McGrew (2000).

13. For example, this topic was influentially raised in anthropology by Ulf Hannerz (1987) who described the "world in creolisation" as well as Arjun Appadurai (1990) who focused on media and the role of imagination. Others who have used the "global" as a framework for ethnographic work include Miller (1995) and Freeman (2000). See also Inda and Rosaldo (2002) for a collection of essays on the topic as well as two edited volumes in the journal *Public Culture* (Appadurai 2000; Comaroff and Comaroff 2000).

14. Ginsburg, Abu Lughod, and Larkin (2002) and Larkin (1997) make a similar point although, at least in the former volume, it is less explicitly tied to frameworks of globalization.

15. In the introduction to *The Anthropology of Globalization*, the only mention of history and the possibility that global dynamics might not be "new," occurs in footnote 4 (Inda and Rosaldo 2002:4).

16. Cooper, however, usefully cautions against projecting the concept of the "global" backwards, arguing that the same theoretical problems can plague the use of the concept for the past as well as the present (2001:190).

17. For example, see Berman's (1988) insightful reading of the modernist aspects of Marx evident in the language and imagery of the *Communist Manifesto*.

18. Among others, helpful ethnographies of "global" dynamics include Freeman (2000) and Ong (1999). Ong deserves particular mention for offering both a useful

critique of the concept of the global and an important ethnographic case study. Because of her difficulties with abstract analyses of the global, she instead uses the term, "transnationalism."

19. In particular, this work draws on the framework of competition among groups over natural resources found within political ecology. For works in this genre, see Blaikie (1985), Blaikie and Brookfield (1989), Watts (1983), Bryant and Bailey (1997), Neumann (1992, 1998), Peet and Watts (1996), Peluso (1992), and Schroeder (1999), among others. Although this book does not draw upon older ecological models, it does utilize more contemporary anthropological research that has sought to move beyond this framework; for example, Moore (1993), Milton (1993), Brosius (1997), Palsson (1991), and Descola and Palsson (1996). Environmental accounts from other disciplines useful to this perspective include Cronon (1983, 1991, 1996), Adams (1995), and Zerner (2000), among others.

20. See Hodgson (2001:11) for a similar position.

21. Abu Lughod (1990), for example, has offered an important cautionary corrective to the many celebratory accounts of "resistance" that emerged during the 1980s. This account builds upon her suggestion that apparent points of resistance may instead be productively used as a diagnostic of broader power relationships.

22. Such ideas appear among postcolonial and subaltern scholars (e.g., Bhabha 1994). See also Guha (1997) and Guha and Spivak (1998) for an overview and sampling of the large literature on postcoloniality and Gaonkar (2001) for the newly emergent and related literature on "alternative modernities."

23. For a critique of such assumptions, see Cooper (1983).

24. For an excellent example of this regarding the importance of cattle as wealth for wage earners in Lesotho, see chapter 5 in Ferguson (1994).

25. Since my fieldwork, Pat Caplan has produced a new work on Mafia, "African Voices, African Lives: Personal Narratives from a Swahili Village" (1997).

26. The "Maritime Division" is a pseudonym.

Chapter One

1. Adult women and men preferred to be taught in separate classes to accord with coastal standards of politeness and sex segregation. Teenagers, however, were taught in mixed-sex settings.

2. *Wageni* in KiSwahili can suggest connotations of visitor, stranger, guest, or outsider. Thus, calling someone a "guest" can be a polite way of drawing attention to their status as outsiders.

3. See endnote 8 in Introduction for discussion of governmentality.

4. For example, Zanzibaris, along with the international press, speculated that some European-owned coastal hotels had ties to the criminal mafia and were covers for money laundering and drug running (Greenberger 1996). In addition, on Mafia in 1994 there were rumors among both European expatriates and Mafia residents that Juani Island was to be "given" to an Irish arms dealer to whom government leaders were indebted for help during the war with Uganda's Idi Amin. (See chapter 7.)

5. The development worker had trained a man from Jibondo who was only temporarily residing on Chole. This man then brought members of his own family from

Jibondo to train as apprentices at the boatyard, excluding Chole residents from this respected and relatively lucrative occupation.

6. For a discussion of German colonialism in Tanganyika, see Illife 1969. The British colonial administration neglected education partly because it did not want to spend the necessary money on a "low-priority" territory and partly because of fears that education, particularly above the primary level, would contribute to political unrest among Africans (Coulson 1982; Illife 1979).

7. Responding to rivalries between competing Lutheran and Catholic mission schools, leaders of the Chagga ethnic group in the 1920s persuaded the colonial government to create a committee that would supervise all the schools in Kilimanjaro. In addition, a special tax was levied to contribute to teachers' wages (Illife 1979:35).

8. Once again, for an important caution against the romanticizing of resistance, see Abu Lughod (1990) and Mitchell (1990).

9. The estimated costs for five years of implementing the Mafia Island Marine Park were 2.3 million (US) dollars. While WWF contributed 235,000 USD and NORAD 513,000 USD, WWF was to provide core staff and technical expertise to set up the park. The remaining 1.55 million USD was requested from the European Development Fund of the European Union although a decision was still pending at the conclusion of this research.

10. The demographic survey had been undertaken in 1993 as part of Operation Dynamite Project, which was sponsored by WWF in the time preceding the establishment of the park. According to official documents on the subject, eleven residents from Mafia worked for forty-one days. The payment records submitted by the Acting Warden indicated that residents worked for half that time on a "voluntary" basis and each had been paid 20,000 shillings. Most residents denied having "volunteered" or having been paid the 20,000 shillings.

11. For an analysis of very similar political techniques and culture in neighboring Kenya, see Haugerud 1993.

12. WWF correspondence, October 24, 1995.

13. During the mid-1990s, there was electricity in only two villages on Mafia, the government seat of Kilindoni and the tourist center of Utende. There were also only a handful of television sets on the islands. As far as I knew, only one set was owned by an individual with origins on Mafia and this was the district member of Parliament.

14. According to notes taken during the minutes of Bwejuu's first marine park committee meeting, many residents on Bwejuu were deeply concerned that the island was being used as a hide-out for dynamiters. The notes suggested that some island residents were in fact cooperating with the dynamiters, in particular, younger men (which invariably means poorer ones). Although some were actively assisting dynamiters, others were showing dynamite fishers from the mainland prime fishing areas or renting them canoes. The Bwejuu committee recorded that it had begun to take independent action to deal with this situation. It had authorized ten cell leaders to record in special notebooks those *wageni* or "outsiders" who were residing in their areas and their permit statuses. The committee also sought to bring charges against any *wenyeji* or local residents assisting dynamiters.

15. WWF correspondence, February 3, 1997.

16. District Councils are a contemporary offshoot of colonial native authorities and

were viewed by residents with similar ambivalence. Although popularly elected, these representatives were accountable upwards in the political hierarchy rather than toward their fellow residents. In addition, many members of the District Council were assumed to engage in corruption by Chole residents. Indeed, during the time I stayed on Chole, District Council appointees tried at several points to extort money from Chole community development funds. For a detailed description, see chapter 6.

17. In KiSwahili: Baruti ile tulikuwa tunapiga kilele sana sisi hapa. Tukafanya utaratibu, tukaletewa mtalamu mmoja. Alhamdullilah. Tunashukuru. Lakini tunapigwa vita vikubwa mno. Anataka aondolewe yule mtalamu mwenye ujuzi wa kazi hiyo, aletwe mwingine. Mtu huyu mwingine tukiletewa sisi tumekufa wanachi wa Mafia. Kwa sababu ndiyo mazao yetu na sisi—watu wengine hawapati kitoweo, hawapati kitu cho chote kwa sababu ya uvuvi haramu. Kwa hiyo, Bwana Waziri Mkuu, tunakuomba mtaalamu yule mzungu asituondokee hapa Mafia atulinde Mafia na bahari yetu hii.

18. In KiSwahili: WWF wana boti ya patroli, ile ya kwenda na patroli na polisi, wanakamata watu hawa wanaofanya uharibifu. Sasa mimi nilivyosoma, watu wa marine park wana interest ya watu wa baruti, itoke boti hapa Mafia ile baruti iendelee. Nilivyosoma mimi.

19. This perspective also in some cases resonated with the forced labor projects of the colonial era (Mushi 1978). See Ribot for a similar dynamic with some international projects (1996, 1999, 2000).

CHAPTER TWO

1. *Boma* in KiSwahili suggests a protective wall for defensive purposes and is sometimes translated as "fort." Under European colonialism, the term was used for government administrative offices. Chole's first Boma was apparently built in the early to mid-1800s during the reign of Seyid Said and his sons in Zanzibar (Saadi 1941).

2. For example, on Zanzibar's popular "Spice Tours," tour guides visiting the palaces of the former sultans stress the number of concubines in the sultan's "harem" and suggest scenes of naked, nubile women splashing in palace fountains awaiting the Sultan's sexual desires. Tours of the Anglican cathedral and former slave market are dominated by sensationalistic accounts of slavery. Such accounts draw on the legacy of Christian abolitionist discourse in East Africa, which suggests ideas of moral superiority to Muslims as much as it does moral outrage at slavery.

3. This observation also parallels comments made in the Zanzibar Visitor Departure Survey conducted by the Zanzibar Commission of Tourism in 1995. See chapter 7.

4. For a discussion of the strident ahistoricism of development discourse, see Crush 1995 and Ferguson 1994.

5. An American performance studies professor from the University of Iowa named Fred Woodward came to Chole for a short time to collect oral narratives about slavery. He was invited to Chole by one of the tour operators who was involved in the community-based tourism development project. Local community groups had already expressed their interest in the project, and I agreed to help organize interviews.

6. There was another way of speaking about the past, shaped by the Islamic ideas

about the coming end of the world, a concept described in KiSwahili as *aheri zamani*. The way in which this doctrine could be used to analyze the hardships of the present will be discussed in chapter 7.

7. While Gray refers to this man as Hassan bin Ali (1951), Freeman-Grenville refers to him as Ali ibn al-Husain ibn Ali (1958) and James Kirkman, as Ali bin Husain (1964). According to Kirkman, it was said that Ali bin Husain was a son of a sultan of Shiraz by an Ethiopian mother and he emigrated to Africa to escape the disparagement of his mother's slave origin (1964:193).

8. Also see references in Trimingham (1964) to the Shirazi-MaShatiri immigrants from Mafia who later settled in Zanzibar. A similar account told from the perspective of Mafia appears in the oral accounts collected by Kadhi Amur Omar Saadi (1941).

9. References to women rulers during the Shirazi period are scattered throughout the historical literature. Patricia Caplan has noted that women rulers were not uncommon historically along the East African coast, a practice that was later discouraged by the Omani Sultans at Zanzibar (Caplan 1982). Kirkman refers to a Queen Fatima of Zanzibar in the mid-1600s. Trimingham refers to female leaders on Pemba, Tumbatu, and Unguja (Zanzibar) (1964:17). See also Romero on Lamu (1997:4). Interestingly, on Chole, Mwanzuwani is referred to as an *mfalme* [ruler] not as *malkia*, the gender specific word that is translated into English as queen. Since pronouns in KiSwahili are nongendered, the sex of actors is not apparent unless named. This raises the possibility that English translations that assume historical actors to be male may obscure more complex gender dynamics in coastal history.

10. According to the Saadi collection of oral accounts, Mwanzuwani's [*sic*] mother had been the Shirazi ruler of Kua and was married to a man named Alawi (the name of a prominent Kilwa family according to Trimingham 1964:16). Mwanzuwani had married a MaShatiri Arab who was named Aidarus who later returned to Hadhramaut and died. They had a child named Alawi, who later ruled in his grandmother's (and mother's) place although he died before his mother (Saadi 1941:25–26). Both Mwanzuwani and Alawi moved to Chole following Kua's sacking. According to the conflicting account of Sheikh Mwinchande, Mwanzuwani was married to a man who was named Mohammed Raasi, who later went to Siu near Lamu on the northern Swahili coast during the period of the Sakalava attacks on Kua to ask for help. Rather than returning, he and his followers settled in Zanzibar. Presumably this is the migration of Shirazi-MaShatiri elites to Zanzibar mentioned by Trimingham (1964).

11. Later dates are given by Baumann (1896), and Saadi (1941). However, Alper's account (1977) is based on in-depth research on the Sakalava and is presumably the most accurate. See also Piggott (1941:39).

12. This, however, contradicts other oral accounts like Saadi (1941) which argue that Mwanzuwani survived the sacking and moved to Chole.

13. Saadi notes the expedition consisted of three groups of soldiers, Shihiri (also from contemporary Yemen), WaGunya (or WaBajuni from near Lamu on the northern coast), and WaBaluchi (from contemporary Iran) (1941). He also notes that the leader of the expedition Abdulla bin Jumaa built the first Boma at Chole during the reign of Sultan Said.

14. Although slaveowners clearly did not always follow Islamic dictates of proper treatment of slaves, prestige in coastal society generally came from being a *mtu mkubwa* (big person) or respected patron, which included amassing the support of

followers who included slaves. Thus, slaveowners could seek to enhance their social position by periodically manumitting slaves, offering slaves support in their old age, or allowing former slaves the use of land without rent (Cooper 1977; Glassman 1991, 1995; Fair 2001)

15. The KiSwahili word for slave—*mtumwa*—literally means a person who is able to be "sent," whether to do work or run errands.

16. The relationship between those accounts told on Chole and those along other parts of the coast is uncertain. Clearly, however, such stories did not spread by official means given that Mafia was under the mainland government rather than the Zanzibari government. People on Chole say that they learned such accounts from their elders and not from schools or by other routes.

17. Although this conflict is generally known as the Maji Maji Rebellion in English (Illife 1979) it is known as the Maji Maji War in KiSwahili (*Vita vya Maji Maji*).

18. After a preliminary bombardment by the guns of the *H.M.S. Kinfauns Castle*, a British Expeditionary Force landed at Kisimani Mafia and briefly encountered resistance at Ngombeni from a handful of Germans and about sixty askaris before taking the island the next day (Revington 1936, Saadi 1941).

CHAPTER THREE

1. Ideas of community have also had a profound effect on two disciplines of concern to this study—anthropology and ecology. In the emerging division of labor between the social sciences in the later nineteenth and early twentieth century, sociology was conceived as studying "modern" societies. In contrast, anthropology, through its concern with "premodern" or "primitive" peoples, was conceived as focusing on "communities." However, *gemeinschaft* was also assumed to exist among rural peasants, the urban poor, and ethnic minorities in Europe and the United States, encouraging a "community"-studies tradition within sociology based at the University of Chicago from the early to mid-1900s. Not coincidentally, this community studies approach was heavily influenced by the ideas of the Ecology Group, also at the University of Chicago and led by Warder Allee, which exhibited its own fascination in ecological terms with the concept of community (Worster 1994:326–321). Such theoretical cross-fertilization resulted in both the "human ecology" paradigm developed by University of Chicago sociologists (Robert E. Park 1915, 1936; Park and Burgess 1921; McKenzie 1926), as well as an ethnographic "community studies" approach which influenced the work of such scholars as William Whyte (1981 [1943]), Robert and Helen Lynd (1929, 1937), Robert Redfield (1930), Herbert Gans (1962), and William Kornblum (1974).

2. Chole, like the small islands of Jibondo and Juani, are considered "villages" for purposes of government administration. (The other small island within the marine park, Bwejuu, is administered as part of Kilindoni).

3. A kinship survey that I conducted on Chole, which notes the place of origin of all persons living on Chole including those who recently married onto the island, supports this finding. For example, the vast majority of links to other areas are in the south of Mafia, almost half of such links being to Juani, a fifth to Jibondo, and the remainder to villages on Mafia's main island. However, the large majority of such

villages on the main island are located in the south, a minority in central Mafia, including Baleni and Kipingwe, and a mere handful from northern Mafia (and these only as far north as Kirongwe). It is actually ten times more likely that a person will be from a more geographically distant place off of Mafia, such as Kilwa, Dar es Salaam, the Rufiji, or Zanzibar than from a village in the north of Mafia.

4. However, rights through *ukoo* are tempered by the occurrence of different kinds of land in different areas of Mafia (Caplan 1975). Land planted with trees follows different patterns of ownership. Possession of trees also confers usage rights to the land beneath the trees, and trees, following patterns established during the era of Arab plantations, are inherited according to Islamic law in which women inherit half of what their brothers inherit.

5. A research assistant from Chole, Ally Ahmadi, helped me to create a kinship map of the entire island of Chole. As I came to know more people over time, I was able to verify this kinship information and ask more questions about interrelationships. Rachel Eide, a Norwegian anthropologist who arrived on Chole in 1996, kindly agreed to help check the accuracy of this survey. Ally Ahmadi also helped create a household map, which plotted actual houses as well as residence and kinship patterns. Because it would have been considered rude to quiz people about their property, the wealth survey consisted of two parts. I asked three friends on Chole to rank the various households on the island according to whether they were better off, average, or poor by local standards. The results were remarkably consistent. Toward the end of my stay on Chole, I asked a very close friend to help me estimate the assets of everyone on the island. While I was aware that everyone knew who owned the few boats and canoes on Chole as well as the handful of tiny selling stalls (or *maduka*), I was also surprised by the extent to which individual tree holdings (the most common form of wealth on Chole) were common knowledge. Although this survey is clearly based on estimates and may well be inaccurate for individuals, I believe it provides an accurate indication of the range of holdings that mark people as being well-off, middling, or poor on Chole.

6. People do not refer to "my home," as is customary in English, but invariably use the plural "our home."

7. Pat Caplan has suggested that this tendency toward patrilocality stems from the reality that men inherit more trees than women; hence it makes sense to live closer to the husband's family to enable better care of trees (1982:37).

8. In patrilineal and matrilineal kinship arrangements, relatives of the parent through whom descent is not traced are still considered "relatives" but they are not "family" in the same sense as those within one's own lineage.

9. For example, while describing a very different kind of kinship arrangement, Carol Stack has noted the role that fictive kinship and the maintenance of wide social networks play for poor African-Americans in dealing with poverty (Stack 1974).

10. Eastman (1988) usefully suggests the impact that slave culture had upon coastal society, including kinship arrangements. However, in linking men primarily to Arab/Islamic culture and women to African culture, she makes overly rigid distinctions that downplay shared beliefs between men and women.

11. This analysis relies heavily on Pat Caplan's discussion of the tensions between *sheria* and *mila* on Mafia (1982, 1984).

12. For example, for property such as trees and boats, which are inherited ac-

corded to Islamic law, women received half the inheritance of their brothers. For other kinds of property and for the division of marital assets upon divorce which follow *mila,* women and men equally divide property following the logic of bilateral kinship arrangements.

13. Older men also made similar comments about the young, including the village religious leader or *sheha,* who noted wistfully that in the past the young would show their respect by kneeling when they greeted elders. Although this is not an "Islamic" practice, it was one he associated with "proper" social relationships.

14. In Zanzibar, *sheria* and other practices associated with the Arab world went into a sharp decline after the Revolution of 1964. However, renewed contact with oil-rich Oman and other Arab countries over the last two decades, has once again meant that Arab cultural practices are being more closely associated with upward social mobility.

15. This skill also underscores the irony of organizations like the United States Information Services (USIS) seeking to "educate" Tanzanians on "democracy," as they did before the 1995 multiparty elections. USIS published booklets in KiSwahili that inexplicably focused on the history of the French and American revolutions and the impact of ancient Greece and Rome on European governments. African contexts and realities were never discussed, nor was there any consideration that there might be "democratic" traditions within Africa.

16. In general, women and men engaged in freer sexual relations than is often assumed to occur in Muslim societies. In part, this relates to the gender dynamics encouraged by bilateral kinship forms in which women are strong social actors in their own right and where there is less desire to control their sexuality for the good of a patrilineal kin group. Although it was considered respectable for girls to be virgins at their first marriage, married women sometimes engaged in extramarital affairs and divorced women freely took lovers. It was also not unusual for children to be born outside of marriage (such children took the second name of Abdallah in place of a father's name). There seemed to be relatively little opprobrium attached to such births. When I asked whether such children were stigmatized for lacking "family," I was told that this was not the case since the children belonged to the *ukoo* of maternal relatives and that the only disadvantage stemmed from their inability to inherit through both maternal and paternal lines.

17. Tourism in poor countries like Tanzania, which is based on vast disparities in wealth between tourists and hosts, is often associated with such dynamics as petty theft, begging, and the phenomenon of "beach boys" (referred to derogatorily in Zanzibar as *mapapasi* [ticks]). The developers of the Chole Kisiwani tourism development (as well as Chole residents who also objected to such transformations) sought to curb such phenomena.

18. Some people also offered the interpretation that opponents of the project included many former residents of Juani who had recently moved to Chole. They attributed this opposition once again to *wivu* (jealousy), believing that newer arrivals or *wageni* would not want Chole's *wenyeji* to improve their lot in life.

19. The money in the community development fund came from donor organizations, such as the British Council, which helped finance the school and the clinic; from the entrance fee charged to day tourists visiting the island; and from a percentage of the profit for each tourist staying on Chole.

CHAPTER FOUR

1. *Vijidudu*, literally refers to little bugs and can mean bacteria or even microbes. It was at times used colloquially on Mafia, however, to mean "little thingies."

2. For interesting explorations of social and cultural dynamics relating to marine life in various parts of the world, see Palsson (1995); McEvoy (1986); and Johannes (1981).

3. For a discussion of "remote" places, see Tsing (1993).

4. This is a similar question to that raised by Talal Asad (1993) in relation to religion. Do all societies have a concept of religion that is defined in the particular ways it is understood in European modernist thought? Asad has offered a powerful Foucauldian argument that this is not the case.

5. *Samaki hana bei* meaning "fish have no price" is in the present tense. In Bi Rehema's account, like many others on Chole, people often used the present tense in giving ongoing descriptions of the past.

6. Prices for selling coconuts in 1997 ranged from 60 to 120 shillings per nut.

7. Although some Chole residents claim that they were at times forced to pay bribes to gain access to medicines or health care (for a similar account, see Caplan 1992).

8. This company also bought lobster and other fish at certain periods and appeared to have complex relations with district government officials. During one meeting, the district commissioner spent much of his talk extolling the virtues of this company. In 1997, however, the company seemed to fall out of favor with officials and was charged with depleting the number of octopus on Mafia.

9. At the time I conducted research, there were only eight sailboats (*mashua*) and six canoes (*ng'alawa*) on Chole for a population of approximately eight hundred.

10. Although as Glaesel (1997) notes, such methods may no longer be effective in areas where the numbers of near-shore fish have decreased.

11. Large catches in the past are also described in the June 1957 edition of the "Kua" newsletter (published briefly by the district government in Kilindoni). Among colonial officials and travelers, Mafia was reputed to be one of best fishing spots in the world (Conan Doyle 1953).

12. Although the word for fishing (*kuvua samaki*) is commonly used, residents also use vocabulary for land-based activities to describe fishing. Occasionally people refer to "farming" (*kulima*) the sea and describe their catch using the same word as that for crops (*mazao*). The word used for conserving fish populations (*kufunga*) is also the same word used for rearing livestock or other land animals.

13. Other natural resources besides fish and land were also not fully commodified on Mafia. For example, when I offered to pay for unripe drinking coconuts for an outing to sun-baked Juani, I was told that unripened coconuts "had no price" and could only be given as gifts.

CHAPTER FIVE

1. For example, ideas of "nature" (in both the human and environmental sense) were profoundly shaped by images of "savages" and the non-Western world even before European colonialism (Trouillet 1991; L. Marx 1964), and Grove notes that conservation itself first emerged in European colonies rather than at "home" (1992).

For other observations on the centrality of non-European histories to the making of the "modern" world, see Comaroff and Comaroff (1991, 1997) and Piot (1999).

2. In a similar example, William Cronon (1983), Eric Wolf (1982) and others, have explored the role that international fur markets played in transforming hunting patterns among Native Americans and Canadians in the seventeenth and eighteenth centuries.

3. Such terminology holds disturbing parallels with that of some contemporary environmental groups that depict "indigenous" groups as part of the natural "biodiversity" of particular regions.

4. For example, mass evictions occurred in 1974 and 1988. In the latter instance five thousand people were forcibly evicted from Umba-Mkomazi game reserve, despite the 1951 legislation that allowed pastoralists continued rights to residence and grazing in their home areas (Neumann 2000:126).

5. Not to be confused with the Arusha Declaration in 1967 in which Nyerere proclaimed Tanzania to be a socialist country.

6. Public Records Office, London. CO 822/654, Progress Report, Development of Mbulu District, January 1, 1952–December 31, 1952.

7. Public Records Office, CO 822/654, comments by R. Browne 2/4 and Progress Report of Mbulu District, January 1, 1952—December 31, 1952.

8. TNA (Tanzanian National Archives), D 3/5/26. Memo from Regional Commissioner S. J. Kitundu to the Mafia District Development Committee, June 22, 1962.

9. Presumably the hippos originated in the Rufiji Delta and made their way to Mafia. Interestingly, a British colonial report dated December 18, 1933 noted that a full-size hippo from the Rufiji had swum across the channel and ended up on Jibondo island although it was unable to walk due to its feet being lacerated by the coral (TNA G1/2/39).

10. TNA, G1/5000/1, G1/5000/2, G1/5000/6, G1/5000/7, G1/5000/33, G1/5000/34.

11. TNA G1/5000/33.

12. During my time on Mafia, *chesi* were widely found in the remoter areas of Juani Island but were to my knowledge largely ignored. During the drought of 1997 when water supplies on Juani dried up, *chesi* began to die from dehydration (at that time Juani residents themselves crossed over to draw water from Chole's wells). Since the dehydrated *chesi* moved slowly, some residents began hunting *chesi* (suggesting that *chesi* themselves formed a famine food for people). However, hunting does not mean a generalized callousness for life as some assume. At one point, several camp workers on Chole brought in a dehydrated and shivering pregnant *chesi* hoping to keep it for a "pet." When the cook killed it for food, arguing that it was going to die anyway, a male camp worker from Chole like myself was too filled with revulsion to join in eating the remains of the gentle creature. This led to a general discussion among camp workers about how difficult it is to overcome *huruma* or "sympathy" when slaughtering animals.

13. TNA G1/5000/33.

14. TNA G1/5000/432.

15. Public Records Office, CO 822/326/C.F.A.C. (52)10.

16. Public Records Office, CO 822/326/C.F.A.C. (52)10.

17. Public Records Office, CO 822/1079.

18. Public Records Office, CO 822/1079.

19. For tales of modernist emancipatory projects in Ethiopia which also had deeply distressing outcomes, see Donham (1999).

CHAPTER SIX

1. The initial General Management Plan for the marine park suggested entry fees of US$10 per day for nonresident visitors and that the park be taxed by the national government at the rate of 50 percent and the district government at the rate of five percent.

2. Funding to develop this legislation was provided by the Food and Agricultural Organization of the United Nations (FAO). At the time of the creation of the Marine Parks and Reserves Acts in 1994, there were seven existing reserves that had been created in the 1970s (two of which were located on Mafia), but all have been described as ineffectual "paper parks." At the time, plans were also being laid for a new marine park at Menai Bay in Zanzibar.

3. According to the general management plan: "The prime task of the warden will be the administration, coordination, monitoring, development and operation of all matters, pertaining to MIMP [Mafia Island Marine Park]. These include: MIMP staff; MIMP accounts; MIMP projects; enforcement including prosecution; all directives given by the BoT [Board of Trustees]; and the monitoring of the management strategy for MIMP with regard to its effect on the environment, resource use, the socio-economies of the local communities, and the District as well as national economies." (GMP 1993:55–56).

4. According to the general management plan, the board of trustees (BoT) is appointed by the Minister for Tourism, Natural Resources and Environment on advice from the Principal Secretary. The BoT is designed to govern not only the Mafia Island Marine Park but any other marine parks and reserves. Its board of ten members includes the principal secretary for Tourism, Natural Resources, and Environment; director for "Maritime;" director of forestry; one regional executive director from an area with a marine park; one member of parliament for an area with a marine park; one representative from an international NGO; the head of a scientific institution dealing with marine resource management; a representative from a private business with interests in a marine park; a marine protected area/coastal zone management expert and a representative from a nationally or regionally based marine conservation NGO working in Tanzania. Other than the member of parliament, no position was allotted for a local representative from any area with a marine park.

5. The Advisory Committee (described as the Technical Committee (TC) in the General Management Plan specifies the composition as follows: a representative from the "Maritime" Department; the district executive director; a district natural resources officer; a regional natural resources officer; two local community representatives; a marine scientist from a Tanzanian institution; two private business representatives (one extractive use, one nonextractive use); one representative from an NGO working within the marine park.

6. Written communication, 11/18/97.

7. In a consultancy review of the project conducted between December 14 and January 15, 1996, Dr. Walter Pfluger (Germany) and Mr. Winley Sichone (Tanzania)

argued "concerning the implementation of the Plan of Operations, the Warden should be accountable also to the Advisory Committee and Mafia residents, as well as to the Board. If this is not taken into consideration, MIMP will never be a 'park for the people and by the people.'" However, the authors also conclude that "frictions" within the park are due simply to "lack of effective management" and that a clear Memorandum of Understanding between WWF and other parties is all that is required for "fruitful cooperation." They argue that goodwill and mutual understanding are required in "open systems like the democracies of our times" where it is not possible to "regulate everything." The review of the project sponsored by NORAD in 1997 under Ian Bryceson, also called for increased representation of local communities on the Advisory Committee and Board of Trustees. Much like the earlier report it also attributed conflict within the park to personality conflicts and resolvable institutional misunderstandings.

8. While Mafia residents in general have been excluded from national government positions due to their limited access to education, Tanzania's post-independence government followed their British colonial predecessors in maintaining what Mamdani (1996) has called a "bifurcated" structure split between local levels of governance and a highly centralized national system (with almost no mobility between levels). Mafia, like other districts, possesses a district council (the contemporary heir to the British colonial "Native Council" and one that is viewed with equal skepticism by residents) that is accountable upward in a way that supports the centralization of the state.

9. The visitors received a "ticket" describing the history of the island and helpful advice (including tips on appropriate dress). Visitors in turn were to be charged a standard price for the ferry and were not to be asked for money for taking photos or by "begging."

10. When visitors began staying in the Chole tourism camp in 1996, $5 out of the $20 per night charge went into the community development fund.

11. The following account of bureaucracy as a terrain for struggle draws on written documents selected from a range of letters, memos, c.c.'s, reports, reviews, and planning documents housed in the WWF-Utende office on Mafia. This discussion clearly would have been impossible without open access to the files in the WWF office during the period of the park's implementation between 1994 and 1997. I am grateful to "David Holston," the WWF technical adviser at the time, for his principled belief that institutional "transparency" should mean exactly that.

12. In KiSwahili: "Ukizingatia kuwa mshauri wa kiufundi si raia wa nchi hii hivyo haruhusiwi kuitisha mkutano wowote ule wa kiutawala bila idhini ya wilaya au MIMP na hii ni hatari pia kwa usalama wa Taifa."

13. Such dynamics were not only evident during a historical era of "ward bosses" in cities like Chicago and Boston, but are currently evident in the politics of regions like rural Appalachia (Duncan 2000).

14. I use the term "popular knowledge" rather than indigenous, local, or traditional knowledge. I find the terms "indigenous" and "traditional" problematic because of the strong connotations of bounded, static societies cut off from contemporary historical dynamics and interaction with other groups. The term "local" knowledge implies that such knowledge exists as separate from—rather than as intertwined with—"global" dynamics, suggesting a false spatialization of social processes. Although not without

its own problems, the term "popular knowledge" is helpful in that it is less symbolically loaded and can refer to non-institutionalized forms of knowledge in Europe and the United States as readily as countries in Africa (for example, Lave, 1996). I would like to thank MaryBeth MacPhee for suggesting this term.

15. Some very old men, trained in the *madarasa* or Quranic schools, were also literate in KiSwahili written in Arabic script; however, they had become "illiterate" in practical terms when KiSwahili came to be written in the Roman alphabet or *kizungu*, as the British colonial era progressed. Many older women had had no access to formal education at all.

16. It should also be noted that the disdain often experienced by fishers in Tanzania is not unique to the so-called Third World. North American and European small-scale fishers are often treated in a similar way in relation to "experts." Such fishers similarly deal with fisheries managers and conservation experts who often are more highly educated and who base their perspectives on bioeconomic models that ignore human dynamics and who find the knowledge of such fishers to be largely irrelevant (McGoodwin 1990).

17. I have also seen this spelled by Chole residents and others as Myewe and Miewe. Some maps indicate that "Jina" is an island behind and adjacent to Miewi, but Chole residents did not seem to make this distinction.

18. For the long debates over these issues within anthropology and related disciplines, see Goody (1968, 1977), Horton (1967), Street (1984).

CHAPTER SEVEN

1. *Maendeleo* is a noun derived from the KiSwahili verb, *kuenda*, meaning "to go." *Maendeleo* suggests a forward movement and is often translated as "progress" or development.

2. However, other Chole residents attribute the greater prosperity of Jibondo to its being favored as a source of development funding by international organizations.

3. While it might be tempting to attribute the individualizing quality of this language to the impact of recent neoliberal development paradigms, such interpretations do not appear to be valid for Mafia. Such comments were already widespread in 1994 when a new generation of development projects was first beginning to appear in the region. Although the necessity of individuals scrambling to get ahead economically might sound reassuringly familiar to neoliberal economists, the ideas and practices associated with such outlooks are not easily encompassed by theories of self-maximizing rational market actors, as chapter 4, clearly demonstrates. The individualizing quality of development talk appeared to instead stem from a sense of disillusionment in which the promises of broader societal transformation previously made by the post-independence government and international organizations had proven hollow. Given this sense of disillusionment, Chole residents implied that scrambling to make ends meet was the only route available to gain *maendeleo*.

4. This comment emerged in a discussion of the use of banks on Mafia. After Mzee Bakari described the practices of the island's *wazee,* he noted that the state and other development bodies castigated contemporary Mafia residents as "backward" for also not putting their money in banks. Mzee Bakari defended such choices by arguing that bank officials were often reluctant to let the "uneducated" have free access to

their accounts, that the poor often needed quick access to money in order to survive, and that the Tanzanian shilling was prone to devaluation and had become increasingly "worthless" (*hamna thamani*) making it a risky proposition to store assets in cash.

5. See, for example, www.zanzibar—holiday.com/kinasi/mafia.htm. Accessed on 2/10/03.

6. ZNA (Zanzibar National Archive) T. 42 AK 19 17.

7. The survey was entitled "The Zanzibar Visitor Departure Survey" and was distributed by the Zanzibar Commission for Tourism at the airport and port. Tourists identified themselves as being from France, Germany, Italy, Switzerland, Australia, New Zealand, the United States, China, and Hong Kong, with Europeans predominating.

8. The overriding fiction that tourism seeks to generate, especially in high-end tourism is that such commodification is in fact "hospitality." For example, hotel workers in Zanzibar and Mafia, as elsewhere, speak of "guests" not "customers." At luxury establishments in particular, hotel operators discuss the need to keep billing as discreet as possible, lumping separate charges into one bill, thereby reducing the sensation that each encounter is a separate, commodified activity. Such concerns also led some of Mafia's hoteliers to initially oppose their guests paying an entrance fee to visit Chole, arguing that it created a "bad feeling."

9. Here, I draw upon Pruitt and LaFont's terminology for a similar phenomenon in Jamaica (1995).

10. Similar dynamics were also apparent in the past. For example, archival records from 1950s Zanzibar document discussions among British colonial officials about whether it would be possible to station police at the port to prevent scantily clad European women from leaving the ocean-going liners and disturbing the sensibilities of residents of Zanzibar Town (ZNA T. 8 AK 19/6A).

11. See Stonich 2000 for a similar example from the Honduras.

EPILOGUE

1. According to the revised version of the General Management Plan (2000:14), between 1997 and 1999, Mafia had only 140 tourist beds between 4 lodges. It received no more than four thousand bed nights per year, with occupancy hovering at only about 10 percent. As the 1990s progressed, once-eager investors appeared to lose interest in the park due to ongoing difficulties with transportation.

2. As mentioned in previous chapters, the purchased limestone for such ostensible projects as improving the airport landing strip was made from high-grade white lime derived from live sea coral (Andrews 1999; Horrill and Ngoile 1991). This grade of limestone involved much more destructive and extensive coral mining methods than residents generally used for local consumption.

3. As described elsewhere, there were small and sporadic efforts to develop alternative building materials. WWF commissioned a report on alternative building techniques, Frontier attempted a mud brick project and one of the tour developers attempted to encourage research into alternative kilns that could fire hard land-based coral. However, the kiln never materialized, the mud brick project was thoughtlessly planned and caused a major social controversy on Chole that left lasting hard feelings about mud brick construction, and WWF's efforts to revive kiln research in 2000

occurred several years after the enforcement of the ban and had not yet produced any viable alternatives.

4. Disagreements and tensions among Tanzanian governmental bodies had long been apparent in relation to the marine park. In the early days of the park's formation, there had been a heated debate whether the park should fall under the jurisdiction of TANAPA (Tanzanian National Parks Service) or the Maritime Division. Although both divisions were located within the Ministry of Tourism, Natural Resources, and the Environment, they were evaluated in very different ways by representatives of non-governmental organizations and tour operators on Mafia who generally perceived TANAPA as a more efficient and "honest" body than the Maritime Division. Although Mafia residents were excluded from such debates, they also had reason to be nervous about TANAPA, given that this body administered national parks that were built in the exclusionary preservationist mold. However, they were also adamant that they did not want the marine park to be located under the Maritime Division. Although the park, in the end, *would* be placed under the Maritime Division, efforts to relocate the park to TANAPA continued as late as 1998–1999 when it was once again proposed in Tanzanian conservationists' evaluation the park (Ngoile et al. 1998: 41–2).

5. I was explicitly told by these men that the reason they were being so straightforward was because of our now lengthy association and that they would not feel comfortable discussing such issues with people they did not know. Revealingly, people now thought it was important that I use pseudonyms to disguise their identity, while in previous years when I mentioned this anthropological convention, many people were puzzled by it and said it was unnecessary.

6. Residents argued that in the initial two zoning trips only a handful of individuals had accompanied park planners. Different individuals had been selected on each trip (without consultation between the two groups), and, on the latter trip in particular, young fishers had been asked to represent the island who did not have the authority to make such decisions in the mind of older residents. Residents further argued that what might be acceptable zones for users of a particular type of fishing gear might not be acceptable for users of different gear. Such concerns go to the heart of the issue of representation both within the marine park and other "participatory" community projects in general. The assumption that representatives necessarily express the best interest of all or that they can adequately represent communities when no mechanisms have been established for the channeling of the information to other residents (particularly in contexts in which there is no popular media to convey such information) reflects stereotypical assumptions about how homogeneous "communities" function rather than a serious concern for social process.

7. The "political ecology" school has been attempting to offer such a focus, although as Moore (1993) rightly argues it has largely neglected cultural dynamics. For a wonderful example of such work from a historical viewpoint, see Cronon (1983, 1991). For marine environments, see McEvoy (1986) and Lowe (2000).

Bibliography

Abu-Lughod, Janet L. 1989. *Before European Hegemony: The World System* A.D. *1250–1350*. New York and Oxford: Oxford University Press.

Abu-Lughod, Lila. 1990. "The Romance of Resistance: Tracing Transformations of Power Through Bedouin Women." *American Ethnologist* 17:41–55.

———. 1991. "Writing Against Culture." In *Recapturing Anthropology*, ed. Richard G. Fox, Santa Fe: School of American Research.

———. 1993. *Writing Women's Worlds: Bedouin Stories*. Berkeley: University of California Press.

Acheson, James M. 1981. "Anthropology of Fishing." *Annual Review of Anthropology* 10:275–316.

Adams, Jonathan S., and Thomas O. McShane. 1992. *The Myth of Wild Africa: Conservation Without Illusion*. New York: Norton.

Adams, W. M. 1990. *Green Development: Environment and Sustainability in the Third World*. London: Routledge.

———. 1995. "Green Development Theory? Environmentalism and Sustainable Development." In *Power of Development*, ed. J. Crush. London and New York: Routledge.

Agrawal, Arun. 1995. Dismantling the Divide between Indigenous and Scientific Knowledge. *Development and Change* 26:413–39.

Agarwal, Bina. 1992. "The Gender and Environment Debate: Lessons from India." *Feminist Studies* 18:119–57.

Ake, Claude. 1996. *Democracy and Development in Africa*. Washington, D.C.: The Brookings Institution.

Alcorn, Janis. 1997. "Dances Around the Fire: Conservation Organizations and Community-Based Resource Management." Unpublished paper presented at the conference, Representing Communities: Histories & Politics of Community-Based Resource Management. Helen, Georgia, June 1–3.

Alpers, Edward A. 1977. "Madagascar and Mozambique in the 19th Century: The Era of the Sakalava Raids (1800–1820)." *Omaly sy Anio* (Antananarivo) 5/6: 37–53.

Anderson, David, and Richard Grove. 1987. *Conservation in Africa: People, Policies and Practice*. Cambridge: Cambridge University Press.

Andrews, Greg. 1998. "Implications of Applying a Marine Park Paradigm in a Developing Country." Conference paper given at the International Tropical Marine Ecosystems Management Symposium, Townsville, Australia, November 23–26.

Appadurai, Arjun. 1988. "Putting Hierarchy in its Place." *Cultural Anthropology* 3(1):37–50.

———. 1990. "Disjuncture and Difference in the Global Cultural Economy." *Public Culture* 2(2):1–24.

———. 1996. *Modernity At Large: Cultural Dimensions of Globalization*. Minneapolis: University of Minnesota Press.

Appiah, Kwame Anthony. 1992. *In My Father's House: Africa in the Philosophy of Culture*. Oxford: Oxford University Press.

Asad, Talal. 1993. *Genealogies of Religion: Discipline and Reason of Power in Christianity and Islam*. Baltimore: Johns Hopkins Press.

Baumann, Oscar. 1957 (1896). "Mafia Island." *Tanganyika Notes and Records* (46): 1–24.

Beckerleg, Susan. 1995. "'Brown Sugar' or Friday Prayers: Youth Choices and Community Building in Coastal Kenya." *African Affairs* 94:23–38.

Beinart, William. 1987. Introduction. In *Conservation in Africa: People, Policies and Practices*, eds. David Anderson and Richard Grove. Cambridge: Cambridge University Press.

Benjamin, Martin. 2000. "Development Consumers: An Ethnography of the 'Poorest of the Poor' and International Aid in Rural Tanzania." Ph.D. dissertation, Yale University.

Berman, Marshall. 1988. *All That is Solid Melts Into Air: The Experience of Modernity*. New York: Penguin.

Bhabba, Homi. 1994. *The Location of Culture*. New York: Routledge.

Bishop, Ryan, and Lillian S. Robinson. 1998. *Night Market: Sexual Cultures and the Thai Economic Miracle*. New York and London: Routledge.

Blaikie, P. 1985. *The Political Economy of Soil Erosion in Developing Countries*. London: Longman.

Blaikie, Piers, and Harold Brookfield. 1987. *Land Degradation and Society*. London and New York: Methuen.

Boddy, Janice. 1989. *Wombs and Alien Spirits: Women, Men and the Zar Cult in the Northern Sudan*. Madison: University of Wisconsin Press.

Boo, Elizabeth. 1990. *Ecotourism: The Potentials and Pitfalls*. Washington, D.C.: World Wildlife Fund.

Boorstin, Daniel. 1972. *The Image: A Guide to Pseudoevents in America*. New York: Atheneum.

Bourdieu, Pierre. 1984. *A Social Critique of the Judgement of Taste*. Cambridge: Harvard University Press.

———. 1998. *Acts of Resistance: Against the Tyranny of the Market*. New York: The New Press.

Bornstein, Erica. 2001. "The Verge of Good and Evil: Christian NGOs and Economic Development in Zimbabwe." *Political and Legal Anthropology Review (PoLAR)* 24(1): 59–77.

Brohman, John. 1996. "New Directions in Tourism for Third World Development." *Annals of Tourism Research* 23(1):48–70.

Brokensha, David, D. M. Warren, and Oswald Werner. 1980. *Indigenous Knowledge Systems and Development*. Lanham, Md.: University Press of America.

Brosius, J. Peter. 1997. Endangered Forest, Endangered People: Environmentalist Representations of Indigenous Knowledge. *Human Ecology* 25(1):47–69.

———. 1999. "Anthropological Engagements with Environmentalism." *Current Anthropology* 40(3):277–309.

Brown, Mervyn. 1976. "Some Historical Links Between Tanzania and Madacasgar." *Tanzania Notes and Records* 79 and 80: 49–56.

Bruner, Edward M. 1991. "The Transformation of Self in Tourism." *Annals of Tourism Research* 18:238–50.

Brush, Stephen, and Doreen Stabinsky. 1996. *Valuing Local Knowledge: Indigenous People and Intellectual Property Rights*. Washington, D.C.: Island Press.

Bryant, Raymond L., and Sinead Bailey. 1997. *Third World Political Ecology*. London and New York: Routledge.

Bryceson, I. 1981. "A Review of Some Problems of Tropical Marine Conservation with Particular Reference to the Tanzanian Coast." *Biological Conservation* 20: 163–71.

Caplan, Patricia Ann. 1969. "Cognatic Descent Groups on Mafia Island, Tanzania." *Man* 4(3):419–31.

———. 1975. *Choice and Constraint in a Swahili Community: Property, Hierarchy, and Cognatic Descent on the East African Coast*. London: Oxford University Press.

———. 1982. "Gender, Ideology, and Modes of Production on the Coast of East Africa." *Paideuma* 28:29–43.

———. 1984. "Cognatic Descent, Islamic Law and Women's Property on the East African Coast." *In Women and Property—Women as Property*, ed. R. Hirschon, New York: St. Martin's Press.

———. 1992. "Socialism from above: The View from Below." In *The Tanzanian Peasantry: Economy in Crisis*, eds. P. G. Forster and S. Maghimbi. Brookfield, Vt.: Avebury, 103–123.

———. 1997. *African Voices, African Lives: Personal Narratives from a Swahili Village*. London and New York: Routledge.

Carr, Edward. 1998. "Survey: The Sea." In *The Economist*. (Special pullout section pp. 1–18). May 23–29.

Castells, Manuel. 1996. *The Rise of Network Society*. London: Blackwell.

Chami, Felix A. 1997. "The Archaeology of the Mafia Archipelago." Unpublished article.

Chaudhuri, K.N. 1985. *Trade and Civilization in the Indian Ocean*. Cambridge: Cambridge University Press.

Chittick, Neville. 1959. *"Notes on Kilwa." Tanganyika Notes and Records* 53:179–204.

———. 1965. The "Shirazi" Colonization of East Africa. *Journal of African History* 6(3):275–94.

———. 1966. *Report on the Excavations at Kisimani Mafia and Kua*. Annual Report of the Antiquities Department for the year 1964. Ministry of Community Development and National Culture, United Republic of Tanzania, Dar es Salaam.

Clifford, James. 1988. *The Predicament of Culture: Twentieth-Century Ethnography, Literature, and Art*. Cambridge: Harvard University Press.

Clifford, James, and George Marcus. 1986. *Writing Culture: The Poetics and Politics of Ethnography*. Berkeley: University of California Press.

Cohen, Erik. 1972. "Towards a Sociology of International Tourism." *Sociological Review* 22:164–82.

Comaroff, Jean. 1985. *Body of Power, Spirit of Resistance: The Culture and History of an African People*. Chicago: University of Chicago Press.

Comaroff, Jean, and John L. Comaroff. 1991. *Of Revelation and Revolution: Christianity, Colonialism and Consciousness in South Africa*. Vol. 1. Chicago: University of Chicago Press.

———. 1997. *Of Revelation and Revolution: The Dialectics of Modernity on a South African Frontier*. Vol. 2. Chicago: University of Chicago Press.

————. 2000. "Millennial Capitalism: First Thoughts on a Second Coming." *Public Culture* 12(2):291–343.

Conan Doyle, Adrian. 1953. *Heaven Has Claws*. New York: Random House.

Cooke, Bill and Uma Kothari, eds. 2001. *Participation: The New Tyranny?* London and New York: Zed Books.

Cooper, Frederick. 1977. *Plantation Slavery on the East Coast of Africa*. New Haven: Yale University Press.

————. 1980. *From Slaves to Squatters: Plantation Labor and Agriculture in Zanzibar and Coastal Kenya 1890–1925*. New Haven: Yale University Press.

————. 2001. "What is the Concept of Globalization Good For? An African Historian's Perspective." *African Affairs* 100:189–231.

Cooper, Frederick, ed. 1983. *Struggle for the City*. London: Sage Press.

Cooper, Frederick, and Randall Packard. 1997. *International Development and the Social Sciences: Essays on the History and Politics of Knowledge*. Berkeley: University of California Press.

Coulson, Andrew. 1982. *Tanzania: A Political Economy*. Oxford: Clarendon Press.

Cowen, Michael, and Robert Shenton. 1995. "The Invention of Development." In *Power of Development*, ed. J. Crush. London and New York: Routledge.

————. 1996. *Doctrines of Development*. London and New York: Routledge.

Craig, Gary, and Marjorie Mayo. 1995. *Community Empowerment: A Reader in Participation and Development*. London: Zed Books.

Crapanzano, Vincent. 1980. *Tuhami: Portrait of a Moroccan*. Chicago: University of Chicago Press.

Crick, Malcolm. 1989. "Representations of International Tourism in the Social Sciences: Sun, Sex, Sights, Savings and Servility." *Annual Review of Anthropology* 18:307–44.

————. 1994. *Resplendent Sites, Discordant Voices: Sri Lankans and International Tourism*. Switzerland: Harwood Academic Publishers.

Cronon, William. 1983. *Changes in the Land: Indians, Colonists, and the Ecology of New England*. New York: Hill and Wang.

————. 1991. *Nature's Metropolis: Chicago and the Great West*. New York and London: W.W. Norton.

————. 1996. *Uncommon Ground: Rethinking the Human Place in Nature*. New York: W. W. Norton.

Cruikshank, Barbara. 1999. *The Will to Empower: Democratic Citizens and Other Subjects*. Ithaca: Cornell University Press.

Crush, Jonathan. 1995. *Power of Development*. London and New York: Routledge.

Curry, Steve. 1990. "Tourism Development in Tanzania." *Annals of Tourism Research* 17:133–49.

Davis, Hannah. 1989. "American Magic in a Moroccan Town." *Middle East Report* July–August; 12–7.

de Kadt, E. 1978. *Tourism. Passport to Development?* New York: Oxford University Press.

Descola, Phillipe and Gisli Palsson. 1996. *Nature and Society: Anthropological Perspectives*. London and New York: Routledge.

Donham, Donald. 1999. *Marxist Modern: An Ethnographic History of the Ethiopian Revolution*. Berkeley: University of California Press.

Dorman, M. H. 1938. "The Kilwa Civilization and the Kilwa Ruins." *Tanganyika Notes and Records* 6:61–71.

Duncan, Cynthia. 2000. *Worlds Apart: Why Poverty Persists in Rural America*. New Haven: Yale University Press.

Durkheim, Émile. 1933. *The Division of Labor in Society*. New York: The Free Press.

Eastman, Carol. 1971. Who are the WaSwahili? *Africa*, 41, no. 3:228–36.

———. 1988. "Women, Slaves, and Foreigners: African Cultural Influences and Group Processes in the Formation of Northern Swahili Coastal Society." *The International Journal of African Historical Studies* 21(1):1–20.

Eco, Umberto. 1986. *Travels in Hyperreality*. San Diego: Harcourt, Brace, Jovanovich.

Edensor, Tim. 1998. *Tourists at the Taj: Performance and Meaning at a Symbolic Site*. London and New York: Routledge.

El-Zein, A.H.M. 1974. *The Sacred Meadows: A Structural Analysis of Religious Symbolism in an East African Town*. Evanston: Northwestern University Press.

Ellen, Roy F. 1986. "What Black Elk Left Unsaid: On the Illusory Images of Green Primitivism." *Anthropology Today* 2(6):8–12.

Engels, Frederick. 1978. "The Origin of the Family, Private Property and the State." In The *Marx-Engels Reader*, ed. R. Tucker. New York: Norton, 734–59.

Errington, Frederick, and Deborah Gewertz. 1989. "Tourism and Anthropology in a Post-Modern World." *Oceania* 60:37–54.

Escobar, Arturo. 1995. *Encountering Development: The Making and Unmaking of the Third World*. Princeton: Princeton University Press.

Evans-Pritchard, E. E. 1937. *Witchcraft, Oracles and Magic Among the Azande*. Oxford: Oxford University Press.

Fabian, Johannes. 1983. *Time and the Other: How Anthropology Makes its Object*. New York: Columbia University Press.

Fair, Laura. 1994. "Pastimes and Politics: A Social History of Zanzibar's Ng'ambo Community 1890–1950." Ph.D. dissertation, University of Minnesota.

———. 2001. *Pastimes and Politics: Culture, Community, and Identity in Post-Abolition Urban Zanzibar 1890–1945*. Athens: Ohio University Press, and Oxford: James Currey.

Featherstone, Mike. 1990. *Global Culture: Nationalism, Globalization and Modernity*. London: Sage Publications.

Feierman, Steven. 1991. *Peasant Intellectuals: Anthropology and History in Tanzania*. Madison: University of Wisconsin Press.

Ferguson, James. 1994. *The Anti-Politics Machine: "Development," Depoliticization, and Bureaucratic Power in Lesotho*. Minneapolis and London: University of Minnesota Press.

———. 1997. "Anthropology and Its Evil Twin: 'Development' in the Constitution of a Discipline." In *International Development and the Social Sciences*, eds., F. Cooper and R. Packard. Berkeley: University of California Press, 150–175.

———. 1999. *Expectations of Modernity: Myths and Meanings of Urban Life on the Zambian Copperbelt*. Berkeley: University of California Press.

Ferguson, James and Akhil Gupta. 2002. "Spatializing States: Toward an Ethnography of Neoliberal Governmentality." *American Ethnologist* 29(4):981–1002.

Finnemore, Martha. 1997. "Redefining Development at the World Bank." In *Interna-

tional Development and the Social Sciences: Essays on the History and Politics of Knowledge, eds. Frederick Cooper and Randall Packard. Berkeley: University of California Press.

Fisher, William F. 1997. "Doing Good? The Politics and Antipolitics of NGO Practices." *Annual Review of Anthropology* 26:439–64.

Foucault, Michel. 1972. The *Archaeology of Knowledge and Discourse on Language*. New York: Pantheon Books.

———. 1977. *Discipline and Punish*. New York: Vintage Books.

———. 1978. *The History of Sexuality, Vol. 1: An Introduction*. New York: Vintage Books.

———. 1994. *Power*, ed. James D. Faubion. New York: The New Press.

Frank, Andre Gunder. 1998. *Re-Orient: Global Economy in the Asian Age*. Berkeley: University of California Press.

Freeman, Carla. 2000. *High Tech and High Heels in the Global Economy*. Durham and London: Duke University Press.

Freeman-Grenville, G.S.P. 1957. "Prefatory note to Mafia Island by Oscar Baumann." *Tanganyika Notes and Records* 46:1–24.

———. 1958. "The Chronology of the Sultans of Kilwa." *Tanganyika Notes and Records* 50:85–93.

———. 1962. "The History of Kua, Juani Island, Mafia." In *The East African Coast: Selected Documents from the First to the Early 19th Century*, ed. G. S. P. Freeman-Grenville. Oxford: Clarendon Press.

Friedman, Thomas. 2000. *The Lexus and the Olive Tree*. New York: Anchor Books.

Gans, Herbert. 1962. *The Urban Villagers*. New York: Free Press of Glencoe.

Gaonkar, Dilip P., ed. 2001. *Alternative Modernities*. Durham: Duke University Press.

Gewertz, Deborah and Frederick Errington. 1989. "Tourism and Anthropology in a Post-Modern World." *Oceania* 60:37–54.

GMP (General Management Plan). 1993. Mafia Island Marine Park: General Management Plan (draft version). Compiled by the Institute of Marine Sciences (Zanzibar) for the Ministry of Tourism, Natural Resources, and the Environment, Dar es Salaam.

GMP (General Management Plan). 2000. Mafia Island Marine Park: General Management Plan (final version). Compiled by WWF and Park Staff for the Board of Trustees, Marine Parks and Reserves, Ministry of Natural Resources, and Tourism, Dar es Salaam.

Ghosh, Amitav. 1992. *In an Antique Land: History in the Guise of a Traveler's Tale*. New York: Vintage Books.

Gibson-Graham, J. K. 1996. *The End of Capitalism (As We Knew It): A Feminist Critique of Political Economy*. Oxford: Blackwell.

———. 1996/1997 "Querying Globalization." *Rethinking Marxism* 9(1):1–27.

Gibson-Graham, J. K., Resnick, Stephen K., and Wolff, Richard D. 2001. *Re/Presenting Class: Essays in Postmodern Marxism*. Durham, N.C.: Duke University Press.

Giddens, Anthony. 2000. *Runaway World: How Globalization is Reshaping Our Lives*. New York: Routledge.

Gilbert, Erik. 2003. *Dhows and the Colonial Economy of Zanzibar: 1860–1970*. Athens and London: Ohio University Press and James Currey.

Giles, Linda. 1987. "Possession Cults on the Swahili Coast: A Re-Examination of Theories of Marginality." *Africa* 57(2):234–58.

Ginsburg, Faye, Lila Abu-Lughod, and Brian Larkin, eds. 2002. *Media Worlds*. Berkeley: University of California Press.

Glaesel, Heidi. 1997. "Fishers, Parks, and Power: The Socio-Environmental Dimensions of Marine Resource Decline and Protection on the Kenya Coast." Ph.D. dissertation, University of Wisconsin.

Glassman, Jonathan. 1991. "The Bondsman's New Clothes: The Contradictory Consciousness of Slave Resistance on the Swahili Coast." *Journal of African History* 32:277–312.

———. 1995. *Feasts and Riot: Revelry, Rebellion, and Popular Consciousness on the Swahili Coast, 1856–1888*. London: James Currey.

Gluckman, Max. 1958. "Analysis of a Social Situation in Modern Zululand." Rhodes-Livingstone Paper 28. Manchester: Manchester University Press.

Goody, Jack. 1968. *Literacy in Traditional Societies*. Cambridge: Cambridge University Press.

———. 1977. *Domestication of the Savage Mind*. Cambridge: Cambridge University Press.

Gordon, April A., and Donald L. Gordon. 1996. *Understanding Contemporary Africa*. Boulder: Lynne Rienner.

Gray, Sir John. 1951. "A History of Kilwa: Part I." *Tanganyika Notes and Records* 31:1–24.

———. 1952. "A History of Kilwa: Part II." *Tanganyika Notes and Records* 32: 11–37.

———. 1962. *A History of Zanzibar from the Middle Ages to 1856*. London: Oxford University Press.

Green, Maia. 1997. "'Development,' Change and the Appropriation of Agency in Southern Tanzania." Unpublished paper presented at the American Anthropological Association Meetings, Washington, D.C., 1997.

Greenberger, Robert S. 1996. "Are One Isle's Hotels Better at Laundering Cash Than Towels?" *Wall Street Journal* December 13, 1.

Griffiths, Jay. 1998. "Mixed Blessings: Plans for a New Tourist Complex in Zanzibar will Mean Displacement of Tens of Thousands of Locals From Their Homes." *The Guardian*. Special Sunday Travel Section: World-Wise: How to Get More From Your Holiday.

Grove, Richard. 1987. "Early Themes in African Conservation: The Cape in the 19th Century." In *Conservation in Africa: People, Policies and Practice*. eds. D. Anderson and R. Grove. Cambridge: Cambridge University Press.

———. 1992. "Origins of Western Environmentalism." *Scientific American* 267(1): 42–7.

Guha, Ranajit, ed. 1997. *A Subaltern Reader*. Minneapolis: University of Minnesota Press.

Guha, Ranajit and Gayatri Spivak, eds. 1988. *Selected Subaltern Studies*. Oxford: Oxford University Press.

Gupta, Akhil. 1995. "Blurred Boundaries: The Discourse of Corruption, the Culture of Politics, and the Imagined State." *American Ethnologist* 22(2):375–402.

———. 1998. *Postcolonial Developments: Agriculture in the Making of Modern India*. Durham and London: Duke University Press.

Gupta, Akhil, and James Ferguson. 1997. *Anthropological Locations: Boundaries and Grounds of a Field Science*. Berkeley: University of California Press.

Gurnah, Abdulrazak. 1994. *Paradise*. New York: The New Press.

———. 1996. *Admiring Silence*. New York: The New Press.

———. 2001. *By the Sea*. New York: The New Press.

Hannerz, Ulf. 1992. *Cultural Complexity: Studies in the Social Organization of Meaning*. New York: Columbia University Press.

———. 1987. "The World in Creolization." *Africa* 57(4): 546–59.

Haugerud, Angelique. 1993. *The Culture of Politics in Modern Kenya*. Cambridge: Cambridge University Press.

Haraway, Donna. 1983. "Situated Knowledges: The Science Question in Feminism and the Privilege of Partial Perspective." *Feminist Studies* 14(3):575–99.

———. 1989. *Primate Visions: Gender, Race, and Nature in the World of Modern Science*. New York: Routledge.

———. 1991. *Simians, Cyborgs, and Women: The Reinvention of Nature*. New York: Routlege.

Hardin, Garrett. 1968. "The Tragedy of the Commons." *Science* 162:1243–48.

Hardt, Michael, and Antonio Negri. 2000. *Empire*. Cambridge and London: Harvard University Press.

Harvey, David. 1989. *The Condition of Postmodernity*. Oxford: Basil Blackwell.

Hatchell, G. W. 1954. "Maritime Relics of the 1914–1918 War." *Tanganyika Notes and Records* 36:1–21.

Haugerud, Anqelique. 1993. *The Culture of Politics in Modern Kenya*. Cambridge and New York: University of Cambridge.

Hay, Douglas. 1975. "Poaching and the Game Laws on Cannock Chase." In *Albion's Fatal Tree: Crime and Society in Eighteenth-Century England*, eds. Douglas Hay et al., New York: Pantheon Books.

Held, David, and Anthony McGrew. 2000. *The Global Transformations Reader*. Cambridge, UK, and Malden, Ma.: Polity Press.

Herzfeld, Michael. 1987. *Anthropology Through the Looking-Glass: Critical Ethnography in the Margins of Europe*. Cambridge: Cambridge University Press.

Hodgson, Dorothy. 2001. *Once Intrepid Warriors: Gender, Ethnicity and the Cultural Politics of Maasai Development*. Bloomington and Indianapolis: University of Indiana Press.

———. 2002. "Precarious Alliances: The Cultural Politics and Structural Predicaments of the Indigenous Rights Movement in Tanzania." *American Anthropologist* 104(4).

Hobsbawm, Eric. 1987. *The Age of Empire 1875–1914*. New York: Vintage Books.

Honey, Martha. 1999. *Ecotourism and Sustainable Development: Who Owns Paradise?* Washington, D.C.: Island Press.

Horrill, J. C., and C. J. Mayers. 1992. *Marine Resource Users in the Proposed Mafia Island Marine Park, Tanzania: A Preliminary Survey*. Dar es Salaam: Institute of Marine Sciences (University of Dar es Salaam) and the WWF Country Office for Tanzania.

Horrill, J. C., and M.A.K. Ngoile. 1991. *Mafia Island Project, Report No. 2. Results of the Physical, Biolgoical and Resource Use Surveys: Rationale for the Development of a Management Strategy. A Report for the Mafia Island Marine Reserve Steering Committee.* Dar es Salaam: The Society for Environmental Exploration and University of Dar es Salaam.

Horton, Robin. 1967. "African Traditional Thought and Western Science." *Africa* 37(1–2):50–71, 155–87.

Humphries, Jane. 1990. "Enclosures, Common Rights, and Women: The Proletarianization of Families in the Late Eighteenth and Early Nineteenth Centuries." *The Journal of Economic History* 50(1):17–42.

Hutnyk, John. 1996. *The Rumour of Calcutta: Tourism, Charity and the Poverty of Representation.* London: Zed Books.

Illife, John. 1969. *Tanganyika under German Rule, 1905–1912.* Cambridge: Cambridge University Press.

———. 1979. *A Modern History of Tanganyika.* Cambridge: Cambridge University Press.

———. 1995. *Africans: The History of a Continent.* Cambridge: Cambridge University Press.

Inda, Jonathan Xavier, and Renato Rosaldo. 2002. "Introduction: A World in Motion." In *The Anthropology of Globalization: A Reader*, eds. Jonathan Xavier Inda and Renato Rosaldo. Oxford and Malden, Mass.: Blackwell.

Jameson, Frederic. 1991. *Postmodernism or the Cultural Logic of Late Capitalism.* Durham: Duke University Press.

Jameson, Frederic, and Masao Miyoshi, eds. 1998. *The Cultures of Globalization.* Durham: Duke University Press.

Johannes, R. E. 1981. *Words of the Lagoon: Fishing and Marine Lore in the Palau District of Micronesia.* Berkeley: University of California Press.

Joyce, Patrick, ed. 1995. *Class.* Oxford and New York: Oxford University Press.

Keck, Margaret E., and Kathryn Sikkink. 1998. *Activists Beyond Borders: Advocacy Networks in International Politics.* Ithaca: Cornell University Press.

Kempf, Elizabeth, ed. 1993. *The Law of the Mother: Protecting Indigenous Peoples in Protected Areas.* San Francisco: Sierra Club Books.

King, Anthony D. 1991. *Culture, Globalization and the World System.* Albany, N.Y.: SUNY.

King, Norman. 1917. "Mafia." *Geographical Journal* 50:117–125.

Kirkman, James. 1964. *Men and Monuments of the East African Coast.* London: Lutterworth.

Kirshenblatt-Gimblett, Barbara. 1988. "Authenticity and Authority in the Representation of Culture: The Poetics and Politics of Tourist Production." *Kulturkontakt, Kulturkonflikt* 28:59–69.

———. 1998. *Destination Culture: Tourism, Museums, and Heritage.* Berkeley: University of California Press.

Kjekhus, Helge. 1977. *Ecology Control and Economic Development in East African History.* London: James Currey.

Kornblum, William. 1974. *Blue Collar Community.* Chicago: University of Chicago Press.

Koth, Barbara. 1990. *Integration of Tourism and Environmental Issues: A Strategy for Zanzibar.* University of Minnesota Tourism Center, Minneapolis on behalf of the Government of Zanzibar with support from FINNIDA.

Kuper, Adam, 1973. *Anthropology and Anthropologists: The Modern British School.* London and New York: Routledge.

Lash, Scott, and John Urry. 1987. *The End of Organized Capitalism.* Cambridge: Polity.

Latour, Bruno. 1987. *Science in Action.* Cambridge: Harvard University Press.

———. 1993. *We Have Never Been Modern.* Cambridge: Harvard University Press.

———. 1999. *Pandora's Hope: Essays on the Reality of Science Studies.* Cambridge: Harvard University Press.

Lave, Jean. 1996. "The Savagery of the Domestic Mind." In *Naked Science: Anthropological Inquiries into Boundaries, Power, Knowledge,* ed. Laura Nader. New York: Routledge.

Leve, Lauren. 2001. "Between Jess Helms and Ram Bahadur: Participation and Empowerment in Women's Literacy Programming in Nepal." *Political and Legal Anthropology Review (PoLAR)* 24(1): 108–28.

Lévi-Strauss, Claude. 1969. *The Elementary Structures of Kinship.* Boston: Beacon Press.

———. 1968. *The Savage Mind.* Chicago: University of Chicago Press.

Lévy-Bruhl, Lucien. 1926. *How Natives Think.* London: G. Allen & Unwin, Ltd.

Lowe, Celia. 2000. "Global Markets, Local Injustice in Southeast Asian Seas: The Live Fish Trade and Local Fishers in the Togean Islands of Sulawesi." In *People, Plants and Justice,* ed. Charles Zerner. New York: Columbia University Press.

Lubeck, Paul. 1992. "The Crisis of African Development: Conflicting Interpretations and Resolutions." *Annual Review of Sociology* 18:519–40.

Luke, Timothy W. 1997. "The World Wide Fund for Nature: Eco-colonialism as Funding the Worldwide 'Wise Use' of Nature." *Capitalism, Nature, Socialism* 8(2):31–61.

Lynd, Robert S., and Helen M. Lynd. 1929. *Middletown: A Study in Contemporary American Culture.* London: Constable.

———. 1937. *Middletown in Transition: A Study in Cultural Conflicts.* New York: Harcourt, Brace.

Maack, Pamela A. 1996. "'We Don't Want Terraces!': Protest and Identity under the Uluguru Land Usage Scheme." In *Custodians of the Land: Ecology and Culture in the History of Tanzania,* ed. G. E. A. Maddox. London: James Currey.

MacCannell, Dean. 1989. *The Tourist: A New Theory of the Leisure Class.* New York: Schocken Books.

———. 1992. *Empty Meeting Grounds: The Tourist Papers.* New York: Routledge.

MacKenzie, John M. 1987. "Chivalry, Social Darwinism and Ritualised Killing: The Hunting Ethos in Central Africa Up to 1914." In *Conservation in Africa: People, Policies, and Practice,* eds. D. Anderson and R. Grove. Cambridge: Cambridge University Press.

———. 1988. *The Empire of Nature: Hunting, Conservation and British Imperialism.* Manchester: Manchester University Press.

Maddox, Gregory, James Giblin, and Isaria N. Kimambo. 1996. *Custodians of the Land: Ecology and Culture in the History of Tanzania.* London: James Currey.

Mamdani, Mahmood. 1996. *Citizen and Subject: Contemporary Africa and the Legacy of Late Colonialism.* Princeton: Princeton University Press.

Marcus, George E. 1998. *Ethnography through Thick and Thin*. Princeton: Princeton University Press.

Marcus, George E., and Michael Fischer. 1986. *Anthropology as Cultural Critique*. Chicago: University of Chicago Press.

Marine Parks and Reserves Act. 1994. Compiled for the Ministry of Natural Resources, Tourism and the Environment by T. Young and the Institute of Marine Sciences, University of Dar es Salaam, Zanzibar.

Marx, Karl. 1995. *Capital*. Oxford: Oxford University Press.

Marx, Leo. 1964. *The Machine in the Garden*. Oxford: Oxford University Press.

Matzke, Gordon. 1976. "The Development of the Selous Game Reserve." *Tanganyika Notes and Records* 79 and 80:37–41.

McCay, Bonnie J., and James M. Acheson. 1987. *The Question of the Commons: The Culture and Ecology of Communal Resources*. Tucson: The University of Arizona Press.

McCormick, John. 1989. *Reclaiming Paradise: The Global Environmental Movement*. Bloomington: Indiana University Press.

McEvoy, Arthur. 1986. *The Fisherman's Problem: Ecology and Law in the California Fisheries, 1850–1980*. Cambridge: Cambridge University Press.

McGoodwin, James R. 1990. *Crisis in the World's Fisheries: People, Problems, and Policies*. Stanford: Stanford University Press.

McKenzie, R. D. 1924. "The Ecological Approach to the Study of the Human Community." *American Journal of Sociology* 30:287–301.

———. 1983 (1926). "The Scope of Human Ecology." In *Origins of Human Ecology*, ed. G. L. Young. Stroudsburg, Pa.: Hutchinson Ross, 35–48.

Merchant, Carolyn. 1980. *The Death of Nature: Women, Ecology and the Scientific Revolution*. San Francisco: Harper Collins.

Middleton, John. 1961. *Land Tenure in Zanzibar*. London: Her Majesty's Sationary Office.

———. 1992. *The World of the Swahili: An African Mercantile Civilization*. New Haven: Yale University Press.

Miers, S., and I. Kopytoff. 1977. *Slavery in Africa*. Madison: University of Wisconsin Press.

Miller, Daniel. 1995. *Worlds Apart: Modernity Through the Prism of the Local*. London and New York: Routledge.

Milton, Kay. 1993. *Environmentalism: The View from Anthropology*. London and New York: Routledge.

Mitchell, Timothy. 1988. *Colonising Egypt*. Berkeley: University of California Press.

———. 1990. Everyday Metaphors of Power. *Theory and Society* 19, no. 5:545–77.

———. 1995. "The Object of Development: America's Egypt." In *Power of Development*, ed. J. Crush. London and New York: Routledge.

———. 1995. *Origins and Limits of the Modern Idea of the Economy*. Advanced Study Center, University of Michigan, Working Paper Series, no. 12, November.

———. 1998. "The Market's Place." In *Directions of Change in Rural Egypt*, eds. N. Hopkins and K. Westergard. Cairo: American University in Cairo Press.

———. 2000. Introduction. In *Questions of Modernity*, ed. Timothy Mitchell, Minneapolis: University of Minnesota Press.

Mitchell, Timothy, ed. 2000. *Questions of Modernity*. Minneapolis: University of Minnesota Press.

Monson, Jamie. 1996. "Canoe Building Under Colonialism: Forestry and Food Policies in the Inner Kilombero Valley 1920–1940." In *Custodians of the Land: Ecology and Culture in the History of Tanzania*, eds. G. Maddox, J. Giblin, and I. N. Kimambo. London: James Currey.

Moore, Donald S. 1993. "Contesting Terrain in Zimbabwe's Eastern Highlands: Political Ecology, Ethnography, and Peasant Resource Struggles." *Economic Geography* 69:390–401.

Morton, Fred. 1990. *Children of Ham, Freed Slaves and Fugitive Slaves on the Kenya Coast*. Boulder: Westview Press.

MTNRE (Ministry of Tourism, Natural Resources, and the Environment, Tanzania). 1992. *The Proposed Mafia Island Marine Park, Tanzania*. Proceedings of the Planning Workshop Mafia Island. October 20–24.

Muhando, Christopher. n.d. Status Report on Corals from Different Regions 6(10). Institute for Marine Studies, University of Dar es Salaam, Zanzibar. Posted at www.cordio.org/Repstatus6.htm. Accessed on 10/30/00.

Mushi, S. S. 1978. "Popular Participation and Regional Development Planning: The Politics of Decentralized Administration." *Tanganyika Notes and Records* 83:63–97.

Mwanjisi, R. K. 1967. *Ndugu Abeid Amani Karume*. Nairobi: East African Publishing House.

Nash, June. 1989. *From Tank Town to High Tech*. Albany: SUNY Press.

Nash, Roderick. 1982. *Wilderness and the American Mind*. New Haven: Yale University Press.

Nelson, Nici, and Susan Wright. 1995. *Power and Participatory Development: Theory and Practice*. London: Intermediate Technology Publications.

Neumann, Roderick P. 1992. "Political Ecology of Wildlife Conservation in the Mt. Meru Area of Northeast Tanzania." *Land Degradation and Rehabilitation* 3:85–98.

———. 1996. "Dukes, Earls and Ersatz Edens: Aristocratic Nature Preservationists in Colonial Africa." *Society and Space* 14:79–98.

———. 1998. *Imposing Wilderness: Struggles over Livelihood and Nature Preservation in Africa*. Berkeley: University of California Press.

———. 2000. Land, Justice and the Politics of Conservation in Tanzania. In *People, Plants and Justice*, ed. Charles Zerner. New York: Columbia University Press.

Ngoile, Magnus, Lota Melamari, and Solomon Makoloweka. 1998. *Assessment of the Mafia Island Marine Park (MIMP), Tanzania*. Dar es Salaam: World Wide Fund for Nature (Tanzania Country Office).

Nicholls, C. S. 1971. *The Swahili Coast: Politics, Diplomacy, and Trade on the East African Littoral, 1798–1856*. London: Allen and Unwin.

NORAD 1997. Preliminary Conclusions and Recommendations in the MNRT Mafia Project. Unpublished report commissioned by the Norwegian Agency for Development Cooperation, Oslo. Received by WWF Tanzania Programme Office on March 4.

Nybakken, James W. 1997. *Marine Biology: An Ecological Approach*. Menlo Park, CA: Benjamin Cummings.

Nyerere, Julius K. 1966. *Freedom and Unity: Uhuru na Umoja*. Dar es Salaam: Oxford University Press.

———. 1968. *Freedom and Socialism: Uhuru na Ujamaa*. London: Oxford University Press.

Ong, Aihwa. 1987. *Spirits of Resistance and Capitalist Discipline: Factory Women in Malaysia*. Albany: SUNY Press.

———. 1999. *Flexible Citizenship: The Cultural Logics of Transnationality*. Durham, NC: Duke University Press.

Ortner, Sherry. 1974. *Is Female to Male as Nature is to Culture?* In Woman, Culture and Society, edited by M. Rosaldo and L. Lamphere. Stanford: Stanford University Press.

Paley, Julia. 2001. *Marketing Democracy: Power and Social Movements in Post-Dictatorship Chile*. Berkeley: University of California Press.

Palsson, Gisli. 1995. *Coastal Economies, Cultural Accounts: Human Ecology and Icelandic Discourse*. Manchester: Manchester University Press.

Park, Robert E. 1915. "The City: Suggestions for the Investigation of Human Behavior in the City Environment." *American Journal of Sociology* 20:577–612.

———. 1936. "Human Ecology." *American Journal of Sociology* 42:1–15.

Park, R. E., and E. W. Burgess. 1921. *Introduction to the Science of Sociology*. Chicago: University of Chicago Press.

Peake, Robert. 1989. "Swahili Stratification and Tourism in Malindi Old Town, Kenya." *Africa* 59(2):209–20.

Peet, R., and M. Watts. 1996. *Liberation Ecologies: Environment, Development, Social Movements*. London: Routledge.

Peluso, Nancy. 1992. *Rich Forests, Poor People: Resource Control and Resistance in Java*. Berkeley: University of California Press.

Pepper, David. 1984. *The Roots of Modern Environmentalism*. London: Croom Helm.

Peters, Pauline E. 1994. *Dividing the Commons: Politics, Policy and Culture in Botswana*. Charlottesville and London: University Press of Virginia.

———. 2000. *Development Encounters: Sites of Participation and Knowledge*. Cambridge, Ma.: Harvard Institute for International Development.

Pigg, Stacy. 1992. "Inventing Social Category Through Place: Social Representations and Development in Nepal." *Comparative Studies in Society and History* 34(3): 491–513.

———. 1996. "The Credible and the Credulous: The Question of 'Villagers' Beliefs' in Nepal." *Cultural Anthropology* 11(2):160–201.

———. 1997. "Found in Most Traditional Societies: Traditional Medical Practitioners between Culture and Development." In *International Development and the Social Sciences*, eds. Frederick Cooper and Randall Packard. Berkeley: University of California Press.

Piggott, D.W.I. 1941. "History of Mafia." *Tanganyika Notes and Records* 11:35–40.

Piot, Charles. 1999. *Remotely Global: Village Modernity in West Africa*. Chicago: University of Chicago Press.

Polanyi, Karl. 1944. *The Great Transformation: The Political and Economic Origins of Our Time*. Boston: Beacon Press.

Pottier, Johan. 1993. *Practising Development: Social Science Perspectives*. London and New York: Routledge.

Prins, A.H.J. 1965. *Sailing From Lamu: A Study of Maritime Culture in Islamic East Africa*. Assen: Van Gorcum.

Pruitt, Deborah, and Suzanne LaFont. 1995. "For Love and Money: Romance Tourism in Jamaica." *Annals of Tourism Research* 22(2):422–39.

Rabinow, Paul. 1977. *Reflections on Fieldwork in Morocco*. Berkeley: University of California Press.

Ranger, T. O. 1975. *Dance and Society in Eastern Africa, 1890–1970: The Beni Ngoma*. London: Heinemann.

Redclift, M. 1984. *Sustainable Development: Exploring the Contradictions*. London: Methuen.

Redfern, Paul. 2000. "Multinationals Have an 'Obligation' to the Poor." *The East African*. July 3–9:5.

Redfield, Robert. 1930. *Tepoztlan, a Mexican Village: A Study of Folk Life*. Chicago: University of Cihcago Press.

Revington, R. M. 1936. "Some Notes on the Mafia Island Group." *Tanganyika Notes and Records* 1:33–37.

Ribot, Jesse. 1996. "Participation without Representation: Chiefs, Councils and Forestry Law in the West Africa Sahel." *Cultural Survival Quarterly* 20(3):40–44.

———. 1999. "Decentralization, Participation and Accountability in Sahelian Forestry: Legal Instruments of Political—Administrative Control." *Africa* 69(1):23–65.

———. 2000. "Rebellion, Representation and Enfranchisement in the Forest Villages of Makacouilbantang Eastern Senegal." In *People, Plants and Justice*, ed. Charles Zerner. New York: Columbia University Press.

Robertson, Claire, and Martin Klein. 1983. *Women and Slavery in Africa*. Madison: University of Wisconsin Press.

Rocheleau, Diane, B. Thomas-Slayter, and E. Wangari. 1996. *Feminist Political Ecology: Global Issues and Local Experience*. London: Routledge.

Rodgers, W. A. 1976. "Past WaNgindo Settlement in the Eastern Selous Game Reserve." *Tanganyika Notes and Records* No. 77 and 78:21–25.

Rofel, Lisa. 1998. *Other Modernities: Gendered Yearnings in China After Socialism*. Berkeley: University of California Press.

Romero, Patricia. 1997. *Lamu: History, Society and Family in an East African Port City*. Princeton, N.J.: Markus Wiener.

Rouse, Roger. 1999. "Global Discourse and the Pursuit of Hegemony." Conference paper presented at the American Anthropological Association Meetings. Chicago, IL, November 17–21.

Ruddle, Kenneth, and R. E. Johannes. 1985. The Traditional Knowledge and Management of Coastal Systems in Asia and the Pacific: UNESCO.

Saadi, Kadhi Amur Omar. 1941. Mafia—History and Traditions. *Tanganyika Notes and Records* 25:23–27.

Sackett, Lee. 1991. "Promoting Primitivism: Conservationist Depicitions of Aboriginal Australians." *Australian Journal of Anthropology* 2(2):233–46.

Safina, Carl. 1999. *Song for the Blue Ocean*. New York: Owl Press (Holt).

Salm, R. V. 1983. Coral Reefs of the West Indian Ocean: A Threatened Heritage. *Ambio* 12:349–53.

Sassen, Saskia. 1992. *The Global City*. Princeton: Princeton University Press.

Schroeder, Richard. 1993. "Shady Practice: Gender and The Political Ecology of Resource Stabilization in Gambian Garden/Orchards." *Economic Geography* 69(4):349–65.

———. 1999. *Shady Practices: Agroforestry and Gender Politics in Gambia*. Berkeley: University of California Press.

Scherl, Lea M. 1995. *Participatory Planning Process for Mafia Island Marine Park Management*. Mission report submitted to WWF-Tanzania, Dar es Salaam. October.

Scott, James C. 1985. *Weapons of the Weak: Everyday Forms of Peasant Resistance*. New Haven: Yale University Press.

———. 1998. *Seeing Like a State: How Certain Schemes to Improve the Human Condition Have Failed*. New Haven: Yale University Press.

Seabrook, Jeremy. 1996. *Travels in the Skin Trade: Tourism and the Sex Industry*. Chicago: Pluto Press.

Semesi, Adelaida K., and Magnus Ngoile. 1995. "Status of the Coastal and Marine Environment in the United Republic of Tanzania." In Integrated Coastal Zone Management in Eastern Africa including the Island States, ed. O. Linden. Arusha, Tanzania: Swedish Agency for Research Cooperation with Developing Countries Marine Science Program.

Sheriff, Abdul M. H. 1987. *Slaves, Spices and Ivory in Zanzibar*. London: James Currey.

Sheriff, Abdul, and Zanzibar National Archives. 1995. *Historical Zanzibar: Romance of the Ages*. London: HSP Publications.

Shiva, Vandana. 1988. *Staying Alive: Women, Ecology and Survival in India*. London: Zed Books.

Shivji, Issa. 1973. *Tourism and Socialist Development*. Dar es Salaam: Tanzania Publishing House.

———. 1976. *Class Struggles in Tanzania*. London: Heinemann.

———. 1998. *Not Yet Democracy: Reforming Land Tenure in Tanzania*. Dar es Salaam: IIED/Hakiardhi/Faculty of Law—University of Dar es Salaam.

Silbey, Susan. 1997. "'Let Them Eat Cake': Globalization, Postmodern Colonialism, and the Possibilities of Justice." *Law and Society Review* 31(2):207–35.

Slyomovics, Susan. 1998. *The Object of Memory: Arab and Jew Narrate the Palestinian Village*. Philadelphia: University of Pennsylvania Press.

Smith, M. Estellie. 1977. *Those who Live From the Sea: A Study in Maritime Anthropology*. St. Paul: West Publishing Co.

Smith, Valene L., and William R. Eadington. 1992. *Tourism Alternatives: Potentials and Problems in the Development of Tourism*. Philadelphia: University of Pennsylvania Press.

Snyder, Katherine. 2001. "Being of 'One Heart': Power and Politics among the Iraqw of Tanzania." *Africa* 71(1):128–48.

Sontag, Susan. 1973. *On Photography*. New York: Farrar, Straus, and Giroux.

Spear, Thomas. 1996. "Struggles for the Land: The Political and Moral Economies of Land on Mount Meru." In *Custodians of the Land: Ecology and Culture in the History of Tanzania*, eds. Gregory Maddox, James Giblin, and Isaria N. Kimambo. London: James Currey.

Stack, Carol. 1974. *All Our Kin: Strategies for Survival in a Black Community*. New York: Harper and Row.

Steward, Julian. 1937. "Ecological Aspects of Southwestern Society." *Anthropos* 32:87–104.

———. 1977. *Evolution and Ecology*. Chicago: University of Illinois Press.

Stoger-Eising, Viktoria. 2000. "Ujamaa Revisited: Indigenous and European Influences in Nyerere's Social and Political Thought." *Africa* 70(1):118–43.

Stonich, Susan. 2000. *The Other Side of Paradise: Tourism, Conservation and Development in the Bay Islands*. New York, Sydney, and Tokyo: Cognizant Communication Corporation.

Strange, Susan. 1996. *The Retreat of the State: The Diffusion of Power in the World Economy*. Cambridge: Cambridge University Press.

Street, Brian. 1984. *Literacy in Theory and Practice*. Cambridge: Cambridge University Press.

Strobel, Margaret. 1979. *Muslim Women in Mombasa, 1890–1975*. New Haven: Yale University Press.

Sunseri, Thaddeus. 1993. "Slave Ransoming in German East Africa, 1885–1922." *The International Journal of African Historical Studies* 26(3):481–511.

Swartz, Marc J. 1991. *The Way the World Is: Cultural Processes and Social Relations among the Mombasa Swahili*. Berkeley: University of California Press.

Thompson, E. P. 1963. *The Making of the English Working Class*. New York: Vintage.

———. 1975. *Whigs and Hunters: The Origin of the Black Act*. New York: Pantheon Books.

Thorne-Miller, Boyce. 1999. *The Living Ocean: Understanding and Protecting Marine Biodiversity*. Washington, D.C.: Island Press.

T.I.P. (Tourism Infrastructure Project) 1995. *Zanzibar: Draft Final Report, Executive Summary*. Compiled by the Nicholas and Vanos O'Dwyer Joint Venture Partnership for the World Bank, the United Republic of Tanzania, and the Commission for Tourism Zanzibar.

Tordoff, William. 1997. *Government and Politics in Africa*. Bloomington: Indiana University Press.

Trimingham, J. S. 1964. *Islam in East Africa*. Oxford: Clarendon Press.

Tripp, Aili Mari. 1997. *Changing the Rules: The Politics of Liberalization and the Urban Informal Economy in Tanzania*. Berkeley: University of California Press.

Trouillot, Michel-Rolph. 1991. "Anthropology and the Savage Slot: The Poetics and Politics of Otherness." In *Recapturing Anthropology*, ed. Richard G. Fox. Santa Fe: School of American Research Press.

Tsing, Anna Lowenhaupt. 1993. *In the Realm of the Diamond Queen*. Princeton: Princeton University Press.

———. 2001. "The Global Situation." *Cultural Anthropology* 15(3):327–60.

Turner, Victor. 1957. *Schism and Continuity in an African Society*. Manchester: Manchester University Press.

———. 1974. *Dramas, Fields and Metaphors: Symbolic Action in Human Society*. Ithaca: Cornell University Press.

United States Information Services. 1991. "Demokrasia ni Nini? (What is Democracy?)" October. Dar es Salaam: Shirika la Habari La Marekani.

Urry, John. 1990. *The Tourist Gaze*. London: Sage Publications.

Vaughan, Megan. 1987. *The Story of an African Famine: Gender and Famine in Twentieth-Century Malawi*. Cambridge: Cambridge University Press.

———. 1992. *Curing Their Ills: Colonial Power and African Illness.* Palo Alto: Stanford University Press.

Verdery, Katherine. 1996. *What Was Socialism, and What Comes Next?* Princeton: Princeton University Press.

Volkman, Toby Alice. 1990. "Visions and Revisions: Toraja Culture and the Tourist Gaze." *American Ethnologist* 17(1):91–109.

von Freyhold, Michaela. 1979. *Ujamaa Villages in Tanzania: Analysis of a Social Experiment.* New York and London: Monthly Review Press.

Wallerstein, Immanuel. 1974. *The Modern World-System: Capitalist Agriculture and the Origins of the European World-Economy in the Sixteenth Century.* New York: Academic Press.

Walley, Christine J. 2002. "'They Scorn Us Because We are Uneducated': Knowledge and Power in a Tanzanian Marine Park." *Ethnography* 3(3):265–97.

———. 2003. "'Our Ancestors Used to Bury their 'Development' in the Ground:' Modernity and the Meaning of Development on Mafia Island, Tanzania." *Anthropological Quarterly* 76(1):33–54.

Watts, Michael. 1983. *Silent Violence: Food, Famine and Peasantry in Northern Nigeria.* Berkeley: University of California Press.

———. 1995. "A New Deal in Emotions: Theory and Practice and the Crisis of Development." In *Power of Development*, ed. J. Crush. London and New York: Routledge.

Weber, Max. 1958. *From Max Weber: Essays in Sociology.* New York: Oxford University Book.

Western, David, and R. Michael Wright. 1994. *Natural Connections: Perspectives in Community-based Conservation.* Washington, D.C.: Island Press.

Wheeler, Sir Mortimer. 1955. "Archaeology in East Africa." *Tanganyika Notes and Records* 40:43–47.

White, Leslie. 1949. *The Science of Culture.* New York: Grove Press.

Whyte, William. 1981 [1943]. *Street Corner Society.* Chicago: University of Chicago Press.

Wilkinson, Clive. 1996–1999. Status of Coral Reefs of the World: 1998. Australian Institute of Marine Sciences. Posted at: www.aims.gov.au/pages/research/coral-bleaching/ser1998/ser-ol.html. Accessed on 10/30/00.

Williams, Raymond. 1973. *The Country and the City.* Oxford: Oxford University Press.

———. 1976. *Keywords: Vocabulary of Culture and Society.* New York: Oxford University Press.

———. 1980. *Problems in Materialism and Culture.* London: Verso.

Wilson, Richard A., ed. 1999. *Human Rights, Culture and Context: Anthropological Perspectives.* Pluto Press.

Wolf, Eric. 1982. *Europe and the People without History.* Berkeley: University of California Press.

Worster, Donald. 1994. *Nature's Economy: A History of Ecological Ideas.* Cambridge: Cambridge University Press.

WWF (World Wide Fund for Nature). 1994. Support for Establishment of Mafia Island Marine Park. WWF Tanzanian Programme Office. June 28.

———. 1995. Proceedings and Response from Group Discussions at the Ecotourism Workshop, Mafia Island. October 6–7.

———. 1996. *Village Holistic Study: Community Development Staff Report (WWF)*. Mafia Island Marine Park, Tanzania.

Young, Crawford. 1994. *The African Colonial State in Comparative Perspective*. New Haven: Yale University Press.

Young, Tomme R. 1993. "Legal and Institutional Issues on Integrated Coastal Zone Management Programs in East Africa." In *Integrated Coastal Zone Management in Eastern Africa including the Island States*, ed. O. Linden. Arusha, Tanzania: Swedish Agency for Research Cooperation with Developing Countries Marine Science Program.

Zerner, Charles. 1994. "Transforming Customary Law and Coastal Management Practices in the Maluku Islands, Indonesia, 1870–1992." In *Natural Connections: Perspectives in Community-based Conservation*, eds. D. Western and R. M. Wright. Washington, D.C.: Island Press.

Zerner, Charles, ed. 2000. *People, Plants and Justice*. New York: Columbia University Press.

Zukin, Sharon. 1991. *Landscapes of Power: From Detroit to Disney World*. Berkeley: University of California Press.

Index